STRUGGLE, REFORM, BOOM AND BUST

AN ECONOMIC HISTORY OF PAPUA NEW GUINEA SINCE INDEPENDENCE

STRUGGLE, REFORM, BOOM AND BUST

AN ECONOMIC HISTORY OF PAPUA NEW GUINEA SINCE INDEPENDENCE

STEPHEN HOWES WITH
MARTIN DAVIES, ROHAN FOX, MAHOLOPA LAVEIL,
MANOJ K. PANDEY, KELLY SAMOF AND DEK JOE SUM

We do not want to build a modern society if that means a society in which only the powerful and wealthy can get the benefits. It is not right for a few to have a fancy car—or even two cars—while most of our people still walk along bush tracks.

—Chief Minister Michael Somare, 1973
(cited in Samana 1985, 210)

Australian
National
University

ANU PRESS

PACIFIC SERIES

*To the people of Papua New Guinea, on the occasion of the nation's
50th anniversary of independence*

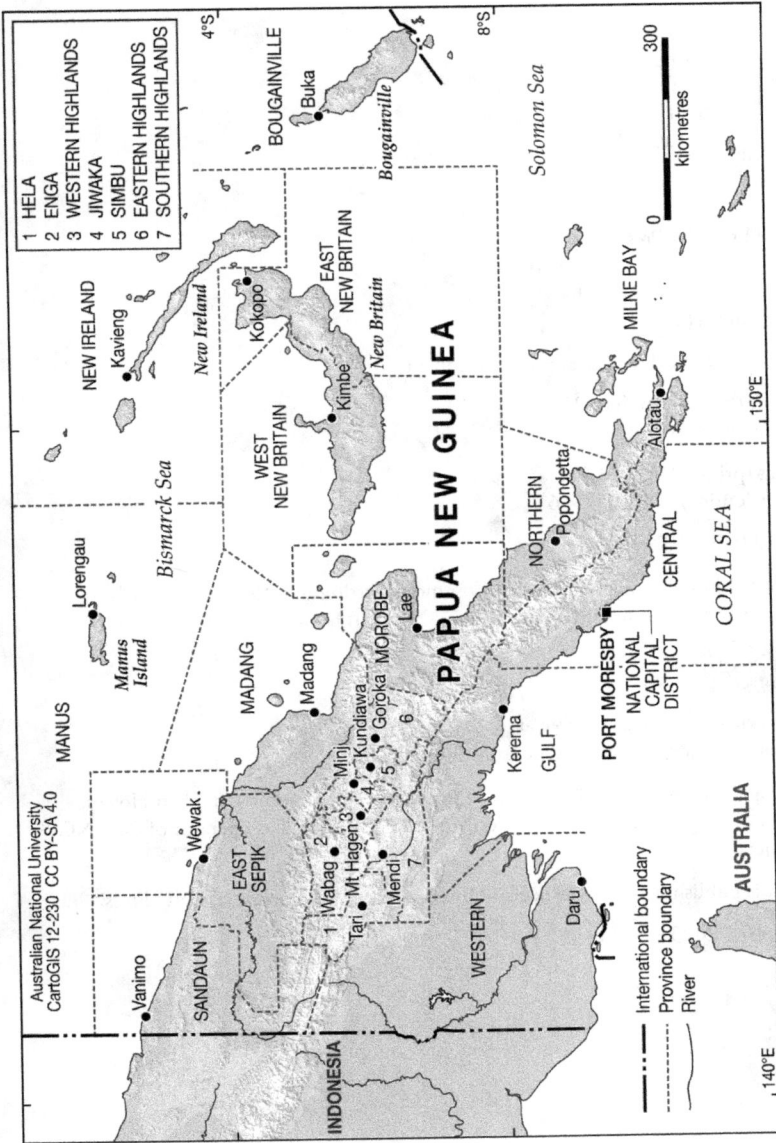

Map 0.1: Papua New Guinea

Source: The Australian National University, CartoGIS 12-230 CC BY-SA 4.0.

Australian
National
University

ANU PRESS

Published by ANU Press
The Australian National University
Canberra ACT 2600, Australia
Email: anupress@anu.edu.au

Available to download for free at press.anu.edu.au

ISBN (print): 9781760466992
ISBN (online): 9781760467005

WorldCat (print): 1524051254
WorldCat (online): 1524052506

DOI: 10.22459/SRBB.2025

Cover design and layout by ANU Press. Front cover photograph by Stephen Howes. Back cover photograph courtesy of ExxonMobil PNG Limited as operator of the PNG LNG Project.

This book is published under the aegis of the Pacific editorial board of ANU Press.

Contents

Part IV: 2014–22: The tens: The quiet bust

List of illustrations

Figures

Tables

Authors

Dr Stephen Howes is professor of economics and director of the Development Policy Centre, Crawford School of Public Policy, The Australian National University (ANU).

Dr Martin Davies is professor of economics at the Washington and Lee University, and has been a visiting lecturer at the University of Papua New Guinea (UPNG) since 2016.

Rohan Fox was a research officer at the Development Policy Centre, ANU, from 2016 to 2021 and a visiting lecturer in the Economics Division in the School of Business and Public Policy at UPNG in 2015 and 2020.

Maholopa Laveil is a lecturer in the Economics Division in the School of Business and Public Policy at UPNG.

Dr Manoj K. Pandey was a lecturer at the Development Policy Centre, ANU, and a visiting lecturer in the Economics Division in the School of Business and Public Policy at UPNG from 2016 to 2022.

Kelly Samof was a lecturer in the Economics Division in the School of Business and Public Policy at UPNG from 2019 to 2024.

Dek Joe Sum was ANU–UPNG partnership coordinator and a visiting lecturer in the Economics Division in the School of Business and Public Policy at UPNG from 2018 to 2021.

Preface and acknowledgements

Writing this book has been a team effort. Early on we decided to split the post-independence period into four, and we gave responsibility for each of the four periods to two authors: Manoj Pandey and I took the eighties, Rohan Fox and Maholopa Laveil the nineties, Martin Davies the noughties, and Kelly Samof and Dek Joe Sum the tens. We all provided comments on each other's work. I provided the introduction and the three concluding chapters, and, more than once, revised the period chapters for consistency and completeness, with comments from my co-authors.

We are indebted for their research assistance and substantial inputs to Taylor Ey, John Howes, Bobby Kunda, Alyssa Leng, Luke McKenzie, Estelle Stambolie and Ajay Tambay. Thank you to Rani Kerin for her meticulous editing of the book.

I would also like to thank everyone who has provided comments and answered queries, and who has provided stimulating discussion and insights that have enriched this book, including colleagues at the Development Policy Centre and the School of Business and Public Policy; and, in particular, from these two institutions and from elsewhere: Michael Burke, John Conroy, Colin Filer, Ross Garnaut, Mudowo Gumoi, Matt Morris and Terence Wood. Paul Flanagan not only shared his wisdom but also made available to us copies of earlier budgets.

The *Devpolicy Blog*, which I edited from 2011 to 2023, has been an invaluable reference for the more recent years we cover, and I thank everyone involved with it.

I learnt a lot from my work from 2021 to 2023 on the Independent Advisory Group to the PNG Treasurer on the Central Banking Act and thank my colleagues in that group, Robert Igara, its chair, and Sir Wilson Kamit, who sadly passed away in January 2023.

This book is a product of the partnership between The Australian National University's Crawford School of Public Policy and the University of Papua New Guinea's School of Business and Public Policy. That partnership took off in 2013 and has been supported by the Australian Department of Foreign Affairs and Trade since 2015. It has provided the basis for many fruitful collaborations, of which this book is one.

Economics is a male-dominated profession, and it shows in this book. That is a pity. But we are glad that the partnership between ANU and UPNG has been able to select three female UPNG economics graduates for further study at ANU. Two are already lecturers at UPNG and we look forward to the future contributions of all three.

Finally, as lead author, I take responsibility for the views expressed in this book and for any errors that remain.

Stephen Howes
31 December 2024

Acronyms and disambiguation

ADB	Asian Development Bank
AIDAB	Australian International Development Assistance Bureau
ANU	The Australian National University
ATM	automated teller machines
AusAID	Australian Agency for International Development
BCL	Bougainville Copper Ltd
BNL	Barrick Niugini Limited
BPNG	Bank of Papua New Guinea
BRA	Bougainville Revolutionary Army
BSP	Bank of the South Pacific
CBB	central bank bills
CLRC	Constitutional and Law Reform Commission
CPI	consumer price index
CRR	cash reserve requirement
DAL	Department of Agriculture and Livestock
DDA	District Development Authority
ECP	Enhanced Cooperation Program
EDF	Electoral Development Fund
FASU	Financial Analysis and Supervision Unit
FRA	Fiscal Responsibility Act
GDP	gross domestic product
GFC	global financial crisis
GIWPS	Georgetown Institute for Women, Peace and Security

GNI	gross national income
GoPNG	Government of Papua New Guinea
GST	general sales tax
HDI	Human Development Index
ICCC	Independent Consumer & Competition Commission
IDA	International Development Association
ILG	Incorporated Land Groups
IMF	International Monetary Fund
INA	Institute of National Affairs
IPA	Investment Promotion Authority
IPBC	Independent Public Business Corporation
IRDP	integrated rural development projects
KCH	Kumul Consolidated Holdings
KFR	Kina Facility Rate
KPHL	Kumul Petroleum Holding Limited
LGL	Lihir Gold Limited
LNG	liquefied natural gas
MCC	Millennium Challenge Corporation
MLAR	minimum liquid asset ratio
MP	member of parliament
MRDC	Mineral Resources Development Corporation
MRSF	Mineral Resources Stabilisation Fund
NCD	non-communicable disease
NDS	National Development Strategy
NEER	nominal effective exchange rate
NGO	non-government organisations
NIDA	National Investment Development Authority
NPEP	National Public Expenditure Plan
NRA	National Roads Authority
NRI	National Research Institute
NSO	National Statistical Office
OLIPPAC	Organic Law on the Integrity of Political Parties and Candidates

OLPG	Organic Law on Provincial Governments
OTML	Ok Tedi Mining Company Ltd
PACER	Pacific Agreement on Closer Economic Relations
PEFA	Public Expenditure and Financial Accountability
PNG	Papua New Guinea
PNGBC	Papua New Guinea Banking Corporation
PNGFA	Papua New Guinea Forest Authority
PNG FIU	Papua New Guinea Financial Intelligence Unit
PPP	People's Progress Party
PRIO	Peace Research Institute Oslo
PSC	Public Services Commission
READ	Resources, Environment and Development
REER	real effective exchange rate
RNZ	Radio New Zealand
RRT	Resource rents tax
SABL	Special Agricultural and Business Leases
SARV	sorcery-accusation-related violence
SDP	Sustainable Development Program
SEZ	special economic zones
SGS	Societé Generate de Surveillance
SOE	state-owned enterprise
SWF	sovereign wealth fund
TI	Transparency Index
TPA	Tourism Promotion Authority
TRP	tariff reduction program
UPNG	University of Papua New Guinea
US	Unites States
VAT	value-added tax
WGI	Worldwide Governance Indicators
WHO	World Health Organization
WTO	World Trade Organization

1

Introduction

As I became further engaged in this process, I realised that it was also important to look back at the road we had travelled since independence and to mark out the significant events, the gains and losses that we had made, the results of decisions by governments and the impacts of national and global events. I realised that we needed to document the lessons we had learnt from the past and the mistakes to be avoided.

—Deputy Prime Minister Puka Temu (cited in Webster and Duncan 2010, Foreword)

1.1 Introduction

Much has changed in Papua New Guinea (PNG) since its independence in 1975. The economy is about four times as big. Income per person has grown only very slowly, but the population is more than three times the size it was at independence. In its half century of independence, PNG has experienced both booms and busts. The seventies and eighties were a period of relative stability, the nineties a decade of crises. A major boom began in the early noughties (2000s) and lasted almost a decade. This was followed by a long bust. Three other booms—one in the early eighties, one in the early nineties and one in the mid-tens (2010s)—were anticipated, but either ended quickly or did not eventuate at all, illustrating just how difficult the challenges of economic management are in this resource-rich country.

Commodity exports are now dominated not by coffee, copra, cocoa and copper as at independence but by gas and gold. Timber, palm oil and fish exports have also grown in importance. Domestic food and betel nut markets have expanded rapidly. People are much more connected, via the technological miracle of the mobile phone. The capital Port Moresby has been transformed and is now home to sprawling settlements and subject to traffic jams. Infrastructure and service delivery have worsened over large parts of the country, and some of the country's social indicators are now among the worst in the world.

PNG has enjoyed macroeconomic stability, except in the nineties. This decade of crises was also a decade of reform, in which the government deregulated, liberalised and redesigned some of its key institutions.

While the nineties was PNG's most intensive reform period, there have been important changes in economic policy throughout the post-independence period, not all of them linear. PNG moved from the pegged exchange rate regime it adopted at independence to a floating one in 1994, and then back to a peg in 2014, but without the convertibility that had been present till then. On the fiscal front, to smooth and save resource revenue, PNG created at independence, but then abandoned in the late nineties, the Mineral Resources Stabilisation Fund, then built up and ran down a set of trust funds in the noughties, before finally legislating a new but yet-to-be-operationalised sovereign wealth fund in 2015, after the long boom ended. The country has been through periods of trade liberalisation and protection, of fiscal austerity and expansion, and of privatisation and state-led development. Overall, Washington Consensus reforms have given way to growing nationalist sentiment. Resource policy has been alternately less and more friendly to investors.

We write this economic history of Papua New Guinea for two reasons. One, it will be the first in about 15 years. Earlier decades produced their own syntheses to summarise what had gone before, and those efforts need to be continued. Two, as economist John Williamson (2005, 45), of Washington Consensus fame, has written, 'recognition of the importance of institutions was perhaps the key innovation in development economics in the nineties'. Institutions matter for the economy, and institutions are the outcome of political processes. Earlier economic histories of PNG have not linked economic performance and policies with politics and governance. This book attempts to.

In this chapter, the next section provides some introductory context and sets out our approach. The following four introduce the four periods on which the subsequent chapters are based. The final section concludes with a summary of the book's main arguments.

1.2 Context, data, resources and approach

For those less familiar with Papua New Guinea, a little background. This section also explains the approach we take in this book, the data we use and the earlier research we build on.

1.2.1 An introduction to PNG

Papua New Guinea is an island nation located in the north of Oceania. It comprises the eastern half of New Guinea, the second largest island in the world, and hundreds of much smaller inhabited and uninhabited surrounding islands.

Papua New Guinea's geography is as diverse as its people. The lowlands consist of a myriad of freshwater swamp and mangrove forests, savannah grasslands, wetlands and plantations, and are humid and malaria infested. Inland of the main New Guinea island are the Highlands, a highly populated, cooler, mountainous region comprising tropical rain forests and numerous fertile river valleys.

PNG is endowed with significant mineral and petroleum resources, the world's third-largest forest and large tuna resources, but it also faces significant resource weaknesses, including its dispersed islands, inhospitable and unstable mountainous terrain, and mixed soil quality. Of a total landmass of 46.4 million hectares, 72 per cent is mountainous and 13 per cent swampy (Allen 1983, 215).

Archaeological evidence indicates that the first humans arrived on New Guinea about 45,000 years ago. Three distinct modes of production developed over time: hunting and gathering; the cultivation of root crops (the PNG Highlands was one of the first areas in the world to develop agriculture independently, around 7000 BC); and the raising of domestic pigs (Wesley-Smith 1989; Bourke 2009).

The estimate this book uses for PNG's population in 2022 is 9.3 million. Some think the population is higher, but there has not been a reliable census since 2001, and even that might have involved undercounting (10.2).

PNG is the world's most ethnolinguistically diverse country (UNESCO 2009), with over 820 indigenous languages and thousands of clans or tribes. 'Papua New Guinean societies were small, fragmented and isolated. They remain largely so today' (Allen 1983, 215). According to World Bank statistics, PNG is the least urbanised country in the world. Even in urban and certainly in rural areas, most Papua New Guineans identify closely with their clan or sub-clan, in what is called the *wantok* (one-talk) system.

Ninety-five per cent of the population is Christian; however, religious syncretism is prevalent. While English is an official language of PNG, the lingua franca is Tok Pisin—an English-based creole language. In the southern region of Papua, people often use the third official language, Hiri Motu, from the Austronesian language family.

The first European navigators came to New Guinea during the sixteenth century, but the impact of Europeans on the island was minimal for the next 300 years. As one report puts it:

> The island of New Guinea was the last inhabited land area of any size to be explored systematically by the western powers. Unlike most developing countries that have had a four or five hundred year history of contact with outsiders, many areas of PNG have had less than a hundred, and, in the highlands, prolonged contact did not occur until after World War II. (World Bank 1982, 1)

European colonisation of PNG did not start until the late nineteenth century. The Dutch claimed the western half of New Guinea in 1828. The German Empire established a protectorate (German New Guinea) in the north-eastern part of what is now PNG in 1884, and soon thereafter in the same year the British Empire proclaimed a protectorate (British New Guinea) in the southern part of the main New Guinea island. In 1906, the British protectorate of Papua was formally transferred to the newly formed Commonwealth of Australia. In 1914, German New Guinea came under Australian military rule, and in 1921 Australia was given a mandate by the League of Nations to rule what was then called New Guinea. World War II deeply affected PNG. Japan took control of New Guinea, and over 100,000 Japanese surrendered there at the end of the war. In all, it is estimated that some 1.5 million foreigners came to PNG during the war years (Nelson 2009). In 1946, New Guinea was combined with Papua into a single trust territory, placed under Australian rule by the United Nations, and called Papua-New Guinea, then Papua and New Guinea and finally Papua New Guinea.

Australia ruled over its colony (earlier, two colonies) in a manner that defies simple judgement. Smallholders were supported to produce more (MacWilliam 2013), and Australia invested heavily in the decades prior to independence. Few colonies received so much aid or had so many expatriates relative to their population (Conroy 1976, 2–3). But this was a curse as well as a blessing: the heavy Australian influence pushed up prices, including wages, and led to over-regulation (Daniel and Sims 1986). Primary education and health were major foci, but a policy of uniform development, premised on a belief that independence was many decades away, undervalued the importance of education beyond primary. In 1975, only 846 children were enrolled in a high school (Gupta 1992, 178). The country's first university was opened only in 1965, just 10 years before independence.

For most of the postwar period, it was expected that PNG's independence would come much later than it did in 1975. There was even a flirtation with the idea that the colony, or at least Papua, would become part of Australia. But from the late 1960s, there was a rush to independence, with self-rule commencing in 1972 and Australia insisting on independence by 1975, something PNG achieved, despite significant domestic opposition and a flurry of secessionist movements (Denoon 2005; Abaijah and Wright 1991).

PNG developed its own constitution but inherited many of its institutions from Australia—more specifically, from Queensland, including the latter's unicameral Westminster system. Elections are held every five years. Most members of parliament (MPs) represent districts. There were 89 district (or open) MPs until 2022, when the number was increased to 96. There is also one regional MP per province (who is now also the province's governor). There were 20 provinces until 2012, and now there are 22.[1]

The 22 provinces are commonly grouped into four regions:

1. The Highlands—referred to above, consisting of the provinces of the Southern, Eastern and Western Highlands, Chimbu, Hela, Enga and Jiwaka; home to approximately 39 per cent of the country's population

2. Momase—the northern provinces of Morobe, Madang and East and West Sepik; 26 per cent

3. Southern—the six provinces in the south-east of the main island: Central, Gulf, Milne Bay, Oro, Western and the National Capital District; 20 per cent

4. New Guinea Islands—the multitude of smaller islands to the east, dispersed among the provinces of East and West New Britain, New Ireland, Manus and the Autonomous Region of Bougainville; 15 per cent.

1   The provinces of Southern Highlands and Western Highlands were split into two in 2012 and the new provinces of Hela and Jiwaka, respectively, were created.

1.2.2 Data and resources

To write this history, we created a database of key economic variables going back to independence, something that had been missing. The PNG Economic Database is available online at devpolicy.org/pngeconomic. Basic trends in the data across the entire post-independence period are analysed in a companion paper (Howes, Fox et al. 2022), and a number of graphs sourced from the database are included in Annex B. For details on how the series was constructed, and what sources were drawn on, see the database.

We also, in this book, go well beyond the numbers to draw out the narrative and to tell the story in as interesting a way as possible. To this end, we draw heavily on the large, though by now out-of-date, volume of secondary material on PNG's economy.

PNG's pre-colonial economy is surveyed in Wesley-Smith (1989) and Gupta (1992). The country's colonial economic history has been more extensively analysed than its post-independence counterpart. Histories of the colonial period include Nelson (1982), Griffin et al. (1979), Lātūkefu (1989) and Denoon (2005), with economic overviews provided by Gupta (1992), MacWilliam (2013) and Conroy (2023), and more detailed economic studies on specific topics by Denoon (2000), Epstein (1968) and Finney (1973) among others.

Policies at independence are discussed in detail in John Ballard's 1981 edited volume, *Policy Making in a New State: Papua New Guinea 1972–77*. In the mid-eighties, three reviews of the PNG economy were written: *Exchange Rate and Macroeconomic Policy in Independent PNG* by Ross Garnaut, Paul Baxter and Anne Kreuger (1984); *The Economy of PNG: An Independent Review* by Raymond Goodman, Charles Lepani and David Morawetz (1985); and *Foreign Investment in Papua New Guinea: Policies and Practices* by Philip Daniel and Rod Sims (1986).

Academic Mark Turner's *Papua New Guinea: The Challenge of Independence* (1990), journalist Sean Dorney's *Papua New Guinea: People, Politics and History since 1975* (1991), and economist Desh Gupta's *Political Economy of Growth and Stagnation in Papua New Guinea* (1992), all published in the early nineties, provide broad and useful perspectives on PNG's first 15 years of independence.

In 1997, another two overviews were published: John Connell's *Papua New Guinea: The Struggle for Development* and *Papua New Guinea: A 20/20 Vision* edited by Ila Temu, both of which reflect on the first 20 years of independence.

A number of surveys and reflective pieces also appeared in the first decade of this century. *Building a Nation in Papua New Guinea: Views of the Post-Independence Generation*, edited by David Kavanamur, Charles Yala and Quentin Clements, was published in 2003. The 2007 book from the Bank of Papua New Guinea (BPNG) *Money and Banking in PNG* has a much wider coverage than the title suggests.[2] John Waiko's *A Short History of PNG* was published in 2007. Ron May's edited 2009 volume, *Policy Making and Implementation: Studies from Papua New Guinea*, mainly covers the period up to 2000. *Papua New Guinea's Development Performance 1975–2008* is edited by Thomas Webster and Linda Duncan and was published by the National Research Institute (NRI) in 2010.

There has been a drop-off in social science writing on PNG since 2010. The 2022 volume edited by Stephen Howes and Lekshmi Pillai *Papua New Guinea: Government, Economy and Society* is the only survey since, with May (2022) and Lea (2023) other recent additions.

In addition to these major histories and overviews, there have been any number of reports, snapshots and analyses of the PNG economy. Collections from various annual 'Waigani Seminars' (3.1.2), as well as a range of Institute of National Affairs (INA), NRI, and ANU monographs are invaluable sources. The Australian aid agency published a series of annual reports on the PNG economy over the nineties (AIDAB 1990–94 and then, after a name change, AusAID 1995–2000).[3] The *Pacific Economic Bulletin* published a survey on the PNG economy more or less every year from the mid-nineties to 2010, and many other interesting articles along the way. More recently, an ANU–UPNG team published an annual survey of the PNG economy between 2015 and 2019. There are now annual International Monetary Fund (IMF) reports and a growing number of World Bank and Asian Development Bank reports on the PNG economy. The *Devpolicy Blog* provides a rich catalogue of articles on many aspects of the PNG economy since 2010. On the political front, *PNG Political Chronicles* were published semi-annually or annually from 1967 to 1991 (and are collected in Moore and Kooyman 1998). More recent annual updates can be found in issues of the *Asian Survey* and *Contemporary Pacific*. Regular election reports are also available (Hegarty 1983; King 1989; Oliver 1989; Saffu 1996; May and Anere 2002; May et al. 2013; Haley and Zubrinich 2018).

---

2   The book's foreword indicates that it was written by Guy Kause and Jacob Weiss. However, the official author is the Bank of Papua New Guinea.
3   Including AIDAB (1990, 1991, 1992, 1993, 1994), Duncan, Warner and Temu (1995) and AusAID (1995, 1996, 1997, 1998, 2000).

1.2.3 Approach and structure

We could have followed the path navigated by Webster and Duncan (2010) and written this history along thematic lines, with separate chapters on fiscal policy, monetary policy and so on. However, the longer the period to cover, the harder that approach becomes to sustain. With now not 35 years but almost half a century of history to write about, separate chapters on separate topics would have involved too much repetition across chapters and would not have outlined in sufficient clarity the main arcs of the PNG narrative.

The four periods we use to structure the book are the seventies and eighties (1975–88), the nineties (1989–2003), the noughties (2004–13) and the tens (2014–22). These periods more or less define themselves.

The first is a period of 'stability and low growth' (BPNG 2007, 40). The stability of this period was superficial: growth was much slower than expected, and the period was storing up problems that would hinder development in the decades to come. We call it a period of 'early struggles'.

Things changed drastically in 1989 with the closure, following violence, of the Bougainville copper mine, PNG's largest. What followed was another decade of low average growth; but also a period of volatility, crisis and reform.

The third period was a boom. In exactly which year it began can be debated, but we chose 2004, the year in which government resource revenue started growing strongly. The last year of the boom was 2013, the year in which construction of PNG's largest resource project to date, the PNG liquefied natural gas (LNG) project, was completed, and the year before a sharp fall in oil prices signalled the start of a prolonged resource revenue drought and decline in employment.

The fourth period, of weak economic growth and macroeconomic stability but also mismanagement, called by us the 'quiet bust', lasted from 2014 to 2022, which is where, by and large, this book ends.

Two chapters are devoted to each of the four periods. The first in each pair covers growth and the macroeconomy: that is, the growth record and the macroeconomic performance and policies of the period. The second examines each period's policies and institutions: that is, the economic policies of the period (other than macroeconomic management ones, so focusing on structural policies such as trade and competition policy), as well as developments in politics and governance (the civil service, decentralisation, law and order, corruption, etc.).

This introduction and the three concluding chapters ensure that the history we are writing is more than the sum of its parts.

To facilitate cross-referencing of the same subject in different periods, we direct readers to specific sections and subsections via section and subsection numbers in parentheses, for example, for this section '(1.2.3)'. To avoid the repetition of graphs, we rely mainly on the figures in Annex B, which cover the post-independence period. Annex A provides some basic data on PNG politics and elections, and Annex C provides information on the country's main resource projects.

Figure 1.1 starts the analysis by plotting gross domestic product (GDP) growth since independence. (GDP growth is always presented in this book in real terms, i.e. adjusted for inflation, as measured by the GDP deflator.[4] Multi-year average growth rates are calculated by comparing end and start values only. In this and other graphs, the dotted vertical lines show the four periods.) The graph shows the slow growth of the eighties, the mini boom of the early nineties, the volatility of the nineties as a whole, and the higher but inconsistent GDP growth of this century. The susceptibility of the economy to shocks, positive and negative, is evident.

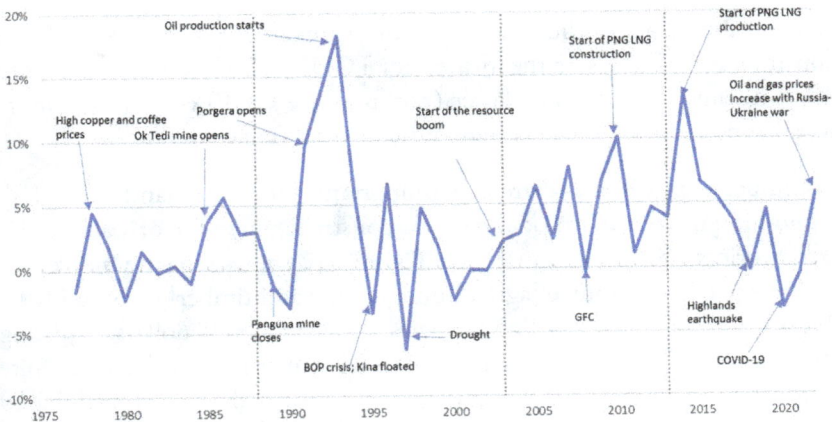

Figure 1.1: GDP growth, 1976–2022 (kina, constant prices)
Source: PNG Economic Database.

---

4   An alternative method is to use CPI to deflate GDP. The issues involved in this choice and the implications are discussed in Howes, Fox et al. (2022).

Questions around the accuracy of GDP data arise in all economies. In PNG, the National Statistical Office is weak, resulting in periods in which the Department of Treasury has actually been responsible for collecting GDP data. GDP does include an estimate of the value of the subsistence and informal economy, but it is out of date, updated annually by a fixed amount and no doubt wildly inaccurate. We also rely on other data, especially relating to formal sector (private and SOE) employment, which BPNG collects every quarter via a business survey. Most working adults are engaged in agriculture or other informal economic activities. However, there is little information on total employment and none on underemployment.

We rely heavily on analysis of 'non-resource GDP'—that is, GDP excluding the value-added (output minus intermediate inputs) of the resource (mineral and petroleum) sector. Given the extensive foreign ownership of PNG's large resource sector, and its enclave, capital-intensive nature, non-resource GDP is the best measure of national PNG economic activity. This measure does not ignore the resource sector; instead, it looks to the contribution it makes to the broader economy via spillover effects, such as through taxation.

Non-resource GDP per person is the basis for our categorisation of PNG's economic history post-independence into four periods. The variable, plotted below in Figure 1.2 (as the solid blue line), traces the stagnation of the first period, the volatility of the second, the boom of the third and the bust of the fourth.

Figure 1.2 also shows the importance of distinguishing between total and non-resource GDP. Using the former (total GDP), PNG's boom lasted until the pandemic of 2020. The latter (non-resource GDP) conveys the more accurate picture that the tens were difficult years economically.

Commodity prices are extremely important for understanding PNG's economic growth. To track them, we construct an index of commodity export prices, shown in Figure 1.3. (Figure B12 shows separate indices for resource and non-resource [agricultural, marine and timber] commodities.) Prices for the commodities PNG exports (measured in US dollars, adjusting for inflation) fell until the early 2000s, but have since increased, and, despite a dip after the boom of the noughties, in 2022 reached a record level due to the war in Ukraine, which pushed up oil and therefore gas prices.

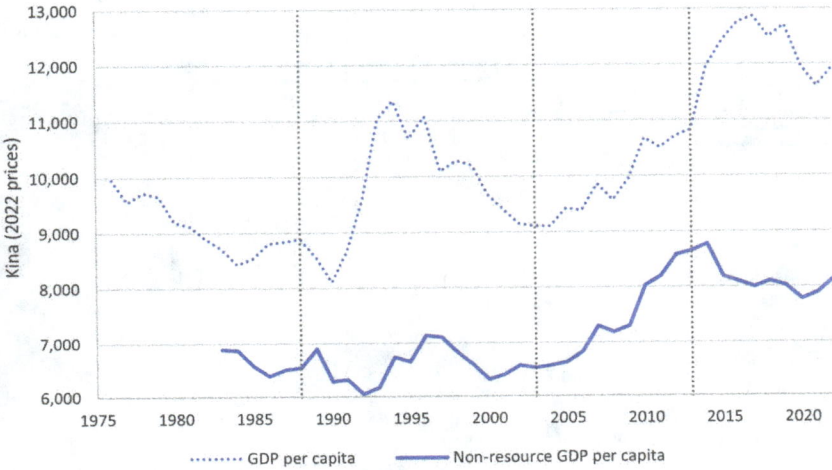

Figure 1.2: GDP and non-resource GDP per person, and the four periods of PNG's economic history, 1976/1983–2022 (kina, constant prices)

Source: PNG Economic Database. The GDP constant prices series is provided in 2013 prices. It is then rebased to 2022 prices.

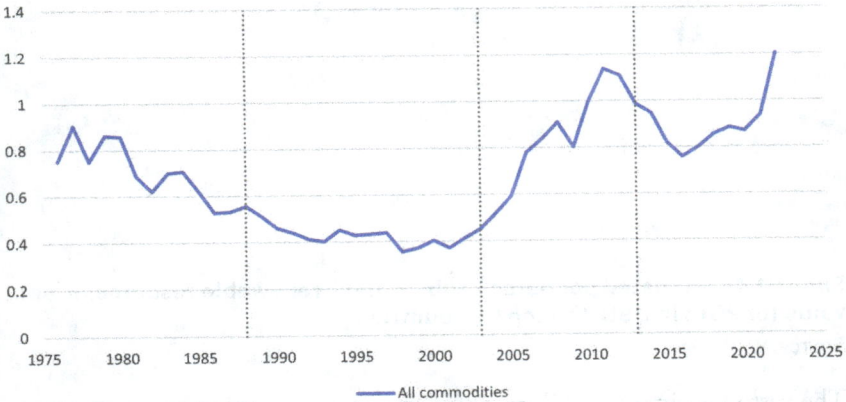

Figure 1.3: PNG commodity export price index (2010 = 1), 1976–2022

Source: See the notes to Figure B12.

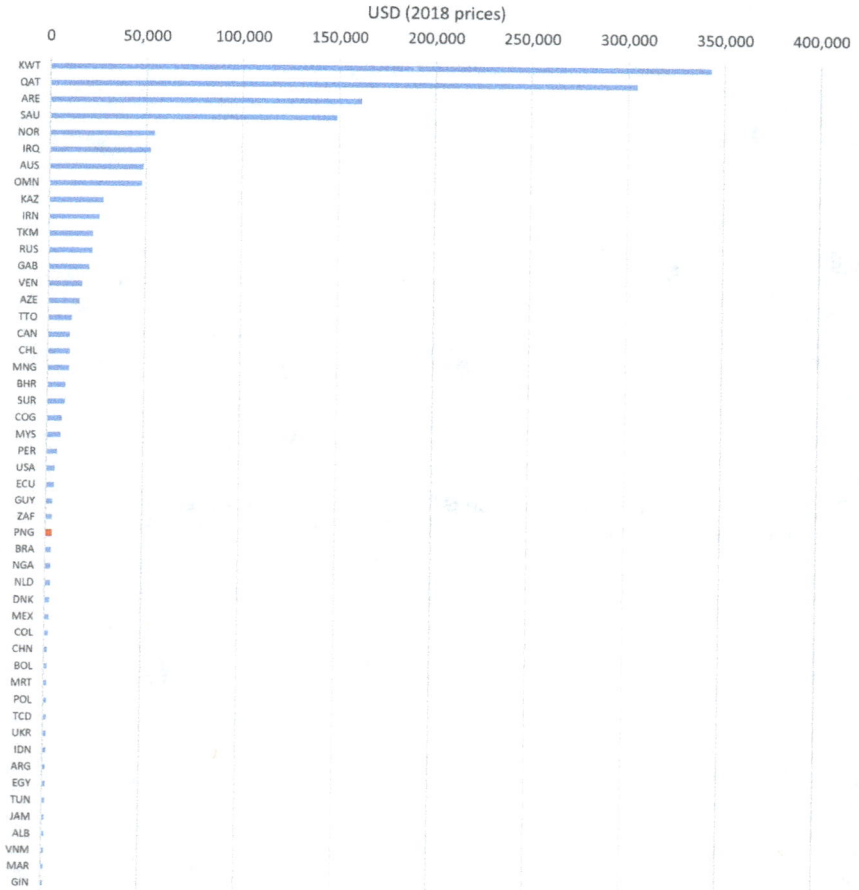

Figure 1.4: Estimated per person subsoil (non-renewable resource) asset value for 2018 in USD, the top 50 countries

Source: World Bank (2021b).

The vast majority of PNG's commodity exports today are resource exports: gas, oil, gold, copper and nickel. Resource dependency—the share of the resource sector in the total economy—has grown from about 10 per cent in the early eighties to 32 per cent in 2022. When writing about PNG, it is easy to become mesmerised by the resource sector. Each project tells a compelling story, and many continue to believe that new resource projects are essential for progress in PNG. International estimates of resource wealth place PNG in 29th place in per person terms (Figure 1.4). But the country's resource wealth is a fraction of countries in the Middle East, and of resource-rich developed countries like Norway, Australia and Canada.

The estimate for PNG's per person resource wealth is USD3,045 in 2018, only about 20 per cent more than its GDP that year. For all the attention PNG's resource sector commands, it is important to keep it in perspective.

A brief summary of each of the four periods follows below to whet the reader's appetite.

1.3 The seventies and eighties (1975–88) — early struggles

The story of the first 14 years, 1975–88, is told in Part I of the book, in Chapters 2 and 3. PNG came to independence with the 'hard kina' policy, which pegged the new PNG currency first against the Australian dollar, and then against a basket of currencies, with the aim of avoiding nominal devaluation. The no-devaluation stance had to be abandoned in the early eighties, but the kina was pegged until 1994.

The hard kina policy was introduced to promote confidence in a new currency, to provide a macroeconomic anchor and to constrain deficit financing. In these regards, the policy was a success: most of this period was characterised by low deficits and moderate inflation.

Behind this solid macroeconomic performance, however, lurked a number of disturbing developments. First, PNG emerged as a high-cost economy, in part because of a doubling of urban real wages between 1972 and 1975, something quite contrary to the emphasis at the time on equity and rural development. Second, defying the optimistic expectations at independence, economic growth was slow, cruelled by those high costs as well as heavy regulation and falling Australian aid and commodity prices. Slow growth was bad for the welfare of ordinary Papua New Guineans, made macroeconomic restraint a less tenable proposition going forward, and worsened law and order. However, there was little by way of economic reform over this period, with the exception of the deregulation of the financial sector. Third, though foreign exchange reserves did not run out until 1994, they fell over the seventies and eighties relative to imports, making a pegged kina policy more difficult to sustain.

Fourth, a distinctively Papua New Guinean political culture began to assert itself, one that was conducive to the stability of the country's adopted Westminster political regime but not to development. Elections continued to be regularly held, but a political culture of clientelism and precarity became entrenched, with MPs elected on the basis of local issues and a high rate of turnover of MPs every election. More and more were attracted to politics, and, as the business interests of politicians grew, no distinction developed between the political and the business class. As parties weakened, politics became increasingly attractive, but as an arena for never-ending power contestation rather than for competing policies.

Fifth, corruption and law and order both emerged as serious problems. Sixth, government effectiveness weakened and service delivery standards started to decline. Seventh, PNG embarked on a program of radical decentralisation to its (then) 20 provinces. Whether or not this was a good idea, it proved to be unsustainable. A quasi-federal system with elected provincial MPs and premiers lasted until the nineties, but not beyond. The lack of an agreed, stable basis for sub-national governance in PNG remains to this day and handicaps the country's efforts to deliver services and provide infrastructure.

In summary, Papua New Guinea's first 14 years passed without major economic crisis. That itself must count as success. But the negative legacy of this foundational period was its subterranean trends.

1.4 The nineties (1989–2003) — volatility, crisis and reform

The second period, from 1989 to 2003, covered in Part II of the book, in Chapters 4 and 5, is the most action-packed of the four. Indeed, the nineties can appear bewildering in its quick succession of booms and busts, economic and political crises, prime ministers (six in all), and repeating episodes of reform and mismanagement. Three of the four times that PNG has turned to the IMF occurred in this period. So too did the country's only insurgency.

Late 1988 marks the start of the Bougainville crisis—the violent uprising on the north-eastern island of Bougainville that permanently shut down the nation's largest mine and revenue earner, and that led to a decade-long civil war.

The closing of the Bougainville copper mine was only the first of several shocks—negative and positive—to hit the PNG economy over the decade. Others include the withdrawal of Australian budget support over the course of the decade; new mineral and petroleum projects (causing GDP to grow in 1993 by 18 per cent—a record that has never since been matched); a drought and the East Asia crisis in 1997 (leading to GDP growth of –6 per cent, another record); and further falls in commodity prices.

Macroeconomic stability gave way over the nineties to extreme instability: inflation was regularly in double digits, the currency lost three-quarters of its value and twice the country ran out of foreign exchange. This is often blamed on fiscal indiscipline. However, while deficits were too high in some years, they were, on average, no higher than in the previous period. Other problems included the growing tendency to finance deficits domestically (including through the central bank) and a reduction in foreign aid, both of which made it harder to find the dollars needed to finance imports. The low level of foreign exchange going into the nineties reduced the margin for error. Monetary policy became less effective. A decline in confidence, on account of political instability and misbehaviour as well as the emergence of high inflation and depreciation, did not help either.

It is not surprising that the nineties is typically remembered as a decade of chaos and failure. Instability increased, corruption intensified and service delivery worsened.

Yet this period was also one of important reforms, many of them of the liberalisation-deregulation sort that were then popular worldwide as per the Washington Consensus. The country's high minimum wage was abolished, prices and foreign investment were deregulated, the currency was floated, superannuation was restructured, the central bank was made independent, a program of tariff reduction was put in place, a value-added tax was introduced and decentralisation was overhauled. The nineties are such a dizzying period that they are difficult to generalise from, but if we were to take one lesson from that decade it would be that crisis and reform in PNG, as in many other countries, go together.

PNG transitioned in 1999 from a prime minister widely regarded as the worst economic manager in its history, Bill Skate, to one heralded as the best, Mekere Morauta. Despite the ability this demonstrated for self-correction, the Morauta government, though magnificent in reform, was unable to restore business confidence, and the overriding sentiment in the early 2000s was one of deep pessimism. In 2003, academic Henry Okole (2003, 62) wrote that PNG was in an 'abyss of despair' and that 'everything resembles a shattered dream'.

1.5 The noughties (2004–13) — the boom

And then, around 2004, quite unexpectedly, everything changed. The economy started to grow again, and political stability returned. No doubt some of the earlier reform efforts did yield a growth dividend, but the most important cause of the unexpected take-off was the global commodity boom. Resource prices, which had fallen over the eighties and nineties, started increasing in 2003 and pushed PNG's commodity price index to above levels last seen at independence (Figure 1.3). Record levels of revenue flowed into the PNG budget from a number of 'revenue-ready' resource projects (projects that yield high revenue for government when prices are high). This underpinned a massive expansion of economic activity and caused the kina at last to strengthen. The economy was further stimulated by deficit spending starting in 2009, and by the construction between 2010 and 2013 of the country's biggest (by far) resource project yet, the PNG LNG project.

The boom, covered in Part III, in Chapters 6 and 7, generated a new optimism that now, at last, things were changing for the better. The return of macroeconomic and political stability helped. Inflation fell as the kina appreciated. On the political front, the country's first prime minister Michael Somare returned to that position after an absence of almost 20 years and stayed in it from 2002 to 2011, forced out only by a long period of ill health. Peter O'Neill took over in controversial circumstances but stayed as prime minister until 2019, making him the country's second-longest serving prime minister.

Unfortunately, the boom was mismanaged. In response to the acute fiscal stress of the nineties, the Morauta government had abolished the Mineral Resources Stabilisation Fund. This meant that there was no vehicle to save the large volume of resource revenue that was now flowing into government coffers. Temporary trust funds were established, but only for short-term savings, and by the end of the boom most of the amount saved earlier in the period had been spent, and, indeed, the government had started to borrow. PNG ran its largest deficits to date in 2013 and 2014 on the back of expectations that the good times were only just starting, with PNG LNG due to start operations in 2014. Earlier reform efforts, such as privatisation, were put on the backburner. Efforts to improve law and order and crack down on corruption were made but not sustained. There were huge increases in the funds given to MPs, and much spending was simply wasted.

The fall in oil prices in 2014, together with the ending of PNG LNG construction the year before, ended PNG's longest boom. This was a period that showed that sustained, broad-based growth is possible in PNG, but also that the conditions for it—some combination of high commodity prices, revenue-ready projects and the construction of large resource projects—are demanding and have been in place for less than a quarter of the post-independence period.

1.6 The tens (2014–22) — the quiet bust

From 2014 to 2022, the period analysed in Part IV of the book, in Chapters 8 and 9, PNG experienced slow growth once again, with non-resource GDP growth not keeping up with population growth. GDP growth, of course, benefited from the massive PNG LNG project, which now makes up almost half of the country's exports. But most of the revenue from that project has gone offshore.

The most obvious causes for the bust were the completion of the PNG LNG project, an absence of new resource projects and a massive shrinking of resource sector revenue, but the downturn was also accentuated by poor economic policy, particularly on the exchange rate front.

The O'Neill government was determined to avoid a crisis, and, in particular, not to have to turn to the IMF, as PNG had so frequently in the nineties. Facing acute fiscal stress, the government borrowed heavily (including, once again, from the central bank), cut expenditure and ran up arrears. At the same time, the Bank of Papua New Guinea, which had been given responsibility for the exchange rate in the reforms of the 2000s, ended the floating of the kina in 2014 to stem a rapid depreciation that had commenced with the conclusion of PNG LNG construction, declining resource revenues and excessive domestic borrowing. Since then, nominal depreciation has been constrained to the extent that, by 2022, the real exchange rate had recovered to above its end-of-boom high. To minimise the need for devaluation, BPNG discontinued the practice of current account convertibility and started rationing foreign exchange. From 2014 onwards, PNG businesses have listed foreign exchange shortages as one of their most important problems, frequently *the* most important.

High fiscal deficits have continued; however, now that foreign exchange rationing has been introduced, politicians no longer need to worry that too high a deficit will lead to a balance of payments crisis. The stability that PNG's economic managers have engineered has undermined both economic growth and support for reform.

To his credit, O'Neill's successor, James Marape, who came to power in 2019, called in the IMF to help with fiscal and exchange rate reform, but the reform program is timid, as it has to be absent any sense of a crisis.

There has also been a turn back towards nationalism and state-led development. This started under O'Neill and was intensified by Marape, whose chief slogan is 'Take back PNG'. The shift away from the Washington Consensus reforms of the nineties is manifest both in the push to have national champions in the resource sector and in increases in tariffs. The shift, while real, has been tempered by pragmatism. A number of more radical policies, such as one to expand greatly the number of sectors reserved for national businesses, have been floated or even adopted but not implemented.

PNG's economy was hit by the negative shock of the global pandemic in 2020. However, in 2022, commodity prices hit a record high, and government resource revenue and economic growth both increased, ending the quiet bust. At the time of writing, foreign exchange rationing continues, and business leaders still speak of a lack of confidence. The PNG economy is out of the bust, but not out of the woods.

1.7 Conclusion

The early struggles of the seventies and eighties, the volatility, crises and reforms of the nineties, the booming noughties and the quiet bust of the tens make PNG's economic history extremely interesting to research, and, we hope, to read. The next four parts, comprising eight chapters, tell that story. The three concluding chapters in Part V contrast, compare and synthesise performance over the four periods (Chapter 10), and link PNG's post-independence economic performance to its policy settings (Chapter 11) and institutions (Chapter 12).

As Chapter 10 notes, of the four periods, the third and fourth are opposites in terms of economic performance: the noughties were the best of times and the tens the worst. The first and second periods are opposites with respect to volatility: the eighties were PNG's most stable period, the nineties the most volatile. The fourth is the most unusual in terms of macroeconomic outcomes, with its sustained fiscal deficits, huge current account surplus and collapse in imports, all in part due to it being the only period of currency non-convertibility.

While each period is distinctive, overall PNG's post-independence development record has been disappointing. John Connell's (1997, 317) conclusion two decades ago that 'neither consistent growth nor sustainable development have been achieved' since independence remains valid today. The last two periods have seen a slightly better performance than the first two; however, for the entire post-independence period, the growth rate of non-resource GDP per person has only averaged 0.4 per cent per year, and formal sector employment only 1.5 per cent, well below the population growth rate. PNG's growth performance is not the worst in the world, but it is certainly well below average. Non-income indicators are alarmingly low by international standards and, in some cases, have worsened: In recent years, PNG has had the lowest rate of immunisation, the fourth-highest rate of child stunting and risk of premature death from non-communicable disease, and the seventh-lowest doctor–population ratio in the world.

Chapter 11 argues that managing the PNG economy is an intrinsically difficult task. A small, open, resource-dependent economy, it is prone to numerous shocks. It is also highly monopolistic, so liberalising policies may not increase welfare. For example, the liberalisation of interest rates in the eighties has led to exorbitant spreads. Even sensible policies have risks. Currency non-convertibility is very damaging for growth and encourages fiscal profligacy, but reintroducing convertibility may lead to a balance of payments crisis as it did, twice, in the nineties. Economic reforms may have a limited return because other constraints are binding and cannot be removed, such as insecurity. The current emphasis on economic stability means that reforms are less likely. And there is a lack of consensus around what reforms are appropriate, with a loss of support for Washington Consensus reforms, and more backing for nationalistic policies.

There are thus many difficulties for any would-be Papua New Guinean reformer. Nevertheless, reform is needed. Chapter 11 argues that the key current priority for macroeconomic reform is a permanent end to foreign exchange rationing. On the microeconomic front, policies that promote competition and market entry should be encouraged, but regulatory approaches, while inherently risky, may be needed where competition is weak. The informal economy is PNG's key strength. It has benefited, and will continue to benefit, from a policy of benign neglect.

While the resource sector has grown at a decent rate, especially compared to the rest of the economy—leading to increasing resource dependency—the return from large resource projects has undoubtedly been disappointing. Resource sector policy has been subject to frequent and radical change over the post-independence period, but the reasons for the sector's disappointing revenue performance need to be determined to guide future reforms in the sector.

Land reforms are regarded by some as PNG's top challenge. Though there is a lack of consensus about which reforms should be pursued, none of the ones tried so far have worked, and insecurity of land title remains an important constraint on development. This is a case in which governance has trumped policy: until land administration improves, PNG's land markets will remain overwhelmingly informal.

Finally, Chapter 11 argues for a return to the emphasis on equality present at independence, including gender equality, with a special emphasis on improving appalling vaccination and nutrition outcomes.

Reforms are needed for faster growth and better development outcomes. Whether or not they will be undertaken depends on deeper institutional factors, which are the subject of Chapter 12. It emphasises what it calls a pattern of 'hyper-politics': hyper or very local, popular and insecure politics, with weak parties, a constant contestation for power, and no clear distinction between the political and the business class. Hyper-politics has been conducive to political regime stability, but has not otherwise been supportive of development. The chapter also draws attention to PNG's weak state, high levels of litigiousness and corruption, unsettled framework for decentralisation, and widespread insecurity, with both high crime rates and weak property rights. Business surveys suggest that, in general, these factors are as or more important as constraints to growth than any of the various policy deficiencies diagnosed in Chapter 11, several of which they help explain.

The idea that explanations for economic growth performance should be sought in the sphere of institutions (the 'rules of the game') has become accepted wisdom. There are, by now, a whole range of theories that explain economic performance in broadly institutional terms. We find very useful for the PNG case those theories that emphasise the damaging effects of dysfunctional politics on development, as well as the longstanding argument that security is important for development, noting that law and order topped the list of concerns for PNG businesses from 1982 to 2012, and that property rights are often tenuous. We argue on the basis of the evidence accumulated from our historical survey that PNG's development outcomes can be explained by its hyper-politics and pervasive insecurity, and the feedback effects generated by the weak state and the low growth these two factors cause. Political regime stability provides a positive countervailing force, meaning that the constraints on development in PNG have led, not to collapse, but to a weak-state and low-growth equilibrium.

Simplistic arguments that resource wealth is a curse are not helpful, but it is true that PNG's growth is not only low, but also increasingly resource dependent, and that, in terms of exports to GDP, PNG is now one of the most resource-dependent economies in the world. The various constraints to broad-based growth are less constraining of big resource projects. While positive as well as negative (Dutch disease) impacts of resource growth are evident in PNG, an increasingly resource-dependent economy is one in which a weak state becomes ever more important as a distributor of economic rents, and perhaps weaker as it is distracted from other policy challenges. It is probably also one that is even more prone to conflict. These feedback loops constitute Papua New Guinea's institutional resource curse.

The picture painted of a hyper-political, insecurity trap is not an optimistic one, but traps are not for ever. However, we refrain from recommending any political or institutional reforms. Papua New Guinea will have to find its own way forward. Rather, the book concludes with five reflections on what this history has taught us, and what the future might hold.

First, the drop-off in academic writing on PNG's economy over time is striking and unfortunate. This volume is only a partial corrective. Second, a lot of what we see in PNG is evident in other countries as well, especially in Africa. The book draws on these comparisons, but more international comparative work is needed to better understand the PNG economy. Third, development in PNG is much more difficult than it was at independence. That the optimism at independence was unfounded should make us sceptical about new aspirational statements, such as the goal of *Vision 2050*, published in 2009, to place PNG among the 50 countries with highest Human Development Index by 2050. Development challenges in PNG have intensified since independence. Optimism and hope are important, but not helpful if disconnected from reality.

Fourth, the prophets of collapse have also not seen their predictions vindicated. Many things have got worse, and there are certainly serious risks, but, so far, the pessimism of the doomsday merchants has been as misplaced as the optimism of PNG's boosters. Fifth, in assessing the country's prospects, too much weight is still given to the country's resource potential. The growth of PNG's resource sector has been quite respectable, yet overall economic growth has been slow. PNG's longer-term outlook depends not on its subsoil assets but on the quality of its policies and, above all, its institutions.

Beyond this, divining what the future holds for PNG we leave for others. The nation is young and has embarked on a long journey. Whatever happens, the next five decades in Papua New Guinea's post-independence economic history will surely be as interesting and as difficult to predict as the first five.

Part I: 1975–88: The seventies and eighties: Early struggles

There are ample reasons for optimism about the long-run outlook for economic development in Papua New Guinea. (World Bank 1978, 64)

The politically independent Papua New Guinea will inherit intractable economic problems ... Independence will come to Papua New Guineans not as a great victory, and not as a great gift from Australia; but as a prelude to a task which they must accept. (Nelson 1972, 114, 230)[1]

---

1   In fact, Nelson refers to 'Niugini' and 'Niuginians' and adds the words 'as men' before 'they must accept'. The second sentence is the concluding sentence in his book.

2

Slow growth and austerity

Despite what we used to be told in the past, Papua New Guinea is a country of very rich and abundant resources. There is no shortage of firms and investors eager to develop those resources. Our problem at the moment is not that we have to go out and search for capital; it is rather that we must be able to control and restrict all the foreign capital that is being offered. Not only must the government make sure of negotiating a hard bargain with foreign companies, we must also determine how much development we want, the most desirable pace for that development, and the price we are willing to pay in terms of the drastic changes that it will force in our way of life.

—Prime Minister Michael Somare (1975, 144)

The over-riding characteristic of the PNG economy today is that, since Independence, average per person income has grown little, if at all, in real terms.

—Finance Minister Julius Chan (1992, 5)

2.1 Introduction

Australia is commonly, and fairly, criticised both for doing too little to prepare Papua New Guinea for independence, and then, in the early seventies, pushing for a rushed independence.[1] As a result, it is often said, PNG was not ready for its independence on 16 September 1975, after just

---

1   As late as 1967, Australia's foreign minister speculated that PNG might never become independent (Ley 2014, 145). When Andrew Peacock became the coalition foreign minister in early 1972, he shifted Australian policy towards a more pro-independence stance. Labor, with its new Prime Minister Gough Whitlam, came to office in late 1972 promising a quick independence for PNG.

three years of home rule. However, at least in terms of economic policy, the new nation arrived well equipped. Legislation passed in 1974 established the Mineral Resources Stabilisation Fund (MRSF) to smooth out volatile revenue flows from the Panguna copper mine in Bougainville, one of the biggest in the world, the tax terms of which PNG had just renegotiated in its favour. The major agricultural commodities—coffee, cocoa and copra—had their own stabilisation schemes. To avoid high inflation and fiscal profligacy, PNG adopted a hard currency policy, known as the 'hard kina', which fixed the new PNG currency against first the Australian dollar, and then a basket of currencies. To promote progress for all, PNG wrote five principles of equitable development into its constitution.

There was confidence in the air, as illustrated by the quote from the founding prime minister, Michael Somare, with which this chapter begins. And, indeed, much seemed to go well in the first decade or so following independence. The government showed exemplary fiscal restraint in the face of a reduction in aid from Australia. There was an expansion in the national ownership of the capital stock. A second major mine (Ok Tedi) opened, and exploration was undertaken and plans made for others. The MRSF helped stabilise mining revenue inflows, the exchange rate was stable and inflation relatively low, at least by global standards.

On the other side of the ledger, economic growth, expected to be rapid at independence, was slow, below the rate of population growth, due to a poor investment climate and declining aid and commodity prices. Formal sector employment was unable to keep up with the growing population. The first challenges to fiscal stability were seen. Foreign exchange reserves fell over time and commodity stabilisation funds were depleted.

Meanwhile, deeper problems started to build. Away from Port Moresby, dissatisfaction on Bougainville with the Panguna mine grew. Many of the newly created provincial governments established in PNG's first round of decentralisation ran into trouble and were dismissed. A distinctive PNG style of governance became apparent. The political class grew in strength, but political precarity and clientelism became entrenched. The party system weakened; bureaucratic quality fell. Crime and corruption became serious problems.

Not all of these problems can be attributed to low growth, but the growing gap between expectations and performance certainly exacerbated them.

We draw a line under this initial post-independence period (which we refer to as the seventies and eighties, or sometimes just as the eighties) in 1988. At the end of 1988, violence broke out on Bougainville, directed against the Panguna mine, and, by May 1989, the mine was closed, never to reopen. The nineties was a very different decade.

This chapter includes an analysis of PNG's growth record over the eighties as well as of macroeconomic policies and performance. The next evaluates (structural) economic policies and explores political and institutional developments during the period.

2.2 Economic growth

PNG had a population of 2.8 million at independence. Outside of agriculture, the economy was dominated by foreign-owned firms and by Australian aid and expatriates. Economic integration was very low. One mine, on Bougainville, contributed about half the country's exports. Manufacturing and other modern business activity was very limited and nearly all foreign owned. Agriculture was both subsistence and market-based, the latter including cash crops, vegetables and *buai* (betel nut). Cash exports came from both foreign-owned plantations and smallholders. In the year of independence, 67 per cent of coffee production, 36 per cent of cocoa and 42 per cent of copra was from smallholders (MacWilliam 2013, 180). Only about 6 per cent of the population was in formal sector employment, and more than one-quarter of that group worked for the government (Figure B16). The informal urban economy was very limited. In the early seventies, 'urban artisan and service activities … [were] virtually non-existent' (Faber et al. 1973, 25).

The optimism at independence notwithstanding, economic growth was in fact slow. Agricultural commodity production grew particularly slowly; the resource sector did somewhat better, but problems at PNG's first two mines that were neglected would subsequently explode. There was little growth in formal sector employment, but the informal economy expanded.

2.2.1 Slow growth

From a global perspective, PNG's independence was poorly timed. The postwar 'golden age' of high growth came to a halt with the first oil crisis of the early seventies. Prices for PNG's agricultural exports rallied sharply just after independence: for example, coffee prices doubled between 1975 and 1976 and then increased by another two-thirds in 1977. However, the national benefits of this were offset by the second oil crisis of the late seventies as PNG then met all its oil needs via imports. The second oil crisis also kicked off the global recession of the early eighties, which dashed the anticipation of a boom induced by the conclusion in 1980 of an agreement for the construction of PNG's second large mine, Ok Tedi. Commodity prices started falling and continued to decline through the eighties and nineties. Our PNG-specific commodity price index has a value of 0.75 in 1976 and 0.86 in 1979, but then falls to 0.62 in 1982 before recovering to 0.71 in 1984, and then falling again to only 0.55 in 1988 (Figure B12).

The eighties was a difficult decade for developing countries—a lost decade for Latin America and a 'disastrous' one for Africa (Singer 1989)—and it was certainly a difficult period for PNG. Declining commodity prices discouraged agricultural production and reduced resource revenue to government. Facing these headwinds, and given the poor investment climate (3.1.3) and falling aid (Figure B25), it is not surprising that growth was slow.

PNG's GDP grew at about the rate of population in the late seventies, but there was no growth at all from 1980 to 1984, a particularly difficult period (Figure 2.1). The Panguna mine went into the red for the first time in 1982. Economic growth only resumed in 1985, the first full year of production for PNG's second mine, Ok Tedi, and it then returned to around the rate of population growth. The same pattern can be observed of government expenditure. It increased ahead of inflation in the late seventies and late eighties, but fell in the early eighties as part of the government's austerity program (Figure B24 and Section 2.3.1).

We emphasise non-resource GDP in this book as a measure of national economic activity, and argue that, due to high levels of foreign ownership and capital intensity in the resource sector, it is a better indicator than GDP itself (1.2.3). Since PNG has become more resource dependent over time, the difference between non-resource GDP and GDP is least important for this first period, and, in any case, non-resource GDP data are only available from 1983 onwards. The simple message from Figure 2.2 is that this first period of independence was one of regression in terms of average living standards, whether measured by GDP or non-resource GDP per person.

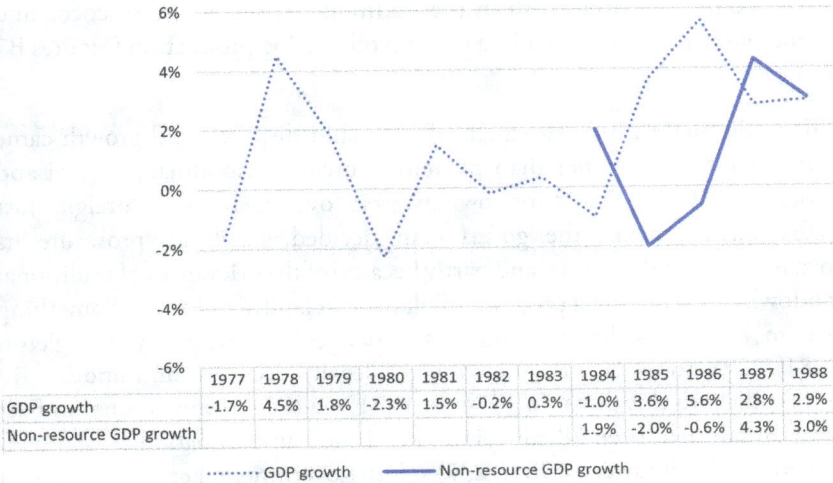

	1977	1978	1979	1980	1981	1982	1983	1984	1985	1986	1987	1988
GDP growth	-1.7%	4.5%	1.8%	-2.3%	1.5%	-0.2%	0.3%	-1.0%	3.6%	5.6%	2.8%	2.9%
Non-resource GDP growth								1.9%	-2.0%	-0.6%	4.3%	3.0%

········ GDP growth   ——— Non-resource GDP growth

Figure 2.1: GDP and non-resource GDP growth, 1977–88 (kina, constant prices)

Source: PNG Economic Database.

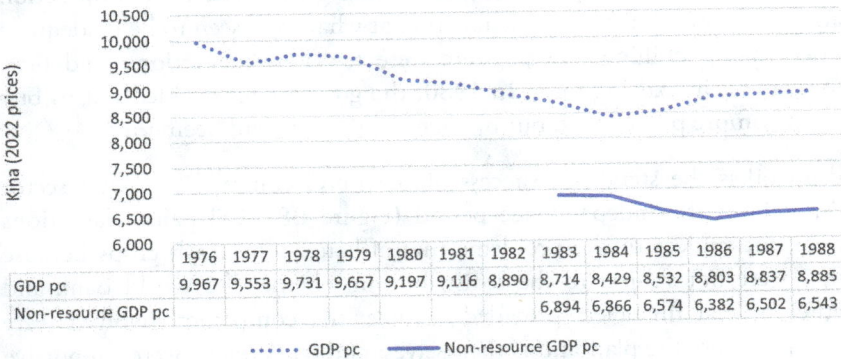

	1976	1977	1978	1979	1980	1981	1982	1983	1984	1985	1986	1987	1988
GDP pc	9,967	9,553	9,731	9,657	9,197	9,116	8,890	8,714	8,429	8,532	8,803	8,837	8,885
Non-resource GDP pc								6,894	6,866	6,574	6,382	6,502	6,543

······ GDP pc   ——— Non-resource GDP pc

Figure 2.2: GDP and non-resource GDP per person, 1976–88 (kina, constant prices)

Source: PNG Economic Database.

2.2.2 Agriculture and manufacturing

Most Papua New Guineans farm, and most grow cash crops. According to the 1980 Census, in that year, 48 per cent of PNG households grew coffee, 19 per cent copra and 13 per cent cocoa (Connell 1997, 81). The performance of non-resource commodities was mixed over this period. If we compare production at the end of the period with that at the start of it, we see little or no growth in the traditional crops of coffee, cocoa and copra, but a more than doubling of palm oil and log production (Figures B7 and B8).

The traditional cash crops struggled with land disputes, and growth came from smallholders rather than plantation owners (Goodman, Lepani and Morawetz 1985). Plantation owners were overwhelmingly foreign. Just before independence the government decided, partly to prosecute its localisation agenda (3.1.1), and partly because of the grievances of traditional landowners, to initiate a program of plantation land acquisition. Something had to be done—the situation was a 'dangerous emergency' (Fingleton 1981, 222); some 60 plantations were illegally occupied and another 40 were subject to this threat in 1974; in 1971, a district commissioner in East New Britain had been killed trying to end such an occupation (Goodman, Lepani and Morawetz 1985, 237)—but government action came at a high cost. The plantation redistribution scheme led to the purchase of 68 plantations (Daniel and Sims 1986, 84), often by politically well-connected rural development corporations, many of which failed (MacWilliam 2013). Much of the land acquired ended up being removed from production altogether, and the threat of acquisition at what were seen to be inadequate prices had a chilling effect. There were few new plantations, and little investment in existing ones. In 1980, the government decided not to buy out any more plantations, but by then the damage had been done.

Palm oil is the stand-out success of the PNG commodity export sector throughout the independence period (Figure B8). Oil palm plantations were not subject to the problems that afflicted other cash crops because they were not subject to the redistribution scheme; the World Bank and other official financiers provided finance; the companies involved were larger, as were the plantations themselves; and landowners were supportive because they were involved through the 'nucleus estate' model, in which the plantation supported and bought produce from surrounding smallholders.

Growth in logging was also impressive over the eighties, and logging prices rose rapidly (Figure B13). Nevertheless, this sector can hardly be considered a success. Performance in terms of processed timber and government revenue was disappointing. When Paias Wingti became prime minister in 1987, he established the Barnett Forest Industry Inquiry 'amidst rumours of massive corruption and scandalous malpractices in the timber industry' (Saffu 1998d, 442). Attempts to reform the forestry sector were a major focus of the nineties (5.1).

One consequence of the prolonged fall in many agricultural prices was the demise of the commodity stabilisation funds for copra, coffee and cocoa. Predicting agricultural prices was next to impossible, and the funds were almost completely depleted by the end of the decade (World Bank 1993; Gumoi 1993, Table 2). From the nineties onward, the government has provided some small support to farmers from revenue and aid, but the era of commodity price stabilisation was over.

As with most discussions of PNG agriculture, our focus is on commodities, because that is what we have data on. And these cash crops are important to ordinary farmers. But so too is the much-more-difficult-to-measure production of crops for own consumption or for sale in domestic markets. Marketed fresh food has been hailed by PNG's leading agricultural expert as 'one of the big success stories in the PNG economy' (Bourke 2005a, 22).

An important non-exported agricultural commodity is *buai*. Again, there are no quantitative estimates, but Tim Sharp, who has examined the *buai* trade in detail, writes that 'since the 1970s the betel nut trade has effloresced, and has fundamentally changed the nature of highland and lowland marketplaces' (Sharp 2012, 275).

PNG seas cover important tuna migration routes, and the tuna caught in its waters make it a significant global producer, with a share of up to 10 per cent of the global catch in some years (Kumoru and Koren 2006). Tuna are caught by a combination of resident and non-resident fishing vessels. The latter pay license fees to fish in PNG waters; the former provide export revenue and some employment. PNG's first plans to have a domestic tuna processing sector were made during this period (Daniel and Sims 1986, 93). However, the first tuna cannery did not open until 1997 (4.3.2).

PNG has never been a manufacturing nation. Manufacturing was about 4 per cent of GDP in 1980, and that share stagnated over the decade.

Food self-sufficiency was an important theme of this period (McKillop 1981, 244). The most notable result of import substitution efforts was the decision to grow and process sugar at a commercial scale. Ramu Sugar Ltd, a joint venture mainly sponsored by the government and the UK Commonwealth Development Corporation, began production in 1982 behind a ban on sugar imports (Laveil 2019a). Notwithstanding the initial agreement that sugar would be priced at import parity, by 1984 Ramu Sugar was selling sugar at six times the world price (Daniel and Sims 1986, 88–9).

The tale of Ramu Sugar takes us well beyond the confines of this period but here we briefly peek ahead to examine its fate. The policy to support Ramu Sugar was controversial. Economists have generally opposed it: John Gibson called it a 'major policy blunder' (cited in Errington and Gewertz 2004, 288). The project's backers point to the 2,500 jobs it has created and the 'community of between 15,000 and 20,000 people, not just our employees but surrounding villages who, to one degree or another, rely on Ramu Sugar' (Errington and Gewertz 2004, 234).

On the positive side, the ban on sugar imports was replaced by an 85 per cent tariff in 1997, and that tariff has been further reduced to 30 per cent, thereby reducing the cost to consumers of this intervention. On the negative side, Ramu Sugar's production is only 30,000 tonnes, about the same level as when the project began in the 1980s. The company, now called Ramu Agro-Industries, has diversified into oil palm and cattle. Probably this should have been the focus from the start: PNG's climate is not in fact suited to sugar, the crop is subject to indigenous diseases and the Ramu mill is too small to be efficient (Anderson and Bosworth 2009).

2.2.3 Resource sector

Production in copper and gold was stable over the first decade of independence and increased when Ok Tedi—another gold, silver and copper mine, this one high in the Star Mountains of the Western Province, close to the border with Indonesia, and at the other end of PNG to Panguna—commenced production in 1984.

There was also extensive exploration in the eighties, leading to the commencement of construction of the smaller Misima gold mine in 1988, and of the massive Porgera gold mine in 1989, as well as preparation for PNG's first oil exports in the early nineties. In 1988, there was a gold rush at Mt Kare on the Enga-Southern Highlands. At its height, some 10,000 diggers worked the field unconstrained by any state supervision. Plans to construct a mine there never materialised due to landowner disputes (Ryan 1991; Henton and Flower 2007).

At independence, the government stated that it supported large mines 'not for any direct benefit they can bring, but for the financial support that they can provide for progress towards other national goals' (Department of Finance 1977, cited in Daniel and Sims 1986, 4). In other words, the aim was to maximise resource revenue to the national government. The government operationalised this objective in relation first to the Panguna mine (the agreement for which was renegotiated just before independence), and then to the Ok Tedi project (negotiations for which began in 1976 and were concluded in 1980). The negotiating stances developed in relation to these two projects were then generalised in 1978 into mining and petroleum policies and laws.

The government relied mainly on the corporate income tax (35 per cent) to extract its share of resource rents. It also introduced a 15 per cent tax on dividends sent abroad,[2] and took a minority equity stake: about 20 per cent in the case of both Panguna and Ok Tedi. The PNG government also became the first in the world to introduce a super-profits tax, which would tax profits above a certain benchmark at a higher rate. This was the resource rents tax (RRT) of Garnaut and Clunies-Ross (1979), developed in PNG just prior to independence. Royalties were seen as distorting and kept low, just 1.25 per cent of the value of sales; they were given to the provincial governments and landowners, on which more below.

The RRT was not often triggered (in Panguna in 1974, 1979, 1980 and 1988). Nevertheless, data from 1974, when the mine agreement was renegotiated, to 1989, when it was closed, indicate that the state ended up with 75 per cent of Panguna's net earnings before tax (Gupta 1992, 206–7; see also O'Faircheallaigh 1986). In other words, from the stated and sensible objective of national government revenue maximisation, PNG's resource policies worked very well.

Panguna was renegotiated when power was in the hands of the government: the mine had already been built, and the country was moving to independence. As a result, it set benchmarks that have not been matched since, and not only in terms of the government's take. The original agreement with Panguna included a provision for review every seven years. More recent agreements allow developers to sign up to a fiscal stability clause that, for a modest charge, prevents any change in terms and conditions at all (4.3.2). Panguna was also a transparent operation with the publication of its project profit and loss, something rarely seen since.

---

2   For petroleum projects, the corporate income tax rate was 50 per cent, and there was no dividend withholding tax.

In hindsight, the two failures of policy in the resource sector in the eighties were to prevent conflict at Panguna and environmental disaster at Ok Tedi. In 1974, in the face of secessionist pressures, it was decided that nearly all royalties from Panguna would be given not to the national but to the provincial Bougainville government. Only 5 per cent of royalties was earmarked for the mine's landowners. The small volume of royalties was one of a number of grievances of the landowners who closed down the mine in 1989 and plunged the island into a decade of conflict (5.2.4). Other problems included the environmental damage the mine was doing—mine waste was simply discharged into the Kawerong River causing lasting damage (Human Rights Centre 2020); the influx of workers from other parts of PNG; the uneven and perceived inequitable sharing of royalties among landowners (O'Callaghan 2002); and an intergenerational battle for control over royalties and power more generally among the landowners (Filer 1992). Although the Panguna agreement had a provision for renegotiation every seven years, the opportunity was not seriously pursued after 1974 (Manning 1994; Wesley-Smith 1992). This looks negligent in hindsight; however, prior to the violence on Bougainville, the possibility that landowners could close an operating mine was not seriously contemplated.

Whether greater distribution of Panguna profits to landowners would have avoided the civil war that followed will never be known, but it surely would have made conflict less likely. While the Bougainville uprising was impossible to predict, it revealed the flaw with the otherwise sound approach of government to resource projects at the time of independence. It was not sufficient only to maximise the central government take; rather, the sharing of national benefits between various stakeholders—national, provincial and landowner—had to be negotiated to the satisfaction of all parties. Over time, this lesson has been well learnt, perhaps too well learnt. Formal negotiations with landowners were introduced in the nineties through the Development Forum, and, over time, an increasing share of resource projects has gone to local interests (4.3.2).

The Ok Tedi mine was constructed in the PNG mainland's mountainous interior. Tailings were meant to be stored in a tailings dam, but the site for the dam was damaged by an earthquake during construction. Rather than delay the mine opening, tailings were directly deposited into the Fly River, where they did significant environmental damage (Zorn 2018), which forced a corporate reckoning in the nineties (5.1.3).

2.2.4 Employment and the informal economy

Given a lack of data on total employment, we are forced to examine formal sector employment, which grew during this period (Figure B16), but not enough to keep up with population growth. Public employment was almost flat due to austerity. Private employment (including at state-owned enterprises) did better, growing at an annual average rate of 2.1 per cent. The bulk of the growth came in agriculture (Figure B17), which expanded from 44,000 workers in 1978 to 64,000 in 1988, presumably reflecting the growth in oil palm (only employees in the formal agricultural sector are captured).

As with non-commodity agriculture, which it encompasses, informal economic activity is hard to measure; however, it seems to have performed better than the formal economy. Informal economic activity had been constrained by the stifling effect of colonial regulations, as well as by 'subsistence affluence', the idea that well-fed villagers were not motivated to work more (Fisk 1971; Conroy 2020), and by the lack of a pre-colonial mercantile tradition. A World Bank (1978, 55) report just after independence noted 'the almost total absence of handicraft workers and the small-scale traders, shopkeepers and service repair establishments that provide such a large volume of employment, especially urban employment, in many other countries'. But the non-agricultural informal economy took off over the eighties. Whereas Conroy (2020, 344) observed that informal activity was 'insignificant in the capital on the eve of independence', Dorney (1991, 92), writing at the end of our first period, remarked that 'Port Moresby's markets are bustling'.

2.3 The macroeconomy

In most years in this period, the government achieved its goal of fiscal prudence, but, in the absence of real revenue growth, this required severe expenditure restraint. Inflation was successfully contained. The exchange rate remained pegged, and the policy of currency convertibility was adhered to; however, the hard kina policy that there should be no devaluation was abandoned over the eighties and the gradual depletion of foreign exchange reserves increased macroeconomic risks.

2.3.1 Fiscal policy

Fiscal policy in the early post-independence years had four goals: (a) revenue smoothing, given the volatility of Panguna revenues; (b) reduced reliance on Australian aid; (c) low deficits, because too high a level of borrowing would lead to external imbalance, and ultimately require a devaluation, which was inconsistent with the hard kina policy; and (d) real expenditure growth, essential given the country's development needs and the high expectations of the time. PNG achieved the first three, at least in part, but not the fourth.

Revenue smoothing was partly achieved. All resource sector government revenue entered the MRSF; only an amount that was considered sustainable for the next 20 years, given price and production projections, was meant to come out. Although some criticised the MRSF for not doing enough smoothing (Guest 1987), outflows from the MRSF were less volatile than inflows (Figure B30). Note, too, that the smoothing was downward. The MRSF saved at peak revenue times, but did not boost revenue as much when inflows were low. This admirable conservatism meant that the MRSF acted as a savings as well as a stabilisation fund.

The surplus accumulated by the MRSF proved a tempting target and, in the late eighties, the government started withdrawing more from the MRSF than its legislated entitlement (Oliver 1998, 465; Duncan and Temu 1995). But, even so, by 1989, the MRSF's balance had reached a handy 2.9 per cent of GDP.

The second goal of reduced aid dependency was clearly achieved (Figure B25). This was part of PNG's self-reliance policy, and also a necessity given agreements with Australia that its aid would fall.[3] Adjusting for inflation, aid measured in kina fell on average by 5.3 per cent a year between 1977 and 1988. As a result, aid became a much smaller share of government revenue, falling from 45 to 22 per cent of total revenue between the same years.

On average, over the period, and adjusting for inflation, own revenue grew at an impressive 4.7 per cent, well above average economic growth for the period. Due to the reduction in aid, however, the average post-inflation growth in total revenue was only 1.3 per cent.

---

3   In 1976, PNG signed a five-year aid program with Australia for AUD1 billion. In 1980, a new agreement introduced a real decline of 5 per cent per year. In 1985, this was changed to 3 per cent (BPNG 2007, Appendix B)

The third goal of fiscal prudence was achieved for most of the period. The deficit went up when revenue went down or stagnated (1979, 1981, 1982, 1983, 1985 and 1986), but it never stayed high for long, averaging just 1.7 per cent of GDP for the period (Figure B27 and Table 10.10). As a result, government debt was moderate, kept to 30 per cent of GDP or below. Most debt was foreign, initially commercial (including to help purchase equity in the Ok Tedi mine), but increasingly from the multilateral banks. Treasury bills were introduced in 1981 to facilitate domestic borrowing, but the share of domestic debt was only 26 per cent by 1988 (Figure B29).

The final fiscal objective of the eighties was real expenditure growth. Expenditure policy was set by the National Development Strategy (NDS) of 1976, which attempted to operationalise Somare's Eight-Point Plan (3.1.1). In turn, the NDS was implemented via the National Public Expenditure Plan (NPEP), a four-year rolling plan updated every year (Yala and Sanida 2010, 50). Eight NPEPs were produced between 1978 and 1985; typically they aimed for real expenditure growth of 3 per cent. In 1980, Somare revised the target up to 5 per cent on the back of the Ok Tedi agreement and a favourable resource price outlook. A few months later, a less favourable outlook forced Somare to return to 3 per cent (Conroy 1980). But even that was unattainable. Average expenditure growth for this first period was only 1.1 per cent after inflation, including negative real growth every year from 1982 to 1985.[4] Paias Wingti, then deputy prime minister, defended his government's austerity policies in 1982 as unavoidable:

> PNG must adjust to a much lower level of available resources to support domestic expenditures … The alternative to such an adjustment is that the nation will begin to follow the path of so many other less-developed countries. The stepping stones on this path are unmanageable government borrowing, large balance of payments deficits, devaluation, higher inflation, further devaluation and an inflationary spiral leading to economic and political instability. At the end of the path lies anarchy and the destruction of our social fabric. (Wingti 1985, 19)

It was responsible fiscal policy, but the inability to grow expenditure at least in line with population put downward pressure on government services, employment and growth.

---

4   The spike in expenditure/GDP in 1981 (Figure B23) is due to a decline in nominal GDP that year.

2.3.2 Monetary policy

The Bank of Papua New Guinea (BPNG) was established in 1973 to administer monetary policy and supervise the financial system. From independence, monetary policy was intended to keep inflation low. This goal was certainly achieved in the first period, especially by global standards, as inflation was contained by avoiding a large devaluation (Figure B31 and Table 10.9).

Until the financial deregulation of the mid-eighties (3.1.2), the central bank was able to manage demand by directly changing interest rates. Then, until the early nineties, the minimum liquid asset ratio (MLAR) became the primary instrument used by BPNG to influence liquidity and, therefore, loanable funds. The MLAR was raised from 15 to 25 per cent in 1977 (a year of strong growth) but eased from 1979 when growth weakened, and ranged between 10 and 15 per cent in the second half of the eighties. Meanwhile, bank lending to the private sector grew rapidly, with outstanding loans to the private sector increasing from 7 per cent of GDP in 1977 to 17 per cent in 1986 (Figure B32). The loan-to-deposit ratio increased from just 52 per cent in 1977 to 100 per cent in 1982 and 105 per cent by 1989. By the eighties, the MLAR was binding, and actual bank liquidity tracked the minimum closely (Figure B33).

2.3.3 Exchange rate policy and the balance of payments

The hard kina policy that PNG took to independence was a commitment to 'at least maintaining the foreign exchange value of the freely convertible kina against major world currencies' (Goodman, Lepani and Morawetz 1985, 53). This was done to keep inflation down (inflation of 20 per cent plus in 1974 had led to public protests in Port Moresby [Hegarty 1998a]), to promote fiscal discipline, and because it was felt that, given the policy of full wage indexation, a real depreciation would be impossible. The hard kina policy had three constituent parts: convertibility, the avoidance of nominal depreciation[5] and the maintenance of healthy foreign exchange reserves.

---

5   In 1975, Finance Minister Chan said that he could not 'forsee circumstances in which it would be sensible to devalue the kina in terms of world major currencies' (quoted in Griffin 1998, 260).

Convertibility on the current account was achieved. Demands for foreign exchange to finance imports and to repatriate capital earnings were honoured. Regarding the avoidance of nominal depreciation, at first the kina was pegged to the Australian dollar, and, in 1976, it was revalued upwards by 13 per cent (Figure B20). From 1977, the kina was pegged to a basket of currencies, with the aim of maintaining its average value against that basket (Garnaut, Baxter and Krueger 1984, 14). However, following the deterioration in the terms of trade in the early eighties, there developed a perception that the kina was overvalued. Even though there was limited formal sector wage flexibility due to indexation (3.1.2), there was a policy shift in 1983 to one of gradual depreciation:

> In a marked departure from previous policy, the kina was depreciated early in the 1983 in step with the devaluation of the Australian dollar. Without any formal announcement of a policy change, the kina was allowed gradually to depreciate further, until by mid-1984 the kina-basket exchange rate was about 10 per cent below what it had been two years earlier. (Goodman, Lepani and Morawetz 1985, 54)

In all, there was a real depreciation over the eighties of about 12 per cent (Figure B21). Clearly, the earlier commitment not to devalue the kina had been set aside. The decision in 1990 to devalue by 10 per cent after the shock of the closure of the Bougainville mine (4.4.2) only confirmed this.

The current account showed a small surplus for the first few years after independence, but went into deficit in the early eighties due to lower export prices and heavy imports associated with the construction of the Ok Tedi mine (Figure B19). The current account deficit reached as high as 14 per cent of GDP in 1981 and 1982. This deficit remained for the rest of the decade, but the trend was towards balance as imports went down and exports recovered relative to GDP. By 1988, it had fallen to 6 per cent. Persistent current account deficits were mainly financed by resource-related capital inflows, but also came at a cost to foreign exchange reserves. While reserves of above USD400–500 million were maintained over the eighties, with the economy growing, and imports growing relative to the economy, this amount covered a progressively smaller number of months of imports: from five or six in the late seventies to only three in 1981 (after a series of relatively high fiscal deficits) and only just above two in 1988 (Figure B22). Such a low level of reserves undermined the credibility of the government's hard kina policy, which relied on 'the accumulation and maintenance of adequate international reserves to assure the credibility of policy', to use the words of Finance Minister Julius Chan (speaking in 1975, cited in Dorney 1991, 84).

In summary, the exchange rate regime remained convertible and pegged throughout this early post-independence period, but commitment to the hard kina weakened in two ways, both of which presaged the radical changes of the nineties. First, the government started to show a willingness to engage in nominal, albeit modest, depreciation. Second, the reduction in foreign exchange reserves relative to imports made it more likely that any kina peg would end in crisis. More generally, the absence of strong economic growth in this period undermined the sustainability of sound macroeconomic policy, leading eventually to crisis, not in this period but the next.

3

Harder than expected

The system of centralised wage fixing that Papua New Guinea inherited ... is totally inappropriate for a country at Papua New Guinea's level of development. The Government might well consider scrapping the system and starting again. (Goodman, Lepani and Morawetz 1985, 67)

Being or becoming a politician has [become] an attraction to many Papua New Guineans from all walks of life. (Pokawin 1986, 136)

3.1 Economic policies

We discussed macroeconomic policies in the previous chapter. In this chapter we focus on microeconomic or structural (growth) policies. Assumptions of growth at independence were optimistic, and policy statements at the time placed all the emphasis on equity. That changed as economic growth in fact proved difficult to achieve, but the period was characterised more by policy stasis than reform. The economy suffered from high costs and over-regulation. Rural development was a major focus of the period, but not a successful one. Land policy reform was largely deferred, not for the last time.

3.1.1 Economic policy at independence

Most striking about the various policy statements from the time of independence is their lack of any mention of economic growth. In the decade prior to independence, following an influential 1964 World Bank report and a change in ministerial responsibility in Australia for its colony, economic policy had shifted from protecting smallholders to also emphasising economic growth or 'accelerated development' as it was called (MacWilliam 2013). In the run-up to independence, growth was de-emphasised by PNG's emerging leaders not due to strong anti-growth sentiment, but rather to signal a new approach, and on the basis of the optimistic assumption that growth, which had been rapid in the immediate pre-independence period, would be the easy part of the post-independence journey.[1]

In 1972, a group of UK consultants commissioned by the United Nations Development Program wrote the Faber Report that argued that 'the emphasis of the next plan should be on localisation/indigenisation, rather than growth' (Faber et al. 1973, 4).[2] PNG had just entered into a period of self-rule in preparation for independence. Chief Minister Michael Somare immediately converted the Faber Report into an Eight-Point Plan that emphasised equality, the decentralisation of economic activity, self-reliance and national ownership.[3] A similar manifesto of five 'national goals and directive principles' became the preamble to PNG's constitution. Some two pages of (non-justiciable) prescriptions were bundled together at the start of the constitution under five headings: integral human development, equality and participation, national sovereignty and self-reliance, (protection of) natural resources and the environment, and (reliance on) PNG ways.

---

1   Langmore (1973, 198) notes that 'in the period 1965–71, Australia's objectives for Papua New Guinea emphasized maximisation of the current rate of growth of national income'. Garnaut (1981, 166) writes about 'the confidence about growth [at the time]: a feeling that growth would come, and that what mattered was the form it would take and the distribution of the resulting benefits'.

2   The team led by British economist Mike Faber visited in 1972 and delivered its report in August. Somare released his Eight-Point Plan in December 1972 (Langmore 1973, 198). The report was officially authored by the Overseas Development Group, University of East Anglia, where Faber worked, but is better known as the Faber Report.

3   The Faber Report was even more radical than the Eight-Point Plan. Several of its recommendations were included in the Eight-Point Plan only in watered-down form or not at all, namely: 'Elite creation is inimical to the welfare of the majority. The advantages of the highly educated and of the urban population in general must therefore be diminished'; 'An equitable distribution of employment and income opportunities should have priority over supply of high level manpower to manage the state bureaucracy'; 'The main emphasis in infrastructure development should be in rural areas' (Faber et al. 1973, 21). These three points were watered down in the Eight-Point Plan to calls for a 'more equal distribution of economic benefits including a move toward equalising incomes' and 'decentralised economic activity, planning and government spending with emphasis on agricultural development and village industry'. See also Conroy (2020, 353), who notes the call by Keith Hart, one of the authors of the Faber Report, for the PNG elite to 'accept reduced living standards and look at policies which are inspired by local needs and availability'. Conroy rightly refers to this as a counsel of perfection.

Although the five goals, like the eight points, avoided any mention of economic growth, they contained aspirations that could only be supported by its occurrence, such as increased revenue and better health, nutrition and education. Much of the content of the five goals is compelling and has maintained its relevance, most notably the calls for a rapid move towards gender equality. Other parts made less sense—even at the time, given PNG's aspirations to develop its mineral and petroleum resources. There is a wariness in the constitutional preamble in relation to globalisation, with calls for 'strict control of foreign investment', for the PNG economy to be 'basically self-reliant' and for the state to 'control major enterprises engaged in the exploitation of natural resources', as well as a warning against 'dependence [on] imported skills'.

Parts of the constitutional preamble and Eight-Point Plan were taken seriously. There was rapid localisation of the civil service (3.2.2), and plans were adopted shortly after independence to buy out plantations (2.2.2) and other foreign businesses.

Other parts of official economic policy at independence, in particular the emphasis on equality, were honoured more in the breach than the observance. It is difficult to think of a more extreme form of policy incoherence than the priority given in the Eight-Point Plan to agriculture and rural development, and the doubling of the minimum urban wage over the years immediately preceding independence. No point was more emphasised by the Faber Report than the importance of *not* increasing urban wages. If the PNG government 'has the welfare of the rural majority at heart', the Faber Report cautioned, it will have to 'adopt a tough line to all sections of the urban workforce' (Faber et al. 1973, 31).

This was a big ask. PNG's first major and then dominant party, Pangu, had made increasing wages for national civil servants a major policy plank in the sixties (Kiki 1968). Industrial relations in the private sector were governed by a central system of wage setting, transplanted from Australia. PNG's Minimum Wages Board sided with the trade unions in the pre-independence years and the urban minimum wage was doubled after inflation between 1972 and 1975 (Figure B18). The PNG government did nothing to prevent or even oppose the large increases awarded by the board in 1972 and 1974, making submissions to neither and ignoring its own income policy that it developed in 1974 and which urged wage restraint (Somare 1974). Indeed, in 1974, the minister for labour sacked the board for not increasing wages enough, and put in place one more sympathetic to union demands (Conroy 2020, 349–53; Langmore and Berry 1978; Gupta 1992).[4]

If support for equality was a reflection of the emerging elite's idealism, the sharp growth in urban wages was a product of its urban base (indeed, union base, in the case of Pangu). The fusion of, and unreconciled tension between, the two was captured early on by university students who, in 1974, went on strike both to demand higher allowances for themselves and to urge the government to do more to promote an egalitarian society (Howie-Willis 1980, 228–9).

Some, including the Wages Board itself, made the argument that increasing urban wages was consistent with equity because workers would redistribute their higher wages to their rural kin or *wantok* (Lepani 2014).[5] However, this ignored the logic central to the government's income policy, namely that increases in the minimum wage would shift government revenue to the payment of salaries and away from rural development. The high minimum wage would also make future economic expansion more difficult. PNG's wages became very high by international standards (3.1.3).

In any case, at the political level, talk of redistribution, while useful as a rhetorical device, was far from a shared ideology. Some aspects of PNG culture were egalitarian, but others were not. According to one observer, in the PNG Highlands what was valued was 'power and wealth and the ostentatious display of both' (Connolly 2005, 94). Few villagers were even aware of the Eight-Point Plan and it had little ownership among the elite either (Allen 1983, 227–9). PNG's politicians had growing links to business, and were more pragmatists than ideologues (Voutas 1981, 46–7).[6]

---

4   In later years, ministers would refer to this as the 'disastrous experience in the early 1970s' (Kaputin 1984, 7).

5   In this, the board was supported by UPNG and then ANU anthropologist and Marxist economist Chris Gregory, whose famous 1982 book *Gifts and Commodities* was a critique of neo-classical economics in the context of colonial Papua New Guinea.

6   'The pseudo-socialist overtones of the aims were acceptable at the level of public rhetoric. They even appeared to be related to the traditional restraints that existed in village societies. But for some ministers I believe that repressed entrepreneurial ambition whispered: "I don't want redistribution applied to me personally; I would rather be a millionaire businessman." The most cynical interpretation that can be made of the general philosophy announced by the Coalition government in the Eight Aims and elaborated in the Constitution is that it reflected an intellectual trend of the late sixties and seventies keenly felt by the expatriate Western liberals and by the Papua New Guinean graduates and undergraduates. The politicians, however, merely clothed themselves with these ideas because other political purposes were served in doing so' (Voutas 1981, 46).

Consistent with this, Pangu's 1972 election platform, while 'calling for rural improvement, came down heavily in favour of improved wages and houses for urban workers, and avoided reconciling the competing demands for urban and rural areas' (Voutas 1981, 34).

To the extent that there was a firm ideological commitment, it was to economic nationalism rather than equality.[7] Hence the emphasis on localisation, the first of the Eight-Point Plan's goals, and one of only two to which the adjective 'rapid' was attached—the other, ironically, was gender equality (Garnaut 1981). From a nationalistic point of view, urban wage increases could easily be, and were, supported as shifting income from foreign capitalists to national workers. The support for redistribution from richer to poorer was much more muted. In 1978, Hegarty (1998e, 327) commented that 'the rhetoric of redistribution is still current but the essentially accommodative political and governmental style ultimately works in the interests of those with the most economic and political clout'.

Apart from the selective way in which they were implemented, the other problem with the Eight-Point Plan and the Faber Report on which it was based is that they were too optimistic. While the latter argued that GDP growth should not be maximised, it nevertheless assumed GDP growth in excess of 7–9 per cent a year and national employment growth of 5–6 per cent a year, which is rapid by any standards (Faber et al. 1973, 4, 18, 19).

It is true that the economy had been growing rapidly in the years prior to independence: gross national product was estimated to have grown by more than 10 per cent on average between 1963 and 1973 (Goodman, Lepani and Morawetz 1985, 28). Growth in the early seventies had been especially rapid with the construction of the Panguna mine in 1971 and 1972, followed by high copper prices in 1973 and 1974 (Chowdhury 2018, 95). If it had been reasonable to assume that high growth would continue, then trading off some of that growth for greater equity would have made good sense. But the rapid pre-independence growth was an unrealistic benchmark. Apart from the risks of deeper disruptions to do with such

---

7   In the words of one radical critic: 'The issues most important to the members of the Bully Beef Club, later to become Pangu Party, were to improve salaries, and to localise. These were more important than anything else. Of course a marked injustice was supported by colonial policy at that time. Housing conditions for workers also became mobilising issues. The workers were more conscious of this discrimination than villagers and provided a base for the development of unionism, which was itself used by the educated elites as a political wheel and a stepping stone in the higher echelons of state positions' (Samana 1988, 99).

a fundamental change as decolonisation, the pre-independence growth in plantation output and mineral production was in any case not sustainable, and the withdrawal of the Australian administration and the departure of many expatriates was always going to be a drag on growth. Moreover, a temporary plunge or a longer-term decline in commodity prices (the latter as per the popular Prebisch-Singer hypothesis) was an ever-present risk for a commodity exporter such as PNG. Finally, the risks of low growth were underestimated. The belief expressed at independence that even 'no growth at all' could lead to 'an increase in human welfare and happiness' (Somare 1975, 108) was naive.

In hindsight, the underlying weakness of economic policy in the seventies and eighties was an underestimation of how important achieving growth was and how difficult it would be to achieve. There were a few warnings that it might not be that easy, but these came more from political scientists and historians (such as Nelson 1972, quoted at the opening of Part I) than economists, and related more to threats of disunity and secession than to economic risks.[8]

3.1.2 Economic policy through the eighties

It did not take long for the realisation to dawn that things were not going to plan. Finance Minister John Kaputin (1982, 57) said that he was:

> quite worried about the future non-mining growth rate of the Papua New Guinea economy. A lack of agriculture replanting, land problems, government inefficiency and a general attitude of wanting to get something for nothing are problems that must be tackled.

However, absent a crisis, there was inadequate impetus to change course.

Economic policy was therefore characterised more by stability than by change through the eighties. The emphasis on economic growth increased due to slow growth. This change was particularly marked from 1985 to 1988 under PNG's third prime minister, Paias Wingti, who talked about 'the imperative for economic growth' and said he would 'not repeat the mistakes of previous governments by compromising its growth objectives to the achievement

---

8   Woolford (1976, 257) was also prescient: 'From whatever perspective one looks at Papua New Guinea, the future appears difficult. It is politically unstable, with party alignments volatile; there is a serious danger that part of the country will break away; some important institutions are inappropriate; self-reliance, whether economic or psychological, exists only at the level of political rhetoric; and everywhere there is a gulf between promise and performance.'

of subsidiary social goals'.[9] The 1985 National Development Plan had as its first aim 'economic growth' (Yala and Sanida 2010, 50). Then, when Rabbie Namiliu took over as prime minister after a vote of no confidence in 1988, his government tried to switch the focus to education.[10] However, fiscal constraints throughout the whole period, political instability from the eighties onwards and the absence of an economic crisis that necessitated a tough response limited the influence of these largely rhetorical policy shifts.

The early years of independence were a period in which radical thinking and experimentation were popular. The 'Melanesian way' continued to be promoted, reminding audiences of the constitution's five directives and emphasising distribution and grassroots community engagement rather than accumulation and foreign investment (Narokobi 1986; Samana 1988).[11] An appropriate technology centre was established in Lae. Tanzania and China were role models for many, and radical ideas were often espoused at the annual academic–policymaker confab, the Waigani Seminar, which started in 1967 and ran (with some breaks) until 1997. However, in most respects, economic policy was, in fact, relatively orthodox. Governments were not against private enterprise but saw a role for themselves as well. A mixed economy developed:

> By 1982, the Government had equity holdings in mineral, palm oil, sugar and logging projects and responsibility for 37 statutory bodies engaged in commercial activities. The State owned the Papua New Guinea Banking Corporation, the largest commercial bank, which controlled around half of the banking business in the financial sector. Two government financial institutions, the Investment Corporation and the Development Bank, had shareholdings in approximately 80 businesses, while most provincial governments had established development corporations. (BPNG 2007, 36).

---

9   From the Wingti government strategic plan (Dorney 1991, 90).

10   In his first speech as prime minister, Namaliu (1988) decried his predecessor's spending on wasteful commercial projects and said that what Papua New Guineans wanted was 'a government that will attack the nation's law and order problems head on … a government that will give new hope of improved education and health opportunities to the underprivileged masses'.

11   Many years later, Gewertz and Errington (1999, 119) wryly commented: 'Bernard Narokobi, after writing *The Melanesian Way*, was widely rumored to have acquired considerable wealth in the course of his long political career … We met him at a meeting in Wewak where, as Wewak's Member of the National Parliament, he was explaining new government policies (including the 'structural adjustments' imposed by the World Bank and IMF). In describing forthcoming stringencies, he said that villages should no longer aspire to Toyota Land Cruisers; instead of holding these unreasonable expectations, they should be content with "appropriate technology" such as water buffalo. Following the meeting, he was driven away in a new Land Cruiser.'

Foreign investment was welcome in principle, but approvals and regulations were cumbersome (Goodman, Lepani and Morawetz 1985). A large number of sectors were reserved for local investors (Daniel and Sims 1986, 31). Even where allowed, foreign investors were tightly regulated by the National Investment Development Authority (NIDA), a product of the thinking at independence of the need to 'control and restrict all the foreign capital', as per the quote from Prime Minister Somare with which the previous chapter began.[12] For such enterprises, 'all overseas marketing, loan, management, royalty, etc. agreements require[d] prior NIDA approval' (Daniel and Sims 1986, 32). There were long delays in granting those approvals. Having to deal with provincial governments as well only added to the process, as did the stringent rules placed around the hiring of foreign workers.

Price controls were widespread—covering some 56 per cent of the typical urban consumption bundle—but not implemented in a way that kept prices artificially low (World Bank 1991, 95–6; 1993, 36).

Tariffs were not high at independence but were increased over time. A uniform tariff at independence of 4 per cent was increased to 10 per cent and, starting in 1979, supplemented by higher tariffs (at first, 17.5 but then 30 per cent) for all goods for which there was domestic production (Gupta 1992, 168–9). From the eighties to the mid-nineties:

> increasing use was made of protective tariff rates and ad hoc bans and quotas to protect a range of both primary and manufactured goods such as sugar, animal feed, plywood, matches, canned meat and soap. (BPNG 2007, 42)

Industrial policy was, and has remained, an area of contention. Daniel and Sims (1986) provide an account of the debate between the 'production', 'valuation' and 'nationalist' schools of thought. The first group wanted more domestic production, the third more national ownership and the second group (the economists) wanted the best value proposition, regardless of location or ownership. Over time, the first and the third group combined to make trade policy more protectionist.

---

12   The Constitutional Reform Commission wanted controls on foreign investment written into the constitution, but this was rejected except in relation to the (non-justiciable) five goals. One prominent businessman talked about NIDA ('which has probably had to do more in the past seven years with deterring investment rather than encouraging it') as 'a body to *control* overseas investment already in Papua New Guinea and to promote further investment from overseas, while warning potential investors in the strongest possible terms of the dire consequences should they fail to toe the line' (Corden 1982, 134).

Hardly anything was done to tackle the problem of high wages, despite the repeated warnings from the economic reports of the time. The government acknowledged the need for action but put it in the too-hard basket. Finance Minister Kaputin (1982, 55) said that a reduction in real wages 'would clearly be desirable as our basic cost structure is too high', but went on to excuse inaction on the grounds that, 'in our Melanesian society, a degree of consensus is required'.

Indeed, there was not only protection for real wages by indexation to inflation, but also a further increase in real wages with the introduction of superannuation in the eighties (Garnaut 2000). Economic reports called for real wages to be cut by 25–30 per cent (Garnaut et al. 1984, 234) and for the system of centralised wage setting to be scrapped (Goodman, Lepani and Morawetz 1985, 67; see the quotation at the start of this chapter). The only nod in these directions was the introduction of partial indexation over the course of the eighties.[13] This saw a modest 9 per cent real reduction in the urban minimum wage between 1982 and 1992 (Figure B18), about enough to offset the superannuation impost.

It is not easy to give an overall verdict on the economic development policy stance of the eighties. It is surely an exaggeration to say that 'the founding fathers of Papua New Guinea were followers of the Dependency Theory approach to economic management' (BPNG 2007, 238). This is no more convincing than the opposite argument, put forward by dependency theorists shortly after independence, that the PNG government was implementing a 'neo-colonialist strategy' (Mortimer 1979, 239) and that PNG was being 'integrated into the world capitalist system' (236) without opposition or resistance via a ruling class of 'politician[s], bureaucrats and foreign interests' (232).

Somewhere in between pro- and anti-market (including pro- and anti-foreign investment) would be one way to describe economic policy in the post-independence years; complacent would be another.

The only area where there was deregulation in the eighties was in the financial sector. PNG's financial system has always been dominated by a small number of banks. The biggest in this period was the state-owned

---

13   In 1976, there was no adjustment of minimum wages; in 1977, they were increased in line with inflation; in 1980, a cap of 8 per cent on wage increases was introduced; in 1983, that cap was lowered to 5 per cent; in 1986, half-indexation was allowed for inflation above 10 per cent; and in 1989 the cap was adjusted to 6 per cent (BPNG 2007, Appendix B).

Papua New Guinea Banking Corporation; three others were subsidiaries of Australian banks (Westpac, ANZ and National). In 1983, two other foreign banks were given licenses to establish local subsidiaries: Indosuez and Lloyds. Until 1984, interest rates were regulated by the central bank, but lending rates were deregulated that year, and deposit rates the following year. Sectoral lending targets, and targets for loans to nationals, were also done away with over the course of the decade. This was a move that had profound implications in the following decades, unexpectedly increasing interest spreads as the financial sector became less competitive (4.3.3).

By and large, however, the eighties was a period of policy stasis. Systemic reforms—privatisation, trade liberalisation and wage deregulation—were talked about, but were a feature of the crisis-prone nineties, not the stable eighties.

3.1.3 High costs and the investment climate

World Bank Chief Economist Nicholas Stern popularised the term the 'investment climate', by which he meant the 'policy, institutional, and behavioural environment, both present and expected, that influences the returns and risks associated with investment' (Stern 2002, 88). With its high costs and long delays, PNG's investment climate was weak at independence, and weakened further during the eighties.

Daniel and Sims (1986, 27–30) were perhaps the first to emphasise the structural constraints hindering PNG's economic development:

> Papua New Guinea provides a small domestic market for local production ... Urban wages in Papua New Guinea are higher than those in comparable countries. In terms of human resources Papua New Guinea was one of the world's least developed countries at Independence[14] ... Virtually all land (97 per cent) is under customary ownership where title is determined by historical occupation and is not effectively registered, making commercial loan finance impossible ... Most land-based activity ... faces long delays. Papua New Guinea is vastly over-regulated ... The main regulations facing land, labour and capital ... provide a barrier to entry ... and expansion ... and raise costs and prices.

---

14   The World Bank commented a decade before independence that 'among adult indigenes, the paucity of educated persons is extreme, under 1 per cent having received a full primary education and probably less than 100 having completed a secondary course, while the first university graduate was expected at the end of 1964' (cited in Garnaut 2000, 30).

It is not surprising, given the rapid wage increases in the run-up to independence described earlier in this chapter, that PNG became a high wage country. In the mid-1980s, Goodman, Lepani and Morawetz (1985, 61) showed that the country's 'urban minimum wages are between 2 and 10 times greater than those in neighbouring competing countries'— for example, almost double the minimum wage in Malaysia. But it was not only wages. PNG became a high-cost country in which electricity, land and transport were all expensive. The figures below come from a World Bank 1993 report. By then PNG had the highest, sometimes by far the highest, labour, electricity, rental and sea freight costs of the nine comparator countries shown.[15]

Table 3.1: International comparison of costs (1993)

Country	Labour (USD/hour)	Electricity (USD/kwh)	Rental (USD/sq ft/yr)	Sea freight (USD/20 ft container)
Papua New Guinea	2.00	0.19	4.24	2,500
Indonesia	0.42	0.06	0.42	2,250
Philippines	0.55	0.07	0.77	2,185
Thailand	0.58	0.07	1.72	2,050
Dominican Republic	0.72	0.07	2.40	1,730
Jamaica	0.88	0.10	3.10	1,685
Colombia	0.94	0.09	3.30	1,920
Costa Rica	1.15	0.08	3.50	1,700
Cameroon	1.56	0.06	3.65	1,625

Source: World Bank (1993, Table 4.6).

To what extent these costs were high due to geography, regulation, land tenure, governance, the Australian legacy and/or the resource sector can be debated. It is likely a product of them all. Costs were already high at independence because PNG inherited 'Australian standards of investment, consumption and incomes' (World Bank 1978, 29). They grew over time. For example, as crime worsened (3.2.5), security costs became another burden.

---

15   Booth (1995, 209) looked at data from the United Nations International Comparisons Program and concluded that 'over the past fifteen years, PNG has emerged as a high-cost economy in comparison with most of its neighbours in Asia and the Pacific'.

3.1.4 Rural development

There are significant and persistent geographical differences in development across PNG, and, consistent with the emphasis on equality, helping rural areas in general and backward areas in particular were priorities for the early independence period. 'Increasing rural welfare' and 'Helping less developed areas' were the first two of the eight objectives in the National Public Expenditure Plan of the seventies and early eighties (2.3.1) (Conroy 1980, Appendix A).[16]

Between 1976 and 1986, the government funded integrated rural development projects (IRDPs) in five of the country's least developed provinces: East and West Sepik, Southern Highlands (which then included Hela), Enga and Simbu. IRDPs were a type of project being promoted by the World Bank around the world, and the PNG IRDPs had financial backing from both the World Bank and the Asian Development Bank. They included a mix of income generation, infrastructure and social welfare investments. In PNG, as globally, integrated rural development delivered a lot less than it promised. Connell (1997, 117) provides a good summary, writing that 'though the IRDPs contributed to rural welfare gains, they failed to provide and develop opportunities where villagers could raise their economic productivity and increase their incomes over time'.

This is a problem that remains to this day. Allen, Bourke and Gibson (2005, 13) provide compelling evidence that the patterns of geographical disadvantage in PNG stretch back to before independence, and that poor areas are those that face 'a number of severe environmental constraints: very high altitude, high rainfall, steep slopes, flooding and poor soils'. These constraints make it difficult for disadvantaged areas to engage with the market and keep them poor.

More broadly, government support for rural development was a victim to forced expenditure restraint (2.3.1) and the rapid civil service localisation policy (3.2.2). On the former, Conroy and Curtain's (1978, 47) early reflection holds good for the entire period: 'notwithstanding a good deal of rhetoric to the contrary, little has been done to tilt the balance ... towards rural life'. On the latter, Allen (1983, 228) observed that:

---

16 Urban management was the seventh and environmental management the last of the eight objectives (Conroy 1980, Appendix A).

field positions were immediately affected [by localisation], and overseas officers were replaced by young Papua New Guineans. Many were inadequately trained and lacking in experience and confidence. Sent to isolated posts as administrators, agricultural or health extension officers, they faced immediate suspicion from villagers. With some outstanding exceptions, very few of these officers succeeded in delivering services.

3.1.5 Land policy

Nearly all of PNG's land is under customary ownership. This has long been seen as a barrier to development. The 2005–10 Medium Term Development Strategy put it this way:

> PNG's customary land tenure system is firmly entrenched in the nation's culture, and it is recognised under the country's legal system. It underpins PNG's robust village farming system and provides a welfare safety-net for the vast majority of the people. Customary owned land, however, is also widely viewed as a major constraint to economic development.
>
> As a general rule, customary land cannot be used as collateral by landowners seeking investment funds due to the absence of secure legal title. As well, individual landowners have little incentive to improve the land if the resulting benefits accrue to a large number of people who did not contribute to the improvement effort. Mobilising customary land for large-scale economic projects is also viewed as costly, time-consuming and is characterised by ongoing uncertainty. (GoPNG 2004, 10)

And it is not only customary land that is problematic. The small (about 3 per cent), but high-value share of land that has been alienated can also be subject to challenge, including from customary owners, who might reclaim ownership of the land and/or claim additional compensation for it (3.2.5). As early as 1982, one commentator noted the 'preoccupation with land issues in the life of the country', and gave a list of news reports such as the following:

> After the National Government had recently allocated government land by way of a lease to a ready-mixed concrete company for development of a cement bulk-handling facility on the Lae waterfront, 700 squatters moved on to the land and constructed traditional houses, following a dispute with other customary

> landowners from whom they previously rented land, and have defied all legal and other efforts to induce them to move; the K3-4 million project is in abeyance. (Trebilcock 1983, 193)

Land reform was a priority at, and indeed before, independence, but follow-through was limited. Although the '[colonial] administration's ultimate objective was to introduce a single system of individual registered titles to land' (Fingleton 1981, 213), it took few steps to realise that objective. Only a small amount (i.e. that 3 per cent) of customary land was alienated by the state, and there was hardly any registration of customary land, or conversion to individual ownership. (In rural PNG, individual households traditionally have exclusive use rights to the land they farm, but not ownership.) An attempt was made by the colonial administration to introduce a framework for customary land dispute resolution and registration, but this was blocked by the new home rule government that, in 1973, instead set up a Commission of Inquiry into Land Matters.

The priorities of the commission and of the government at this time were legislation to support the plantation redistribution scheme (2.2.2), and customary land dispute resolution to help prevent tribal violence (3.2.5). To deal with the latter, the Land Disputes Settlement Act was passed in 1975. The Act relied on mediation, but, in the face of constrained resources and deep-seated disputes, had only limited success. In 1981 the World Bank (1982, 2) noted that disputes over landownership were 'a major constraint on development'.

Another legislative milestone was the 1974 Land Groups Incorporation Act that, as its name suggested, aimed to give groups of landowners the ability to form a company to negotiate with and receive benefits from developers, such as in forestry. There are now some 20,000 Incorporated Land Groups registered in PNG (Allen and Monson 2014, 4), but hardly any of them are based on registered land. Rather, they are largely used as vehicles for the distribution of benefits from resource or forestry projects, and are often plagued by governance problems (Koyama 2004; Antonio, Wagi and Kari 2010).

Commercial transactions in customary land were banned, but an exception was made for the government, and this was used to get round the commercial ban. Customary landowners could lease their land to the government, who would then lease it back to the customary landowners who, since they were now themselves lessees of the land, could do whatever they wanted with it, including leasing it to developers. This was called the lease-leaseback scheme, 'a very unusual—probably unique—legal institution' (Filer 2017, 169). At one time, it was thought it could provide the basis for widespread commercial use of land. Amendments to the pre-independence Land Act were made in 1984 and again in 1996 (5.1.2) to further define this approach to land mobilisation, but the state could not keep up with the demand. The 1983 Taskforce on Customary Land Issues estimated the backlog to be between 8,000 and 10,000 applications (Cooter 1991, 776).

The same taskforce recommended, as had the pre-independence commission of inquiry, that customary owners be able to lease their land without the intermediation of government following a process of formal registration (Antonio, Wagi and Kari 2010). Some provinces took matters into their own hands: the East Sepik government initiated a registration scheme in 1982 (Filer, Dubash and Kalit 2000, 33). The national government approved the drafting of legislation, but it never got to parliament. 'Land law reform drifted into the wings' (Fingleton 1981, 235). It was not until the 2000s that the national government finally implemented a direct customary land leasing scheme and, unfortunately, it met with little success (9.1.5).

In the absence of channels to bring customary land into the formal sector, there was rapid growth in informal and often non-customary dealings in customary land:

> including clan land usage agreements permitting an individual member of a clan exclusive use of given land for agricultural production for a certain period of time; group projects involving inter-clan agreements as to common working and development of both groups' lands; [and] leasing and outright sale of land, often to migrants. (Ward cited in Trebilcock 1983, 210)

3.2 Politics and governance

The early post-independence era is one in which many of the features of PNG governance, as we know it today, were bedded down. The seventies and eighties saw the development of a distinctive style of politics, a decline in the quality of public services and a losing battle against corruption. It also saw a decisive though troubled shift to decentralisation, and the emergence of crime as a serious problem.

3.2.1 Politics

Papua New Guinea is often called the land of the unexpected, but one predictable thing is that elections will be held every five years. Given the high rate of turnover, incumbent MPs are united in wanting to avoid an early election. The first post-independence general elections were held in 1977, five years after the 1972 elections that had ushered in home rule. The surprise pro-independence coalition that the 1972 election had produced between the more left-wing and larger Pangu (Papua and New Guinea Union) Party and the smaller, pro-business People's Progress Party (PPP) was returned to power in 1977 under Pangu Party leader Michael Somare, who had been chief minister from 1972 and prime minister from 1975. This coalition gave PNG almost a decade of political stability, but started showing signs of strain in the late seventies, especially over a disagreement on anti-corruption policy (3.2.3). PPP ended its alliance with Pangu in 1978, and, after the country's first successful vote of no confidence, Julius Chan, the PPP leader, became prime minister in 1980, with the support of the United Party, which had its base in the Highlands and had been the main opposition.

Pangu bounced back in 1982 with an emphatic election victory—the most successful performance by any single party in PNG before or since (Table A2)—and Somare again became prime minister. However, the party itself then started to fracture, as younger leaders jostled to take power from Somare, who had intimated that he was contemplating retirement. He eventually decided against retirement but was unable to retain authority over the party he had helped to found. He lost the leadership of it in 1988 and left the following year over a dispute relating to the ownership of the Pangu business arm, Damai (Callick 1997, 111). Before that, Paias Wingti, who had first entered parliament in 1977 in his final year of tertiary economics studies, broke away from Pangu in 1985 to form his own party. He came to power in the same year, again via a parliamentary vote of no confidence. The 1987 elections delivered another shake-up and, after some wild jostling and a brief extension of the Wingti reign, Rabbie Namaliu, who had succeeded Somare as Pangu leader in May 1988, became prime minister a month later, and served in that role until the elections of July 1992.

Through this period, the shape of PNG's politics was taking form. PNG's first House of Assembly had been established in 1964. Democracy suited PNG, a country whose traditional, tribal organisation was 'distinguished by a lack of inherited status' (Allen, Bourke and Gibson 2005, 203) and where 'political manoeuvring was a constant all-pervading activity' (Allen 1983, 215).[17] The Melanesian 'big man', the archetypal Papua New Guinean leader, was focused on 'prestige, power and wealth', above all, some argued, the first of these three (Conroy 1976, 14–15).[18] The distinguished academic and politician Stephen Pokawin (1986, 136) commented that even before independence 'it became obvious … that the short cut to prestige and wealth was by becoming a political leader'. The growing primacy of politics can be seen most clearly in the increasing numbers of candidates who stood for election, from an average of eight per seat in 1977 to 10 in 1982 and 14 in 1987 (Table A2). While the numbers were to double again in subsequent decades, these levels of political interest and competition were already high by global standards. The creation of provincial assemblies provided further opportunities for aspiring politicians to enter the field. Pokawin (1986, 134) wrote that 'the ratio of salaried political leaders per person [in PNG] should be one of the highest anywhere'.

The pull of politics was irresistible even, or especially, for those who had already proven themselves as leaders in other fields. Membership of parliament became PNG's most valuable prize. In the mid-seventies, people spoke of a 'Gang of Four'—a group of talented, young and powerful bureaucrats. Two of the four became MPs in the eighties, a third followed in the nineties and the fourth attempted to become one.[19] PNG's first head of the armed forces, Ted Diro, subsequently became an MP, as did the country's first governor-general, John Guise.

Such transitions strengthened democratic traditions, as they confirmed that the path to power lay through the ballot box. However, they were also representative of a politicisation of society that was hardly helpful for development. 'This is a country where politics permeates society at all levels' (Clifford, Morauta and Stuart 1984, 101). According to Pokawin (1986, 136):

---

17   In his memoir, one of PNG's first politicians Albert Maori Kiki (1968, 185) said: 'I think we have democracy in our blood'.

18   'Our culture has an ancient entrepreneurial tradition … Material wealth was not an end in itself, but a means to gain renown, the esteem of one's people' (Bougainville and national leader John Momis, cited in Denoon 2000, 195).

19   Two became prime ministers (Mekere Morauta and Rabbie Namilau); a third became a minister (Anthony Siagaru); the fourth (Charles Lepani) ran unsuccessfully as a candidate in the 1982 and 2022 elections.

Even simple decisions are highly politicised. Any decision or action taken by an incumbent leader is questioned by the prospective leaders, who are considering how it would affect their own chances in the next election. Thus, even if a decision is in the best interests of the community, they would not support it if its success would strengthen their chance of the incumbent and weaken their own in the next election.

The primacy of the political class was reinforced by the merging of business and political interests. Several commentators noted this. Finney (1973, 118) wrote of 'the prominence of businessmen-politicians in the first House of Assembly [1964–68]'. Lapani (cited in Fitzpatrick 1980, 206) commented in 1976 that, 'at the political level, most leaders are involved in business ventures'. Not long after, Hegarty and King (1998, 356) wrote of the creation of a 'politician-businessman ruling class'.[20] With no government funding, politicians and their parties had to self-fund their election campaigns. Politicians therefore either had to be in business themselves or have a link to business. As first national army chief turned disgraced minister Ted Diro admitted: 'It is common in PNG for politicians to use the returns from business to secure votes' (Saffu 1998d, 443). Parties also got in the act, establishing business arms.

If business was a way to cover political costs, politics was a route to business wealth. Hegarty (1998b, 288; 1998c, 306) commented just after independence that many politicians 'have rapidly moved into business and are maximising their opportunity to enhance their private wealth', and that 'politicians have come to power not from a distinct class base but in search of economic power'.

Political parties emerged in the run-up to, and were a critical part of, the political scene at independence (Woolford 1976). Pangu's success in 1982 with 30 per cent of the vote and almost half the seats (50 out of 109) made it look like political parties were becoming more important (Jackson and Hegarty 1983), but its subsequent disintegration—and moves against Somare as party leader, despite his electoral success—gave a different perspective. Parties were not coherent enough to discipline and

---

20   Hegarty (1998c, 299) also wrote of the 1977 elections that they 'saw the demise of the older style big-men and the rise of the "new men" drawn from the rural and urban elites. The bulk of candidates tended to be "businessmen" of some sort or to have had a corporation or a salaried income as a base.' He quoted the ombudsman as saying in 1980 that 'many leaders have got themselves involved in private businesses' (Hegarty 1998f, 344). See also MacWilliam (2013).

unite competing interests and ambitions. The tendency was to more parties and fewer differences between them, as politicians began to 'party hop' and create their own. In 1987, Pangu was again the most successful of the 10 parties that won seats in that election, but this time it won only 15 per cent of the votes and 24 per cent of seats (Table A2)—never again has a party come close to getting half the seats on offer, as Pangu did in 1982.

The fragmentation and weakening of the party system in PNG is the flipside to the clientelism and localism of the country's politics (Hegarty 1998c; Wood 2018). In the 1977 elections, 'neither parties nor national issues were of concern to the voters' (Hegarty 1983, 12–13).[21] Over time, politics became even more local as, with more candidates, it became easier to win with fewer votes. The mean winner vote share fell from 35 per cent in 1977 to 26 per cent in 1987 (Table A2).

The political class was growing in importance, but not in stability. In the 1977 elections, only 39 per cent of sitting MPs were returned; this ratio increased only slightly in 1982 and 1987 to just above 50 per cent (Table A2), and it has largely remained there ever since.

At first, notwithstanding this micro-level churning, political stability prevailed at the macro level. But the first and loyal opposition leader Tei Abel was deposed in 1977, and politics quickly became more combative. PNG's first vote of no confidence occurred in 1978. Such votes could be held at any time from six months after an election to a year before the next one.[22] Somare survived three votes of no confidence before losing the fourth in 1980 (Pokawin 1998, 331). Many more were to follow. From 1977 to 2002, no government survived a full term.

Unconstrained by differences in ideology or by party allegiances, PNG politics became increasingly a game in which the most important objective of politicians, once elected, was to accumulate power. General elections were only for electing MPs; the choice of the prime minister and, more broadly, the government was a matter for those MPs, and never a settled one. Opposition leaders openly declared that their aim was to change the government not at the ballot box, but within the current term of

21 'The linkages or relationship between politicians and constituents is based not on mass mobilization but on patronage and clientelism' (Hegarty 1998c, 306–7).
22 The length of time after an election during which votes of no confidence are prohibited was increased to 18 months in the nineties (5.2.1). If a vote of no confidence is successful within a year of when the next election is due, that election is brought forward, a scenario no MPs want.

parliament—to 'expose, oppose and depose' in the words of Highlands leader Iambakey Okuk (cited in Pokawin 1998, 331) who orchestrated one vote of no confidence after another against Somare until he succeeded in replacing him, not by himself, but by the more acceptable Julius Chan; Okuk became his deputy.[23]

Even if a prime minister was able to survive a vote of no confidence, the fight took a lot of their effort and attention. Ministers had an even more fragile hold on power as they were reshuffled between portfolios and in and out of cabinet in response to the latest power struggle (Ivarature 2022).

Reforms to enhance stability and bolster the party system were attempted from as early as 1982, when the Pangu Party took to the election a number of related proposals: to give the prime minister the right to dissolve parliament, thereby reducing the incentive for backbenchers to bring on a vote of no confidence; to force members who left their party to face a by-election; and to introduce preferential voting at elections. Bills were drafted, but did not even make it to the floor of the parliament (Dorney 1991, 78). MPs did not want to be restrained, and political, like economic, reform was put on the backburner until the nineties.

The creation of a political system in which participation was highly prized has ensured the stability of PNG's political (Westminster) regime. This itself has been supportive of development: PNG has not been plagued by coups and periods of one-party rule. Beyond that, however, the political culture that became entrenched in this first period has not provided the foundations needed for the sort of long-term planning and national decision-making essential for development.

First, politicians inevitably developed short time horizons. The hard kina policy was often defended on the grounds that it involved 'facing up to the difficult choices before, rather than after we get ourselves into big trouble', to use the words of PNG's first finance minister, Julius Chan (cited in Garnaut, Baxter and Krueger 1984, 10). However, if time horizons were short, the risk of later getting into trouble would be heavily discounted: it would likely be someone else's problem.

---

23 Okuk is also quoted as telling his fellow MPs: 'If you are not hungry for power then you should be working for the missions and reading the Bible all the day' (Hegarty 1998e, 323).

Second, party systems discipline political elites through electoral accountability to take into account broader social interests. As one political leader from the time wrote: 'due to the absence of an ideological framework … the country's leaders are succumbing to the temptations of power and privilege for themselves, to the detriment of the people' (Samana 1988, 96).[24]

Third, politicians were distracted. As Dorney (1991, 78) commented, 'smooth, steady government [was] practically impossible'. Or, as Saffu (1998f, 491) put it:

> The impact of the MPs' gamesmanship, the ferment and the turmoil, on government efficiency and performance was manifested in many ways, not least in the strong impression … that nobody seemed to be really in charge, and that vital decisions were not being made.

Fourth, the intermingling of business and political interests had pernicious effects. MacWilliam (2013) argues that politicians represented bourgeois rather than national interests. But perhaps they did a good job of neither. In an article reflecting on PNG's early independence, Garnaut (1980, 451) wrote:

> There is no doubt that the opportunities for personal gain provided by contact with the international economy can turn the minds of the controllers of a new state, where internal and external constrains on the use of public office for private gain are weak … No-one who has been close to the controllers of the new Papua New Guinea state can doubt the strength of these pressures.
>
> … The first casualty of the passion for increased ownership of business assets by the controllers of a new state is devotion to public duty; there is simply less nervous energy, and time, for solving the complex problems of a new state. The second casualty is the gradual loosing of constraints on the exercise of state power in ways that are favourable to particular business interest, that is, the drift into conflict of interest in policy-making, and corruption.

---

24   Bill Standish (1981, 303) found in relation to his case study of Simbu province that, absent party disciplines, the interests of politicians 'as members of a tiny elite are not the same as those of the mass'.

3.2.2 Public services

Shortly after independence, a World Bank report commented that 'an effective set of institutions for economic and financial management had been developed'. It noted that 'education and health care and some of the country's infrastructure—harbors, electricity supply, telecommunications and air services—are comparatively advanced', and praised the country's well-designed 'network of rural health care' (World Bank 1978, 4–5, 18).

Post-independence, there was some expansion of services, especially more schools. However, by the late seventies and early eighties, commentators were noting serious service delivery problems. Allen (1983) wrote that 'people everywhere complain of a deterioration of services' (228) and about the 'general breakdown in government services which followed independence' (235). 'Port Moresby hospital—to name but one—seemed on the point of collapse several times early in the year', commented Hegarty and King (1998, 355–6). Trebilcock (1982b, 114) surveyed PNG's state-owned enterprises and concluded that their performance was 'weak by almost any measure of performance that might be applied'. The same author, in another report, spoke to the:

> widespread concern that in many areas of government policy-making and administration, [policy-making] proceeds by way of individualised, high-level, case-by-case review or decision that has resulted in a bureaucratically intensive, delay-ridden, often highly politicised treatment of individual cases. (Trebilcock 1983, 133)

The primary explanation for this decline in government effectiveness is the consolidation of the political culture described in the previous section. The increasingly powerful political class, increasingly preoccupied with jostling for power and their own business and local interests, failed to provide developmental leadership.

The judiciary weathered the rise of the political class well. In the late 1970s, a government minister, Nahau Rooney (PNG's first female minister and one of only 10 female MPs since independence), was jailed for contempt of court, but then immediately pardoned by the prime minister. There was a mass resignation of (largely expatriate) senior judges to protest this challenge to judicial authority. But judicial independence in the long run was little affected, and, in fact, the courts have carved out a very broad role for themselves as PNG has become an extremely litigious society (9.2.2).

The rise of the political class was much more at the expense of the bureaucracy. There was nothing intrinsically wrong with this. The interests of the bureaucracy and the broader population were not necessarily any more aligned than the interests of the politicians with the latter.[25] However, politicians and bureaucrats found it difficult to build an effective modus operandi. In an environment of 'mutual suspicion' (Standish 1981, 304) and 'basic distrust' (Ballard 1981, 84), politicians increasingly saw bureaucrats as non-responsive and expensive, and bureaucrats increasingly saw politicians as corrupt and self-interested. Politicians asserted themselves and took into their hands decisions previously left to bureaucrats. A bureaucratic expenditure prioritisation committee that was powerful in the early years of independence was dismantled. Iambukey Okuk (1982, 237), as deputy prime minister, said of the 1982 budget that for the first time it had been ensured that 'Cabinet decides the final budget, not the non-elected, non-accountable bureaucracy'. Pieper (2004, 3) summarises the views of early senior bureaucrats about politicians:

> There was an increasing feeling amongst politicians that the bureaucracy was too powerful and independent, and not astute to political needs … [B]y the mid-eighties they were generally much better educated, and a belief grew that they 'knew it all' and did not need to rely on the advice of public servants. Public resources increasingly became controlled by politics rather than public policy, and politicians began involving themselves in administration, project management, and senior appointments.

As early as 1979, the government established a high-level committee 'to investigate the poor performance of the public service' (Allen 1983, 228). In 1985 the Public Services Commission (PSC), a constitutional and extremely powerful body controlling public service appointments and promotions, was sidelined via amendments to the constitution. The changes to the constitution and associated new legislation, introduced on the advice of the World Bank and consistent with new public sector management thinking, delegated the responsibilities of the PSC to departmental heads (Cochrane 1986). While a well-intentioned move to increase government efficiency and responsiveness, this reform also opened up the public service to political interference and nepotism. Factors other than merit quickly

---

25   In an early radical critique, Good (1979, 158) labelled the bureaucracy a 'parasitic group' because it 'acts as if the control of the state for administrative purposes was an end in itself'.

came to be salient for recruitment and promotion. In fact, as early as 1980, it was commented that 'ethnicity is an influential factor in the advance of officials within the public bureaucracy' (Fitzpatrick 1980, 208).

There were other problems as well. It was inevitable that there would be some decline in service delivery following independence. The pre-colonial model 'cost too much and depended on a highly educated [expatriate] workforce' (Firth, cited in Denoon 2005, 145). Expatriates dominated, especially at the senior level. Indeed, until 1955 there had been no indigenous civil servants at all (Gupta 1992, 28). By 1972, there were only four senior nationals in the civil service (Ballard 1981, 79). It is not surprising that localisation was the new government's top priority (3.1.1), but the pace was excessive. The Public Service Board (forerunner to the PSC), impervious to the mood of the time, put out a statement in 1972 that the number of expatriate civil servants that would be needed in 1976 would be 7,000, not much less than the 7,800 then employed. Somare took exception to this and said that the target for 1976 should be 3,000. This shocked many in the expatriate workforce into leaving, and the 15 per cent annual reduction targets put in place following Somare's announcement were more than exceeded (Ballard 1981, 80–1). The number of expatriate public servants continued to fall, reaching 1,700 by 1988 (Turner 1990, 44). While some excellent national public servant leaders emerged, the outcome of localisation was 'a sharp decline in effective performance and responsiveness to policy objectives in the field' (Ballard 1981, 92–3). Section 3.1.4 highlights the cost of localisation in the context of rural development. Nelson (1982, 208) gives the example of a nursing tutor who, four months after qualifying for that job, was appointed as principal of the nursing school.

The controversy and, at times, chaos around provincial governments (3.2.4) was another influence on government effectiveness. Moreover, there were shortages in most provinces of 'the trained, experienced, competent and confident staff required for coherent policy formulation, advice and implementation' (Standish 1981, 303).

Finally, the controls on civil service numbers due to low revenue growth meant there could be no increase in frontline workers despite rapid population growth. Significant pay increases to national public servants in the run-up to independence worsened inherited problems of affordability. Fiscal stringency meant there was virtually no growth in the civil service, with employment of 46,000 public servants in 1975, 55,000 in 1981 and only 49,000 in 1988 (Figure B16).

3.2.3 Corruption

Its framers, anticipating problems with corruption, included a Leadership Code in the constitution to be administered by an Ombudsman Commission and a Leadership Tribunal. The code is broad in scope and covers not only politicians but also senior bureaucrats. The Ombudsman Commission was very active: Dorney (1991, 217) observed that there was 'no other country in the South Pacific or Asia where such a proportion of those occupying positions of power and privilege have had to face the criminal courts'.

In 1978, corruption in PNG was judged to be 'still low by world standards' (Mortimer 1979, 233). But things quickly got worse. 'National concerns about corruption arose ... during the late 1970s and in the early eighties' (Payani 2003, 91). Somare put forward a proposal, when he was returned to office after the 1977 elections, to strengthen the Leadership Code to require MPs to sell all business interests (and not to relatives) in return for a substantial pay rise. (The business activity of ministers was already constrained by the code, though it is not clear whether this has ever been seriously enforced.) Somare justified this radical move as necessary to prevent the entrenchment in power of 'the interests of a small elite' (Hegarty 1998d, 317).

Perhaps he was right, but the reform flew in the face of the substantial business interests even then of many of PNG's political leaders and parties. If there was a 'politician-businessman ruling class' (3.2.1), Somare's proposal was an existential risk to it, and it was opposed and doomed from the start. Julius Chan quit the ruling coalition partly on account of this issue and went on to briefly replace Somare as prime minister in 1980.[26]

Other anti-corruption efforts were made in the eighties, including the strengthening of the police fraud squad. In 1988, Prime Minister Namiliu put forward the first proposal for an anti-corruption agency (Oliver 1998, 458). One was finally legislated for 32 years later (9.2.3). As this long delay itself suggests, the anti-corruption battle was a losing one, in the eighties and, indeed, in subsequent decades, for a range of reasons.

---

26 Ironically, in hindsight, the Australian High Commission lobbied against the proposal on the grounds that it had 'socialist implications' (Hegarty and King 1998, 317).

First, as Somare recognised, the growing business interests of MPs were an intrinsic risk to integrity. Second, ministries and chairs of boards were handed out as inducements to join and stay with a ruling coalition. This might not in itself have been corrupt, but it created an environment in which rules governing accountability and conflicts of interest got short shrift. Politicisation breeds corruption. Third, the efforts of the Ombudsman notwithstanding, a number of prominent scandals went unpunished or lightly punished. Ted Diro, mentioned earlier, was forced to resign twice as a result of corruption allegations, once as a minister, once as an MP, and in both cases bounced back. Over time the perceived balance between risk and reward led to the normalisation of corruption.

3.2.4 Decentralisation

It is an exaggeration to say that decentralisation was foisted on PNG at independence because of Bougainville, but not a huge one (Howes, Sause and Ugyel 2022). Given PNG's demographic and cultural diversity, it is hard to imagine that its governance structure would not, at least to some extent, involve decentralised government. Decentralisation was also consistent with the ethos of self-determination that prevailed at this time, and MacWilliam (2016) argues that it was part of a drive to transform political power into commercial opportunities. Nevertheless, it was Bougainville that forced the pace and type of decentralisation. The fact that this remote province—that happened to contain the country's one, massive mine—was threatening to secede in the pre-independence years (and, at one point, did, if briefly and ineffectually, declare its independence) meant that the national government had to counter with an offer of autonomy. At that time, there was no reason to give Bougainville special treatment, so autonomy for one meant autonomy for all.

The process was not a smooth one: there was no national movement for regional autonomy, there was no obvious 'right' level of autonomy to aim at, decentralisation was a threat to national politicians and whatever was agreed had to be acceptable to Bougainville. A sign of the sensitivity and difficulty of the issue is that decentralisation and provincial governments are not even mentioned in PNG's original constitution. Despite the heavy emphasis on the subject by the Constitutional Planning Committee (tasked with drafting the constitution), it was simply not possible to reach agreement in time. However, the issue could not be assigned to the too-hard basket for long. In 1976, agreement was reached on arrangements for Bougainville, and in 1977 PNG passed the Organic Law on Provincial Governments, which extended those arrangements to all of PNG's then 20 provinces, or districts as they had been called. (An organic law in PNG is one that amends the constitution; it requires a two-thirds majority in parliament, twice.)

Wide-ranging responsibilities—including for health, education, agriculture and transport—were given to the provinces, initially on a selective basis (to those that wanted more autonomy), but, over time, to all. Bureaucrats were still formally regarded as belonging to the national government, but those working in a province were subject to the authority of the top provincial bureaucrat. Modest equalisation grants were provided.

However, the emphasis was not on fiscal or administrative decentralisation, but on political participation and mobilisation. Provincial assemblies (parliaments) were created. These had elected representatives and were headed by a premier (normally indirectly elected, but in a few cases directly) and a cabinet.

It soon became clear that the system adopted did not provide a stable basis for governance or development. In some cases, decentralisation worked well, at least initially (Kolma 2021, 2022 on Morobe); in others it failed from the start (Standish 1981 on Simbu). In most provinces, provincial assemblies had little public support and tended to replicate the problems seen at the national level: 'instability of coalitions and political alliances; the over subscription of elections and the super-rapid circulation of elites; the weakness of financial controls' (Saffu 1998c, 424).

Given the local nature of PNG politics, provincial premiers, ministers and assembly members were often seen as a threat to the national members of parliament. 'With the establishment of provincial governments, national politicians lost considerable influence in their home areas and personal jealousies became inflamed' (Allen 1983, 230). In 1983, the national government passed an amendment to allow for the suspension of provincial governments for non-performance, and, over the next decade, most were suspended. But this simply led to increased conflict and confusion. Sean Dorney (1991, 166) provides an example of the sort of problem that arose:

> The Western Highlands provincial government had been suspended early in 1987 by Prime Minister Wingti [from the same province]. Prior to the lifting of the suspension, Mr Wingti appointed Gabriel Waipek to the job [of provincial secretary, the top provincial bureaucrat]. Then the reinstated premier, Philip Kapal, reappointed

his former provincial secretary, Peter Wama. Both Wama and Waipek claimed legitimacy, and each issued orders suspending the other from duty. The farcical situation dragged on for months, with the public service in the Western Highlands cleaving down the middle, half supporting and taking directions from one man and half from the other.

By the mid-eighties, national leaders were talking about the need for major decentralisation reforms.[27] These were finally implemented in 1995, when provincial assemblies and elections were abolished (5.2.4).

Meanwhile, national MPs were reasserting their fiscal influence with decisions in the early eighties to allocate sectoral funds for roads, health and agriculture to MPs rather than provincial governments (King 1998, 348). They were also developing a completely different model of decentralisation, based on discretionary funds under their control. The antecedents were funds created in the 1970s, such as the Village Economic Development Fund and the Prime Minister's Discretionary Fund, which provided resources for local projects. As time went on, these funds came to be allocated per MP. The Electoral Development Fund was created, and, in 1984, MPs were given funding of PGK20,000 each (Connell 1997, 278). This increased to PGK100,000 by 1990 (Dorney 1991, 223) and MPs manage millions of kina in discretionary electorate funding today (Figure A1). Through these funds, national MPs would come to challenge both provincial politicians and national departments.

3.2.5 Law and order

Tribal violence and urban crime were problems before and at independence, but they and other law and order problems became much more serious and widespread over the seventies and eighties.

Even before independence, in parts of the Highlands 'traditional warfare, suppressed for a generation, was breaking out' (Nelson 2009, 267). Saffu (1998b, 415) succinctly enumerates the causes of tribal violence as 'tradition, absence of trusted and effective state institutions, pressures of the modern economy on land and customary relations, [and] alcohol'. Urban violence, and perhaps tribal as well, was exacerbated by low employment growth, and by low conviction rates (Clifford, Morauta and Stuart 1984).

---

27 In 1985, reflecting on a decade of independence, 'Somare put decentralisation at the top of his list of mistakes he believed the country had made' (Saffu 1998b, 412).

Crime was not only a matter of urban gangs and fighting between tribes. The stealing of coffee and other cash crops became widespread as did hold-ups on the country's main road, the Highlands Highway (Good 1986, 59–60). During this period, landowners increasingly used coercion to claim resources and to protest. By the late seventies, there was an 'increasing tendency for the people to demand high compensation for work done on their land' (Pokawin 1998, 336). Various groups threatened to close roads, stop water supply and interrupt electrical services if their demands for increased compensation were not adhered to (Saffu 1998e, 475).[28] One of the daily newspapers said that promoting compensation claims was the 'biggest growth industry in the country' (Trebilcock 1983, 193).

Election violence also worsened. Of the 1987 elections, Saffu (1998d, 436) commented:

> in terms of violence, the Highlands region was the worst, with ballot boxes being burnt in the Kandep area of Enga, and officials being assaulted and rivals being axed. Worse violence often followed the declaration of results.

More generally, Saffu (1998d, 436) noted: 'The tendency for aggrieved groups to take the law into their own hands and unleash their own brand of justice is a familiar problem in Papua New Guinea.'

The widespread public dissatisfaction with the law and order situation was as much with the unsatisfactory response to criminality as with growing criminality itself (Dorney 1991). As early as 1980, the police were 'accused of widespread indiscipline and ineffective performance' (Pokawin 1998, 334). The army, too, started to have 'significant problems with indiscipline' in the eighties, with army riots in February 1989 in the nation's capital (Dorney 1998, 70). 'Renewed fighting in the Highlands [after independence] represented a return to forms of violent self-help in the absence of effective government alternatives for managing disputes' (Walton and Dinnen 2022, 90). Some argued that rising crime was a response to 'the crumbling of integrity in the structure of the state itself' (Clifford, Morauta and Stuart 1984, 103).

---

28 'Where the people felt their claims had gone unheard, they did not hesitate to blockade towns and companies' (King 1998, 353).

As early as 1982, a survey of businesses found law and order to be the private sector's biggest concern 'by a substantial margin' (Trebilcock 1982a, 75). Saffu (1998a, 394–5) described 'lawlessness and lack of order' as PNG's Achilles' heel, and commented that crime had become a national obsession, with large protests (25,000 people) in Port Moresby in October 1985. Writing at the end of the eighties, another commentator, Sean Dorney (1991, 333), nominated law and order as the biggest problem the country would face in the coming decade. The eighties also saw a 'mushrooming of security companies' (Saffu 1998b, 402), and they are now, collectively, the country's biggest private sector employer (9.2.5).

Policy responses emerged even before independence, with a Committee to Investigate Tribal Fighting and a Peace and Good Order Committee both established by the chief minister in the early seventies (Fingleton 1981, 225; Clifford, Morauta and Stuart 1984, 114). In 1977, two new Acts were passed: the Inter-Group Fighting Act made it illegal to participate in any sort of tribal violence; and the Vagrancy Act made it unlawful to be in an urban area without lawful means of support, as it had been in colonial days. The former has been ineffectual (witnesses fear payback). The latter was ruled unconstitutional on the grounds that it restricted freedom of movement. Calls for its reintroduction have been a constant refrain from politicians ever since.

More committees were established and reports commissioned in the eighties: one on law and order in 1981, another to review the police force in 1982 and one on the justice system in 1984. The last resulted in the Clifford Report, which called for an emphasis on 'informal and community institutions in the maintenance of order' (Clifford, Morauta and Stuart 1984, v). However, the government preferred a get-tough approach. In 1979, tribal violence led to a state of emergency being declared in the Highlands, and, in 1985, urban crime precipitated a state of emergency for Port Moresby. The Curfew Act of 1987 made it possible to implement curfews without a state of emergency. Minimum sentence laws and mobile squads were introduced. Some of these responses helped to contain the problem temporarily, but all failed to have a sustained impact.

3.3 Conclusion

In an interview that is part of the audio history series *PNG Speaks*, prominent PNG trade unionist Lawrence Titmur tells the story of when, in 1976, just after independence, he, a 20-year-old public servant, was sent by government to negotiate a pay dispute with a group of mosquito sprayers in Maprik in the Sepik. (Malaria control was a major pre-independence priority [Nelson 1982].) The sprayers had expected independence to bring increased wealth for the PNG government and, therefore, had expected a pay increase. 'We've got independence ... We know you have the money ... We want some of it', Titmur recalls them saying. When they did not get the massive pay increases they demanded, the workers started sharpening their knives, blockaded the road and took Titmur hostage, relenting only when they had won a pay increase, albeit much smaller than the one they were demanding.

The sprayers, like many in PNG, had high expectations from independence: consider Somare's (1975, 144) remark used to open Chapter 2 that it was up to PNG to 'determine how much development we want'. But the reality was much less favourable. To its credit, the government was fiscally responsible, as in this instance, but the fiscal stringency required by low commodity prices and declining aid together with a poor and worsening investment climate put rapid or even modest growth out of reach. For the period as a whole, GDP (and, to the extent we have the data, non-resource GDP) per person fell, as did the formal sector workforce relative to population.

If this period had laid the foundations on which more rapid growth could subsequently be built, it could be looked back on as a successful start in difficult circumstances (Garnaut 2000, 31). The early years of independence did, in the main, deliver macroeconomic stability, but, even on this front, the reduction in foreign exchange reserves was a sign that macroeconomic problems were being stored up for the future. A number of other problems also emerged in this first period that only intensified over subsequent decades. These included the growing primacy of a political class with short time horizons, focused on local issues and increasingly preoccupied with achieving power and with their business interests; a significant reduction in the quality of public services; deepening corruption; and increasing insecurity.

Kurer (2006) argues that the adoption of the redistributive recommendations of the Faber Report is to blame for PNG's subsequent governance problems. This is too harsh, because the government was not actually that serious about redistribution; the drag on growth from low commodity prices and declining aid would have remained whatever policies were in place; and many of PNG's governance problems would have likely emerged in any case. Nevertheless, slow growth must surely have made the law and order situation worse, and perhaps weakened the party system, since no party in power was able to deliver development. The bottom line is that PNG's development strategy at independence was both founded on the assumption of rapid growth and undermined by its absence. In hindsight, much greater attention should have been given from the start to the very real risk that rapid growth would not be realised. If it had been, more might have been done sooner to improve PNG's investment climate and tackle its high cost structure.

There were attempts at reform over the eighties, but not successful ones. Political reforms—to promote political stability, to combat corruption—were proposed but failed to garner support from MPs. Economic policy changes, except for financial sector reform, remained largely rhetorical. Absent a crisis, even as the optimism inherited from independence faded, the distractions caused by the (by now) never-ending struggles for political power and the focus of politicians on local issues and their business interests made it too difficult to execute major changes to the political and economic rules of the game the country had taken to independence.

The nineties changed all that and became a decade of reform precisely because it was a decade of crisis. This is the story of the next two chapters.

Part II:
1989–2003:
The nineties:
Volatility, crisis
and reform

We find ourselves in 1995 perching on a landscape of simmering volcanoes. Essential social services are starved of operating funds; the Government is sending companies broke through late and lack of payment of bills; the war still rages in Bougainville; there has been a surge of crime, particularly in urban areas; there is evidence of corruption at the highest level.

—Shadow Minister for Finance and Planning Masket Iangalio
(1995, 3)

The transformation has been both massive and amazing. After being left with a major fiscal and external crisis, we have stabilised both the budget and the external situation.

—Deputy Prime Minister and Minister for Finance and Planning
Chris Havieta (1995, 51)

4

A decade of volatility

Prime Minister Sir Julius Chan stated in his Christmas address that 1994 was the most turbulent, painful and unpredictable of the nation's nineteen years of independence. Most who witnessed the sudden change of government in August, the volcanic destruction of Rabaul in September, the dramatic collapse of peace talks on war-weary Bougainville in October, the ominous confrontations over provincial government reform, the confusion surrounding the giant Lihir gold project, and the multi-billion-kina environmental lawsuit against the operators of the Ok Tedi mine would agree. Affecting all of these issues and events was an unprecedented financial crisis, whose impact will be felt for some time. (Wesley-Smith 1995, 364)

4.1 Introduction

Our second period, 1989–2003, the nineties for short, was highly volatile. It began with the closure of PNG's biggest mine, Panguna in Bougainville, due to civil strife, and was punctuated by the opening of other resource projects, by natural disasters and by poor economic management: the country twice ran out of foreign exchange reserves. The period contains the year with PNG's highest economic growth rate (1993, 18 per cent) and with its lowest (1997, –6 per cent).

On average though, economic growth during the nineties, as in the eighties, was slow and, worse than the eighties, there was no expansion of formal sector employment opportunities outside of the government. The late 1990s and early 2000s was a particularly bad period for the economy.

If PNG's politics gained its distinctive form in the eighties, in the nineties the financial sector took on its current form, one that was no more supportive of development, with the emergence of high spreads and profits, and a growing reliance on lending to government rather than the private sector.

Governance and service delivery worsened. Ross Garnaut (2000, 34) writes that the nineties were characterised by a 'radical decline in the quality of government services, and grotesque corruption in public life'. And yet this was also PNG's most reform-minded period, with three distinct reform programs, at the start, the middle and the end of the decade, supporting a mix of important homegrown and externally imposed policy and institutional changes.

Was the nineties, then, a decade of reform or one of decline? Our answer is both. The nineties was such a roller-coaster of a decade that it is useful to begin with a summary narrative. Subsequent sections examine this period's growth record and macroeconomic policies and performance. The next chapter covers economic reforms, politics and governance.

4.2 A brief chronology

Between 1989 and 2003, the period covered by this and the next chapter, PNG had no fewer than six prime ministers.[1] Rabbie Namaliu was elected prime minister after a vote of no confidence ended the government of Paias Wingti in 1988, just one year after the latter's election by parliament following the 1987 general elections. After the closure of Panguna, the Bougainville copper mine—so important for government and export revenue—in May 1989, Namaliu's government devalued the currency by 10 per cent in January 1990; negotiated with the International Monetary Fund (IMF) and the World Bank for financial support in the same year; and abolished the urban minimum wage in 1992, a reform that was earlier unthinkable, and that effectively deregulated the formal labour market.

The Bougainville crisis was to last right through the nineties, and, indeed, though peace was restored by the late nineties, the province's political future is still unresolved. However, the economic crisis induced by Panguna's closure was remarkably short lived as its dominant role in the economy was

---

1   Acting prime ministers are not included in this total.

quickly replaced by new mines and oil projects. GDP growth went from marginally negative in 1989 and 1990 to double-digit positive in the next three years.

Paias Wingti became prime minister again after the 1992 elections. Anticipating a boom, he loosened fiscal policy and ignored the fact that foreign exchange reserves were low and falling. By mid-1994, reserves were at crisis levels, covering only two weeks of imports.

While the economic crisis was deepening, there was also, at the same time, and by complete coincidence, a change in government. In September 1993, to avoid having to face yet another vote of no confidence, Wingti had, cleverly he thought, resigned in secret and got himself re-elected in parliament the next morning, arguing that he should once again be protected by the post-election bar on votes of no confidence, which by then had been increased to 18 months (5.2.1). Opposition members were not impressed, went to the courts, and, in June 1994, just when the country's balance of payments crisis was at its most serious, Wingti's re-election was ruled invalid. Julius Chan, who had briefly been prime minister in the early eighties, was elected by his fellow members of parliament to replace the prime minister he had been deputy to.

Chan, who, ironically, had been finance minister to Wingti's expansionary 1993 and 1994 budgets, now had no choice but to adopt emergency measures. He slashed spending, reversed his earlier tax cuts and implemented a 12 per cent devaluation in September 1994. When that did not turn things around, the next month the architect of PNG's hard kina policy floated the currency. Chan also entered into negotiations with the World Bank and the IMF. The reform program jointly agreed to the next year was substantial, but also controversial.

In early 1997, politics intervened once more. Chan was consumed that year by controversy over military resistance to, and protests about, his plan to send foreign mercenaries into Bougainville (the so-called Sandline affair). In March, Chan had first to abort that plan and then resign while an inquiry was held. He returned to the position of prime minister in June, but lost both the prime ministership and his own seat at the 1997 elections.

William 'Bill' Skate emerged as the new prime minister. Many of his policies were reformist, but his administration was marred by corruption, scandals, instability, poor donor relations and severe financing problems. Drought and the Asian financial crisis in 1997, plunging confidence and extensive domestic (including central bank) deficit financing led to the exchange rate losing 30 per cent of its value in a single year (1998) against the US dollar. In the end, unable to fund his budget, running out of foreign exchange and facing mounting domestic and international criticism, Skate resigned in mid-1999 rather than face certain defeat in a vote of no confidence.

Skate's departure led to the election as prime minister of Mekere Morauta, one of the 'gang of four'[2] of leading bureaucrats that emerged shortly after independence, and a former secretary of Finance and governor of the Bank of Papua New Guinea. Morauta had only become a member of parliament in 1997 but put himself forward just two years later as the man to rescue PNG at this time of crisis. In the three years before the next elections, he pushed through a comprehensive reform plan, including a third structural adjustment program. While his reforms did a lot of good, economic growth and macroeconomic stability remained elusive.

The 2002 elections ended Morauta's tenure as prime minister. Indeed, three-quarters of MPs (though not Morauta himself) lost their seat—by far the highest turnover ever seen at an election, and perhaps a sign of the tough economic conditions. Michael Somare, PNG's first prime minister, became prime minister once again, after a gap of some 17 years. The first sign of the boom that was to follow came the very next year when, for the first time in a decade, the currency gained in value. Then, in 2004, government revenue grew unexpectedly quickly, and PNG's long boom was underway.

4.3 Economic growth

GDP growth was volatile during the nineties. However, after all the ups and downs, our key indicator of national economic activity, non-resource GDP per person, was no higher at the end than the start of the period, and formal sector employment was stagnant outside of the public service. Resource dependency grew and resource policy changed. There was a response to the depreciation of the real exchange rate in agriculture, but in most sectors growth was low. The banking sector shifted away from private to public sector lending and a large spread in lending and deposit rates materialised.

---

2   See footnote 19 in Chapter 3.

4.3.1 Volatile growth

Figure 4.1 shows both GDP and non-resource GDP growth rates over this period.

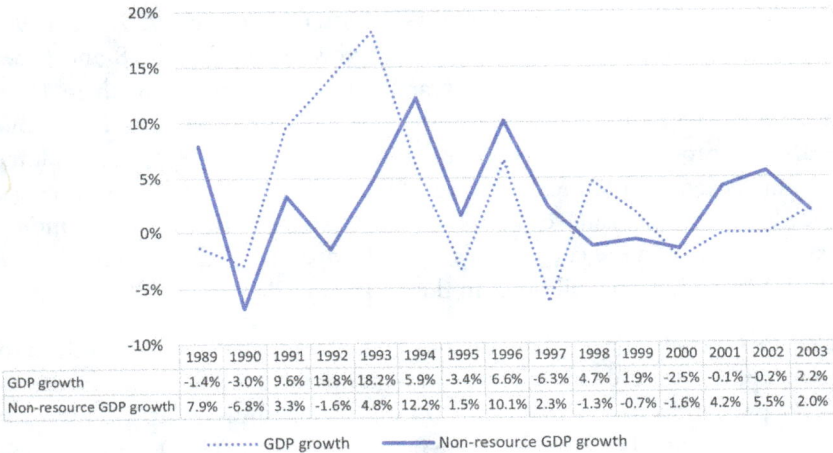

	1989	1990	1991	1992	1993	1994	1995	1996	1997	1998	1999	2000	2001	2002	2003
GDP growth	-1.4%	-3.0%	9.6%	13.8%	18.2%	5.9%	-3.4%	6.6%	-6.3%	4.7%	1.9%	-2.5%	-0.1%	-0.2%	2.2%
Non-resource GDP growth	7.9%	-6.8%	3.3%	-1.6%	4.8%	12.2%	1.5%	10.1%	2.3%	-1.3%	-0.7%	-1.6%	4.2%	5.5%	2.0%

········ GDP growth   ——— Non-resource GDP growth

Figure 4.1: GDP and non-resource GDP growth, 1989–2003 (kina, constant prices)
Source: PNG Economic Database.

Commodity prices fluctuated over the course of this period, ending about where they started (Figure B12). Though timber prices boomed in the mid-nineties, the non-resource commodity price index declined by 40 per cent. Gold and copper prices were mainly stable, and oil prices rose over the decade. Commodity prices did better in kina terms due to currency depreciation (Figures B13 and B14).

The closure of the Panguna mine in May 1989 led to resource output falling in that year by 38 per cent, about 8 per cent of GDP. Ironically, resource revenue remained high (as it was the previous year's profits that were taxed), so government revenue and expenditure did well, and non-resource GDP grew strongly. The next year, 1990, PNG's sovereign wealth fund, the Mineral Resources Stabilisation Fund (MRSF), provided a partial buffer, but, even so, the government was forced to tighten its belt. Confidence took a hit, bank lending started to fall (Figure B32), and non-resource GDP growth was negative in 1990, barely positive in 1991 and negative again in 1992.

The resource economy quickly rebounded, and, in fact, PNG soon embarked on its biggest boom of the independence era. The small Miasma gold mine opened in 1989, followed by the much larger Porgera gold mine the following year. The Kutubu oil fields began production in 1992. The resource sector almost tripled in size (in real terms) between 1988 (before the closure of Panguna) and 1993. GDP, after falling in 1989 and 1990, increased rapidly in the next four years (growing at 10, 14, 18 and 6 per cent in 1991 and the next three years). The 18 per cent growth in 1993 has never been equalled; nor has the 56 per cent growth over the four years. Oil production peaked almost immediately (in 1993), and resource output started to fall in real terms in 1994, though rising oil prices over the decade boosted the value of PNG's resource exports. The resource economy expanded again in the late nineties, with the opening of the Lihir gold mine (1997) and additional oil fields in the Southern Highlands (1998).

Due to spillover effects from the resource sector, non-resource GDP also grew rapidly over the early nineties, though not by as much and with a lag— by 31 per cent between 1992 and 1996. The most important stimulus was the quadrupling of resource revenue in 1993 (after inflation)—a new post-independence record—just four years after Panguna was closed. Resource revenue stayed at this new high until 1997, after which it declined again with the Asian financial crisis.

The nineties was a decade of natural and economic shocks. A volcanic eruption on 19 September 1994 destroyed the town of Rabaul in East New Britain and displaced 45,000 people (Dinnen 1995a). Heavy rains in 1995 led to the collapse of Umi bridge in Morobe, halting food supply to five Highlands provinces and causing serious flooding in Momase and the Highlands. Drought and frosts in 1997 hurt rural food supply (Allen and Bourke 2001), and drought also took a toll on GDP (which fell by 6 per cent), as it forced the temporary closure of some mines. On 17 July 1998, the Aitape tsunami hit the West Sepik coast, killing upwards of 1,600 people.

The Asian financial crisis of 1997 resulted in a steep reduction in the global demand for commodities, reflected in both volume and prices. Log exports, which had boomed earlier in the decade, fell by more than half between 1997 and 1998 (Figure B8). Non-resource GDP growth was low in 1997, and negative in each of the next three years.

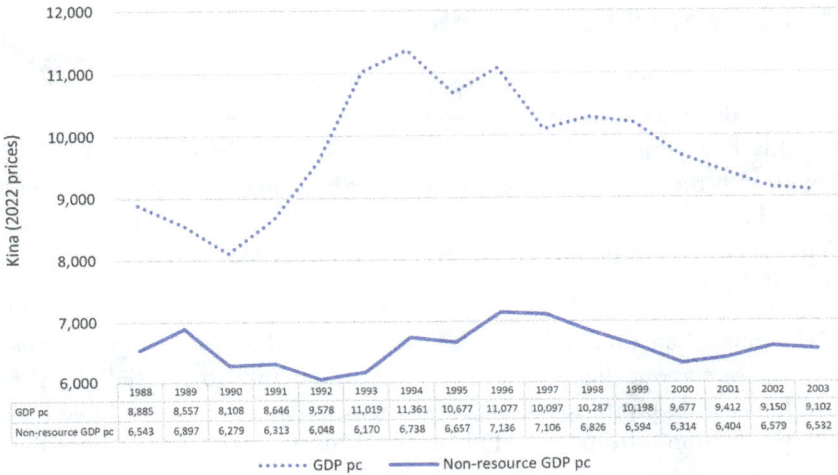

	1988	1989	1990	1991	1992	1993	1994	1995	1996	1997	1998	1999	2000	2001	2002	2003
GDP pc	8,885	8,557	8,108	8,646	9,578	11,019	11,361	10,677	11,077	10,097	10,287	10,198	9,677	9,412	9,150	9,102
Non-resource GDP pc	6,543	6,897	6,279	6,313	6,048	6,170	6,738	6,657	7,136	7,106	6,826	6,594	6,314	6,404	6,579	6,532

Figure 4.2: GDP and non-resource GDP per person, 1988–2003 (kina, constant prices)

Source: PNG Economic Database.

Non-resource GDP growth only modestly rebounded in the early 2000s. The business community supported Morauta as prime minister, but depreciation and inflation stayed high, and business confidence remained low. Adjusting for inflation, private sector wages fell on average by about 8 per cent per year between 1999 and 2002 (Blunch and Davies 2024).

GDP per person hit its maximum for the period in 1994, and non-resource GDP per person in 1996. Thereafter both declined. Non-resource GDP per person was almost exactly equal in the last year of this period, 2003, to the last of the previous period, 1988, while GDP per person was just 2.4 per cent higher (Figure 4.2).

This picture of economic stagnation is confirmed by the very slow growth in formal sector employment (Figure B16): 169,000 in 1988 and 184,000 in 2003. (These figures exclude the public service, in which growth was faster; see 5.2.2.)

Stagnation is not what was expected from the nineties, a decade the country went into with 'expectations of prosperity coming from gold, oil and natural gas development' (Oliver 1998, 457). As discussed in the remainder of this chapter and the next, the difficulties of this period are explained by the negative shocks of the decade; the failure of the economic reforms undertaken to stimulate a broad-based, supply-side response; and economic and political mismanagement.

4.3.2 Sectoral developments

The closure of the Panguna mine notwithstanding, PNG became a more resource-dependent economy. Resource dependency exceeded 20 per cent for this first time in the nineties (Figure B3), reaching 24 per cent in 1993 (with the start of oil production) before falling and then rising again to 23 per cent in 2000 (with more oil and gold). On average, resource dependency for the period was 17 per cent, substantially up from the 10 per cent of the eighties (Table 10.3).

PNG more than doubled its gold exports over the nineties, and copper exports were about the same as in the eighties, thanks to Ok Tedi, Porgera and Lihir, and despite the closure of Panguna (Figure B10 and Table C1). Oil production—from the Highlands—peaked in its second year, but remained important over the decade, its share of resource exports falling from one-half in 1993 to 30 per cent a decade later (Figure B11).

Preparations began in the late nineties for two more resource projects: a nickel mine and processing plant in Madang on the northern coast; and a gas project, originally conceived to pipe gas from PNG to Australia. The nickel project commenced production in 2010, and the pipeline project was repositioned in the 2000s as a liquified natural gas project, and became the PNG LNG project, which started production in 2014 (6.2.2).

There were major shifts in resource sector policy, formalised through the Mining Act of 1992, the Petroleum Act of 1992 and the Oil and Gas Act of 1998. The main thrust of these legislative changes was to take the national government away from its policy of maximising its revenue take (2.2.3) towards one more focused on landowners and provincial governments— hardly a surprising move given that landowners had closed the Panguna mine, and that Bougainville was now engulfed in a civil war.[3] The key reform was the Development Forum, first applied to Porgera. This innovation of the Namiliu government was actually in train before violence erupted at Panguna. At these fora, the national government is obliged to gain consent from (and therefore make concessions to) landowners and provincial governments before the grant of a license to a developer.

---

3   See Filer and Imbun (2009) for a comprehensive account of the reforms and their motivations.

There were other changes as well over the course of the nineties reflecting the increased power of landowners, now described as PNG's 'most powerful pressure group' (Saffu 1998f, 486). Formal procedures were laid down for how affected landowners were to be identified. Royalties were increased from 1.25 to 2 per cent of the value of output, creditable against corporate tax payments (Davis 1995). The share of royalties to go to landowners was increased, with the exact amounts to be determined by the relevant Development Forum. The share given to Porgera landowners was increased from 23 per cent at mine opening to 50 per cent in 1995 (Johnson 2012). A 2 per cent development levy was introduced for petroleum projects, to go to local and provincial governments. Landowners (and, for mining projects, provincial governments) were to be entitled to a minor equity share (about 2 per cent), to be gifted to them by the central government—a world first (Johnson 2012, 61). [4] The central government was now also expected to make infrastructure and business development grants to landowners and provincial governments. Landowners were also to be given preferential access to employment and related business opportunities. A tax credit system was introduced in the early nineties allowing developers to make local investments (the amount has ranged between 0.75 and 2 per cent of assessable income) in lieu of corporate tax payments. The Mineral Resources Development Corporation, which had originally been established in 1981 to hold the state's share in resource projects, became responsible for holding in trust the equity held by landowners and provincial governments, and by that means has become over time a major investor in the PNG economy. [5]

By the end of what had been a turbulent decade, there was a sense that the frequently changing but generally more burdensome tax arrangements now in place had deterred new investment in the resource sector. As part of the reforms of the early 2000s (5.1.3), and following extensive analysis (an official tax review chaired by a former tax commissioner Nagora Bogan and an Asian Development Bank review specifically of resource taxation), the corporate tax rate for mining projects was reduced from 35 to 30 per cent, and for petroleum projects from 50 to 45 per cent for oil and 30 per cent for gas (Department of Mining 2003; Department of Petroleum and Energy 2005). The dividend withholding tax (only for mining projects) was reduced

---

4   The relevant legislation entitled the central government to take up to a 30 per cent share in any mining project, and a 22.5 per cent share in any petroleum project. Shares to other national stakeholders were to come out of these amounts.

5   Landowners do not have to work through the MRDC. Most do, but the Lihir landowners decided not to.

from 15 to 10 per cent, and the resource rents tax, the centrepiece of the government's tax regime at independence, was abolished.[6] A mining levy was introduced in 1999 to counter the windfall the industry had received due to the reduction of import duties as part of a tariff reform program (5.1.3), but this was largely phased out over the 2000s. The period in which losses could be carried forward was increased from seven to 20 years (Banks 2001, 37). A legislative commitment (through the Fiscal Stabilisation Act 2000) was made to not increase tax rates on projects after start up in return for companies agreeing to slightly higher tax rates—a far cry from the first Panguna agreement that authorised reviews every seven years (2.2.3).

Another focus for the decade was equity ownership. Prime Minister Paias Wingti was an early resource nationalist, and an early proponent of the idea that PNG was not benefitting enough from its big resource projects. The government had initially taken a 10 per cent stake in the Porgera gold project (with half of that for the provincial government and landowners), but Wingti, on becoming prime minister in 1992, demanded an increase to 30 per cent, and achieved 25 per cent, with the funds to be provided out of initial dividends. Around the same time, the government also took a share in the Lihir mine of 20 per cent, and increased its share in Ok Tedi from 20 to 30 per cent. These decisions were controversial at the time, but of little lasting consequence. Most resource stakes were sold over the course of the nineties through the sale of the state-owned Orogen company (5.1.3). There was also a push for the pipeline needed to bring oil from PNG's new oil fields in the Highlands to the coast to be built and owned by a national consortium, but that was unsuccessful and the pipeline remained with the project developer (Brunton 1992).

The Fisheries Management Act was passed in 1994, and a 1995 domestication policy provided incentives for firms to set up tuna canneries. Two were established during this period—the first in Madang in 1994 and the second at Wewak in 2003—and the export of marine products grew rapidly (Figure B8). 'Fisheries exports from the late 1970s to 1995 averaged 10 million kina annually. By 2002–3, exports reached 350 million kina, with direct employment growing from about 450 to around 6,000' (Morauta 2005, 161).

---

6   The 2000 (Bogan) review on tax reform had actually recommended that the resource rents or additional profits tax be increased and the mining levy discussed below in the text abolished. However, instead the mining levy was phased out *and* Somare abolished the additional profits tax. Since negotiations had already commenced on what would become the PNG LNG project, the additional profits tax was retained for it (Department of Petroleum and Energy 2005).

The period was relatively good for agriculture, the share of which in non-resource GDP rose from about 20 per cent to about 30 per cent over the decade. Most traditional cash crops did not do well, but logging and palm oil saw strong growth, especially the latter. Agricultural production, including fresh food produce, was positively affected by exchange rate depreciation (BPNG 2007; McKillop, Bourke and Kambori 2009; Conroy 2023). Bourke (2005a, 7) noted that:

> Villagers have responded [to exchange rate depreciation] by producing more food for sale in local and distant markets. Consequently the volume of locally grown food traded within PNG has increased rapidly, particularly since 1998. Fresh food generates significant income for rural villagers; in the mid 1990s it was second in value only to Arabica coffee and worth more than cocoa, betel nut, copra, oil palm and fish.

Manufacturing stagnated at 4 per cent of non-resource GDP. One might have hoped that it would benefit from depreciation as well as labour market deregulation (5.1.1), but the output response to the reforms of the nineties was constrained by growing crime and worsening infrastructure, not to mention a general lack of confidence.

4.3.3 The financial sector

The poor growth performance over the nineties is reflected in declining bank lending to the private sector. The ratio to GDP of loans outstanding to the private sector rose over the eighties but fell over the nineties. On the one hand, banks adopted 'more cautious lending practices following the large losses incurred as a result of the uprising in North Solomons [Bougainville]' (BPNG 2007, 137). On the other, loans to government seemed much less risky, and the government's appetite for domestic borrowing grew. Lending to the private sector plummeted from 18 per cent of GDP in 1989 to only 7 per cent in 2003, while lending to the government increased from 2 to 6 per cent of GDP over the same period (Figure B32).

Interest rates on loans remained high after financial sector deregulation (3.1.2), but deposit rates fell from above 10 per cent to below 5 per cent by the end of the period, and have since fallen to close to zero (Figure B34). The spread between lending and deposit rates increased from around 2 percentage points to above 5 and then 10 by the end of the period, falling slightly to about 8 in 2022 (8.2.2). Related to this, PNG's banks became much more profitable over the nineties (BPNG 2007, 196), and are now among the most profitable in the world (Jamaludin, Klyuev and Serechetapongse 2015).

Once they had the freedom to do so, banks reduced the rates they paid to savers on deposits for two reasons. First, limited competition in the sector meant that there was little incentive for banks to offer higher rates to savers or lower rates to borrowers. PNG is not an easy place to operate in, and, despite high profits, the number of banks fell over the nineties. Niugini-Lloyds exited in 1990 and Indosuez was bought by the Bank of Hawaii, which exited in 2001. By the end of this period, only four commercial banks were operating: ANZ; Westpac; Bank of the South Pacific, which bought the government-owned Papua New Guinea Banking Corporation in 2002 (5.1.3); and Maybank Malaysia, which entered in 1994 (BPNG 2007, 191). Second, because lending fell, there emerged over the decade an excess of deposits, which the banks ended up parking, unremunerated, with the central bank (Figure B36 and Section 4.4.4). Since banks were unable to get a return on the marginal deposit, they reduced their deposit rates.

There was a reduction not only in the number of banks over the nineties but also in their presence around the country (Figure B37). The number of branches increased slightly, but the number of banking agents plummeted from 400 in the mid-eighties to just 100 by the mid-nineties, 'primarily because of insufficient business, though, in some cases, security concerns and misappropriation were cited as the reasons for closure' (BPNG, 2007, 193).

The Port Moresby Stock Exchange (now PNGX Markets Limited) was opened in 1999. Only a handful of companies have ever been listed (at the time of writing 12, with only three added since 2009) and liquidity is extremely low.

The decline in lending and the growth in the interest rate spread were a frustration to politicians in the nineties. Julius Chan, finance minister in the early nineties, leaned on banks to reduce their interest rates and lend more, and threatened them with re-regulation (Callick 1993). He also pressured BPNG to reduce its policy rates. Bank Governor (and former finance secretary) Mekere Morauta publicly resisted this and was highly critical of Chan's expansionary 1993 and 1994 budgets, leading to pressure on Wingti to sack Chan, which he did (the two were not on good terms in any case). Chan briefly became foreign minister before coming back as prime minister after Wingti was disqualified by the courts. He then removed Morauta from the position of central bank governor (Vatsikopoulous 1995).

4.4 The macroeconomy

This section examines the causes of macroeconomic instability in the nineties, arguing that it cannot only be blamed on high deficits. It then covers the floating of the exchange rate, the most important change in economic policy since independence; fiscal policy; and the emergence of excess liquidity, which has become a permanent feature of the PNG economy.

4.4.1 Macroeconomic instability

The nineties were characterised by high inflation and rapid currency depreciation. The average annual rate of depreciation against the US dollar was 9.3 per cent, compared to just 0.3 per cent in the previous period. The kina lost 17 per cent of its value in 1994, 30 per cent in 1998 and 18 per cent in 2001. There is a strong link in PNG from depreciation to inflation (Sampson et al. 2006). Inflation averaged 9.6 per cent, up from 6.4 per cent in the previous period, and was in double digits for seven of the 15 years in this period.

There were two occasions, one in 1994 and one that stretched across 1998 and 1999, when the country virtually ran out of foreign exchange.[7] Domestic interest rates spiked during these crises, reflecting both government desperation and a collapse in confidence: the average lending rate increased from 10 per cent in 1994 to 15.4 per cent in 1995 and then from 10.6 per cent in 1997 to a stunning 20.2 per cent in 1998 (Figure B34).

Why did an economy that had been so stable become so crisis prone? There are, in fact, seven reasons. 'Lost fiscal discipline' (Chowdhury 2018, 162) is the cause normally mentioned, and certainly there were some high deficits in this period, especially in 1992 and 1993, the result of the expectations

---

7   In August 1994, 'foreign exchange reserves were negative at around USD160 million, covered by forward commitments in the interbank market' (BPNG 2007, 244). In May 1999, 'reserves were down to US$124 million (1.2 months of nonmineral imports), compared with US$ 194 million at end-1998' (IMF 1999).

of good times to come that built up with the two new gold mines and the commencement of oil exports. In 1990, a boom that would bring a 'massive injection of revenue' (Dorney 1991, 115–16) was predicted. The 1993 budget, in particular, was presented as something different: 'a revolutionary and aggressive approach' and 'a fundamental departure from traditional fiscal policies pursued in the past', designed to address PNG's slow growth (Department of Treasury 1992, 18–19). Taxes were cut in the 1993 budget and expenditure increased in both years (by 23 per cent after inflation over the two years). Mekere Morauta, PNG's first finance secretary and then its central bank governor, described the budgets of these years as 'the most disastrous and most inappropriate budgets since independence' (Vatsikopoulous 1995).

However, the deficits of the nineties were not in fact particularly large relative to the stable eighties that had preceded it (Figure B27). The average deficit for the two periods is the same (Table 10.10), and the maximum deficits of 3.6 and 4.0 per cent in 1992 and 1993 are indistinguishable from the maximum deficits of the eighties (3.9 and 4.1 per cent in 1981 and 1982). Indeed, large deficits were impossible to sustain because they manifested themselves in a loss of reserves or a depreciation that required a prompt correction. Temporary, large deficits at the wrong time are part, but by no means the whole part, of the story of how the nineties became crisis prone.

Importantly, there was also a change in how those deficits were financed, with a switch from international to domestic financing. In 1976, 75 per cent of the government's debt stock was foreign; the ratio was the same in 1989. However, by 1996, this ratio had fallen to 48 per cent. Commercial bank holdings of government debt increased rapidly, from PGK107 million in 1989 to PGK1.1 billion in 1996. The central bank also engaged in extensive and unprecedented deficit financing during this period, especially during the mid-nineties (Figure B35). The Central Banking Act as it then stood allowed limited deficit financing, but the limits were ignored.

There is a high propensity in PNG for government expenditure to be spent on imports. If that spending is financed by foreign borrowing, then the additional foreign exchange can be used to finance the additional imports. However, if that spending is financed by domestic sources, there is a mismatch, and it is more likely that any deficit would put pressure on foreign exchange reserves and/or the exchange rate.

This reliance on domestic financing was also responsible for the tendency for interest rates to spike over this period in crisis periods. This tendency appears at odds with the emergence of excess liquidity (4.4.4), but the small number of banks meant that the government debt market was not competitive. Banks knew when the government was desperate to borrow from them and priced their lending accordingly. Of course, inflation was very high during this period as well, often well in excess of 10 per cent, and this pushed up interest rates too.

Third, changes in aid made things worse. The reduction in aid—from 32 per cent of revenue in the eighties to 18 per cent in the nineties (Table 10.10)—meant not only less revenue, but also less foreign exchange to fund the high import content of government spending. The increased tying of aid to specific projects (4.4.3), and therefore purchases, also meant that aid was increasingly unavailable to boost foreign exchange reserves.

Fourth, there was less margin for error. The import cover provided by foreign exchange reserves had fallen over the eighties (2.3.3). This increased the risk that the next spending spree, or simply miscalculation, would lead to a balance of payments crisis. In the nineties, even during the resource-driven, high-growth years, foreign exchange reserves never provided more than three months of import cover and often less than two (Figure B22).

Fifth, monetary policy, the other instrument to influence aggregate demand, became ineffective (as explained in 4.4.4). Not surprisingly, with one less instrument at its disposal, the chances of a balance of payments crisis increased.

With the points made so far, it is interesting in hindsight to go back to the late seventies and early eighties. PNG's fiscal position began to deteriorate in 1979.[8] The counterpart of this was a reduction in foreign exchange reserves between 1979 and 1981 from five to three months of imports. The government response was to control expenditure and to restrain private sector credit (ToRobert 1982). With a bigger buffer to begin with, an increase in interest rates to reduce private sector demand (BPNG 2007,

---

8   'Before 1979, the government had a deficit in the range of K15-25 million per annum ... By any measure, the fiscal position was very strong and we had no balance of payments problem. In 1979, the fiscal position began to deteriorate. The deficit in 1979 mushroomed to K67 million and rose again to K78 million in 1980 ... Moreover, by the time the problem was appreciated, the 1981 national budget was formulated at about the same level of deficit and difficulties were being encountered within that budget. In short, a major fiscal problem had emerged' (ToRobert 1982, 149). In fact, the 1980 deficit was controlled to 1.0 per cent of GDP, but larger deficits re-emerged in 1982 and 1983.

125) and corrective fiscal measures, a balance of payments crisis was averted. From this perspective, it is hardly surprising that a decade later, with a much smaller buffer to begin with and without effective monetary policy instruments to deploy, an ill-timed kina-based fiscal expansion would have exhausted the country's foreign exchange reserves.

Sixth, especially towards the end of the decade, political instability and erratic behaviour (and misbehaviour) eroded confidence. This is an especially important explanation for the second crisis that occurred when Bill Skate was prime minister.

Seventh, and completing our list of explanatory factors, in the context of an anticipated boom and expected currency appreciation (Booth 1995), the government worsened the situation for itself by relaxing foreign exchange controls in the early nineties. The central bank increased 'the authority of authorised foreign exchange dealers (the commercial banks) to grant foreign exchange approvals' (BPNG 2007, 132) and access 'by residents and non-residents to offshore accounts' (245). Low levels of confidence meant that, once a crisis hit, those who had dollars were reluctant to hand them over, and those who did not tried hard to get them.

4.4.2 Exchange rate policy and the balance of payments

In response to the closure of the Panguna mine, the government devalued the kina by 10 per cent in January 1990. Although there had been gradual real depreciation over the eighties (2.3.3), this was a much more explicit rejection of the hard kina 'no depreciation' policy.

It was not enough. By mid-1994, foreign reserves had been exhausted. There was another 12 per cent devaluation on 11 September 1994. But reserves continued to fall. The government temporarily suspended kina convertibility, and, the next month, on 4 October, Julius Chan, who, as finance minister, had introduced PNG's hard kina policy, now, as prime minister, floated the currency.

The exchange rate regime that prevailed from late 1994 was a managed rather than a pure float. The central bank became the biggest player in the new foreign exchange market, and its decisions on how much foreign exchange to release into that market were crucial (King and Sugden 1997, 24). Nevertheless, the float was a massive reform, rightly labelled by Chan at the time as 'the most important economic decision … since independence' (cited in Chan 2010, 221). The next big change in exchange rate policy would not come until 2014 (8.3.1).

In 1989, one kina would buy 1.16 US dollars. By 2003, one kina would buy 28 US cents. The consequences were far-reaching. Expatriates became either too expensive to hire (if their salary was dollar denominated) or too poor to stay (if kina denominated) and the number of expatriate workers fell by half in just a couple of years (Duncan and Lawson 1997, 39). Foreign imports and services that had been within the reach of the elite or the middle class no longer were. With high inflation, the real adjustment in the exchange rate was much lower than the nominal adjustment, but nevertheless significant: in total about 30 per cent over the period (Figure B21).

While the real depreciation should have been a benefit to the economy,[9] the kina's fall was extremely unpopular, destabilising and bad for business confidence. The 'overwhelming attitude' of business to the devaluation was 'negative' (Duncan and Lawson 1997, 57). In his memoir, Chan (2016, 154) said he regretted floating the kina, commenting that 'because we were such a small little fly, we ought not to have put our currency on an international market and made it the subject of daily speculation'. It is striking that one of the biggest falls in the currency came in 2001, under the reform prime minister Morauta and when PNG was in receipt of support from the World Bank and IMF. This speaks to Morauta's inability to restore confidence, and also to the fickle nature of currency markets.

The depreciation did help the agricultural sector (4.3.2); however, it also imposed economic costs, including the loss of demand as foreign debt servicing costs increased, real wages fell and expatriates left (Duncan and Lawson 1997, 57). This last was a supply-side as well as a demand-side shock, with the departing workers taking with them skills and supervisory capacity that were not easily replaced.

The current account, that had been in deficit throughout the eighties, went into surplus in 1992 and stayed there for most of the period (Figure B19). This reflected the growth of resource exports and the associated repatriation

---

9   This was certainly the expectation at the time. Minister of Finance Chris Havieta (1995, 9) said: 'The medium to long term benefits of the Kina devaluation and float will be felt more strongly in the rural areas by farmers. At the same time, employment opportunities will become available to Papua New Guineans because job-creating industries will be attracted to employ local labour through a competitive and open economy.'

of revenue. Exports that had been around 30 per cent of GDP in the eighties increased towards the end of the period to 40–45 per cent. Imports continued to average just below 40 per cent of GDP.

It is ironic that PNG's two balance of payments crises came when the current account was in surplus. But the current account balance is a poor indicator of foreign exchange availability in PNG. With large resource projects, exports can exceed imports, but much of the revenue generated from those exports is unavailable for the financing of imports, as it is instead retained offshore to pay debtors and shareholders.

4.4.3 Fiscal policies

Adjusting for inflation, there was hardly any growth over this entire period in either government expenditure or revenue (Figure B24). With high inflation, real government salaries fell;[10] therefore, fully adjusting for inflation, as we do, underestimates real government expenditure growth. Nevertheless, the picture is dire. Recall the aspiration of the eighties for 3 per cent real expenditure growth per year (2.3.1). In fact, in 1980, total real expenditure was PGK8.8 billion, in 1988 PGK8.6 billion and in 2003 PGK9.1 billion (all in 2022 prices).

With fiscal deficits in most years (Figure B27) and little economic growth, the debt/GDP ratio grew: from 24 per cent of GDP in 1988 to a maximum of 47 per cent in 2002 (Figure B28). The interest burden almost doubled after inflation. The salary bill was roughly constant in real terms with public service hiring (5.2.2) offsetting declines in the real wage. The development budget showed an increase, but at least part of this was aid from Australia formerly given as budget support (and spent through the recurrent budget) and now, as discussed later in this section, given through projects (and so part of the development budget). The increase in electorate funding (5.2.4) also benefited the development budget. Something had to give, and it was spending on recurrent goods and services, which was slashed (Figure 5.1). The cost of the Bougainville conflict added to the fiscal stress. In the early nineties, and then in the early 2000s, school fees were abolished; neither policy was sustained, and the pattern was repeated in the next two periods (7.2.2).

---

10   For example, there was a wage freeze in 1997 (AusAID 1999, 59) and only a 3 per cent salary increase in 1996 (AusAID 1997, 59).

On the revenue side, there was little change in policies until the late nineties, when a value-added tax was introduced to replace the sales tax, and tariffs started to be cut (5.1.3). As part of the expansionary fiscal policies of the early nineties, the corporate tax rate was reduced in 1993 from 35 to 30 per cent, while the top marginal income tax rate was reduced from 45 to 28 per cent. This was referred to as a '"big bang" approach' adopted to 'move Papua New Guinea to amongst the lowest taxation regimes in the world' (Department of Treasury 1992, 33–4). However, these changes had to be reversed as part of the subsequent stabilisation. By 1998, the top marginal income tax rate was actually 47 per cent.

With the economy becoming more resource dependent, the government got a lot more revenue from the resource sector in the nineties than in the eighties, with government resource revenue averaging 2.9 per cent of GDP from 1993 to 2003, compared to 1.7 per cent before the closure of Panguna. PNG's sovereign wealth fund, the MRSF, continued to perform its stabilisation and saving function, and, by the late nineties, the fund's balance was at a record level of 7 per cent of GDP (Figure B30). And then it was abolished.

In hindsight, it looks like the MRSF was cut down in its prime, but that is not how it appeared at the time. When the fund was established just before independence, it was envisaged that deficits would be kept low, and most financing would be offshore.[11] It was reasonable then to assume that the decision of how much to borrow (to fund the deficit) would be independent from the decision of how much to save (through the MRSF). However, by the late nineties, given the fiscal stress the government was experiencing, the more that was saved, the more that needed to be borrowed. Moreover, with the cost of borrowing in the double digits and rising, and MRSF balances at BPNG earning a much more modest rate of interest (on average about 6 per cent), maintaining the MRSF was becoming increasingly expensive. By the end of the decade, the government was cash-strapped, accumulating arrears and struggling to pay its debts. The MRSF's PGK677 million balance was viewed as an unaffordable luxury. With the blessing of the World Bank, the MRSF was abolished in 1999. What made sense as a short-term crisis response, however, meant that when a boom did come a few years later

---

11   In 1981, the central bank governor expressed the conventional wisdom of the day that 'the budget deficit should not be much larger than the net amount of concessional financing that can be raised' (ToRobert 1982, 149). The initial fiscal deficits were very low: 1.4, 1.1 and 1.2 per cent of GDP for 1976–78.

there was no mechanism with which to save revenue. Indeed, since it was abolished some 25 years ago, the MRSF has, despite various efforts (7.1.3), not been replaced.

While PNG's fiscal position was helped by resource inflows over the decade, the situation was worsened by a change in aid policy. Australian aid had not kept up with inflation but it had grown over the eighties in nominal terms. Not so in the nineties. Australian aid was AUD338 million in 1999 and it did not exceed that value (even in nominal terms) until the Enhanced Cooperation Program started in 2004 (7.2.6). Moreover, Australia decided to shift away from budget support. The first Development Cooperation Treaty between Australia and PNG signed in 1989 agreed that budget support would be progressively replaced over the coming decade by program aid (aid in support of specific projects, planned together but controlled by Australia, and reported through but not injected into the PNG budget). Given the level of corruption in PNG—not to mention the war in Bougainville—this change seems inevitable,[12] but it did make fiscal management difficult. Whatever the benefits of Australian aid projects (and they were mixed), shifting aid to projects reduced the revenue and foreign exchange available to government without reducing its responsibilities since, from the start, Australia has, with some minor exceptions, notably on road maintenance, refused to consistently fund core PNG government responsibilities, whether recurrent or capital.[13]

4.4.4 Monetary policy

The minimum liquid asset ratio (MLAR) was the main tool of monetary policy in the eighties (2.3.2). However, it lost its relevance in the nineties. The large purchases by banks of government bonds (4.3.3) meant that they far exceeded the MLAR even when the latter was increased. (Most bonds were counted as liquid assets even though they are typically bought and held, and there is no secondary market.)

Over the nineties, the Bank of Papua New Guinea turned to a number of new policies to influence banking behaviour. In 1998 it introduced a cash reserve requirement (CRR)—a percentage of commercial bank deposits

---

12 At, and not long after, independence, there were pushes, then resisted, for Australian aid to be tied to particular projects (Denoon 2005; Conroy 1980). Langmore (2014, 135) reports widespread support in PNG for this in the early nineties on the basis of a loss of confidence in the national government.
13 Garnaut (2000, 34) has argued that the switch weakened public service capacity, authority and morale.

that must be kept with BPNG. This was initially set at 10 per cent, but then to encourage bank lending reduced to 5 per cent in the following year, and then 3 per cent in 2003. However, as bank enthusiasm for private sector lending fell, the share of commercial bank deposits held at BPNG or as cash crossed 10 per cent in 1999 and showed no sign of falling when the CRR was reduced (Figure B36).

A policy lending rate, the Kina Facility Rate, was also introduced in 2001 (Figure B34), but it has also proved ineffective, as banks, flush with funds, have not needed to borrow from the central bank. Indeed, the problem of underlying excess liquidity has worsened since the nineties, as deposits have continued to grow faster than lending (6.3.2).

5

A decade of reform

The high level of wages has contributed to low levels of investment, high levels of unemployment, growing disparity between urban and rural living standards, urban migration, and to reduced international competitiveness of the economy ... The Minimum Wages Board handed down its determination in August 1992. The Board took a firm position on the need for radical change ... The determination recommends deregulation of all wages above the minimum, a uniform minimum wage for new employees ... set at the current level of the rural minimum wage ... discontinuation of the practice of automatic indexation ... and future variations of minimum wages to be determined by employer–employee negotiations, based on productivity and capacity to pay ... The Board has ... set the necessary base for private sector investment, economic and employment growth, reduction in the cost structure and increased competitiveness of the economy.

—From the 1993 PNG Budget (Department of Treasury 1992, 18–19)

Today's decision to float the Kina is undoubtedly the most important economic decision made by any Government since independence.

—Prime Minister Julius Chan, 4 October 1994 (cited in Chan 2010, 221)

There is a lot of energy in our people, which yields income and wealth when it is given a chance. We will give Papua New Guineans their chance by removing the many barriers to small-scale business through more effective government or through privatisation.

—Prime Minister Mekere Morauta, 14 July 1999, from his 'date with destiny' acceptance speech (Morauta 2021)

5.1 Economic reforms

The nineties, while characterised by economic volatility and mismanagement, was also a decade of economic reform. This reform was in part driven by the three structural adjustment programs the country entered into during this period with multilateral donors at strikingly regular intervals: in 1990, 1995 and 2000. All three were preceded by fiscal crises, and so, not surprisingly, all had fiscal stabilisation front and centre. And, in all three, fiscal stabilisation was achieved, though the related emphasis on public sector retrenchment proved ineffectual.

Apart from the common theme of fiscal adjustment, each economic reform episode had its own distinctive areas of focus. In the early nineties, the emphasis was on wage deregulation and investment promotion. In the mid-nineties, the exchange rate was floated, other liberalising reforms were promoted, and, surprisingly, forestry reform took centre stage. The economic reforms of 1999 to 2002 were the most comprehensive of all, and covered, beside fiscal reform, privatisation, financial sector reform and the empowering of the central bank.

This section details the major economic reforms of the decade, in the early, mid and late nineties, respectively, and assesses the contribution of the various donor-backed structural adjustment programs.[1] The focus is on structural reforms. Fiscal, monetary and exchange rate policies were covered in the previous chapter (4.4), and political and governance reforms are covered in the next section of this chapter (5.2).

5.1.1 Early nineties

The keynote reform of the early nineties was wage deregulation. The urban minimum wage had been rapidly increased in the run-up to independence (3.1.1). Economists agreed that it was too high, but a regime of wage indexation imported from Australia prevented inflation from substantially eroding the minimum wage's real value. In 1992, a decisive break with the past was made when the urban and rural minimum wages were unified at the level of the latter—only 37 per cent of the former—and the policy of indexation was abolished (Figure B18). These reforms effectively deregulated the urban labour market. Wages were not immediately cut

---

1   BPNG (2007, Chapter 6) covers some of the same ground.

(except for new workers; existing workers were grandfathered) but fell in real terms, as they were not adjusted in line with inflation (Levantis 1997). The next significant increase in the minimum wage was not until 2005.[2] Unfortunately, this radical reform did not induce the expected growth in employment. Too much else was going wrong with the economy for a strong supply-side response to emerge.

Also in 1992, PNG established the Investment Promotion Authority (IPA) to replace the National Investment and Development Authority (NIDA). The difference between the two entities is suggested by their names. NIDA had exercised 'tight control and cumbersome approval procedures' (World Bank 1991 89), and had presided over a foreign investment regulatory regime in which long delays were the norm (3.1.2). IPA was meant to be friendlier to foreign investors, and more streamlined. IPA continues in existence to this day and has a largely positive reputation. Around the same time, the Small Business Development Corporation and the Industrial Centres Development Corporation were created; their subsequent existence has been less edifying.

Forestry policy and reform were headline issues throughout the nineties (see Filer, Dubash and Kalit 2000; and Bird et al. 2007 for overviews). Customary owners of forested land were allowed to interact directly with developers under the Forestry Private Dealings Act of 1974. The Barnett Inquiry into forestry found extensive corruption (2.2.2), and that Act was repealed in 1991 and replaced by a new forestry policy and Forestry Act. In the same year, the Papua New Guinea Forest Authority was established. The aims of these reforms were to centralise the control of licensing to reduce sweetheart deals with well-connected elites and to ensure sustainability and a higher return to PNG from its tropical forests—the third largest in the world.

Most logging is in coastal areas. When the Highlands prime minister Wingti returned to power in 1992, he put a non-coastal, reforming minister in charge of forestry. Plans were put in place to increase log export taxes, reduce logging and increase domestic processing. In 1994, the government contracted the Swiss company Societé Generale de Surveillance to monitor

---

2   There was a marginal increase in 1998, and a ruling in favour of a wage increase in 2001, which the Morauta government dismissed (Marshall 2001).

all log exports from PNG. Claims of underpricing remain to this day, but the organisation continues to work in the PNG forestry sector, a bright spot in a perpetually troubled sector.

5.1.2 Mid-nineties

Despite it being one of several areas of activity for the World Bank in the early nineties, no-one would have anticipated that forestry would become such a central issue in the relationship between the PNG government and its multilateral financiers. But the World Bank was becoming increasingly interested in both governance and the environment, and increasingly susceptible to the influence of Western non-government organisations (NGOs). Measures such as further increases in log export taxes and reduced logging were made conditions of the World Bank's 1995 support program to PNG, delivered in response to the 1994 balance of payments crisis (4.4.2). These measures were highly controversial with politicians, many of whom were involved in the logging industry themselves: while the aim of the reforms of the early nineties had been to do away with sweetheart deals, in fact they had merely switched the fora in, and mechanisms by which, such deals were negotiated. In 1994, the pro-reform forestry minister mentioned earlier was replaced by one whose electorate accounted for nearly half the country's log exports (Filer, Dubash and Kalit 2000, 29). Forestry became a major sticking point and reason for delay in the World Bank's adjustment loan. A key bone of contention was whether politicians could appoint members to the Forest Authority. In the end, the politicians prevailed, though tax rates were increased.

Land was another controversial issue in the mid-nineties and in the PNG–World Bank relationship. The PNG government had long supported the idea of the registration of customary land, but the only action on this, beyond legislative drafting (Kalinoe and Kiris 2010, 30), had been at the provincial level (3.1.5). The World Bank and Australia had funded a Land Mobilisation Program starting in 1989 to progress the issue. Little headway had been made. To stimulate action, it was proposed that a condition regarding land registration be included in the 1995 structural adjustment loan. The draft condition—'Complete framework legislation for customary land registration. Complete registration in East New Britain and East Sepik'—was leaked (Filer, Dubash and Kalit 2000, 32). While the approach suggested was consistent with longstanding government policy, the leaked condition met with a violent reaction from NGOs, students and some politicians, who contended that the World Bank was trying to undermine customary ownership and privatise PNG land. The condition was dropped, and this reform once again stalled, not to be picked up for another decade (7.1.4). In fact, there were violent protests against land reform not only in the mid-nineties but also in 2001, when four students were fatally shot during a protest against privatisation and land reforms, even though the latter was not actually part of the Morauta reform program.[3]

Ironically though, this controversy over land reform did not stop the government reforming the Land Act in 1996 to further clarify the lease-leaseback arrangement, which dates back to the seventies (3.1.5), and which allows landowners to lease their land provided that the government acts as an intermediary. This reform had little immediate impact, but underpinned a massive land grab the next decade (7.1.4).

Liberalisation was foreshadowed in the early nineties, but more vigorously pursued in the mid-nineties. Reforms included removing goods from the price control regime and pruning back the reserved list (the list of economic activities from which foreign investment was barred). Trade opening was also a major theme, with PNG joining the World Trade Organization in 1996. As the World Bank (1995a, 9–10) reported, the government was committed to:

> Replace quantitative restrictions and import bans by prohibitive tariff rates for cement, canned fish, and beef/lamb, fresh fruits and vegetables, remove other non-tariff barriers on imports, and lower such duty rates to internationally acceptable levels over a five-year period.

It was no coincidence that cement was the first in this list. In 1993, the government had provided protection to a new high-cost cement factory in the form of an import ban, alongside other support (Laveil 2019a). The World Bank (1995a, 10) also persuaded the PNG government to undertake a study on tariffs and indirect taxes. This in turn lead to a 1997 White Paper on the tariff reform program, and, as discussed below, to substantial tariff reductions in the late nineties and over the next decade, as well as the introduction in 1999 of a value-added tax.

---

3   Errington and Gewertz (2004, 289) comment that 'there were widespread rumours that these students were supported by various politicians who, under the guise of populist rhetoric, sought to destabilize the [then] current government and to maintain their own access to the resources of the state-owned enterprises'.

5.1.3 Late nineties and early 2000s

The reforms of the late nineties and early 2000s were PNG's most comprehensive ever. While Bill Skate is mainly remembered now for his scandals, he was also, in his own way, a reformer. His main economic legacy is the introduction of a value-added tax (VAT) in 1999, called the general sales tax (GST), which remains in place to this day. This 10 per cent tax was introduced in place of both a general import tariff and the provincial sales tax, and replaced the decentralised collection of the latter by a revenue-sharing system that excluded imports. To circumvent a successful appeal to the Supreme Court by Governor of Morobe Luther Wenge in 2002, the VAT was renamed the GST, and the provinces were guaranteed 60 per cent of proceeds.[4]

Skate's reform efforts were otherwise consumed by the chaos of his reign, and it was left to his successor, Mekere Morauta, PNG's famous reforming prime minister, to ring the changes. Morauta's 'date with destiny' acceptance speech (Morauta 2021), delivered on the floor of parliament on 14 July 1999, outlined his reform agenda, which he proceeded to implement over the next three years with no fewer than 150 pieces of legislation (Morris 2021a, 2021b).

Perhaps most significantly of all, Morauta changed the legislation governing PNG's central bank. The Bank of Papua New Guinea had come under immense political pressure in the late nineties (three governors in four months at one stage)[5] and its role had been reduced primarily to one of financing the government deficit (Figure B35). The 2000 Central Bank Act made deficit financing by BPNG illegal and gave it a mandate to focus exclusively on controlling inflation. The Act it replaced had given the central bank much vaguer objectives and had capped, rather than banned, deficit financing (though the caps had been greatly exceeded over the nineties). The new Act also gave responsibility for both monetary policy and financial sector regulation to a single person, the governor, who could be neither directed nor easily sacked, in contrast to the earlier Act that had given those responsibilities to a politically appointed board. Discretion over the board's appointment was largely removed by making most positions representative

---

4   Total GST revenue is shown in the budget and then transfers to the provinces of their share are shown as a separate expenditure item.

5   For the details, see footnote 15.

(e.g. of the churches, business and unions). These were some of the most radical reforms PNG has seen. They brought first benefits (6.3.2), but then costs (8.3.4).

Morauta's reforms also transformed PNG's financial sector (Biggs 2007). A new Banking and Financing Institutions Act strengthened bank supervision. Superannuation was a particular reform focus. The National Provident Fund, which managed the retirement funds of private sector employees, had been wracked by scandals in the late nineties, and was loss-making. A commission of inquiry was established, headed by Tos Barnett who had headed the forestry inquiry (2.2.2). Its report (GoPNG 2002) implicated future prime minister Peter O'Neill in one of the scams, though charges against him were later dropped. The National Provident Fund (Financial Reconstruction) Act 2000 wrote down member accounts and provided temporary government support. The Superannuation (General Provisions) Act 2000 set down governance standards for the future, for example, banning governments from appointing members to superannuation fund boards, and put the super funds under BPNG prudential supervision. These reforms transformed the NPF, renamed Nasfund, which has been very profitable ever since, and which has retained its position as effectively PNG's monopoly superannuation fund for employees other than public servants. (The superannuation of public servants is managed by Nambawan Super, which is also regulated by BPNG.)[6]

Morauta privatised PNG's largest bank, the Papua New Guinea Banking Corporation, which had a market share of 60 per cent and was on the verge of bankruptcy. It was sold to, and amalgamated with, the national, private and much smaller Bank of the South Pacific (BSP). The sale was highly controversial at the time and led to a commission of inquiry. However, BSP, which began as a subsidiary of the National Australia Bank and was sold to local investors in 1993, has gone on to become the country's biggest and most successful bank by far.

There was significant trade liberalisation, with the 1997 White Paper (5.1.2) converted in 1999 into a tariff reduction program (TRP) (Scollay 2007; Laveil 2019a). A general import tariff of 10 per cent was abolished, replaced by the new GST. Tariffs were left in place only for goods that were or, it was judged, could be produced in PNG. The TRP divided the remaining tariffs

---

6   In principle, Numbawan Super and Nasfund can compete for clients, but, in practice, virtually no competition occurs.

into three groups—intermediate, protective and prohibitive with rates of 30, 40 and 55 per cent. The upper limit itself replaced various tariffs of as high as 100 per cent. A tariff reduction schedule was put in place to 2006, by which time the three tariffs were to be just 15, 25 and 40 per cent. Although controversial, the reduction schedule was largely adhered to, and, in fact, continued beyond 2006 (Scollay 2007, 15; Laveil 2019a; Section 7.1.2).

In 1999, the Pioneer Industries Act, which had provided tax holidays and other incentives for new entrants, was abolished.

Morauta also oversaw the exit of BHP from Ok Tedi. That mine's dumping of waste into the Fly River was causing environmental damage (2.2.3). Eventually, BHP, the majority owner, was taken to court in Australia in 1994 and successfully sued (Banks and Ballard 1997). BHP wanted out, but the PNG government could not afford to see a second mine closed (after Panguna's closure at the end of 1988). BHP was not willing to gift its shares to the PNG government due to concerns around corruption. The deal struck in 2003 involved the creation of an independent foundation, registered in Singapore, the Sustainable Development Program (SDP). In return for a guarantee of immunity from further litigation, BHP transferred its Ok Tedi shares to SDP to manage on behalf of the people of Western Province and PNG as a whole. The deal only lasted a decade (7.1.3), but the mine was kept open and became fundamental to the boom of the next decade (6.2.1). Waste management practices at the mine were improved.

Forestry was once again an area of reform. There was further haggling and tension with the World Bank, but Morauta restored the logging tax increases put in place in the mid-nineties that had been subsequently reduced.

Finally, an area of effort rather than success. Privatisation had been on the agenda since the early nineties, but the main steps actually taken during the decade had been to corporatise rather than sell state-owned enterprises (SOEs).[7] This had not worked. The quality of services continued to deteriorate, and the underlying problems of corruption and mismanagement remained. Manning (2000, 97) commented that many politicians still saw 'the operation of statutory institutions as their personal fiefdoms to be exploited to the utmost', and that:

---

7   The first Privatisation Committee was established in 1990. In 1995, the government sold 49 per cent of its ownership of Orogen, discussed later in the section. In 1996, it sold its holdings in New Britain Palm Oil.

because governments change so often, and ministers even more often, the appointees are seldom left on a board for longer than one year and, therefore, have no chance to develop a knowledge of the workings of the organisation. (Manning 2000, 98)

Garnaut (2000, 35) noted that:

the increased autonomy, through corporatisation, of virtually all government business enterprises in the mid 1990s was associated with expansion of the scope for directors and senior executives to use the businesses as avenues for personal enrichment.

It was for good reason, therefore, that Morauta put privatisation at the top of his reform agenda. In 1999, the Privatisation Act came into law. This committed the government to sell off its SOEs and established a Privatisation Commission. Then, in 2002, all companies were put under a holding company, the Independent Public Business Corporation (IPBC) to ready them for sale. Actual privatisation, however, proved harder to achieve, and the sale of the government bank to BSP was the only major success of this broader policy, which lacked popular support and was technically complex given the monopoly positions many of the state-owned companies had and the cross-subsidies embedded in their operations.[8]

The IBPC had little success in improving SOE governance. Of more lasting value was Morauta's creation of the Independent Consumer & Competition Commission (ICCC), an economy-wide regulator and competition watchdog. The ICCC had the futile task of regulating public sector utilities (Manoka and Rodrigues 2013) but proved its value a few years later with the vital role it played in liberalising the mobile phone sector (7.1.1).

The government did, over the course of the nineties, sell its minority stake in various resource projects (e.g. the Kutubu oil field and the Lihir and Porgera gold mines) held by Orogen Minerals. In 1995, the government sold 49 per cent of Orogen (4.3.2); in 1999, Morauta sold the rest, to Oil Search. While this was, technically speaking, a privatisation, it made no difference to the operation of the resource projects, which were already majority private-owned. The first sale swapped an expected future stream of revenue flows for funds today in order to reduce fiscal stress; the second swapped a minority stake in various PNG resource projects for a share in a PNG oil company, Oil Search.

---

8   A buyer was selected for the telecom company, but the sale was called off at the last minute.

5.1.4 The three structural adjustment programs

We should not make the mistake of assuming that all the reforms of the nineties were imposed on PNG from the outside. Some were clearly homegrown. The exchange rate was floated in 1994, before the World Bank–sponsored economic reform program of 1995 (approved by the Bank in August 1995). Other far-reaching reforms—such as the introduction of the GST (5.1.3) and the reform of provincial governments (5.2.4)—were also undertaken with little or no donor support at all. But nor should we discount the role of foreign pressure, which was clearly influential in many reforms, and decisive in some.

Table 5.1 provides a summary of the three structural adjustment programs of the nineties. The table focuses on World Bank support, since its reform programs were the most comprehensive, but the IMF also had its own reform and funding agreements with the PNG government. Australia and Japan provided additional funding for all three programs, the EU did for two, and the Asian Development Bank supported the reforms of the early nineties.

These loans have largely been judged unsuccessful. The World Bank's (1995b) own evaluation of its 1990 adjustment loan rated it unsatisfactory. An academic review of the 1995 loan concluded that it was 'an abysmal disappointment' (Barcham 2002, 210). The 2000 loan was the most successful, but even it was only partially successful relative to its objectives.

Reforms were undermined by the instability of the decade. The World Bank review of the 1990 loan complained that 'reforms did not take root. Although the loan supported a successful short-term stabilisation operation, it did not initiate the expected extended process of economic reform' (World Bank 1995b, iv). It was not that politicians were necessarily against the reforms that these adjustment programs promoted. Rather, they had other, competing agendas—mostly staying in power, but also protecting vested interests. These were often given greater weight than the demands of reform.

One can certainly criticise the behaviour of the multilaterals. They failed to recognise that they would only be turned to during a crisis, that the windows for reform would be brief, and that they needed to be realistic in their goals and opportunistic in their approach. Reform conditions became more ambitious over time. Especially in the mid- and late nineties, the World Bank imposed conditions that were politically unrealistic and that the PNG government could not deliver on. Examples include the forestry industry discussed above, in which too many prominent politicians were engaged for reforms to be sustained, as well as public sector retrenchment (5.2.2), electorate funding (5.2.4) and anti-corruption reforms in the early 2000s (ABC News 2002). On land, the World Bank's engagement, however slight, set the cause of reform back at least a decade.

The World Bank and IMF reform programs were always going to be controversial. However, because they were overly ambitious, they became more controversial than they should or could have been, both with politicians and with various aspects of civil society. We have already mentioned protests and deaths. The World Bank's stance on forestry led to a major failing out between it and the PNG government. Wesley-Smith (1997) details the 'extraordinary standoff' between Chan's government and the World Bank in 1995 and 1996, with a visiting mission asked to leave in early 1996 and some non-forestry taxes temporarily raised in September 1996 in a PNG attempt to 'go it alone' (Dorney 1998, 146–7), all before the World Bank's funds were finally released in 1997. The tensions lasted through the next decade. Even the reforming Morauta government had a rocky relationship with the World Bank. In February 2001, his government expelled its representative, Australian economist Daniel Weise, accusing him of overreach (*Saipan Tribune* 2001).

All that said, viewed from a longer-term perspective, and considering the lack of economic reforms in other decades, the three adjustment operations in fact seem highly successful. The financing they provided was critical. One reason Skate came unstuck is that he hired the former World Bank country economist for PNG, Pirouz Hamidian-Rad, as his adviser. Under World Bank rules, this was a conflict of interest and made PNG ineligible for loans. Skate's desperation for funding led him to pursue commercial options; when that failed, he decided to switch allegiances from China to Taiwan and the controversy around that contributed to his toppling. More fundamentally, there was a mood for reform, and the multilateral institutions were right to try to take advantage of that.

Table 5.1: The three structural adjustment programs of the nineties

Name World Bank loan	Years (starting at month of loan approval)	Also supported by	Amount	Key reform areas	Sources
Structural Adjustment Loan	June 1990 to 1991	ADB, EU, Japan, Australia and IMF	World Bank: $50m in two tranches: $25m released in October 1990 and $23m in December 1991, with $2m in technical assistance. Two IMF stand-by agreements valued at about $35m each. Supported by $290m over 1989–91 from ADB, EU, Japan and Australia.	• Macroeconomic reform and fiscal adjustment, including retrenchment • Wage deregulation • Investment promotion.	IMF (1992); Lodewijks Enahoro and Argyrous (1991); World Bank (1990, 1995b).
Economic Recovery Program Loan	August 1995 to 1997	Japan, Australia and IMF	World Bank: two $25 million tranches: first released in 1995, second in 1997. IMF stand-by agreement valued at about $111m. Supported by $45m from Japan, $50m from Australia.	• Macroeconomic reform and fiscal adjustment, including retrenchment • Forestry reform • Trade and domestic liberalisation.	Barcham (2002); IMF (1996); Proctor (1996); World Bank (1995a).
Governance Promotion Adjustment Loan	May 2000 to 2001	Japan, Australia EU, and IMF	World Bank: three tranches: $35m on board approval, $20m first tranche; $35m second tranche. IMF stand-by agreement valued at about $115m in four tranches. Supported by $180m from Australia, Japan and EU.	• Macroeconomic reform and fiscal adjustment, including tax reform and retrenchment • Establishment of independent central bank • Superannuation reform • Privatisation • Forestry reform • Trade and domestic liberalisation.	Filer, Dubash and Kalit (2000); IMF (2000); Weise (2002); World Bank (2000, 2002).

Notes: Tranche information is not available for the 1990–93 and 1995–97 IMF stand-by agreements. Currency is USD.

5.2 Politics and governance

In 1989, the first references to PNG as a 'weak' or 'fragile' state appeared (see Hegarty [1989] for what appears to be the first analysis, and Ketan [2000] for a comprehensive historiographical survey).[9] PNG expert Ron May ([1997] 2001b) was perhaps the first to explain PNG's disappointing economic performance in terms of its governance rather than other more strictly economic factors.

May drew on the work of two scholars. Nigerian academic Peter Ekeh (1975, 91) had argued for the existence in post-colonial African countries of 'two publics instead of one public, as in the West'. The two publics or public realms were, first, 'primordial' or pre-colonial, and, second, 'civic' or colonial. The elite belonged to both, but their primary allegiance was to the former, and this undermined the latter. Since it was seen as 'legitimate to rob the civic public in order to strengthen the primordial public' (Ekeh 1975, 108), the state was made weak through the rise of corruption and patronage. May ([1997] 2001b) argued that that Ekeh's theory applied as well to PNG as it did to post-colonial Africa.

May's (1998) treatment of the work of Joel Migdal (1988) is more complex, but PNG is, in Migdal's framework, a classic case of a strong but fragmented society, co-existing alongside a weak state, where the fragmented nature of social power makes the state weak.[10]

These were pioneering analytical contributions. On the ground, governance continued to deteriorate. Trends and patterns in politics established in the first period of independence continued. Public services deteriorated and public sector retrenchment failed. Corruption and crime grew. Decentralisation policies were radically changed.

---

9   Hugh Tinker's 1964 article on 'broken back states'—that is, states that gained independence without preparation or struggle and that became weak almost immediately—was republished in the journal *New Guinea and Australia, the Pacific and South-East Asia* (Tinker 1967) with an editorial note that it had 'a direct bearing on possible political developments in New Guinea'. However, this 1967 warning appears to have been forgotten in the optimism of independence.

10   As Migdal (1988, 139) writes: 'Where societies have been weblike and where social control has been fragmented among numerous organisations states have faced formidable barriers in seeing their policies through.' See Howes (2024) for further discussion.

5.2.1 Politics

The Sandline affair of 1997 has been described as PNG's 'story of the decade' (Dorney 1998, 224) and the country's 'most serious political crisis' since independence (May, Regan and Dinnen 1997, 3). The very fact that three books were almost immediately written about it (the above two and O'Callaghan 1999) speaks to the interest it sparked. However, while Sandline had major and surprisingly positive implications for the resolution of conflict on Bougainville (5.2.4), it had surprisingly little lasting effect at the national level. The decision by the army chief Jerry Singirok to change his position in February 1997 from supporting to opposing the hiring of UK mercenaries (from the UK Sandline company) to attack the Bougainville rebels certainly posed a major challenge to the idea of civilian rule. Singirok not only successfully instigated a mission to expel the mercenaries but also called on PNG's top political leadership to stand down. However, he pulled back from that latter demand and, while Prime Minister Julius Chan did resign in response to the public anger that followed the military action, he did so only for a few months while a commission of inquiry proceeded to clear him of allegations of corruption related to the deal. In summary, although it looked like Sandline might be giving the army more political power, it did not. A coup today is as unthinkable as it was before Sandline.

In fact, the elections following Sandline—far from being the moment at which, as Singirok put it at the time, in his national radio address of 17 March, 'we the ordinary people, together as a nation, can actually change the system for the benefit of the common people which successive governments have let down for many years' (Singirok 1997, 215)—showed how little national events matter in PNG's electoral processes, and how resilient and resistant to change PNG politics are. Although Chan lost his seat, the two main parties in power before Sandline, Pangu and the People's Progress Party, were returned to power (in a coalition with the People's National Congress, Bill Skate's party) after the 1997 elections. And the deputy prime minister, Chris Havieta, the man whose reputation suffered the most as a result of Sandline, not only kept his seat but also his position as deputy. Three independent members of parliament were elected in 1997 on an anti-corruption platform, but all three joined the government they had so virulently opposed during their campaigning once it had been returned after the elections.[11]

---

11   The three—Father Robert Lak in Western Highlands, Father Louis Ambane in Chimbu and Peti Lafanama in Eastern Highlands—were all associated with the NGO Melsol (Melanesian Solidarity), which campaigned against both World Bank reforms and Sandline (Callick 1997).

More broadly, politics in the nineties continued along the lines established in the eighties (3.2.1). The number of candidates continued to grow, reaching an average of 26 per electorate in 2002 (compared to eight in 1977, see Table A2). About half of all MPs were replaced at each election, except in 2002 when it was three-quarters, a record; parties continued to be weak and small—no party won more than a fifth of the seats at general elections (Table A2); and no prime minister lasted a full term (Table A1).

Politics also continued to grow more violent. Of the Western Highlands, it was said 'that violence is becoming more and more an expected part of political activity' (Strathern 1993, 56). May and Anere (2013, 11) wrote of the 2002 elections that they were:

> marked by inaccurate—often grossly inaccurate—electoral rolls, widespread voting irregularities and manipulation (sometimes by electoral officials), intimidation of voters, hijacking of ballot boxes, and violence among rival candidates and their supporters and in a few instances against polling officials. There were a number of election-related deaths ... The problems were concentrated in the volatile highlands provinces, but were not confined to the highlands.

Votes of no confidence were, by the nineties, an established feature of political life. Rabbie Namiliu, who himself became prime minister in 1988 as a result of one of them, faced down eight attempts in three years (Standish 2007, 148). To avoid them, prime ministers would suspend parliament for long periods of time. Morauta adjourned parliament from December 2000 to July 2001.

PNG's politicians changed the rules of the game to increase political stability. In 1991, the initial grace period during which votes of no confidence are not allowed was extended via constitutional amendment from six to 18 months after government formation (May 2003a, 5).[12]

A more comprehensive approach to political reform was taken at the end of the decade by Morauta, who introduced the Organic Law on the Integrity of Political Parties and Candidates (OLIPPAC). This amended the constitution to strengthen the party system by making it more difficult for MPs to leave their party and illegal for them to vote against the position

---

12 Another attempt was made more than a decade later (in 2003) to further extend the grace period to three years. That was unsuccessful, but then, another decade later (in 2013), the grace period was extended to two-and-a-half years, only for that extension to be struck down by the courts (7.2.1). At the time of writing, the grace period remains 18 months.

of their party on major issues. OLIPPAC was passed unanimously in December 2000, and was described by Morauta as 'the most significant reform since the Constitution was adopted at independence' (cited in Baker 2005, 102).

The Morauta government also amended the Organic Law on National and Local-Level Government Elections to replace the country's first-past-the-post electoral system by one of limited preferential voting. The aim was to ensure that successful election candidates had a broader base of popular support (May and Anere 2013).[13]

Morauta's political reforms, for all their promise, had little lasting impact, at least along the lines intended (7.2.1). Major parts of OLIPPAC were ruled unconstitutional in 2010 by PNG's Supreme Court (Kabuni et al. 2022), and, despite much longer prime ministerial tenures this century than last, neither piece of legislation seems to have changed the underlying dynamics of PNG politics, either at the electorate or the national level (Okole 2012).

5.2.2 Public services

Ther was a 'progressive decline in the quality and delivery of government services' during the nineties (Dinnen 1998, 51). Former prime minister Rabbie Namaliu (1995, 62) commented that:

> many of our people are worse off in terms of basic services and facilities than they were at independence. The rundown in basic services, such as health care and rural roads, is not only a tragedy, it is totally inexcusable.

The nineties was a bad decade for service delivery, partly because of a continuation of the negative governance trends seen in the previous period (3.2.2), and partly because of fiscal retrenchment (4.4.3). Government spending on recurrent goods and services—such as purchases of drugs and petrol—was slashed. As Figure 5.1 shows, after adjusting for inflation, such spending fell by two-thirds over the nineties on a per person basis.

---

13 Interestingly, in colonial times, PNG had had an optional preferential voting system for elections. It had been replaced by first-past-the-post in order to encourage the development of a two-party system (May 2001a, 3).

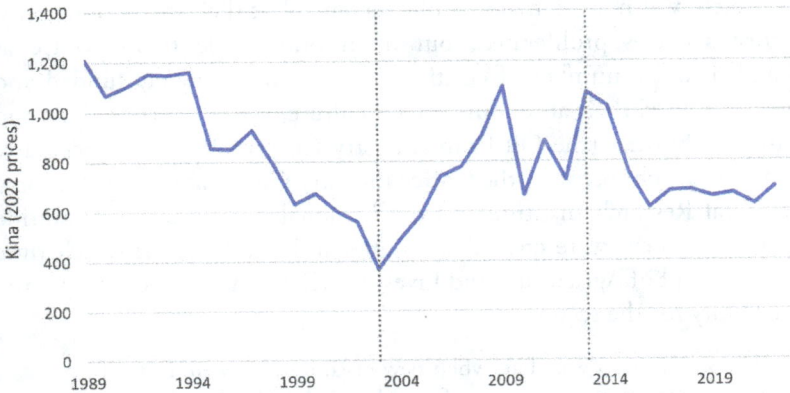

Figure 5.1: Government recurrent goods and services per person, 1989–2022 (kina, constant prices)
Note: Salaries (excluding statutory authorities), interest and development spending are subtracted from total expenditure.
Source: PNG Economic Database.

Public sector retrenchment was a catchcry of the nineties, but not something that was successfully pursued. An initial target of the first structural adjustment loan was retrenchment of 3 per cent of the public service (Stein 1992, 26). The second structural adjustment loan of 1995 required the retrenchment of 7.5 per cent of the public service. The Skate government announced that 7,500 positions would be cut. After Morauta came to power, the target was 6,500–7,000 redundancies (World Bank 2000, 3).

These retrenchments simply did not happen. To the contrary, public service employment, which had been flat in the eighties, grew over the course of the nineties from 50,300 in 1990 to 60,500 in 1995 and 77,800 in 2002 (Figure B16). Looking back, BPNG (2007, 62) concluded wistfully that 'it appears that this nagging reform will never be implemented successfully or effectively'. Retrenching staff is a drastic step. Soldiers mutinied when Morauta undertook to reduce their numbers from 4,150 to 1,900 (Chin 2002, 150–1). This was an extreme case, but others threatened with job loss could make less drastic but nevertheless credible threats of violence.

While the number of government staff increased over the nineties,[14] PNG has never had a large public sector relative to the population (Curtin 2000), and the ratio of the public service to the population was still lower in the early 2000s than at independence.

---

14   To what extent this was a deliberate policy decision versus a loss of control over hiring requires further research.

The problem was not too many public servants, but their low productivity. Statutory agencies proliferated, but often only made things worse as they added to the number of entities that were inadequately funded and frequently abused their autonomy. In agriculture, various corporations and statutory authorities (the Oil Palm Industry Corporation, the Cocoa and Coconut Research Institute, the Coffee Industry Corporation, the National Agricultural Research Institute and the National Agricultural Quarantine Inspection Agency) were created soon after independence, at which time the Department of Agriculture and Livestock (DAL) had sole governmental responsibility for the sector:

> The supposition was that, when new organizations were formed to take on functions formerly performed by DAL, they would take on most of the resources formerly used by DAL for those functions and that DAL would have cost reductions similar to the cost of the new organizations ... This expectation was not born out in practice. In common with other areas of institutional change in Papua New Guinea, weak public administration meant that the changes were never implemented as intended. With a strong nostalgia for the past, DAL actively lobbied to retain its staff and budget, despite the transfer of functions out of the department ... By retaining large numbers of staff without useful functions, DAL has become an aimless organization with low staff morale. Motivated, skilled staff have sought opportunities elsewhere, leaving the 'time servers' to fill the numbers. (McKillop, Bourke and Kambori 2009, 68)

The politicisation of the public service was a growing problem. Over the late eighties and nineties, 'personal connections started to become more significant determinants of who occupied seats on boards of public authorities or filled the higher departmental positions' (Turner and Kavanamur 2009, 13). The behaviour of the Skate government of the late nineties was particularly egregious in this regard. It replaced:

> many competent and experienced senior officials with its own less qualified political clients ... By early 1999 few departmental heads had held their jobs for more than a year and observers described a climate of fear in the bureaucracy. (Standish 1999, n.p.)

Take the Bank of Papua New Guinea as an example. Its first governor was Henry ToRobert, who served an astonishing two decades, from 1973 to 1993, before he was fired (Chan 2016, 136). But then, between 1993 and 1999, there were four governors, with three in 1998 alone.[15] Likewise, 'the telecommunications company had five chief executives between 1996 and 1999, and the postal service three between 1997 and 1999' (Garnaut 2000, 35).

By the time Morauta came to power at the end of the nineties, he was convinced that the politicisation of senior appointments needed to be restrained. This did not mean returning the Public Services Commission (PSC) to its former pre-1986 glory when it had responsibility for all public service appointments (3.2.2), but it did mean giving it a much bigger say in the appointment of the heads of departmental and statutory authorities so that politicians had to follow a highly prescriptive and bureaucratic process, including choosing from a shortlist prepared by the PSC. Morauta himself ran out of time to push through the required constitutional changes but they were completed by Somare in 2003 (Bizhan and Howes 2024).

5.2.3 Corruption

Concerns about widening corruption in the nineties broadened into what was seen as a crisis of governance. Even leaders perceived as relatively clean saw their reputations tarnished. Rabbie Namiliu as prime minister made cash payments to MPs who had been stood down from the ministry in order to retain their loyalty (Saffu 1998f, 489–90). Disturbing allegations were made in parliament in relation to Paias Wingti when he was prime minister (Wesley-Smith 1995, 365). Julius Chan, who had been accused in the eighties of self-dealing in relation to a share placement (Dorney 1991, 216–17),[16] was accused in 1994 of gross impropriety in relation to a property purchase in Cairns (PNGi 2019). The Sandline affair also greatly damaged Chan's reputation. Subsequent inquiries found evidence against his colleagues, but not against Chan himself, of corrupt dealing. But the invitation to mercenaries to enter PNG came to be seen more broadly as symptomatic of governance gone badly wrong.

---

15 Mekere Morauta (July 1993–September 1994), his sacking is explained in Section 4.3.3; Koiari Tarata (September 1994–April 1998); John Vulupindi (April–July 1998); and Morea Vele (July 1998–1999). Wilson Kamit, a beneficiary of the new Central Banking Act, served from 1999 to December 2009.

16 Chan was cleared in the end, but not before the inquiry 'revealed that 40 other national leaders including ministers, judges, and the Chief Ombudsman himself had received Placer Pacific shares without honoring their constitutional obligation to declare their purchases to the Ombudsman Commission' (Hegarty 1989, 4).

Bill Skate took the reputation of the political class to a new low when he was taped discussing political bribes and boasting about a gangland killing (Standish 1999). A video from the same period showed Skate's party deputy having sex with an underage girl. An Australian investigator, initially asked to investigate fraud in the nation's capital, ended up fleeing the country for his life (Standish 1999).

Corruption took on a much higher public profile. The governor-general at the time, Wiwa Korowi, bemoaned in 1995 that corruption had become 'deeply rooted' (Dinnen 1995b). At the height of the Sandline affair, he took the extraordinary step of placing a newspaper ad warning that PNG 'will be destroyed by … greed, corruption, nepotism, malice, selfishness and manipulation' (Walton 2016). A religious movement, *brukim scru* (bend the knee), led by the same governor-general appealed for divine intervention to improve the quality of PNG's political leadership (Eves 2008). The NGOs that took on the World Bank over economic reform also campaigned against corruption (Walton 2016). Future prime minister Mekere Morauta made his famous assessment that corruption in PNG was both 'systematic and systemic'. It had, he said, 'invaded the whole process of policy making and decision making. It has drowned the whole system' (Vatsikopoulos 1995).

Financial scams were also all too common. Bank of Papua New Guinea Governor Loi Bakani later reminisced about how, at the turn of the century, '"pyramid schemes" (scams) … were growing like mushrooms after the first rain' (Bakani 2010, 2). Efforts were made with donor support to counter corruption through this period, especially through improved public financial management. Morauta's was the only government to launch an effective assault, and some of his reforms have had a lasting impact, especially in the financial sector (5.1.3). But Morauta was only prime minister for less than three years.

5.2.4 Decentralisation and Bougainville

An overhaul of sub-national governance was one of the biggest reforms of the nineties (Howes, Sause and Ugyel 2022). By the late eighties, the decision made just after independence to create elected provincial premiers and assemblies (3.2.4) had come to be viewed, at least by national MPs, as a mistake. A series of inquiries and reports led to the repealing in 1996 of the 1977 Organic Law on Provincial Governments, and the passing of a new constitutional law: the Organic Law on Provincial Governments and Local-Level Governments. As the new law's name suggested, it was intended to strengthen local-level government, and it introduced regular elections for them, but its real effect (and intent) was to assert the control of national MPs over provincial governments. It did away with elected provincial representatives and made each province's regional MP its governor. Provincial assemblies remained but were to be constituted by that province's MPs and a few other representatives, none of them directly elected.

Such a centralising reform was only possible because it exempted Bougainville, by then bogged down in bloody conflict. It was resisted by leaders from the island provinces of East and West New Britain, Manus and New Ireland, who at one point threatened to secede to form the Federated Melanesian Republic. These provinces were unable to prevent the passage of the new law, but did ensure that an earlier plan to abolish provincial governments altogether was not successful (Mukherjee 2010).

If the new organic law was a victory for provincial MPs (since it made them into provincial governors, and their rivals, the elected premiers, were done away with), the bulk of MPs (the so-called 'open' MPs, representing districts) were rewarded over the decade by large increases in funding through the Electoral Development Fund (EDF). This reached PGK100,000 per electorate by 1990, and was tripled to PGK300,000 in 1994 (Figure A1). The EDF was then abolished due to World Bank pressure, but re-emerged in the late nineties, reaching PGK1.5 million in 1999 (Middleton 2000, 56–7). The World Bank again tried to kill off electorate funding in its 2000 round of support. In the end, it had to settle for an agreement around its better governance—with guidelines that were comprehensive in scope, but also comprehensively ignored.

In contrast to the growth in electorate funding, that to sub-national governments was squeezed during the nineties due fiscal stress. Sub-national spending fell as a share of total expenditure (excluding interest) from 30 per cent in the eighties to almost 20 per cent in the early 2000s (Gouy n.d.).

The conflict on Bougainville that started in late 1988 continued on and off for a decade, concluding only with the Bougainville Peace Agreement of 1998 (May and Spriggs 1990; Spriggs and Denoon 1992; Regan, Baker and Oppermann 2022). The Panguna mine closed in 1989 and never reopened. In early 1990, all PNG national government staff left the province. The rest of the decade saw thousands of deaths amid various periods of blockade, negotiations and conflict, involving both clashes with the PNG armed forces and between Bougainvilleans, as the insurgency morphed into a civil war, with the PNG military supporting those (the Resistants) opposed to the Bougainville Revolutionary Army (BRA). Some 60,000 Bougainvilleans were displaced out of a population of 150,000; estimates of conflict-related deaths range from 4,000 to 20,000 (Regan 2019). Early attempts at a settlement were 'successively frustrated either by the extreme misbehaviour of PNG troops or selective assassinations by the BRA' (Dorney 1998, 45). Governance collapsed and infrastructure was wrecked. 'Every district office was destroyed and community government buildings in more than thirty locations were burnt down' (Dorney 1998, 46).

Finally, after almost a decade of unsuccessful negotiations, and, ironically, with the abortion of the Sandline mercenary intervention creating a moment of hope and therefore a more favourable atmosphere for negotiations (Regan 1997, 64), Bill Skate, with international support, negotiated a peace agreement—this controversial prime minister's leading achievement. Agreements signed in 1998 and 2001 led to the creation of the Autonomous Bougainville Government, which left Bougainville as the only one of PNG's provinces still to have an elected provincial assembly. Key to that peace agreement was an undertaking that a non-binding referendum on Bougainville's independence would be held between 2015 and 2020 (9.2.4). This successfully kicked the can down the road, probably the best that could be done in the circumstances.

5.2.5 Law and order

A 1996 survey of businesses turned up the same result as in 1982 (3.2.5), namely that PNG's 'law and order problems and the resulting security concerns are having the most adverse impact on the business environment' (Duncan and Lawson 1997, 1). Two-thirds of the firms surveyed said that the cost of security was a serious problem for them: among the many issues put to them, this was the only one to be placed in this category by more than half of them. The violent activities of *raskols* (rascal gangs) were a particular worry (Dinnen 1995a). Research showed that criminal activity was well remunerated given weak law enforcement (Levantis 2000a).

In 1995, former prime minister Rabbie Namiliu wrote of 'an alarming decline in respect for authority, as evidenced by a breakdown in law and order' (Namaliu 1995, 62–3). Crime was not only a problem in the capital, Port Moresby. It had become so endemic that 'daily life had lost its reasonability', according to the middle class of Wewak, the capital of East Sepik (Gewertz and Errington 1999, 105).

Landowners became increasingly militant with their demands for compensation, even in relation to land used to benefit the community, such as schools. These demands were often supported by illegal actions, such as occupations and blockades (Errington and Gewertz 2004, 190–1). This 'resulted in closed hospitals, schools and airstrips, disrupted road construction programs and water supplies, stimulated violence and slowed the pace of social and economic development' (Connell 1997, 254). According to Saffu (1992, 337):

> In case after case ... landowners made hefty compensation demands, backed their demands with threats of violence if not met by a certain date, did indeed resort to the threatened violence, and, in the overwhelming majority of cases, ended up with some compensation and no prosecution for their lawlessness and use of violence.

Tribal violence became more destructive and lethal. Yala (2002, 10) commented:

> The destruction of homes, businesses, schools, health centres, all forms of infrastructure, gardens, and economic trees is a typical consequence of tribal warfare, resulting in the wasting of resources and retardation of development. The increased use of modern and high-powered guns is a national problem and virtually every tribe in the Highlands of PNG has access to high-powered arms. Educated elites, including members of the armed forces and external arms traders, are involved in the illegal arms trade.[17]

Policy responses to crime were ineffectual. Namiliu called a crime summit in 1991, and reintroduced capital punishment in the same year (a penalty that was never enforced, and finally repealed in January 2022). Wingti orchestrated the passage of the Internal Security Act in 1992, which aimed to tackle the problem of violence through a terrorism lens. Chan declared 1996 to be the Year of Law Enforcement. Unrealistic (and unconstitutional) proposals were repeatedly made, but never implemented, to restrict mobility and send people back to the countryside (11.8).

---

17 'Gun-running from other parts of PNG to the Southern Highlands is financed and facilitated by politicians and civil servants up to the highest levels of the educated elite. Many, and perhaps most, illicit high-powered firearms in the Southern Highlands were deployed by political candidates, sitting MPs, and their supporters to impress and intimidate both rivals and voters' (Alpers 2005, 24).

5.3 Conclusion

The nineties were a decade of reform. Important policy changes included wage, price and foreign investment deregulation, the floating of the exchange rate, trade liberalisation, fiscal reform, some privatisation, financial sector reform and the granting of independence to the central bank.

While the reform achievements of the nineties should not be ignored, it is not surprising, given people's lived experience, that it was the negatives—the crises, the declines and the mismanagement—that dominated perceptions at the end of the decade.

Andrew Anton Mako writes about Kolombi, the town in Enga in the Highlands in which he grew up, connected to the world by an airstrip. He describes how, in 1996, that airstrip was shut down due to a lack of maintenance. After this, government services shut down one after the other as the staff that ran them left and were not replaced: the health centre, the school and the police-post all closed (Mako 2013).

There was also private sector contraction. Banking services became harder to access (4.3.3). The number of newspapers fell from four to two. Talair was a PNG airline that started in 1952 and, at independence, served some 150 domestic destinations. But it ran into hard times in the nineties. Finding it difficult to get work permits for his expatriate staff (given the ongoing localisation drive), suffering from worsening law and order, and no doubt affected by the economic downturn, its founder and owner, Dennis Buchanan, said to be PNG's largest individual investor at the time, announced his decision to shut his business in 1990 (Dorney 1991). It finally closed in 1993.

Thus went the nineties. Public service delivery weakened as funding for goods and services was slashed. Private services reduced as businesses folded. The increasing resource dependency of the economy was a sign that the country was more accommodating of large resource projects than a range of other, diversified economic activities. The financial sector became less supportive of development, with fewer banks and banking agents, less lending, and a larger spread between deposit and lending rates. High inflation and rapid depreciation hurt many, though the depreciation was, it is important to note, good for rural producers and did produce a positive agricultural supply response.

Diagnoses of the eighties had blamed PNG's poor economic performance on economic problems—high wages and/or an overvalued exchange rate. Then, in the first half of the nineties, the government addressed both these constraints, going:

> a long way towards putting in place an economic policy regime that should lead to the development of a much more export-oriented industrial sector, generating many more jobs than in the past. (Duncan and Lawson 1997, 4)

And yet the jobs did not come.

Analysts decided, correctly, that the problem must be governance. The 'conditions for investment had deteriorated so badly that wage deregulation [and devaluation] on its own was no longer sufficient to reinvigorate private investment' (Chand and Yala 2005, 12). We have already highlighted Ron May's early analysis of PNG as a weak state (5.2). The World Bank (1999, 6) wrote at the end of the decade that:

> Politics as business and politicized public administration are at the heart of PNG's governance crisis. Together with poor transparency and accountability, the result has been generally poor economic governance, poor public sector performance, mismanagement and a fertile environment for corrupt practices.

In the early nineties, it was still possible to express 'cautious optimism about the PNG economy' (Gupta 1992, 22). But the late nineties and early 2000s was a time of tremendous pessimism. Indeed, there was a sense of imminent collapse. Sandline had been seen as a nadir, but what came after it (the Skate government) was even worse. Morauta's reforms were admired and appreciated; however, as the currency kept falling, inflation stayed high, real wages fell sharply, business confidence remained elusive and the national mood became increasingly pessimistic. It was perhaps a reflection of widespread hardship that, whereas normally about half of PNG's MPs lose their seats every election, in 2002, it was three-quarters (Table A2). The author Regis Stella (2003, 17) wrote:

> Right now, Papua New Guinea is going through the most contemptible period in our history. The political leadership and apparatus is dominated by infantile politicking with a propensity for greed and improbity. Many of these leaders engross themselves with defrauding and embezzling from state institutions and the national coffers. In the process they prevent equitable prosperity for all.

In the same year, another set of prominent PNG academics commented that:

> Media headlines, editorial pieces, letters to the editor, talkback radio shows and casual conversations all point to numerous crises and lament the state of the nation. The common theme is that the nation-state is on the edge of a precipice, facing a complete breakdown. (Kavanamur, Yala and Clement 2003, 1)

A prolonged period of economic expansion must have seemed like the least likely of developments. In fact, it was just around the corner.

Part III:
2004–13:
The noughties:
Boom time

Times are good in PNG … Good times do not last forever.
(Chand 2009, 1)

6

The boom

There are fundamental economic problems [in PNG], including weak domestic demand, and the 2 per cent economic growth experienced in 2003 is not likely to improve. (Parliament of the Commonwealth of Australia 2005)

2009 was the fifth straight year to record non-mining GDP growth in excess of population growth—unprecedented for Papua New Guinea. (Gouy et al. 2010, 1)

By 2016, we expect our budget to be three times bigger due to the monies coming into the country, not only from our LNG but other major projects. (Prime Minister Peter O'Neill, cited in Price 2012)

6.1 Introduction

Once adjusted for inflation, government revenue in 2003, the last year of the 'volatility, crisis and reform' period examined in the last two chapters, was actually lower than in 1989, the first year of that period. Non-resource GDP per person was virtually the same. The reforming Morauta government had been deposed in the 2002 elections. The nineties had shaken confidence, and the future looked at best uncertain; many predicted a crisis or thought that one had already arrived.

And then, unanticipated by all, PNG's resource boom began. There was rapid growth in government revenue: 17 per cent in 2004, 20 per cent in 2005, 16 per cent in 2006 and 10 per cent in 2007 (all after inflation). Government revenue only again reached its 2007 level in 2014, but the economic boom continued based first on the spending of windfall revenues from those early boom years, then on the construction of the mega PNG LNG project—by far the country's biggest resource project to date—and throughout by renewed economic confidence. Average real GDP growth from 2003 to 2013 was 4.5 per cent. Non-resource GDP growth did even better, averaging 5.6 per cent, an unprecedented result. Formal sector employment, sluggish for two decades, grew rapidly at an average of 5.0 per cent. The exchange rate, which had plummeted in value over the nineties, steadily rose. Inflation moderated. Political stability was restored: Michael Somare returned to serve as prime minister from 2002 to 2011, and Peter O'Neill was prime minister from 2011 to 2019. Admittedly, 2011 saw a serious political crisis, but it was quickly resolved by the 2012 elections, and the country moved on.

The transition from Somare to O'Neill was a generational shift. When PNG became independent, Somare was prime minister and O'Neill was 10 years old. Somare's rule had become increasingly lethargic. O'Neill brought a new energy to the position and in his first few years in office introduced a number of important changes: a (temporarily) tougher anti-corruption regime, a more active role for the state in the resource sector, a more expansionary fiscal policy and much more electorate funding.

The resource boom was a good thing for PNG, but not an unmitigated blessing. For one thing, the country was completely unprepared for it. The Mineral Resources Stabilisation Fund had just been abolished (4.4.3) so there was no mechanism in place for saving resource revenues during good times. The government had also recently sold off half of the equity it had accumulated in various resource projects and reduced tax rates on resource projects (4.3.2).

The boom was also mismanaged. Too much was spent too quickly, and, as the years went on, the expectation that the good times were here to stay led to heavy borrowing and rapid growth in real wages; this has made the subsequent bust harder to manage.

Finally, the boom bred complacency. The reform efforts of the previous decade largely stalled, though the opening up of the mobile telecom sector is an important exception.

Booms never last and this one ended, ironically enough, once the PNG LNG project was fully constructed in 2013. With a falling oil price, and belying expectations that were in any case inflated, the expected rivers of LNG revenue failed to materialise. Non-resource GDP per person and formal sector employment started falling, and the kina started depreciating again.

That is the story for the next part of the book. In these two chapters, we study the boom of 2004 to 2013, beginning in this chapter with economic growth and macroeconomic performance and policy, and then turning in the next chapter to economic policies, and politics and governance.

6.2 Economic growth

Economists at the time debated the causes of the boom, but, in hindsight, it is clear that high commodity prices and then PNG LNG construction were the driving forces. As resource prices rose, resource dependency increased to a new high in 2006 but then fell back to where it was at the start of this period as gold and copper production fell and the non-resource economy boomed. While growth was indeed broad-based, the resource boom left a costly legacy in terms of higher housing prices, an appreciated exchange rate and higher real wages.

6.2.1 The boom

Exactly when the resource boom began and ended can be debated. The year 2003 saw low but positive economic growth, rising formal sector employment and, for the first time in over a decade, exchange rate appreciation. However, 2003 was also characterised by high inflation and interest rates and negative real revenue growth. In 2004, which we regard as the first year of the boom, economic growth was still low, but inflation and interest rates moderated and, on the back of a rapid increase in commodity prices, government revenue started to grow, catalysing the boom that followed (Figures B12 and B24).

We take 2013 to be the last year of the boom. Construction of the PNG LNG project was substantially completed that year, and the exchange rate started to depreciate (Figure B20). In 2014, formal sector employment fell, which it continued to do every year for the next four (Figure B16).

Figure 6.1 shows the annual growth rates over this period for GDP and for non-resource GDP. Early growth was driven by resource revenue and ended with the global financial crisis (GFC). The economy quickly recovered due to a massive fiscal stimulus in 2009. PNG ran its largest fiscal deficit to date that year, financed by the spending down of temporary trust fund balances accumulated in the earlier boom years (Figure B30). In 2010 PNG LNG construction began, and this massive project took over from increasing resource revenue as the main driver of rapid growth. Growth slowed after 2010, as, by then, the construction was already built into the base.

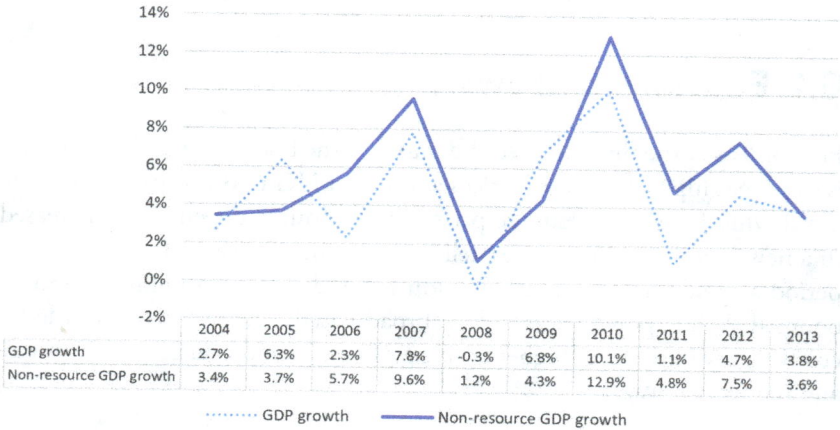

	2004	2005	2006	2007	2008	2009	2010	2011	2012	2013
GDP growth	2.7%	6.3%	2.3%	7.8%	-0.3%	6.8%	10.1%	1.1%	4.7%	3.8%
Non-resource GDP growth	3.4%	3.7%	5.7%	9.6%	1.2%	4.3%	12.9%	4.8%	7.5%	3.6%

········ GDP growth   ───── Non-resource GDP growth

Figure 6.1: GDP and non-resource GDP growth, 2004–13 (kina, constant prices)

Source: PNG Economic Database.

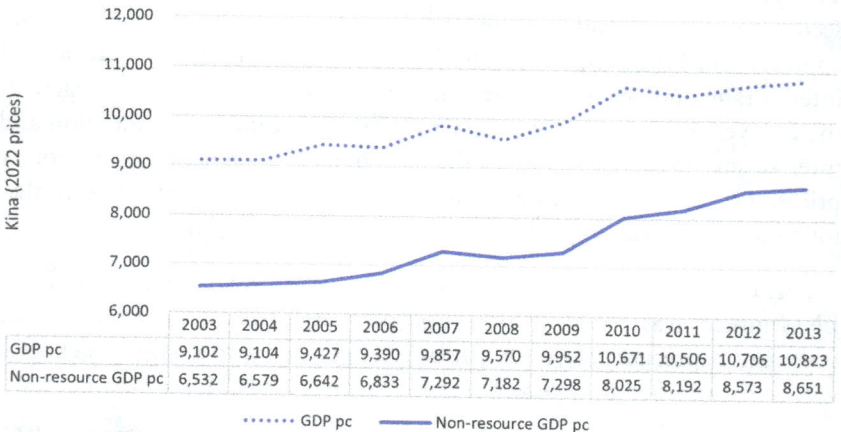

	2003	2004	2005	2006	2007	2008	2009	2010	2011	2012	2013
GDP pc	9,102	9,104	9,427	9,390	9,857	9,570	9,952	10,671	10,506	10,706	10,823
Non-resource GDP pc	6,532	6,579	6,642	6,833	7,292	7,182	7,298	8,025	8,192	8,573	8,651

········ GDP pc   ───── Non-resource GDP pc

Figure 6.2: GDP and non-resource GDP per person, 2003–13 (kina, constant prices)

Source: PNG Economic Database.

The noughties was a period of sustained and significant economic expansion. Between 2003 and 2013, real non-resource GDP per person grew every year except 2008, at an average rate of 2.8 per cent (Figure 6.2). Both before and after this boom period, average non-resource growth per person has been either zero or negative (Table 10.2).

Economists argued whether the growth of the noughties was due to the reforms of the previous period or to high commodity prices, with Gouy et al. (2010) stressing the former and Kauzi and Sampson (2009) the latter. The reforms of the nineties must have helped, but this was a commodity price boom. Our PNG resource price index increases by 19 per cent in 2004, 18 per cent in 2005 and 39 per cent in 2006 (Figure B12). Commodity price growth then slowed; however, by 2010 the resource price index was 26 per cent above its 2006 level, and, by 2012, 15 per cent above 2010. On average, resource commodity prices were more than double the level of the earlier two periods (Table 10.4). The value of resource exports, adjusted for inflation, increased by 25 per cent in 2005 and 34 per cent in 2006 (Figure B15). The export/GDP ratio increased from 44 per cent in 2003 to 55 per cent in 2007, a record never since broken (Figure B19).

Of equal importance, but less emphasised, was the existence of 'revenue-ready' projects—resource projects that yielded large amounts of revenue for government (a high 'government resource take') when commodity prices were high because their production was high and/or they had already depreciated their assets. Ok Tedi was the prime case in the boom period. When prices rose in the early 2000s, its production of copper and gold was close to its maximum, and it had been in production long enough for its investments to have been depreciated. Ok Tedi's corporate tax bill skyrocketed from about PGK50 million in the early 2000s to over PGK1 billion in 2007. Resource revenue, which had been about 2 per cent of GDP in the early 2000s, climbed to 9 per cent in 2007 (Figure B25). This ratio fell sharply with the GFC, but the average for the period was 4.9 per cent (Table 10.10), more than double the average of any of the other three periods.

Then there was the PNG LNG construction, a truly unique event in the country's history. The ratio of the total value of that construction to nominal GDP in the year it started is 133 per cent (Table C1). This far exceeds the construction value of other major projects, such as Ok Tedi (39 per cent) and Porgera (22 per cent). Of course, all these projects have a high import content, but the figure of 133 per cent speaks for itself.

Both the beginning and end of the boom were totally unexpected. Even as the boom was starting, the IMF (2004, 23) was projecting falling government revenue relative to GDP, and GDP growth lower than the rate of population.

The quick end to the boom was even more of a shock. PNG's Treasury had warned in the 2012 budget that PNG LNG revenue would only serve to keep resource revenue at a constant share of non-resource GDP given the depletion of revenue from other projects (Osborne 2014, Figure 2). At the time though, Treasury's forecasts were widely ignored in the face of much more bullish projections. A now infamous 2009 study by ACIL Tasman predicted that PNG LNG (which had commissioned the study) would start paying more than PGK1.5 billion in corporate tax from 2015 onwards (Osborne 2014, Figure 5), and was widely quoted.[1] The PNG Treasury increased its own revenue forecasts in the 2013 budget.

The injection of funds from PNG LNG exports would, it was claimed by many, more than offset the withdrawal of stimulus from the completion of construction. Peter Graham, who headed PNG LNG from 2009 to 2015, commented in 2011 that 'some analysts forecast a doubling of the GDP of the country' (Blades 2011). Another said 'the LNG project's success will reshape the PNG economy and the government's fiscal resource envelope' (Batten 2010b). Australian Foreign Minister Julie Bishop talked about 'huge revenue' flowing from the project to government (Garnaut 2015).

Business figures were also talking up PNG's potential more broadly. These remarks made by the PNG Treasurer Don Polye in a 2013 speech are telling:

> Many learned people ... have given us projections that I find very encouraging. We recently had a visit to PNG by the CEO of the ANZ bank, Mike Smith ... and he said that PNG could be the Tiger of the Pacific. (ANU TV 2013)

Sadly, none of these expectations came close to being realised. Even Treasury's more sober 2012 forecasts turned out to be wildly over-optimistic as resource revenue dried up in the 2010s (8.3.2).

---

1 For example, Gouy et al. (2010) predicted that 'revenues amounting to about one-third of production will flow to the government from the outset in about 2015'.

6.2.2 Sectoral developments, employment and housing

Given that we refer to this period as a boom, it seems paradoxical that non-resource GDP growth should exceed GDP growth for the period (Figure 6.1). But, in fact, in real terms (i.e. using constant prices), there was no increase in resource output and actually a marginal decline (Figure 6.3). Production of gold, copper and oil were lower in 2013 than a decade earlier, and significantly so—by 20, 60 and 45 per cent, respectively (Figure B10). This was a resource revenue boom, not a resource output one.

Confidence was high and growth was broad-based. All sectors grew faster than the rate of population, except the resource sector (Figure 6.3). The non-tradeable sectors (construction, finance, other [mainly government], transport, utilities) grew faster than the tradeable sectors (manufacturing, agriculture). This likely reflects real exchange rate appreciation (Figure B21), government revenue growth (Figure B24), and of course PNG LNG construction.

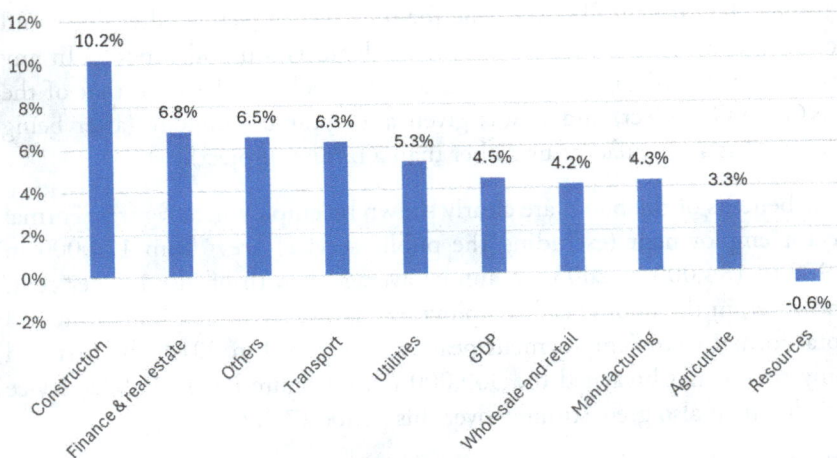

Figure 6.3: GDP growth by sector, 2003–13 (kina, constant prices)
Source: PNG Economic Database.

Although resource output fell, two new resource projects were negotiated and constructed during this period, and one came into production. The PNG LNG project had been under active consideration since the nineties. The initial plan was to pipe gas to Queensland. When it became evident that Queensland was planning to ship gas to Asia where it would fetch much higher prices, it was clear that a new approach was needed. Agreement between the government and the project developers was reached in 2009. Construction commenced in 2010. Major contributors to the USD19 billion price tag included the drilling facility in Hela (a newly created province that was carved out of the Southern Highlands as part of getting the project off the ground); a pipeline to take the gas to near Port Moresby; and a liquification plant and landing dock for ships to take the liquified gas to China, Japan and Taiwan. Exxon is the project operator and the major shareholder with a 33 per cent share. Oil Search, which operated the nearby oil fields and first developed the project, had a 29 per cent share. In 2021, it was acquired by Santos, which became the major PNG LNG shareholder with 40 per cent. The government borrowed to finance its 17 per cent share, later increased to 20 per cent. Production commenced in 2014, ahead of schedule.

The second, much smaller resource project of this period was the Ramu nickel and cobalt mine and processing plant at Madang, agreed to in 2006, with construction commencing in 2008, and production in 2010. This integrated mining-pipeline-processing project was controversial for its deep-sea dumping of tailings, which was opposed by many civil society groups.[2] The tax profile over time for resource projects is often back-end loaded, as companies first pay off their depreciation and interest. In any case, the value of this project's output was much smaller than that of the PNG LNG project, and it was given a 10-year tax holiday (after being classified as a manufacturing rather than a mining project).

The benefits of the boom are clearly shown by employment figures. Formal sector employment (excluding the public service) grew from 129,000 in 1975 to 184,000 in 2003, an annual average growth of just 1.3 per cent. However, in the boom years, employment growth averaged 5 per cent and total formal sector employment peaked at 301,000 in 2013, the first and only time it has breached the 300,000 mark (Figure B16).[3] Public service employment also grew strongly over this period (7.2.2).

The PNG LNG construction workforce peaked at 21,220 in 2012, 7.3 per cent of the formal sector workforce in that year. However, the number of national employees peaked at only 8,421, just 40 per cent of that total (Voigt-Graf and Odhuno 2019, 13). PNG amended its employment

---

2 The Somare government amended the Environmental Act in 2010 to remove the power of the courts to review environmental decisions. The amendments were reversed in 2012.

3 Unfortunately, no annual figures are available on public service employment for this period. However, we know it increased nearly 30 per cent from 2002 to 2015 (Figure B16).

legislation to exempt the LNG project from the requirement to advertise positions in PNG first. The government also prioritised LNG-related work permit applications.

Voigt-Graf (2015a) analyses visa data to show that the number of foreign workers arriving in PNG had been stable at around 14,000 from 1996 to 2003, but thereafter grew explosively to reach 70,000 in 2013 (jumping from 45,000 to 65,000 in a single year, 2012), with particularly rapid growth in Asian nationals, especially Filipinos, arriving for work (Voigt-Graf 2015b). These figures are not directly comparable with workforce numbers. However, the growth in the formal sector workforce over this period was 116,000. If each foreign worker stayed only a year, about half of this increase would have been made up by foreign workers. In other words, national employment grew but not by as much as first appearances indicate.

There is also evidence of strong real wage growth. As confidence built, minimum wages were significantly increased for the first time since they were slashed in 1992: by 50 per cent in 2005 to PGK37 per week. Minimum wages were then almost tripled in three years to PGK49 in 2009 and PGK102 in 2010, and then increased again to PGK131 in 2013 and PGK141 in 2014, at which level they have remained since. These increases were significant, but, after adjusting for inflation, still left the urban minimum at well under half of the minimum wage at independence (Figure B18 and Section 3.1.1; see also Jones and McGavin 2015; Imbun 2015).

Blunch and Davies (2024) provide the first analysis not of minimum but of average formal sector real wages, using 20 years of data on superannuation contributions from the private sector superannuation fund, NASFUND.[4] They calculate that wages rose on average by about 8 per cent per year after inflation in the boom years (which they define as between 2003 and 2013). Men did slightly better than women, but both did extraordinarily well, with average wages more than doubling over this period.

However, the boom was by no means an unmitigated blessing. Its legacy of an appreciated exchange rate and higher wages made the economy less competitive, and likely slowed growth in the next period (8.2.2). This was Dutch disease with a lag. And, even at the time, a painful side effect of the boom was a dramatic escalation in housing prices. Housing prices have always been high in urban PNG, due to limited land supply and demand

---

4   Wages can be backed out from the superannuation data, given compulsory superannuation rates.

from cashed-up resource companies. They fell over the nineties, but then increased rapidly during the boom. Rooney (2015) shows that property prices in Port Moresby fell between 1985 and 1995, and were stable to 2000, but tripled or more between 2000 and 2010 (Table 6.1).[5]

Table 6.1: Advertised property sale prices, 1985–2010 (kina, constant prices)

	1985	1990	1995	2000	2005	2010
Most exclusive (downtown Port Moresby)						
Maximum	669,146	1,048,473	1,138,612	1,221,092	1,202,879	4,000,000
Minimum	669,146	838,778	422,913	469,651	1,076,260	2,800,000
Average	669,146	996,049	817,941	653,989	1,139,569	3,100,000
More exclusive (Boroko, Korobosea, Gordons, Gordons 5)						
Maximum	760,393	671,023	487,976	657,511	443,166	2,500,000
Minimum	425,820	326,192	146,393	65,751	341,871	380,000
Average	554,001	450,501	366,999	358,479	389,353	1,147,692
Less exclusive (Hohola, Gerehu, Waigani, Tokarara, June Valley, Ensisi, Morata, Rainbow Estate)						
Maximum	547,483	121,157	211,456	356,934	443,166	750,000
Minimum	91,247	116,497	32,532	56,358	291,223	175,000
Average	268,875	118,827	94,003	138,051	367,194	424,654

Notes: CPI used to convert to 2010 prices. Sales prices are for two-to three-bedroom houses for the month of June except for downtown Port Moresby in 2005, which is for August.
Source: Rooney (2015).

6.3 The macroeconomy

Fiscal performance was aided by rapid growth in revenue inflows starting in 2004 but undermined by the lack of any long-term saving mechanism for those proceeds, and by profligate spending and, ultimately, borrowing. BPNG, under new legislation, ended its practice of deficit financing, and, with the exchange rate appreciating on the back of resource inflows and PNG LNG construction, inflation moderated. The effectiveness of the central bank's monetary policy management continued to be undermined by the deepening problem of excess liquidity.

---

5   Another estimate is that 'rental rates for high-end residential units in Port Moresby doubled between 2008 and 2012', reaching PGK8,000 per week (Oxford Business Group 2015).

6.3.1 Fiscal policy

The debt/GDP ratio fell from 39 per cent in 2003 to 25 per cent in 2013. This suggests successful fiscal management, but a closer look raises more questions.

The key fiscal fact of this period is explosive revenue growth (Mako 2012). Revenue grew by 79 per cent after inflation between 2003 and 2007 (Figure B24) and from 18 to 25 per cent of GDP (Figure B23).

The 2003–07 revenue spike was due to a resource revenue boom (Figure B25). Resource revenue thereafter started to fall, but total revenue remained high due to broad-based growth (6.2.2). Aid continued to fall relative to GDP (Figure B25).

Both the government and analysts were surprised by this rapid increase in revenue, as they were by the boom more generally. PNG had run deficits every year from 1998 to 2003, leading one commentator to make the reasonable inference that PNG was 'in all likelihood caught in a high debt and persistent deficit spiral' (Chand 2004, 17). While the 2002–07 Medium Term Fiscal Strategy (Department of Treasury 2005) promised fiscal balance by 2009, in fact, surpluses were achieved every year from 2004 to 2008.[6] The 2005–10 Medium Term Development Strategy, also written before the boom was evident, had 'resource availability forecast to remain more or less constant in real terms' (GoPNG 2004, 53). It could not have been more wrong.

PNG had abolished the Mineral Resources Stabilisation Fund in 1999 (4.4.3). Therefore, it had no mechanism in place to save windfall revenues. Efforts were made, with Australian encouragement (7.2.6), to put in place a sovereign wealth fund, but these were unsuccessful (7.1.3). Initially, expenditure restraint was exercised, and between 2003 and 2007 real expenditure increased by an annual average of 7.2 per cent, less than half of the revenue growth being experienced. A small amount of the resulting combined 2004–08 surpluses was used to pay down debt (16 per cent or about 3 per cent of GDP) but most (82 per cent)[7] went into what were known as trust funds, much of it through supplementary budgets brought

---

6   The deficit calculations in the text exclude deposits into trust funds as expenditures; PNG budgets at the time included them as expenditures. If they are included, there were surpluses in 2003, 2004, 2006 and 2007.
7   The 2 per cent residual could correspond to changes in cash balances, for example.

down in the course of the year to allocate unexpected revenues. Trust funds were earmarked for specific spending areas (school rehabilitation, agriculture, etc.), and so were at best only a short-term smoothing mechanism. The balance on all trust funds reached 10 per cent of GDP in 2008, but half of that was spent the following year, as real expenditure increased by 21 per cent following the GFC. By 2012 the balance on trust funds was down to 2.5 per cent of GDP (Figure B30).[8] In other words, by the end of the boom, very little had been saved. Moreover, as discussed in the next chapter (7.2.2), a lot had been wasted.

Meanwhile, the appetite to spend and borrow was increasing. After O'Neill won the 2012 elections, he increased expenditure in 2013 by 26 per cent after inflation, the largest increase ever, financed by a deficit of 6.9 per cent of GDP, the highest to that point (Figure B27).

Revenue growth had slowed in 2012 and 2013, but it was widely believed that LNG exports, beginning in 2014, would deliver a massive revenue boost to government. O'Neill defended his 2013 budget in the following terms:

> The budget is a deficit budget. I make no apology for that, none whatsoever. We are borrowing now certain in the knowledge the revenue inflows from mining and LNG projects will make repayment manageable. I have noted with approval that many analysts have endorsed this strategy. (Flanagan and Fletcher 2018, 35)

This rush to spend and borrow suited O'Neill's impatience, and was, as he said, supported by much of the public commentary (6.2.1).[9] However, in hindsight, it was clearly a policy error. After all, whatever the future held, the economy was already booming. Surely it was time to save or, at a minimum, not run a record deficit. As things turned out, the assumption that revenue would keep growing—let alone triple by 2016 as per the 2012 quote from the former prime minister with which this chapter began—proved to be completely fallacious.

---

8   In 2009, expenditure slightly violated the 2008–12 Medium Term Fiscal Strategy, which restricted trust fund drawdowns to 4 per cent of GDP, but the more important point is that these funds should have been saved for a much longer period of time, and not pre-allocated.

9   For example, Batten (2012) wrote of the 2013 budget that 'the significant economic stimulus that this spending will provide is well timed to counter falling domestic demand as LNG construction begins to wind down next year'.

The expansionary fiscal policy adopted blew PNG's new fiscal targets out of the water. The 2008–12 Medium Term Fiscal Strategy (Department of Treasury 2008) envisaged debt stabilising at 20 per cent of GDP by 2012. In fact, based on the old GDP series that was then being used, debt bottomed out at 26 per cent in 2011, and increased to 38 per cent by 2013. (GDP was rebased upwards in 2016, changing all these ratios.) A Fiscal Responsibility Act was introduced in 2006. This prohibited the 'overall level of debt' from rising and required that the budget be in balance during any term of government. That rule was abandoned as too strict in 2013, and successive amendments have been made to increase the debt cap (8.3.3).

Debt-retirement efforts in the early years of the boom were focused on foreign debt, and the deficits of 2012 and 2013 were largely domestically financed, meaning that by 2014, three-quarters of government debt was domestic, a record (Figure B29).

In summary, serious fiscal policy errors were made during the boom period. In the early boom years, up to 2008, funds were saved, but, given the nature of the trust funds they were put in, only for the short term. It is no surprise then that, in the late boom years, the short-term savings were spent; moreover, there was then too much borrowing.

6.3.2 Monetary policy

Inflation spiked in 2008 at 10.8 per cent, but overall the period was characterised by moderate inflation, an average of 4.4 per cent (Table 10.9). This can be explained by consistent exchange rate appreciation on the back of resource inflows and PNG LNG construction. During this period, the kina gained in value against the US dollar every year except for two (2009 and 2013), at an average rate of 4.9 per cent (Figure B20). As a result, the real effective exchange rate regained all the value it had lost over the nineties, returning to close to its pre-independence level (Figure B21). BPNG was also able to rebuild its foreign exchange reserves, which peaked in 2012 at USD4 billion compared to 490 million in 2003 (Figure B22).

With a bar on deficit financing, and fiscal surpluses rather than deficits in the early years of the boom, central bank holdings of government debt plummeted to almost zero (Figure B35).

Consistent with faster growth and higher confidence, loans from the commercial banks to the private sector rose from just 7 per cent of GDP in 2003 to as high as 17 per cent in 2013, almost matching the levels of the late eighties. Commercial bank deposits rose even more sharply from 15 per cent of GDP in 2003 to 39 per cent in 2013 (Figure B32).

This growth of deposits relative to loans worsened the problem of excess liquidity that had emerged in the late nineties (4.4.4). The cash reserve requirement was gradually increased starting in 2010 from 3 per cent to 10 per cent in 2014. Increasingly, banks parked their deposits with the central bank. The share of commercial bank deposits held at the central bank (or as cash) increased from 10 per cent in 2003 to 16 per cent in 2013 (Figure B36). For a few years in the mid-noughties, BPNG engaged in the sale of central bank bills (CBB). This gave banks another use for their deposits, but it was expensive and inadequate to mop up the excess liquidity, and BPNG eased back on CBB sales.

Excess liquidity remains a feature of the PNG economy to this day. Its solution is greater lending, but this requires more competition among banks and more bankable projects.

7

The stalling of reform

We set up KPHL [Kumul Petroleum Holding Limited] after the Malaysian Petronas model so that we can use it as a vehicle to grow our LNG revenue and make PNG a Dubai or Kuwait of the Pacific …When there was talk of government change, we would run to Wapu [the KPHL CEO] and get cash to pay for MPs to keep the numbers.

—Ben Micah (2020), former minister for state enterprises

7.1 Economic policy

Ending the mobile telecom monopoly in 2007 had a transformational impact. But, overall, this period was characterised by a stalling of the Washington Consensus reforms of the nineties. Trade liberalisation was continued, but privatisation was abandoned. Once O'Neill became prime minister, the first signs emerged of a shift to a more state-led model of development. Land policy was a major focus of reform and contention over this period.

7.1.1 The mobile telecom revolution

In 2004, plans to sell a majority of Telikom PNG, the state-owned telecommunications monopoly—part of a broader, but largely unsuccessful push on privatisation in the early 2000s (5.1.3)—were put on hold in the face of union opposition. In December 2005, however, cabinet agreed to end the state-owned enterprise's mobile phone monopoly. The Independent

Consumer & Competition Commission (ICCC), which the Morauta government had established (5.1.3), was instructed to select two new licensees (Ofa 2011, 75).

Telikom protested these moves, and the government had second thoughts, but ICCC stuck to its mandate and, after a tender process, licenses were granted to two companies, Digicel and GreenCom, in March 2007 (Stanley 2008). GreenCom went into receivership before commencing operations. Digicel paid its license fee and launched in PNG in July 2007. The minister of public enterprises ordered that its license be revoked (*Post-Courier* 2007), but the courts overruled the minister. Digicel reportedly 'secured 20,000 customers in its first three days of business' (Marshall 2007), having already invested AUD170 million in its new network (Burke 2007). Domestic and international call rates were slashed, in some cases by more than 50 per cent (Batten, Gouy and Duncan 2009, 10). In the subsequent years, there was a transformational expansion in the number of mobile phone subscribers (Figure 7.1). Over time, Digicel grabbed almost the entire market, and Telikom was relegated to being a marginal player.

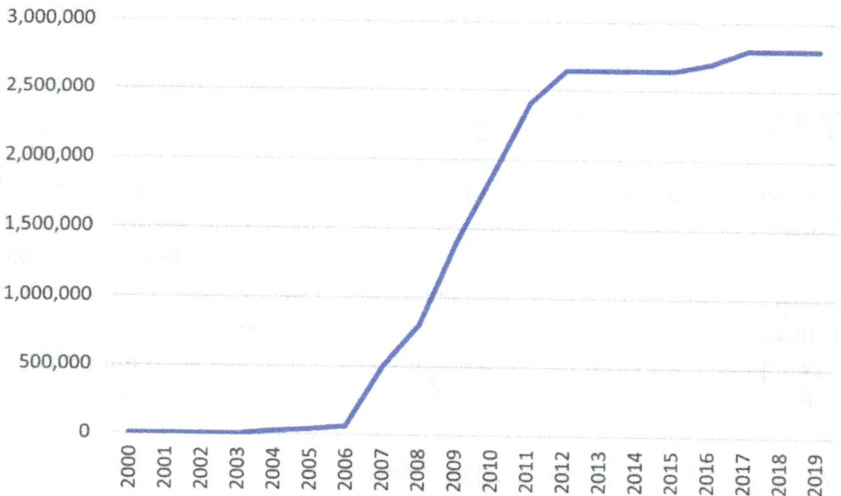

Figure 7.1: Mobile phones in use in PNG over time, 2000–19
Source: Watson (2022).

This is a clear case in which a Morauta-era reform paid rich dividends down the road. Earlier commitments to the World Trade Organization (WTO) made by PNG in the nineties (PNG had joined the WTO in 1996) might also have helped (Duncan 2011); however, without the ICCC, it is unlikely that Digicel would have been able to overcome the incumbent operator's opposition. Three years later, in 2010, the government took responsibility for regulation of the internet and telecom sector away from the ICCC and gave it to a newly created specialised agency, the National ICT Authority (NICTA).

7.1.2 The stalling of reforms

While none of Morauta's reforms were reversed by the Somare government that succeeded it, few of his reform plans were persevered with. Trade liberalisation is a notable exception. The initial tariff reform program ran from 1999 to 2006, and, while controversial at times, it was by and large implemented (5.1.3). A Treasury review in 2007 proposed a further round of tariff cuts, recommending 5 percentage point reductions every year until all tariffs were, at most, 15 per cent. This, too, was implemented, albeit with some delay; by 2015, the lowest rate was 10 per cent, the intermediate rate 15 per cent and the highest 30 per cent (Laveil 2019a, 10). In 2017, however, the tariff reduction program was suspended, and tariffs were increased that year and the next (9.1.3).

Another positive reform concerned international air travel, which had come to be dominated by a code-sharing arrangement between the state-owned Air Niugini and Qantas. In 2006, the government announced an 'open air' policy to increase competition (*RNZ* 2006), and in 2008 the ICCC allowed Airlines PNG (now called PNG Air) to code share flights with the Virgin Australia subsidiary, Pacific Blue. This increased competition and significantly reduced the cost of flying between Australia and PNG (Batten, Gouy and Duncan 2009, 13).[1]

However, other reforms were abandoned. There was no further privatisation. State-owned enterprise (SOE) reforms, discussed in the next section, did nothing to improve performance (ADB 2012a, 2014). When Morauta (2012a) briefly became minister for state-owned enterprises in 2011, he bemoaned the fact that:

---

1   'For both the Brisbane and Cairns to Port Moresby routes, this has meant an almost 65 per cent reduction in prices' (Batten, Gouy and Duncan 2009, 13).

Through a process of mutation IPBC [Independent Public Business Corporation][2] had become a major business empire full of ailing, under-performing businesses, trapped in a vicious circle—lack of capital, lack of management expertise, lack of commercial discipline, and lack of accountability.[3]

Forestry reforms were also shelved. In a 2003 speech delivered in the presence of the visiting Malaysian prime minister, Somare sent a very clear message by attacking the World Bank and reaching out to Malaysia for assistance specifically on forestry (McLeod 2003). World Bank involvement in forest policy reforms ended in 2005 (Filer 2017, 181) and amendments to the Forestry Act in 2007 made it easier for new forestry projects to get up (Filer 2017, 180)—amendments that, by reducing the amount of scrutiny new proposals would be subject to would open the door to PNG's land grab scam (7.1.4).

In 2009, the PNG government released its *Vision 2050* (National Strategic Plan Taskforce 2009). This was a homegrown (non-donor-funded) development strategy that had the aim of placing PNG among the 50 countries with highest Human Development Index by 2050. In 2010, a strategic development plan (Department of National Planning and Monitoring 2010) projected that PNG would grow at an average rate of 8.4 per cent over the next two decades. This plan also introduced the idea of economic corridors, of which 10 were proposed (Hangatt and Momoi 2011) in an aggressive, nationwide investment program. While these documents reflected the optimism of the late boom period, it is hard to detect many links from the 2050 plan, the 2030 one, or the five-year plans that continued to be produced to government policy, let alone economic outcomes.

7.1.3 Resource nationalism

There has always been a nationalistic streak to economic policymaking in Papua New Guinea based on apprehension around over-reliance on primary exports and an aspiration to be more involved in downstream processing. For example, phasing out 'round log' (or unprocessed log) exports has been a long held—so far thwarted, but still aspired to—goal, stretching back to independence (see Daniel and Sims 1986; Tukne 2022).

---

2   IPBC was an SOE holding company Morauta had established (5.1.3).
3   The ADB (2014, 20) commented: 'Deficiencies in the current legal and governance framework and problems with compliance have contributed to SOEs' poor commercial performance … Noncompliance … has been a problem since 2002, leading to weak governance and accountability.'

There is also a history of infant industry protection policy, with government support and protection being given or proposed to be given, over the years, to such industries as sugar, cement, rice and gold refining (see 2.2.2 and 9.1.3; Errington and Gewertz 2004; Laveil 2019a).

From the time he took office in 2011, Prime Minister Peter O'Neill shifted the dial on both nationalism and state intervention, starting in the resource sector. In 2013 a new SOE holding structure was announced that was then implemented over the next few years (Howell, Pertus and Sofe 2018; Fallon 2017). The IPBC was renamed Kumul Consolidated Holdings, and corporatised, signifying that the SOEs were no longer being prepared for privatisation but rather would stay under government ownership, and that state involvement in the economy was going to grow rather than shrink.[4]

In the resource sector, two new holding companies were created, Kumul Petroleum Holdings and Kumul Mineral Holdings (formerly Petromin), both to be taken out from under the IPBC umbrella, and to report directly to the prime minister, their sole shareholder. The PNG government has often taken equity stakes in resource projects, but this policy signified a shift to the creation of 'national champions' to identify and invest in future resource projects. The models were Malaysia's Petronas and Indonesia's Pertamina (Jackson 2022).

This policy had unexpected consequences for another policy domain, resource revenue stabilisation and savings. The story around the creation of a sovereign wealth fund (SWF) to replace the abolished MRSF is a complex one: useful overviews are provided by Osborne (2014) and Voigt-Graf and Sanida (2015). In summary, work on an SWF began in 2010 in anticipation of the large volumes of revenue expected to flow following commencement of the PNG LNG project. The Organic Law on the Sovereign Wealth Fund was certified in March 2012 under O'Neill, but largely reflecting work done under Somare's reign as prime minister. At some point, the claim arose that proper legislative procedures had not been followed, and that the new SWF legislation was not in fact valid. The simple remedy would have been to repeat the process, this time properly. Instead, this claim was used as an opportunity to redraft the SWF legislation. It was not until September 2014 that new, substantially different draft SWF legislation was published, and July 2015 that it was passed.

---

4   The *kumul* is the bird of paradise, PNG's national bird.

There are numerous differences between the 2012 and 2015 Organic Law on the SWF (Voigt-Graf and Sanida 2015; Chand 2015).[5] The key one is that the 2012 Act required all PNG LNG dividends to be paid into the SWF. This would mean no national petroleum champion. The 2015 Act, by contrast, required that all dividends *distributed to government* would go to the SWF, but said nothing about how it would be decided what proportion of dividends would be retained by any state-owned resource company and what proportion would be remitted to government revenue. By killing the 2012 SWF legislation and putting in place a much less stringent alternative several years later, O'Neill was able to keep his national resource champions project alive. The costs of this policy can be measured in terms of the subsequently significantly reduced flow of dividends to government (8.3.2). A final irony is that the 2015 SWF has never, in fact, been operationalised.

Another early move by O'Neill in the resource sector was to nationalise the Ok Tedi mine. O'Neill signalled in 2010 as treasurer (Gridneff 2010), and then in 2012 as prime minister in a Canberra Press Club speech (O'Neill 2012a), his dislike for the deal negotiated by Morauta that had seen BHP pass its majority stake in the environmentally damaging Ok Tedi mine not to the PNG government but to an independent Singapore-based bespoke trust, the PNG Sustainable Development Program (SDP) (5.1.3). O'Neill also in late 2012 banned Ross Garnaut—eminent Australian economist; active in PNG since before independence as an academic, public servant and then business executive; and at the time chair of SDP—from entry to PNG.

In September 2013, O'Neill introduced legislation, unanimously passed by the PNG parliament, that gave the PNG government full ownership of Ok Tedi (in place of its earlier minority share). The special circumstances of SDP meant that this expropriation was not seen as a broader threat to multinationals operating in PNG. The government also tried to get control of SDP itself, which by then had accumulated over USD1 billion in Ok Tedi profits, but that was blocked by the Singapore courts. After a long and expensive court battle that lasted to 2019, SDP is once more funding development projects in PNG, but Ok Tedi now operates under government ownership.

These early moves by O'Neill prefigured a broader shift to economic nationalism that would accelerate in later years (9.1).

---

5   The two acts can be found at pngnri.org/images/Publications/SL_8-4_PNGs_SWF_Bill_CVoigt-GrafOOSanida.pdf and pngnri.org/images/Publications/Issues_paper_17_PNGs_SWF_the_efficacy_of_the_withdrawal_formula_final1.pdf.

7.1.4 Land reforms and controversies

Despite earlier efforts, there had been little progress with land reform since independence. A group of reformers led by the economist Charles Yala decided that something needed to be done, and, with high-level political support, convened a land summit in 2005. Customary landowners already had the right to form Incorporated Land Groups (ILGs), which they did typically to bargain with resource companies and loggers, and to lease land indirectly, via government, through the lease-leaseback arrangement (3.1.5 and 5.1.2). The proposal coming out of the land summit was to improve the transparency of the ILG process, and then to allow ILGs to register their collectively owned land, and then lease that land *directly* to developers, with the process providing a security that would enable the lease to be bankable (Chand 2017). Government policy since the early eighties had backed this type of reform, but there had been hardly any implementation for two decades, with attention from the World Bank in the nineties only making things worse (5.1.2).

There was real hope when the necessary amendments were passed in 2009. However, the legislation was not made effective until 2012, and that was only the first disappointment in the implementation of this reform program (9.1.5).

While the land reform program was designed to make it easier to access land for development, over the same period the government had to deal with a problem of land being too easily mobilised (Filer 2011, 2017). A commission of inquiry was established in 2011 into the grant of Special Agricultural and Business Leases (SABLs) based on the above-mentioned, longstanding 'lease-leaseback' arrangement, whereby landowning groups would lease their land to government for the government to lease it back to them to lease to developers (as SABLs).

The common complaint was that the process was too cumbersome to be impactful, but in the late noughties evidence started emerging that, in fact, the lease-leaseback mechanism was being used, in conjunction with the recently relaxed Forestry Act (7.1.2), for a land grab. The new leases involved some 5.2 million hectares—more than 10 per cent of the PNG landmass—and 72 SABLs (Filer 2017, 176), including several of more than 100,000 hectares each (Filer 2017, 172). Prior to this, according to one estimate, only 200,000 hectares had been made subject to lease-leaseback arrangements since independence (Kimas 2010, 36), so the new leases were of a completely different order of magnitude. The leases were meant to be, as their name suggested, for purposes that went beyond forestry, but their number and size gave rise to suspicions that they were being entered into without genuine landowner consent and had more to do with chopping down trees than with expanding agriculture. After the scale of the issue was made public by Paul Barker, head of PNG's Institute of National Affairs, the resulting public outcry led to a commission of inquiry. This in turn resulted, in 2014, in the revocation of most of the SABLs the commission investigated, and a moratorium on any further use of the lease-leaseback arrangement (Filer with Numapo 2017, 266).[6]

One other land reform was also mooted during the boom period. While nearly all of PNG's land belongs to customary owners, all subsoil assets belong to the state. A perennial sense that landowners are not getting enough from resource projects (even though their share has greatly increased, see 4.3.2), and an argument that state ownership of subsoil assets was inconsistent with customary ways (Donigi 2010) led to a bill brought first by a backbencher and then by the mining minister (in 2009 and again in 2011) to regard the ownership of subsoil assets as lying with the customary owners of the land under which these assets sit.[7] This is not as radical as it sounds—in fact, it is a principle followed in the United States—but it was strongly resisted by resource companies (Callick 2011), who thought it would endanger their projects. In the end, Prime Minister O'Neill reassured them that this proposal would not be taken forward, first in 2011, and then, since the proposal had not gone away, again in 2016 (Blades 2011; Patjole 2016).

7.2 Politics and governance

The boom period saw a return to political stability, but not a fundamental change in political patterns. Funding for service delivery expanded, but the quality of service delivery did not necessarily improve. With more money, there was more scope for corruption. There were once again major

---

6   As one commentator noted, most witnesses to the commission were not opposed to large-scale land development but objected to their exclusion from the process. 'In many cases, different landowner companies, or different factions represented on the board of one landowner company, had formed partnerships with different investors, each one with a view to convincing their partners that they alone were the genuine representatives of all the customary owners of the land to be developed' (Filer with Numapo 2017, 276).

7   A court challenge on the unconstitutionality of denying landowners the ownership of subsoil assets was unsuccessful in the early 1990s (Nonggorr 1993).

decentralisation reforms, resulting in a shift of expenditure to the sub-national level, but reduced autonomy for provinces. Crime levels appeared to stabilise. Australia tried to come to the rescue at the start of the period with a new approach to aid and failed.

7.2.1 Politics

Michael Somare served as prime minister from 2002 to 2007 and then again from the 2007 elections. He was deposed in controversial circumstances in August 2011 when in hospital in Singapore (since March of that year), seriously unwell. His ousting—not through a vote of no confidence, but through one declaring the position of prime minister to be vacant—was, the courts ruled, illegal. However, the new prime minister, Peter O'Neill, leader of the People's National Congress and former Somare minister, had the majority of MPs behind him. The stand-off became a serious political crisis: for a period the country had two prime ministers, two cabinets, and two heads of army and police commissioners (May 2022). Fortunately, the 2012 election intervened. When O'Neill's party was returned with the highest number of MPs, questions about his legitimacy as prime minister disappeared[8] and O'Neill went on to serve in that role until 2019.

There has been much discussion of why stability returned to PNG politics in the noughties. Turnover at the individual MP level remained high (at around the 50 per cent mark), but there clearly was a change at the macro level. One explanation is that it was simply luck. It is not that easy to muster the numbers to remove an incumbent prime minister mid-term, and, given that PNG has never seen more than one change in the position per parliamentary term, it is not surprising that, eventually, the country was to experience one or even two terms with no change.

But if the new-found stability was more than just luck, one theory is that legal changes—specifically the Organic Law on the Integrity of Political Parties and Candidates (OLIPPAC) passed under Morauta to strengthen political parties (5.2.1)—had tilted the playing field in favour of the incumbent. Early assessments were mixed.[9] More recent analyses (Okole 2012; Kabuni et al. 2022) are on the sceptical side, arguing that MPs worked their way

---

8   Illustrating the flexibility of PNG politics, O'Neill and Somare buried the hatchet, and the latter joined the former's ruling coalition.
9   Compare Fraenkel (2004), Gelu (2005) and Standish (2007) to Sepoe (2005) and Reilly (2006).

around the changes or simply ignored them. In any case, the Supreme Court declared much of Morauta's political engineering legislation invalid in 2010 on account of it interfering with the freedom of MPs.

There is one aspect of OLIPPAC not struck down by the courts that has fostered political stability: Section 63, which gives the first chance to form government to the party emerging from the elections with the largest number of MPs (Howes and Kabuni 2022). More than 40 parties competed in the 2012 elections, and more than 20 returned at least one MP (Laveil 2022). Over the life of the parliament, MPs tend to join the party of the prime minister to be close to power. Because of this, the prime minister's party will typically go into the election with by far the largest number of MPs, and therefore emerge with the largest number as well. The same party will then, because of Section 63, get the first (and typically successful) attempt at forming a government. The influence of Section 63 can be seen from the fact that the incumbent prime minister has been returned in the four elections from 2007 onwards. This is quite different to the pre-OLIPPAC era in which, after the period of Pangu dominance ended in 1982, the largest party usually did not provide the prime minister post-election (neither in 1987, 1992 nor 1997).

There were also other legal changes. After O'Neill won the 2012 elections, MPs extended, at his instigation, the grace period (wherein the prime minister at the start of his tenure cannot be subject to a vote of no confidence) from 18 to 30 months. They also reduced the minimum number of sitting days required each year from 63 to 40 (Kabuni 2018), doubled the number of MP signatures required to support a vote of no confidence to 22 and increased the period of notice for such a vote from a week to a month (*RNZ* 2015b). All these amendments were struck down by the Supreme Court in September 2015 as inconsistent with the democratic ethos of the constitution, but they doubtless assisted O'Neill while they were in place.

Another theory to explain PNG's new-found political stability is that politicians have become more adept at hanging on to power. May (2022, Chapter 13) attributes Somare's success between 2002 and 2007 to 'the government's control of parliamentary procedures, through a less than impartial speaker ... dominance of parliamentary committees and adjournment of sittings'.

Finally, the economic boom itself contributed to first Somare's and then O'Neill's prime ministerial longevity. It was hard to mobilise members of parliament against the government when the economy was doing well, and increasingly large sums were going to MPs as electorate funding (7.2.4). As one MP put it, 'so long as you have the money, you will master the numbers' (cited in Mou 2016). The boom meant that the incumbent prime minister had the money.

The economic growth of this period might have fostered political stability, but, though many had argued stability was needed for growth, it is hard to see that it helped much. Perhaps it assisted with the successful negotiations for the complex PNG LNG project, but it did little if anything for the cause of better governance or broad-based growth. Even if unsuccessful, attempts to unseat the prime minister were still a major distraction.

Politics in PNG has been an almost exclusively male endeavour. The 1995 decentralisation law reserved two seats in each local-level government for women and put a women's representative in each provincial assembly. Bougainville introduced a few reserved seats as part of its autonomy set up. But only 10 women have served in PNG's first 11 parliaments (Table A3). In 2009, a plan was hatched to appoint a small number of women to the PNG parliament. This would have been allowed under the constitution, but it did not attract majority support (Sepoe 2021a). Then, after O'Neill became prime minister in 2011, a proposal was put forward to allow for the election of a fixed number of female MPs. The Equality and Participation Act was passed that very year. However, the enabling legislation to specify the size of this new class of female MPs failed to get the requisite support the following year, and this revolutionary initiative has been quietly forgotten (Sepoe 2021a).

7.2.2 Public services

After repeated failed attempts in the nineties (5.2.2), there was no further attempt to downsize the civil service. The multi-donor 'Public Expenditure Review and Rationalization' program (World Bank 2003), started in 2002, languished for a few years and was then disbanded. The number on the government payroll grew from 77,800 in 2002 to 100,500 in 2015 (Figure B16; figures are unavailable for all years).

Despite this growth, the structure of expenditure improved, with the ratio of salaries to total expenditure falling from 29 per cent in 2003 to 19 per cent in 2013. The interest burden also fell, increasing the room for operational and capital spending (Figure 9.1).

Service delivery should have improved during the boom with more and better resourced public servants. Unfortunately, much of the new funding was wasted. The trust funds (6.3.1), which at their height had a balance in excess of PGK3 billion, were an easy target. Money was regarded as spent once allocated to a trust fund (and typically deposited in a commercial bank), meaning there was little oversight of actual expenditure when it occurred. Funds were often given not to line departments but to the Planning Department, which had no experience in actually spending, as against allocating, money. Programs to rehabilitate school infrastructure and to support agricultural development were front and centre in terms of corruption allegations (Transparency International PNG 2010). According to one report, PGK49 million allocated to two provinces in 2019 for school buildings had simply gone missing (Wari 2016). According to former prime minister Morauta (2012b): 'Billions of kina was parked by the last Government in trust accounts, and walked out, seemingly without trace.'

O'Neill introduced policies of free education and health. This was the fourth abolition of school fees, and it lasted to 2019; since then, school fees have again been introduced and eliminated (Walton and Hushang 2022.) Eliminating school fees gave a boost to school enrolments, but eliminating the ability of health centres to charge fees only made them even more cash-strapped and even less effective (Howes et al. 2014).

Easy money led to recklessness. The Solwara project was to be the world's first deep-sea mining project. Despite the obvious risks, the PNG government decided in 2011 to take out a 30 per cent equity share, to be paid upfront, in cash (Nautilus Minerals 2011). Fortunately, it only ever bought 15 per cent, but that was PGK327 million, paid out in 2014 (Kero 2014). The project never got off the ground, and when Nautilus was liquidated in 2019, PNG realised it had lost its investment (about USD100 million) entirely (Filer, Gabriel and Allen 2020).

This period proved to be yet another in which the political and bureaucratic class could not get on. It ended with the sidelining (for the second time, after the reforms of the eighties, see 3.2.2) of the Public Services Commission (PSC). O'Neill was frustrated by the power given to the PSC by Morauta and Somare in the early 2000s in relation to senior appointments such as heads of departments (5.2.2), and so stripped the PSC of these powers via a constitutional amendment in 2013 that transferred them to a Ministerial Executive Appointments Committee (Howes and Bizhan 2024).

7.2.3 Corruption

The resource boom expanded the scope for corruption. In 2008, surveys in four urban centres found that over 80 per cent of the community believed that corruption had been increasing (ADB 2012b). Forty per cent of businesses claimed to be 'highly affected' or 'very highly affected' by official corruption (ADB and INA 2008).

Two major corruption scandals of the period involved the Department of Finance. In one, a commission of inquiry documented a process whereby the state would be sued and, no matter the spuriousness of the case, an out-of-court settlement reached. This scam cost the state up to PGK780 million (GoPNG 2009). In another, a protracted court process finally, in 2023, found prominent lawyer Paul Paraka guilty of charging for and receiving PGK162 million between 2007 and 2011 in fictitious legal fees (National Court 2019).

Corruption went right to the top. Back in the late eighties, the nation's first prime minister, Michael Somare, had been found by the Barnett Commission (2.2.2) to have abused his position for personal gain: he had successfully lobbied in 1988 to get logging rights in his electorate for a company of which he was the majority owner (*Masalai i tokaut* 2006). In the noughties, Somare's corruption became more blatant. A court in Singapore in 2016 heard that USD784,000 had been transferred to him from a couple (Singaporean residents, the husband a close Somare family friend) with funds from one of the period's many poorly monitored trust funds, intended for a PNG government project initiated in 2008 to establish community colleges. The Singapore court found that the couple had paid a total of USD3.6 million in bribes and sentenced them to five to six years in jail for fraud and money laundering. There were multiple beneficiaries, but the agreement was, according to the husband, that 'no one should take more than PM and son combined' (Lasslett 2017).

Somare never faced charges for either the forestry or community college allegations, though, in early 2011, he was suspended from office for two weeks after being found guilty by the Leadership Tribunal on the minor charge of providing incomplete or late financial returns, from as far back as 1991 onwards (Gridneff 2011).

Somare's reputation suffered little from these revelations.[10] Indicative of the forgiving way in which those accused of corruption are treated in PNG, his status as the nation's foremost national hero has only grown, especially since his death in February 2021.[11]

It was symptomatic of the changed attitude of politicians that the same Prime Minister Somare who had, in the eighties, attempted, albeit unsuccessfully, to make the rules against corruption stricter (3.2.3) now presided over efforts to weaken them. In 2006, amendments were passed that created stricter rules of evidence for Leadership Tribunal proceedings (Sangetari 2014, 14). Further changes—under the so-called 'Maladina Amendment' (Jackson 2010)—were pursued starting in 2009 to place time limits on investigations, to limit the ability of the Ombudsman Commission to freeze public funds, and to prevent those found to have breached the Leadership Code from being tried under criminal law (Fox 2010). Despite widespread protests in person and online, the proposed changes were brought into law; however, they were struck down by the Supreme Court when the Ombudsman Commission appealed them (Supreme Court 2013).

O'Neill came to power with serious corruption allegations hanging over him relating to the mismanagement of pension funds (5.1.3). However, to his credit, the new prime minister established Task Force Sweep in August 2011 to investigate corruption. Its 2012 report concluded that corruption was 'systematic' and 'institutionalized' and described PNG as a 'mobocracy' (Fox 2012). The taskforce had some success (May 2022, Chapter 14), most notably obtaining the conviction of Paul Tiensten, former planning minister, for misappropriation of PGK10 million of public funds (Kama 2014). His sentence in 2014 to nine-years imprisonment was the most severe given to a convicted public official since PNG's independence. However, O'Neill disbanded the task force in 2014 after it began to investigate and lay charges against him (9.2.3).

10 A few were critical. The eminent Australian historian, and UPNG's first professor of history and then second vice-chancellor Ken Inglis observed many years after his departure from PNG: 'In every way Somare was a friend of the university and greatly admired by students. Later, there was increasing disenchantment. People wanted so much to believe that Somare was an admirable leader, but they were forced to realise that he went in for a great deal of what we could call corruption, as did a lot of people who had been our friends. Not all of them, by any means, but a lot of them' (Inglis and Spark 2014, 229).
11 'As expressed through the re-election of numerous politicians after being found guilty of misconduct in office, the PNG voters seem to have a remarkable capacity for forgiveness. An explanation may be found in the concept of "us-versus-them", whereby crimes against the state or similar organisations are deemed morally acceptable, whilst offences committed against members of one's own group are not' (Ketan 2000, 9). See also Ekeh (1975), discussed in Section 5.2.

7.2.4 Decentralisation

Booming government revenue was used to massively increase constituency funding for members of parliament. Such funds increased tenfold (even after adjusting for inflation) over this period (Figure A1). That increase came in its entirety in just a few years, between 2005 and 2008. It initially could not be sustained due to the GFC, but MP funding went back up to its 2007 level in 2013 when Peter O'Neill opened the borrowing taps. Large-scale MP funding is now a permanent feature of PNG public finance, through both the District Improvement Support Program (DSIP) for district (open) MPs and the Provincial Improvement Support Program (PSIP) for provincial MPs.

The District Development Authority (DDA) Act was an early O'Neill reform, introduced into parliament in late 2013 and passed in 2014. DDAs became the constitutionally endorsed vehicle for spending the large amounts of money now at MPs' disposal; previously such expenditure was the responsibility of a committee rather than a statutory authority. This reform effectively converted PNG's governance system into a four-tier one, with governments (elected or appointed) now at the national, provincial, district and local level. Not surprisingly, provincial MPs opposed the introduction of DDAs (Sowei n.d.), but they were outnumbered; they have since taken the matter to the courts.

Constituency funding and DDAs are polarising. Those who support them (including O'Neill 2006) argue that the bureaucracy is non-responsive, and that such mechanisms are vital to get more funds into rural areas. Opponents point to the wastefulness of constituency spending, the lack of accountability and the dangers associated with the politicisation of service delivery, which can, for example, lead to infrastructure being destroyed at election time (Duncan and Banga 2018; Auditor-General 2014).

There was also scope in the boom years to provide increased funding for provincial governments (Batten et al. 2009). New legislation in 2009[12] introduced a minimum share of non-resource tax revenue (6.57 per cent) that would be set aside in equalisation grants to go towards the non-salary recurrent costs of provincial governments (provincial capital and salary costs are fully covered by the central government). A small amount was earmarked

---

12 A new Intergovernmental Relations (Functions and Funding) Act was passed, and the Organic Law on Provincial Governments and Local Level Governments was amended.

for local governments as well. This reform resulted in an increase in central government grants to the provinces from PGK101 million in 2009 (one-fifth of provincial government revenue) to PGK280 in 2012 (one-third) (National Economic and Fiscal Commission 2012). Equalisation grants are certainly justified. A few provinces receive significant amounts of mining and petroleum revenue. The National Capital District receives more than half of the provincial allocation of GST revenue (5.1.3) and Morobe another third, leaving little for any other provinces. Own-source revenue is very modest, less than 10 per cent of all provincial revenue (Laveil 2024). However, a commitment to better-off provinces that they would not lose from the reforms meant that the move towards equalisation of provincial government revenue had to come at the expense of the central government, further contributing to fiscal stress once the boom was over.

This increased funding both to provincial governments and to districts led to an increase in the sub-national share of expenditure, which recovered in the noughties to around 30 per cent, its share in the eighties, after falling to 20 per cent during the nineties (Gouy n.d.).

While provincial governments saw their income go up, they also saw their autonomy diminished. DDAs were not the only new, competing sub-national power source. The Provincial Health Authorities Act 2007 took responsibility for health away from the provincial government and gave it to a statutory authority. Regardless of the merits of this exercise—and it was perceived that health services in particular had suffered as a result of decentralisation (Thomason and Kase 2009)—these authorities were run by boards appointed by the health minister in consultation with the province, not by the provincial governor or government. In the succeeding years, encouraged by the central government and donors alike, more and more provincial health authorities were established by the national government.

7.2.5 Law and order

A World Bank 2014 report found that, 'at the national level, crime rates appear to have stabilized since year 2000' (Lakhani and Willman 2014b, 5). This good news notwithstanding, the country's reputation for crime was by now firmly cemented. The same report noted that 'violence victimization rates in PNG are among the highest in the world' (Lakhani and Willman 2014b, 1). In 2012, the ADB (2012b, x) noted that Port Moresby was rated as a 'top five' murder city worldwide, that the 'crime rate is high, and the public perceives enforcement of law and order as weak' and that 'businesses [still] consider the poor law and order situation as the topmost constraint to doing business'.

Tribal conflict continued to rise in profile and severity, with the growing use of 'high-powered weapons, local mercenaries ("hire-men") and guerrilla tactics' (Walton and Dinnen 2022, 92). The border with Indonesia was porous.[13] In 2007, a border electorate MP complained that 'money laundering, sales of illegal firearms, drug trafficking, human smuggling and other illicit activities were becoming common practices' (Nelson 2009, 266).

In 2005, Haley and Muggah (2006, 50) undertook a survey on the basis of which they concluded that 'inflated compensation demands [were] crippling local economies' in some parts of the country; that 'threats, intimidation and extortion with firearms are the most virulent form of violence in their community'; and that there was a link between the 'weakness of the state and these high compensation payments'. One of their informants commented that 'the law is weak so we must pay more in order to obtain peace' (Haley and Muggah 2006, 50). On the positive side, local, hybrid responses proved effective in some areas (Dinnen, Porter and Sage 2010).

7.2.6 Foreign aid and relations with Australia

The story of aid to PNG crosses all four periods of our history but is particularly interesting in this period as it is the one in which Australia most actively tried to influence outcomes in PNG. To recap briefly, aid volumes declined in real terms from independence through to the end of the nineties. The first phase of Australian aid to PNG was one of (unconditional) budget support. This started with independence (or really with home rule in 1972) and was phased out over the nineties (4.4.3). Aid via projects or programs, as they were called, was phased in over the nineties to replace budget support and continues to this day. Australia helped finance the structural adjustment programs of the nineties, and its aid agency, AIDAB then AusAID, produced a number of economic reports on PNG over that decade. Overall though, there was little effort by Australia in the first almost 30 years of PNG's independence to influence government decision-making. That all changed in 2004 with the introduction of the Enhanced Cooperation Program (ECP), agreed to in December 2003 (Joint Standing

---

13   In 1984, 10,000 refugees from the conflict in Indonesian Papua crossed over into PNG.

Committee on Treaties 2005), to be implemented for five years at a cost of AUD1 billion. Some 210 Australian police and 64 bureaucrats were placed in PNG, many in 'in-line' rather than advisory positions.

The ECP emerged from Australia's successful stabilisation mission to Solomon Islands (RAMSI),[14] which commenced in mid-2003, and, more generally, from a more pro-active international stance on the part of the US and its allies post-9/11. It also, if with a lag, responded to the sense of crisis in PNG at the end of the millennium (5.3). But the ECP was also born of a profound naivete and a failure to learn the lessons from the tenuous achievements of a decade of adjustment lending (5.1.4). Replacing advisers with in-line managers had merit (Pieper 2004; Howes 2015a), but Australia's goal for the ECP of 'improved economic and social governance to help boost economic growth and the quality of life' (Australian Treasury 2004, 76) was unrealistic. The Australian Treasury revealed the extent of overestimation of its capability to influence events on the ground by its (supposedly realistic) declaration that 'building up Papua New Guinea's core institutions will involve at least a five year program of assistance' (Australian Treasury 2004, 78).

From the start, PNG politicians viewed the ECP with mixed attitudes. Prime Minister Somare was against it on nationalistic grounds: unsurprisingly since he had been promoting self-reliance his entire political career. Even reformers such as Morauta (2005, 159) warned that 'the ECP is widely seen as an Australian, not a Papua New Guinean initiative' and would likely fail for that reason. The PNG public, however, weary of high crime levels, welcomed the Australian police force presence on the streets of Port Moresby (Squires 2004).

Whatever its merits and deficiencies, the ECP was a short-lived experiment. One MP, Luther Wenge, who likened the ECP to recolonisation, took the matter to the courts (as he had with PNG's value-added tax, see 5.1.3), and in May 2005 PNG's Supreme Court ruled that the immunities provided to Australian personnel serving under the ECP were unconstitutional (Chin 2005). Australia pulled most of its police and moved those remaining into advisory roles. Those in non-policing roles stayed on, but with increasingly limited leverage and in increasingly limited numbers as the diplomatic relationship between Australia and PNG soured.

---

14 The Regional Assistance Mission to Solomon Islands; though regional, it was led by Australia.

Australia was unhappy that PNG had effectively called the ECP off. On the PNG side, Prime Minister Somare was offended in April 2005 when told to remove his shoes in a security check at Brisbane airport; Alexander Downer, Australia's foreign minister, refused to apologise (McLeod 2005). Relations soured further over the extraordinary Moti affair, involving the Solomon Islands attorney general, Julian Moti, an Australian citizen. The Australian government saw Moti as provoking opposition to RAMSI in Solomon Islands, and went after him on spurious legal grounds, eventually thrown out by the Australian courts in 2011. Moti was arrested for extradition to Australia when visiting PNG in 2006, but Somare helped him escape back to Solomons, breaking several PNG laws along the way (as a subsequent official inquiry revealed) and antagonising Australia no end (Nelson 2007a; Rowlings 2011).

A second attempt at influence arose in this period in relation to the PNG LNG project, which Australia helped fund through its export credit agency, Export Finance Australia, in return for PNG agreeing to introduce a sovereign wealth fund (SWF). The champagne was opened at the Australian High Commission in Port Moresby when the SWF Act was passed in 2012—but prematurely, since that legislation was soon replaced by another, and not even the newer one has actually been implemented (7.1.3).

By then Australia's brief attempt to exercise policy influence had come to an end. Prime Minister of Australia Kevin Rudd, following his election in 2007, went on a charm offensive, which helped to repair relations with PNG, but also ended any residual effort by Australia to encourage PNG to reform. In fact, Rudd's election can be seen as the start of a new phase in Australia's relations with PNG, in which power shifted from the former to the latter. A decisive change took place in 2013 when Rudd (briefly returned to the position of prime minister after losing it in 2010) negotiated with O'Neill the processing and settlement of Australian asylum seekers on Manus Island in PNG. In 2001 and 2002, when John Howard was Australia's prime minister, PNG had also agreed to house asylum seekers on Manus while they were being processed. That arrangement, like the new one, was controversial, and Prime Minister Morauta was forced to sack his foreign minister for being publicly critical of it. The new arrangement was more far-reaching because now the asylum seekers were to be PNG's indefinite responsibility (and a few remain on PNG to this day). PNG's opposition leader Belden Namah challenged the constitutionality of the deal, and, in 2016, the Supreme Court of Papua New Guinea ordered the Manus processing centre be shut down,[15] which it was in 2017.

By this time, PNG was increasingly viewed in Australian policymaking circles through a China lens (9.2.6). What mattered from this perspective was not whether Australia was having a beneficial impact on PNG but simply whether it was popular. While budget support was again provided in the most recent period, this time it came with less onerous conditions (8.3.5).

7.3 Conclusion

Anyone living in Port Moresby experienced the 2004–13 boom firsthand. A city that used to be easy to get around in became subject to long traffic jams. More positively, the city got (back) a cinema, and several new, modern shopping malls and new restaurants. Port Moresby benefited the most from the boom (though it also saw the biggest house price increases), but the rest of the country also saw increased demand for domestic produce and increased funds for both households and governments alike.

Of the four periods covered in this book, the third stands out in a positive way. For many key variables—non-resource GDP per person, government revenue, bank loans and deposits, and formal sector employment—the broad pattern is little, no or even negative growth in the first, second and fourth periods, and rapid growth in the third (10.12). The boom years were indeed good ones on a range of dimensions. Third-time prime minister Michael Somare (2010, 215), who had seen the bad times, said that PNG was 'going through a period of resurgence'. Commentators adjudged the country to be 'on the brink of success' (Batten 2008). But the drivers were temporary—high commodity prices, revenue-ready projects and PNG LNG construction—and so the good times did not last. Moreover, the boom, and its mismanagement, exacted a toll on the country's economy that had to be paid in subsequent years.

---

15 The government had by then passed constitutional amendments to authorise the arrangement, but the court rejected these.

In the early boom years, funds were saved; however, given the nature of the trust funds they were put in, they were only saved for the short term. It was no surprise, then, that, in the late boom years, those short-term savings were spent; moreover, there was then too much borrowing. And much of the spending splurge was of low quality, symbolised by the USD100 million lost to the Nautilus deep-sea mining venture.

More saving of the resource boom proceeds would have slowed growth in the boom years but would have helped during the subsequent bust. Higher wages, house prices and a re-appreciated exchange rate also hurt the economy in later years.

The boom period also saw the start of a move that would be intensified in the years ahead away from the Washington Consensus reforms of the nineties towards policies of nationalism and greater state intervention. How all this has played out since is the subject of the next part of this book.

Part IV:
2014–22:
The tens:
The quiet bust

I know that our economy is bleeding and struggling ... This leadership is all about placing this country in the right place and taking back our economy.

—James Marape, in his maiden speech upon becoming prime minister in 2019 (*Business Advantage PNG* 2019)

8

The bust and its macroeconomics

Mr Mackellar [CEO of PNG hardware firm Brian Bell] said for many years businesses have been restricted with their growth potential via this heavily regulated currency situation within PNG.

'It continues to have a negative impact on employment opportunities and reduces taxable income for the government. If businesses can't access what they need in foreign currency, at the time when they need it, it quite genuinely limits their growth potential which in turn impacts the economy negatively', said Mr Mackellar.

He said every business that requires some level of foreign currency is required to apply for that FX through their bank or banks on a daily basis to see if the bank can then provide an allocation, either in part or in full for their currency needs.

'As a business we have been doing this for longer than I can remember now and [there are] no signs of it changing. Our banks have been very supportive but they are limited with the foreign currency they are allocated by the Central Bank.' (Tom 2022)

8.1 Introduction

In Papua New Guinea in 2014, optimism was at an all-time high. The country's mega LNG project made its first shipment in May. These exports were supposed to unleash a flood of revenue for the government. Other resource projects were to follow. Things had been good over the last decade; they were, it was thought, about to get even better. They did not. Government resource revenue in fact plummeted. Formal sector employment fell every year between 2014 and 2018. Non-resource GDP per person started to fall in 2015 and fell every year except one to 2020. Fiscal stress intensified; by 2019, PNG's ratio of debt to GDP was back at pre-boom levels.

Superficially, the period from 2014 to the current times was a return to the eighties. Growth was slow, the exchange rate was once again pegged and there was a return to an emphasis on economic nationalism and state-led development. However, a crucial difference is that current account convertibility was replaced by foreign exchange rationing to limit the need for depreciation. This ensured there would be no balance of payments crisis—hence the term 'the quiet bust'—but also compressed imports, encouraged fiscal profligacy, discouraged investors and prolonged the downturn.

The politics of the period was dominated by Peter O'Neill, PNG's second-longest serving prime minister, who became an increasingly controversial and polarising figure, trapped by his earlier narrative of success. When he was finally defeated in a vote of no confidence in 2019, one of the first statements by his successor and former finance minister, James Marape, was an admission that the economy was 'bleeding and struggling'. Marape turned up the rhetoric on economic nationalism, but also did what O'Neill had long refused to do and call in the IMF. With the onset of the COVID-19 pandemic in 2020, PNG's economic woes intensified. But then, in 2022, oil prices shot up as a result of the Ukraine war, PNG's commodity price index reached an all-time high, resource revenue at last recovered to a healthy level and economic growth increased, ending the bust.

This is the first published retrospective on the 2010s in PNG. This and the next chapter include policy developments up to early 2024, but mainly rely on data up to 2022. This chapter includes an account of the period's growth slowdown and the macroeconomic policies that exacerbated it. The next examines the shift towards nationalistic and statist policies and developments in politics and governance.

8.2 Economic growth

Of the four periods examined, this is the one for which the distinction between GDP and non-resource GDP growth is the most important. Sectoral developments in this period are consistent with a widespread downturn. Employment fared even worse than non-resource output. Throughout the bust, PNG was said to be one resource project away from recovery.

8.2.1 The bust

If we are satisfied with GDP as a good measure of economic activity for PNG, then we should regard this period as a continuation of the previous period's boom. GDP growth averaged 3.8 per cent, not far behind the boom period's average of 4.5 per cent. If, however, as we should (1.2.3), we rely on non-resource GDP growth as a superior measure of national economic activity, then we see average growth of only 2.0 per cent for this period, in stark contrast to the boom's 5.6 per cent.

As Figure 8.1 shows, GDP growth started high and fell during this period as LNG sales were increasingly built into the base (production began midway through 2014). In 2015, there was a drought, which hurt both agriculture and water-reliant mining projects, in particular Ok Tedi. In 2018 there was an earthquake in the Highlands that interrupted resource production. Negative growth in 2020 reflects the closure of the Porgera gold mine (8.2.3) and the impact of the COVID-19 pandemic, which resulted in external and internal restrictions on movement and reduced commodity prices. GDP contracted by 3.2 per cent in 2020, with government revenue falling in the same year from 16.3 to 14.7 per cent of GDP.

The good years for non-resource GDP growth were 2014 and 2018, both years of expenditure expansion in a period of austerity, and the COVID recovery years of 2021 and 2022. Record high commodity prices in 2022 as a result of the war in Ukraine boosted resource revenue in 2022 (Figure B25), fuelling fiscal expansion and pushing that year's non-resource GDP growth up to 5.9 per cent. Non-resource growth of 4.7 per cent in 2023 confirmed that the bust was over.

	2014	2015	2016	2017	2018	2019	2020	2021	2022
GDP growth	13.5%	6.6%	5.5%	3.5%	-0.3%	4.5%	-3.2%	-0.5%	5.7%
Non-resource GDP growth	4.1%	-4.1%	1.5%	1.5%	4.0%	1.6%	-0.4%	4.2%	5.9%

········ GDP growth ——— Non-resource GDP growth

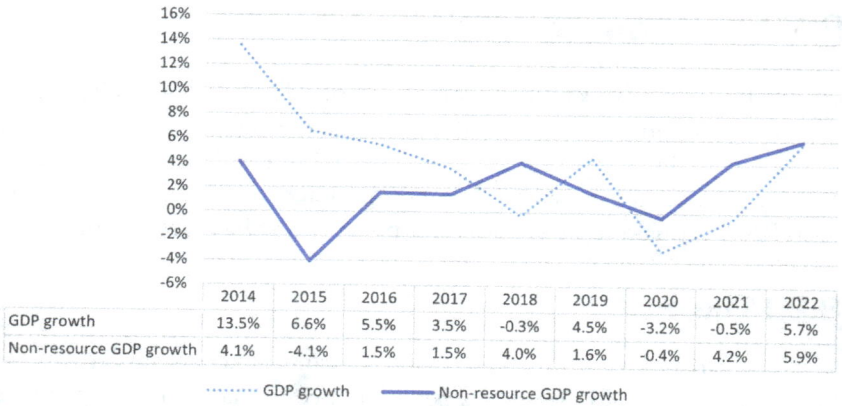

Figure 8.1: Real GDP and non-resource GDP growth, 2014–22 (kina, constant prices)
Source: PNG Economic Database.

Non-resource GDP per person fell every year from 2014 to 2020 except for a marginal increase in 2018 (Figure 8.2). It ended the period some 6 per cent below where it started. GDP per person jumped between 2013 and 2016 by about 18 per cent due to the commencement of the PNG LNG exports before first plateauing and then falling.

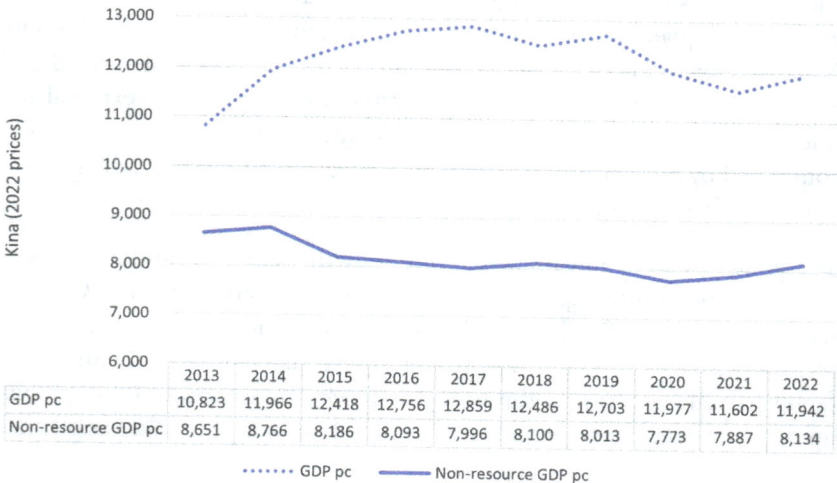

	2013	2014	2015	2016	2017	2018	2019	2020	2021	2022
GDP pc	10,823	11,966	12,418	12,756	12,859	12,486	12,703	11,977	11,602	11,942
Non-resource GDP pc	8,651	8,766	8,186	8,093	7,996	8,100	8,013	7,773	7,887	8,134

········ GDP pc ——— Non-resource GDP pc

Figure 8.2: Real GDP and non-resource GDP per person, 2013–22 (kina, constant prices)
Source: PNG Economic Database.

The impressive GDP figures are explained by the commencement of LNG production, which almost doubled exports. But why was non-resource growth so low in this period? There are a range of reasons. This section provides some sectoral and employment analysis, and discusses the absence of new resource projects coming online during these years. The next section analyses the macroeconomics of the bust.

Before going further, we should note that in 2016 the National Statistical Office revised PNG's GDP series from 2006 onwards, increasing it by about 60 per cent in nominal terms. Though PNG is not the only country to have undertaken such a radical rebasing, no explanation has ever been provided for this. Only data for the rebased series are now produced, and all the GDP figures in this book are either drawn from or (for earlier years) are consistent with the new series (for details, see Howes, Fox et al. 2022, Appendix).

8.2.2 Sectoral developments and employment

Only the resource sector grew quickly in this period. Gold production reached its highest level ever, and LNG came to make up more than half of the resource export bundle. Resource dependency rose over the period, setting a record of 32 per cent in 2022 (Figure B2). Growth in other sectors was harmed by the growth in real wages and property prices, and the appreciation in the exchange rate that resulted from the previous period's boom (6.2.2)—a lagged Dutch disease—as well as by a loss of confidence. PNG businesses were surprised by the economic downturn, as they had expected continuing strong growth. Businesses found that they were in an 'overhang': they had borrowed too much and expanded too rapidly. They were then forced to focus on retrenchment and consolidation rather than expansion (Howes et al. 2019, 275).

Manufacturing contracted with an average annual growth of −0.5 per cent over this period. Agricultural growth recorded average growth of 2.1 per cent. Most agricultural commodities continued to stagnate or contract, though log exports reached a record and palm oil continued to grow (Figures B7 and B8). Marine products (fish exports) grew rapidly, reflecting a growing domestic fleet, as did 'other agricultural products', that is, new crops such as vanilla (Figure B9).

Trends in air arrivals are consistent with our boom-bust story (Figure 8.3). These were stagnant between 1996 and 2002, then more than tripled to 2015 before starting to fall (Liu and Howes 2022).

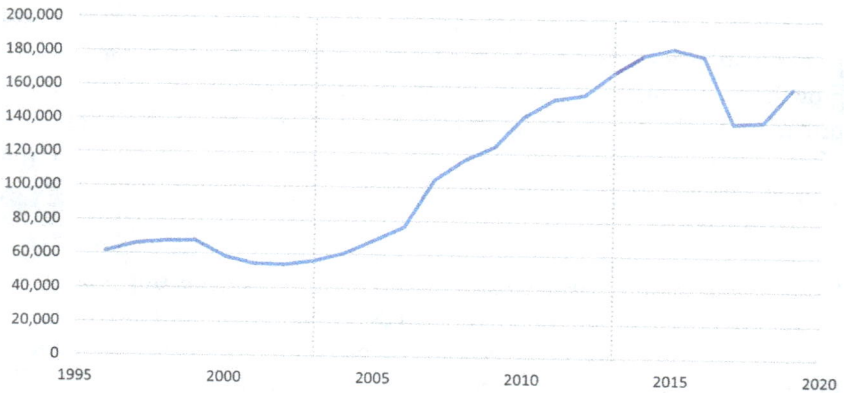

Figure 8.3: Air arrivals to Papua New Guinea, 1996–2019
Source: Liu and Howes (2022) based on data from PNG Tourism Promotion Authority.

Tourism has always struggled in PNG, with high costs and law and order problems negating the country's many attractions. Things went backwards in the tens (Liu and Howes 2022). A positive was that cruises started bringing tourists by sea to PNG. By 2019, 51,400 cruise visitors were recorded. On the other hand, tourists arriving by air (which had been increasing) fell from a peak of 38,300 in 2015 to just 25,200 in 2019. Since airborne tourists spend on average about 18 times as much as cruise arrivals (TPA and Acorn 2021), the net impact of these developments on the economy was negative.

Formal private sector and SOE employment peaked at 301,000 in 2013 and fell every year thereafter, except for 2019 and 2022, to finish at 268,000 in 2022, 89 per cent of the 2013 level (Figure B16). Ongoing decline rather than stagnation or slow growth in employment may also be explained by the boom overhang.

Expatriate employment had grown rapidly during the boom (6.2.2). Arrivals for the purpose of employment fell from their peak of 70,000 in 2013 to around 50,000 in the subsequent years, but recovered to 64,000 in 2019, well above their pre-boom (1996–2003) average of 14,300 (Liu and Howes 2022). This means that the number of national workers is not back at 2011 levels, as suggested by the employment data, but at an earlier year, since the share of foreign workers to the total workforce has grown. Why this is requires further research, but a growing share of foreign workers in a declining pool of formal sector employment opportunities is a worrying sign.

Real wages grew strongly over the boom (6.2.2) but stagnated during the bust. Blunch and Davies (2024) estimate an annual average decrease in formal sector real wages of 0.6–0.8 per cent between 2014 and 2018, the most recent year for which data are available.

Consistent with the downturn, outstanding loans from PNG's commercial banks to private sector and state-owned enterprises (SOEs) declined from 17 per cent of GDP in 2013 to 12 per cent in 2022 (Figure B32). The Kina Group, a set of local financial companies, bought out Malaysian Maybank in 2015, and then acquired ANZ's non-corporate banking business in mid-2018. While ANZ continues to serve the corporate sector in PNG, Westpac decided to exit altogether, which would have left BSP and Kina as the only two remaining retail banks. Westpac agreed on a sale to Kina, but that was overruled by the regulator on competition grounds in 2021, and in 2023 the Australian bank reversed its decision to leave.

The increased competition provided by Kina is evident from the reduction in lending rates in the late tens (Figure B34). Meanwhile, progress in financial inclusion was made on a number of fronts (Figure B37). PNG has had a tradition of credit cooperatives, but their number and customers have stagnated. On the other hand, the number of microfinance institutions (MFIs) increased from one in 2004 to five in 2020, and the number of microfinance customers reached 450,000 compared to the 260,000 customers of credit cooperatives. The reduction in the number of bank branches and agents over the nineties was reversed (Figure B37), and, of course, electronic payment systems and automated teller machines (ATMs) made their entry, though PNG is still a relative laggard (with the 21st-lowest ratio of ATMs to population among all countries in 2021).[1]

The most spectacular change was in the number of adults with a bank account, which, according to data from the IMF Financial Access Survey, grew from under 1 million in 2006 to 6 million in 2021. However, even if these data are reliable (an increase of 2 million in just one year, 2021, is implausible) field research has cast doubt on the number of adults using bank accounts that they were encouraged to open (Hoy and Toth 2020).

---

1   All data in this and the next paragraph are from the IMF Financial Access Survey.

Microinsurance was a success with the entry of the Swedish health company BIMA in 2014, which, in collaboration with Digicel and Capital Life Insurance, started offering life, health and disability insurance, with payments through mobile credit. As of 2017, it had 350,000 active polices (IFC 2018, 19).

8.2.3 Resource sector optimism and delays

Throughout this period, PNG was said to be one project away from recovery. As early as 2012, Prime Minister O'Neill (2012b) said that a second LNG project (Papua LNG) had been approved. Other mines such as Wafi-Golpu and Frieda River have been hailed as imminent more than once over the last decade (Price 2012). In 2019, the then treasurer said that 'Papua New Guinea is in the early stages of an unprecedented economic development phase based on the expansion of the mining and petroleum sector' (Basil 2019). Business commentators were bullish throughout, damaging their credibility in the process (Howes and Mako 2023a). For example, in 2018, the ANZ suggested that PNG was 'on the cusp of another resource boom' (Sen 2018).

And, yet, as of the end of 2023, PNG LNG remains the last major resource project to have been fully negotiated, with its final investment decision reached at the end of 2009. That this last period is the only one of the four without any new resource projects certainly means that it has been uniquely deprived of an important source of economic stimulus.

A second LNG project, named Papua LNG on account of its location in the Gulf Province, is the one that has made most progress. An agreement for that project was signed in April 2019. The change of government and COVID-19 delayed things. The final investment decision date has been repeatedly pushed back, and, at the time of writing, is now expected in 2025 (Pekic 2021; Macdonald-Smith 2023; Reuters 2024). The expansion of the PNG LNG project to include the P'nyang gas fields, preparations for which were underway in 2016, is now expected to follow only after PNG LNG construction is complete (*Business Advantage PNG* 2021b). Agreement on a much smaller offshore gas project has been elusive (Searancke 2021). A memorandum of understanding for the large copper and gold Wafi-Golpu project was signed in 2018, but the project then became stuck in the courts and negotiations are still underway (Badui-Owa 2021).

Globally, many resource projects are subject to delay (Cust and Mihalyi 2017), and there are a number of factors that push out timelines in PNG, in some cases increasingly so. One of the biggest problems for mining projects in PNG is where to put the waste. Panguna, Ok Tedi and Porgera have all demonstrated the risks involved with on-land disposal. Newer mines (Lihir, Ramu Nickel) have disposed of their waste at sea, but this, too, is contentious, and often the cause of popular opposition (*LoopPNG* 2021a, 2021b).

Landowner opposition and protest are common, especially during the preparation stage (Yafoi 2019). Again, this is in part because of past experience. Although the identification of landowner groups is meant to be concluded before the commencement of project construction, so that benefit flows can begin immediately, under the PNG LNG project that determination is still incomplete, long after production commenced.[2] Whatever the reasons for this (Filer 2019b), it is an experience unlikely to inspire confidence in landowners in relation to future resource projects, and some landowners have already taken the Papua LNG developers to court (*Post-Courier* 2019; Harriman 2021). Indeed, with PNG becoming an increasingly litigious society (9.2.2), those opposed to mines, whether on environmental or social grounds, as well as those wanting a better deal from them, whether landowners or provincial governments, can and do often go to court.[3]

Finally, there is the 'Take back PNG' agenda, motivated by a lack of development despite successive large resource projects, and in particular the disappointment around the PNG LNG project. Delays are accepted as the price of negotiating a harder deal, and politically are a way to signal a hard stance, whether one is being taken or not. The Papua LNG project was negotiated by the O'Neill government in early 2019, but then 'reviewed' and 'renegotiated' rather than re-agreed (as it actually was) by the Marape government later in the same year.

In fact, over this period, not only did PNG not gain any new projects, but it lost an existing one. In August 2019, the 30-year operating lease for the Porgera gold mine expired. In April 2020, Prime Minister Marape informed the two major shareholders, Barrick from Canada and the Zijin

---

2   As of November 2021, PGK1.1 billion was reported to be sitting in trust funds for the landowners once they are identified (*Pacific Mining Watch* 2021).
3   The Madang provincial government and a group of landowners sued the Ramu nickel mine in 2020 to stop the dumping of tailings at sea (Fox 2020). The environmental permit granted for the Wafi Golpu mine was stayed by the courts in September 2021 (*National* 2021).

Mining Group from China, that their lease would not be extended, citing longstanding environmental and resettlement issues. In August 2020, the PNG government issued a 20-year special lease for Porgera to its SOE, Kumul Mineral Holdings. Meanwhile, the Porgera shareholders took the PNG government to the PNG courts and to international arbitration for expropriation. While the government was not bound by law to extend the lease, Porgera's owners argued that it had a legitimate expectation to be granted an extension (Burton and Banks 2020). The government backed off on reopening the mine through its SOE, and, in April 2021, announced a new deal with the Porgera shareholders (9.1.4)—one that the prime minister sold as being 'far superior' (Marape 2021) but that informed observers said was actually little different from the deal Porgera had offered prior to its lease expiry (Vailala 2020). Work on recommissioning the mine commenced at the end of 2023 after the Mining Act was amended to remove the requirement that landowner compensation arrangements be worked out prior to the commencement of operations, but its operations are threatened by illegal miners (Pearl and Joku 2024). Porgera has never paid much corporate tax (8.3.2) so its closure had a significant local impact but not a national fiscal one.

8.3 The macroeconomy

Why did the downturn last so long? The previous section provided some answers to this question in terms of the lack of new resource projects, and an overhang from the earlier boom. This section examines two macroeconomic factors that prolonged the downturn. First, on the external front, a move away from currency convertibility compressed imports, allowed the exchange rate to be overvalued and damaged investor confidence. Second, there was record low resource revenue. The section also explains the persistently high deficits of the period as a consequence of non-convertibility, and reviews recent reforms to the Bank of Papua New Guinea and the re-emergence of budget support.

8.3.1 Foreign exchange rationing

PNG has two foreign exchange markets: the open or general market at which anyone can trade currencies, and the inter-bank market, in which only licensed dealers can operate, and into which the Bank of Papua New Guinea (BPNG) buys or, more often, sells US dollars.

PNG's kina, which had appreciated steadily during the boom, fell in 2013 by 6.9 per cent against the US dollar. By the end of May 2014, the kina had lost another 13.6 per cent on the open market. BPNG, which under its 2000 legislation had been handed authority for the exchange rate, decided that enough was enough. In June 2014, it introduced new so-called 'trading bands' that meant that the price of the kina in the inter-bank market became the price in the open market. Since a divergence had opened up between the two markets, this forced the kina up in the open market, resulting in an immediate appreciation of 17 per cent. Suddenly facing a much more attractive conversion rate for their holdings of kina, many rushed to buy dollars, and, in the face of limited supply, a queue developed. Thus ended the time-honoured policy in PNG (and most other but not all countries) of current account convertibility under which importers and those wishing to repatriate profits have automatic access to foreign exchange.

Ever since, foreign exchange shortages have been a deterrent for investors, and a cost for business. In 2021, a US government report noted:

> While there are no legal time limitations on remittances, foreign companies have waited many months for large transfers or performed transfers in small increments over time due to a shortage of foreign exchange. (US State 2021)

PNG's imports fell from close to 50 per cent of GDP during the boom to below 30 per cent during the bust (Table 10.7). Paradoxically, this import compression occurred despite strong export growth, leading to a record current account surplus of 14 per cent on average for the period. The PNG LNG project doubled the value of exports, but its revenue went largely offshore, including to repay construction-related debts. Foreign exchange reserves were protected (via rationing) and were not allowed to fall to the levels they had reached in the nineties, whether in absolute terms or as months of imports (Figure B22).

Figure 8.4, based on annual surveys of PNG CEOs, shows the top two concerns of businesses (on average) since 2014: foreign exchange and security. Between 2014 and 2024, foreign exchange has been the top concern for CEOs in six years and the second- to fourth-most important concern in four. It has, on average, been a more pressing concern than security, normally PNG business's main worry.

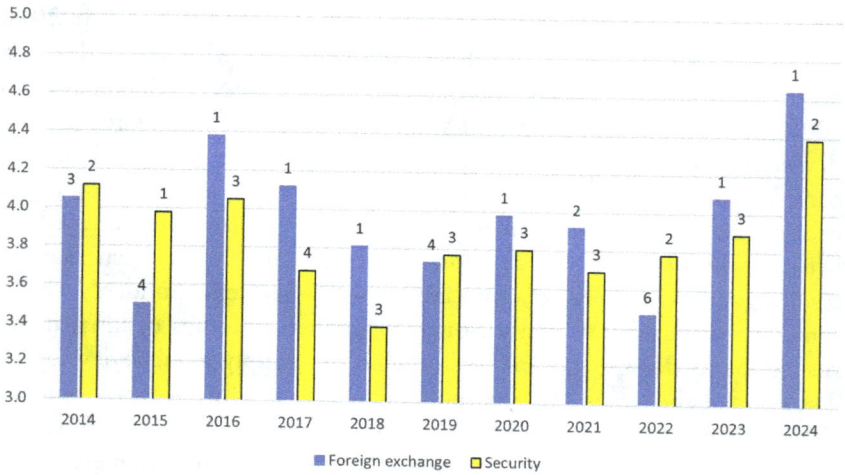

Figure 8.4: Top two business constraints according to PNG CEOs, 2014–24

Notes: Annual surveys published at the start of the year by *Business Advantage PNG*. CEOs are asked to rate concerns on a scale of 1–5, where 5 is reserved for the most serious concerns. The numbers on the top of each columns show the ranking of the two concerns shown out of some 20, where 1 is the concern that gets the highest average rating across CEOs. The two concerns shown have the highest average rating for the period shown. The survey started in 2012, but foreign exchange did not appear as an issue for businesses until 2014.

Source: Updated from Igara and Howes (2023).

Foreign exchange rationing has had all sorts of negative impacts on growth and development. Some import compression was inevitable following the boom, but rationing, by minimising depreciation, has exacerbated it. In 2021, Virgin Australia exited the PNG market on account of foreign exchange shortages. (In 2018, the Independent Consumer & Competition Commission disallowed the Air Niugini–Qantas code share, and these two airlines now provide the only competition on Australia-PNG routes.) Rationing has repeatedly grounded airlines due to shortages of imported fuel, has sometimes resulted in petrol rationing and has led to drug shortages (Salmang 2023). Foreign exchange rationing has also led to rent-seeking and lobbying. The Independent Advisory Group on the Central Banking Act noted in its 2021 report that it had 'heard stories from businesses [about] having to text the Governor or reach him through an intermediary in order to request the release of foreign exchange to finance vital imports' (Igara, Kamit and Howes 2021, 74).

The introduction of rationing meant that the exchange rate was no longer floating (though BPNG insisted that it was). The inter-bank market continued, but the incentive of dealers to bid down the kina was greatly weakened. They could no longer, because of the imposition of trading bands, compete on price outside the inter-bank market, and in the inter-bank market BPNG allocated foreign exchange not through an auction but on the basis of non-price factors, principally the stock of outstanding foreign exchange orders. All this, combined with the use of moral suasion from time to time, undermined the earlier floating regime, and the system became akin to a crawling peg with a bias against depreciation.

The kina was linked to the US dollar rather than a basket of currencies as in the eighties (2.3.3). As the US dollar strengthened over this period, any tendency to depreciation was further weakened: average nominal depreciation of the kina over this period against the US dollar was 5.1 per cent, but on a trade-weighted basis only 2.4 per cent (Table 10.9).

For some periods (June 2016–August 2017 and November 2020–April 2023), the kina was simply fixed against the US dollar (Figure B20). In others, it was allowed to depreciate slowly. The net result is that kina depreciation since the boom has been modest. The real effective exchange rate remained as high as it was at its boomtime peak, and not much lower than at independence (Figure B21). Various analyses have confirmed that the kina is overvalued (Fox and Schröder 2017; Davies 2021), as indeed it must be given the excess demand for foreign currency. While many commentators are sceptical that depreciation will help the PNG economy, noting supply-side rigidities, there can be no doubt that the hard-won competitiveness gains of the nineties have been surrendered and the economy prevented from adjusting to a post-boom era.

While the abandonment of a floating exchange rate suggests a return to the economic policy of the eighties, the reliance on non-convertibility was a major and new shift. A decade after independence, Daniel and Sims (1986, 36) noted that 'all governments since independence have been committed to a strong and convertible currency and there are very few impediments to bringing money in or sending it out'. In his 1991 budget speech, Finance Minister Paul Pora (1990, 4) boasted that, despite the closure of the Panguna mine, 'our currency continues to be easily convertible'. Economists at the time confirmed that the central bank 'since its creation has been highly successful in ensuring a freely convertible kina' (Gupta 1992, 6). Despite the turmoil of the nineties, King and Sugden (1997, 25) awarded the PNG government 'high marks' for convertibility. Current-account convertibility continued through the boom years but was brought to an abrupt end in 2014.

The more BPNG has tried to regulate access to foreign exchange (foreign exchange regulations were tightened in 2016 and then in 2022), the more companies have tried to circumvent them, including by buying coffee and other commodities in kina and at a discount to get access to dollars. However, there has been no suggestion that the black market will grow big enough to force a devaluation. Unlike in many other countries with artificially controlled exchange rates, there is no widely quoted black market exchange rate (Davies 2021).

The costs of this shift towards foreign exchange rationing and an overvalued kina are obvious and massive. Why were they incurred? Rationing was made possible as a result of the 2000 Central Banking Act, one of the cornerstone-Morauta reforms (5.1.3), which not only gave responsibility for the exchange rate to BPNG, but also, perhaps inadvertently, removed the requirement that the exchange rate be managed in compliance with the country's international agreements. When PNG joined the IMF in 1975, it signed up to that body's articles of association, including article VIII, which forbids foreign exchange rationing. The fact that before, but not after 2000, domestic law required this external commitment be adhered to allowed BPNG to ignore it from 2014 onwards.

The shift to rationing was not entered into with any degree of transparency and public deliberation. In fact, according to BPNG governor Lok Bakani, it was introduced as a 'short-term measure to a short-term problem' (Albaniel 2016). The policy of rationing was attractive though and, even as its costs became increasingly obvious, was retained to avoid two features of the nineties: one, a balance of payments crisis; two, significant currency depreciation.

After all, the nineties was seen as a traumatic decade—a time of failure. The large depreciations of the nineties had caused real economic pain to PNG's urban population, which, though only a small proportion of the total population, often seems much more influential than the rural majority. A weaker kina would mean higher prices for imported food for urban dwellers, and higher prices for overseas schools, health care and holidays for PNG's elite.

Finally, the Central Banking Act 2000 set the control of inflation as the only legitimate goal for monetary policy. This meant BPNG could ignore the adverse growth consequences of rationing. With monetary policy continuing to be ineffective due to excess liquidity (Figure B36)—ironically driven in part by the inability of businesses to freely convert kina into dollars—the exchange rate was the only instrument BPNG had to control inflation. Again and again over this period, the IMF in its annual surveillance reports recommended to BPNG that it allow the kina to depreciate; consistently the latter responded that this would increase inflation, as it surely would. It was not until the end of 2021 that the Central Banking Act was amended to force BPNG to consider growth as well as inflation when setting monetary (and thus exchange rate) policy—and this amendment was reversed in 2024 (8.3.4).

This amendment, plus the agreement entered into with the IMF in 2023 (8.3.5), had some positive outcomes: an end to denial by the central bank that there was rationing, increased releases of foreign exchange and a modest devaluation against the US dollar starting in the second half of 2023. However, rationing, while reduced, has outlived the end of the bust (Figure 8.4) and, as of the first half of 2024, businesses continued to complain virulently about foreign exchange shortages (Shlezinger 2024). Absent any commitment to return to convertibility, when this problem will end is unclear. Moreover, if and when it does, there is now the clear risk of a return to rationing.

8.3.2 Low resource revenue

The boom of the previous period was explained in Chapter 6 by reference first to high resource revenue flowing to government and then to a construction boom centred around the PNG LNG project (6.2.1). Construction of that project was completed in 2013, but the boom may well have continued had resource revenue held up, or, as was anticipated by many, increased. Instead, resource revenue collapsed to an average of only 1.5 per cent of GDP for the bust, the lowest of the four periods and just a fraction of the 4.9 per cent average seen during the boom (Table 10.10).

Explaining this collapse first requires understanding why PNG LNG did not deliver the massive revenue that was anticipated of it. The ACIL Tasman report commissioned by Exxon (6.2.1) provided projections of corporate tax revenue from PNG LNG of more than PGK1.5 billion from 2014 to 2023 under the base case, and PGK2.5 billion after that (ACIL Tasman 2009).

Over time, these projections found their way into both public discourse and government forecasts. Yet, until recently, very little revenue from PNG LNG has actually found its way into the budget. Why (beyond the obvious incentives this consulting group faced given who commissioned the study)?

ACIL Tasman projections were based on USD9 billion capital costs. Actual PNG LNG capital costs were USD19 billion. Operating costs may well have been higher than projected as well. Oil and gas prices fell in 2014, but have since recovered, and, offsetting this, production has been higher than expected. Some have suggested tax havens are the culprit: the company responsible for the sale of LNG is registered in Bahamas, a tax haven (TNJ and Make Exxon Pay Coalition 2018). However, large PNG LNG tax payments in 2022 in response to high petroleum prices cast doubt on this argument. It is also possible that ACIL Tasman did not accurately model the tax regime.

Dividend payments from the PNG LNG project have also been much lower than the projected PGK1 billion per year. Here we must distinguish between profits flowing to Kumul Petroleum, and dividends paid by it to the budget. In late 2019, Kumul Petroleum revealed that since 2014 it had received PGK4.2 billion in profits from the project (Kumul Petroleum 2019), which corresponds to about PGK0.76 billion per year. Of this amount, it only paid about one-third (PGK1.3 billion) in dividends to government. Other claims on profits included payments on the Oil Search/UBS loan (9.1.4). PGK0.8 billion was retained by the company. Building up a national champion is not cheap, and will come at the expense of the budget, at least in the short and medium term.

By 2015, as the reality was sinking in that PNG LNG was not going to deliver to the budget in anything like the way anticipated, Finance Minister James Marape made front-page news with his declaration that 'LNG is a myth'. But it was not just LNG. Revenue from all resource projects only exceeded PGK1 billion twice between 2015 and 2020.

One reason is that commodity prices fell, but PNG's commodity price index declined only marginally, back to levels of the mid-noughties, when resource revenue was at record highs (Figures B12 and B25).

Ok Tedi had been the star contributor to government revenue in the noughties, but its annual corporate tax contribution, which had breached PGK1 billion in 2006, fell to less than PGK200 million during the bust, as its production fell. Oil production also continued its slow decline, which left, among the major projects, only Ramu Nickel, which had an extended tax holiday, and the two major gold mines—Lihir and Porgera—which have never paid significant amounts of corporate tax, even when gold prices have been at record highs, for reasons that have never been clear.

While project-specific factors seem to be the most important contributors to the resource revenue drought, one common cause is that the share of the take by the central government has fallen as that by provincial governments and landowners have increased (4.3.2). We should also recall that PNG sold off its equity share in most resource projects over the nineties (5.1.3), and through this period only had a share in two large projects: Ok Tedi (7.1.3) and PNG LNG (9.1.4).

All in all, while we lack a full explanation, we can point to a number of project-specific and sectoral factors that contributed to the collapse in resource revenue flowing to government over this period.

Low resource revenue was also one reason why the sovereign wealth fund (SWF), legislated for in 2015 (7.1.3), was not operationalised over the course of the period. According to that legislation, a portion of resource revenue, no matter how small, should have been saved, but, given the fiscal stress, that was simply ignored. In 2022, when resource revenue rebounded on account of high petroleum prices due to the Russia–Ukraine war, a token deposit was finally made into the SWF, but without any reference to the underlying legislation, which would have required a much more substantial downpayment (Ukama 2022; Leng and Howes 2022).

8.3.3 High deficits

Like the private sector (8.2.3), the government was also surprised by the downturn. Revenue in 2015 was only 79 per cent of the budget target, and only 83 per cent of budgeted expenditure could be financed that year. Indeed, throughout the period, the government found it difficult to set realistic revenue and expenditure targets.

There was no growth in revenue until 2022. Adjusting for inflation, government revenue in 2019 was 2 per cent above that in 2013. That was before the pandemic: real revenue fell in 2020 by a massive 16 per cent, and even in 2021 was 8 per cent below its 2019 level. In 2022, however, on the back of high oil and gas prices, resource revenue jumped from 1.1 to 3.9 per cent of GDP, causing real revenue to rise by 27 per cent in a single year.

We have already attempted to explain the precipitous decline in resource revenue experienced during the tens (8.3.2). Non-resource revenue also performed poorly (Figure B26), reflecting the depressed state of the economy. There was not much by way of tax reform, with little follow-up to the Tax Review Committee established in 2013 (Tax Review Committee 2015a, 2015b)—though it did recommend the resource sector tax reforms implemented during the period (9.1.4). In 2017, a five-year Medium Term Revenue Strategy was put in place that aimed to increase revenue by improving tax administration and compliance (Department of Treasury 2017a).

The Public Money Regularisation Money Act was passed in 2017 to force statutory authorities to remit funds in excess of requirements (set at 10 per cent unless an exception was granted) to the Treasury. However, the Act was ruled unconstitutional by the Supreme Court after it was challenged by the Ombudsman Commission (which wanted to protect its own fee income). A revised version was passed in 2022 exempting the judicial sector, but the extent to which it will be implemented remains unclear.

Given an absence of revenue growth during most of this period, and the fact that deficits were high going into it, there was no room for the government to grow expenditure. In 2019, real government expenditure was equal to its 2013 level (though recall that 2013 expenditure was a 26 per cent increase on 2012 levels) after inflation; this was a permanent increase. Expenditure was little changed (after inflation) in 2020 and 2021, with the decline in revenue due to the pandemic made up for by extra borrowing. But in 2022, with the influx of resource revenue due to the Ukraine war, expenditure growth resumed again, with a single-year real increase of 15 per cent at last taking total expenditure well above peak boom levels, another sign that the bust was over.

There were large deficits and therefore increasing debt during this period. The average deficit for this period was 5.2 per cent, three times or more greater than the average for any earlier period (Table 10.10).

With debt increasing from 25 per cent in 2013 to a peak of 53 per cent in 2021, it is hardly surprising that PNG's credit ratings were adjusted down (Table 8.1). PNG received its first credit rating in 1998 and has, since then, received ratings in the highly speculative range of B1 to B2 (Moody's) or B– to B+ (S&P). Higher (B1 and B+) ratings were received during the reform period of the late nineties (though with downgrades in the early 2000s, reflecting poor investor confidence) and during the boom. Lower grades (B2 and B–) came with the fiscal stress of the quiet bust. The IMF's original assessment of PNG's risk of debt distress was moderate-to-high in 2006. This was reduced to low by the end of the boom (2012 and 2013), but then increased to moderate in 2018 and high in 2020.

Table 8.1: PNG credit ratings, 1999–2022

Agency	Rating	Outlook	Date
Moody's	B2	stable	10 November 2022
S&P	B–	stable	24 May 2022
S&P	B–	negative	3 June 2021
S&P	B–	negative watch	30 April 2021
Moody's	B2	negative	19 April 2021
IMF	high		1 June 2020
S&P	B–	stable	29 April 2020
IMF	moderate		6 April 2020
Moody's	B2	stable	15 February 2019
IMF	moderate		3 December 2018
S&P	B	stable	16 April 2018
Moody's	B2	negative	23 March 2018
IMF	moderate		17 November 2017
IMF	low		11 November 2016
Moody's	B2	stable	25 April 2016
Moody's	B1	negative watch	25 February 2016
IMF	low		18 November 2015
S&P	B+	negative	8 October 2015
Moody's	B1	negative	18 May 2015
S&P	B+	stable	29 October 2015
IMF	low		10 November 2014
IMF	low		3 December 2013
IMF	low		30 April 2012
S&P	B+	negative	27 January 2012
IMF	moderate		3 May 2011
IMF	moderate		4 May 2010 *
IMF	moderate		27 February 2009
IMF	moderate		18 January 2008 **
S&P	B+	stable	13 September 2007
IMF	moderate		21 March 2007

Agency	Rating	Outlook	Date
IMF	moderate–high		13 March 2006
S&P	B	stable	6 December 2005
S&P	B	positive	21 December 2004
S&P	B	stable	21 December 2003
S&P	B	negative	8 October 2002
S&P	B	stable	6 August 2001
S&P	B+	negative	21 March 2001
S&P	B+	stable	29 June 2000
S&P	B+	negative	1 September 1999
S&P	B+	negative watch	26 July 1999
S&P	B+	stable	25 January 1999
Moody's	B1	stable	31 December 1998

Notes: * IMF (2010); ** IMF (2008). In the range shown in the table, the ratings, in ascending order, for Moody's are B3, B2, B1 and, for S&P, B -, B and B+. The risk of debt distress as assessed by the IMF is low, moderate or high.

Source: For S&P and Moody's, see Trading Economics (n.d); for IMF, see IMF (n.d.).

In fact, PNG's risk of default remained extremely low throughout. Even during the extreme stress of the nineties, there was no question that the government would meet its debt obligations. These ratings were more verdicts on the health of the PNG economy; and, with the bust having ended, debt can be expected to fall and credit ratings rise again.

The real puzzle is that, whereas in earlier periods deficits emerged from time to time but were quickly reduced (Duncan 2002), in this period they were persistently high. Why?

One answer is that attempts to limit deficits and the resultant increase in debt via legislation were unsuccessful. PNG's Fiscal Responsibility Act (FRA), which was introduced in 2006 (6.3.1), was amended at the end of 2012 to replace the requirement that debt not be increased by a cap on debt to GDP of 35 per cent for 2013 and 2014, and 30 per cent thereafter. When debt reached 38 per cent at the end of 2013,[4] the FRA was amended again to extend the higher cap by another year, 2015. PNG's GDP was rebased upwards in 2016 (8.2), and this fortuitously made it much easier to hit the original debt target. With the debt/GDP ratio at 34 per cent of GDP in 2016 (49 per cent using the old GDP measure), the FRA was once again amended

---

4   Calculated using the 'old', smaller GDP figure: see the discussion in the text (8.2.1).

in 2017 to make a permanent cap of 30–35 per cent. This amendment also replaced the FRA's balanced-budget requirement (which had not been met since 2010) by a 'zero average annual non-resource primary fiscal balance'. In 2018 and 2019, debt/GDP increased again, reaching 40 per cent by the end of 2019. This required a further amendment, and in 2019, the upper bound on debt in the FRA was increased to 45 per cent. Finally, COVID-19 struck, borrowing was increased, and, in 2020, debt/GDP increased to 49 per cent and the debt limit to 60 per cent. Clearly, the legislative effort to limit debts and deficits did not work, as it was just too easy to amend the legislation whenever there was an actual or potential breach.

Another reason for the failure of fiscal adjustment over this period was the poor state of the economy. Given low growth, and the reluctance of the government to stimulate the economy via depreciation, spending was the only stimulatory tool the government could turn to.

Deficit reform efforts were also undermined by the continued narrative of success and the failure to admit that the boom had come to an end. This in turn allowed demands for salary increases to be met, even when there was no additional revenue to meet those demands (9.2.2). Serious policy efforts to bring down the deficit commenced only towards the end of the period. Under Treasurer Charles Abel, a new Medium Term Fiscal Strategy (Department of Treasury 2017b) was agreed to in 2017 for the period 2018 to 2022, and received backing from the World Bank. However, there was a salary blow out in 2018 (9.2.2), and debt went up relative to GDP rather than down as planned. Ian Ling Stuckey was appointed in August 2019 not long after Marape became prime minister. He undertook a 'due diligence' exercise, with the assistance of the IMF, which found the underlying deficit to be significantly higher than reported due to a build-up of arrears. The 2019 deficit was projected to be 5.8 per cent of GDP. This then became the baseline from which deficit reduction would be measured in future years. However, this second adjustment program was blown off course the next year by the pandemic. Nearly all governments around the world responded to the pandemic by increasing deficits. PNG's fiscal deficits for 2020 and 2021 were this highest it had ever run.

The most important reason, however, for the unusually high average deficits of this period was foreign exchange rationing (8.3.1). In the nineties, high deficits resulted in an actual or at least potential balance of payments crisis, something no politician wanted. The shift to non-convertibility of the kina in 2014 removed that threat. Politicians could run any level of deficit that they wanted; PNG's central bank would ensure that the country would not run out of foreign exchange by rationing it as required. It was a vicious circle. High deficits encouraged the introduction and extension of rationing to prevent greater depreciation and a possible run on reserves, and once rationing had been introduced, it in turn encouraged the maintenance of high deficits.

How were these deficits financed? It was not easy. Recall that the previous period ended with a record reliance on domestic financing. Over this period, commercial banks continued to retain about 40 per cent of their assets in government debt. The government became increasingly reliant on superannuation funds. By the end of the period they too, like the commercial banks, had 40 per cent of their assets in government securities.

There was also a return to deficit financing by the central bank, despite this being outlawed by the Central Banking Act of 2000. Under the so-called 'slack arrangement', between 2014 and 2016 BPNG purchased those government securities that it was unable (as government debt manager) to sell to private buyers. BPNG holdings of government securities rose from PGK0.9 billion in 2013 to PGK3.6 billion in 2016, not as high as the levels seen in the nineties, but not far from it, once adjustments are made for inflation (Figure B35). While this seemed to have no adverse economic effects (no spike in inflation), it did call into question the bank's independence, as well as its accountability, and was one of the issues dealt with by the BPNG reforms of 2021 (8.3.4).

In the later years of this period, the government turned to foreign borrowing. This was first done through a sovereign bond issue in September 2018 (USD500 million), PNG's first foray into international commercial debt markets since the early years of independence. PNG also started, in 2018, to turn to official international lenders (8.3.5), and by 2022 the share of domestic to total government debt was 52 per cent, still high by historical standards but below the 77 per cent peak reached at the start of this period (Figure B29). This official borrowing carried much lower interest rates than either commercial foreign or domestic borrowing. Domestic interest rates on government borrowing also fell partly because there was less demand from government, and partly because the government seemed to take a tougher negotiating stance. PNG's interest/GDP ratio, after rising from 1.1 per cent of GDP in 2013 to 2.6 per cent in 2019 fell to 2.5 per cent of GDP in 2021.

8.3.4 Central bank performance and reforms

In the Central Banking Act of 2000, BPNG was made more independent of political influence, told to focus only on controlling inflation, given control of the exchange rate and prohibited from engaging in deficit financing (5.1.3). BPNG certainly succeeded in keeping inflation moderate, with growth in the consumer price index averaging 4–5 per cent during both the boom and the quiet bust. In other respects it was less successful. The persistence of excess liquidity that first emerged at the end of the nineties (4.4.4) and worsened during the boom years (6.3.2) undermined the effectiveness of monetary policy. This meant that there was no stimulatory impact from BPNG's reduction of both the cash reserve requirement and the Kina Facility Rate during the pandemic (Figures B34 and B36). While this itself can hardly be blamed on the central bank, its return to deficit financing (8.3.3) was in clear contravention of the Central Banking Act, and its introduction of foreign exchange rationing (8.3.1) was deeply damaging to growth.

BPNG was also slow to recognise the headwinds the PNG economy was facing. It was only in September 2019—after Peter O'Neill had been removed as prime minister, and the new prime minister had described the economy as 'bleeding and struggling' (*Business Advantage PNG* 2019)— that BPNG shifted its monetary stance from 'neutral' to 'accommodating'. It might be argued that this did not matter if monetary policy was ineffective, but it did suggest that the central bank was unwilling to be an independent voice on the economy.

The concentration of power in one individual that the 2000 Central Banking Act provided for was highly unusual by international standards. Loi Bakani had become governor in 2009, and was still there in 2021, having become a very powerful figure in the meantime. In 2021, following a review (Igara, Kamit and Howes 2021), the government amended the Central Banking Act to move towards a more collegial model in which responsibility for monetary policy as well as financial regulation was shifted away from the governor to the board. The amendments also shortened the maximum term of governor from 14 to 8 years, which effectively meant that the incumbent was out of a job. The 2021 amendments also removed the deficit financing ban and returned to the pre-2000 arrangement of a cap on central bank holdings of government debt, on the basis that the earlier ban had proved unworkable and that what mattered about central bank purchases of government debt was not their existence but their volume.

The amendments also broadened BPNG's objectives to target growth as well as inflation (appropriately so, given its role in exchange rate setting), though in 2024 the IMF insisted that the Central Banking Act be further amended to once again give primacy to combatting inflation.

8.3.5 The re-emergence of budget support

Policy-based lending was a major theme of the nineties (5.1.4) and returned with the fiscal stress of this period. This time around, the loans were larger, but the conditions fewer and less onerous.

The Asian Development Bank was the first to move, providing USD100 million to the budget in return for health sector reforms in May 2018 (ADB 2018), and an additional USD159 million in 2021 (James 2020). Given the appalling performance of the health sector over this period—PNG's immunisation rates plummeted to be the lowest in the world (Howes and Mambon 2021)—it is unclear what the justification for this loan was or what it achieved.

In September 2018, the World Bank (2018) provided USD150 million in return for fiscal reform. The basis for this was the 2018–22 Medium Term Fiscal Strategy and Medium Term Revenue Strategy. A second, follow-up operation of USD50 million was also planned, but was cancelled and the first loan rated a failure after PNG's fiscal reform strategy went off track (8.3.3; World Bank 2020)

In November 2019, the Australian government provided a condition-free USD300 million loan to PNG through its export finance agency. By 2020, an IMF staff-monitored program (focused mainly on tax administration) was in place, and the Australian government was able to replace the export finance loan by the more conventional vehicle of a direct loan. (The International Monetary Agreements Act requires the Australian government, as against its export finance agency, to only lend to other governments in support of a multilateral program.) Australia provided another AUD140 million at the end of 2020 (Australian Treasury 2020). This was followed by a JPY30 billion, highly concessional loan from Japan in early 2021 (JICA 2021), and by another AUD650 million from Australia at the end of 2021 (Australian Treasury 2022), AUD750 million at the end of 2022 (Australian Treasury 2023), AUD600 million at the end of 2023 (Australian Treasury 2024) and AUD570 million at the end of 2024 (Australian Treasury 2025).

In November 2020, ADB provided the first in an envisaged three loans in support of SOE reform: USD100 million was disbursed in 2020, USD150 million in 2021 (ADB 2021) and USD250 million in 2022 (ADB 2022). These loans supported various legislative amendments—for example, to reduce political interference in the selection of SOE boards—and were made despite little progress on the ground in SOE performance (9.1.1)

The pandemic unlocked additional and largely condition-free foreign funding. The ADB released an additional USD250 million in 2020 (*Xinhua* 2020), the IMF approved USD364 million also in 2020 (IMF 2020) and the World Bank authorised USD100 million in 2021 (World Bank 2021a).

Finally, in March 2023, after three years on a trial staff-monitored program, the IMF signed off on a loan agreement with PNG worth USD918 million over three years. The agreement has three main aims: elimination of the fiscal deficit by 2027; the mopping up of all excess liquidity, a feature of the PNG economy since the 1990s, by the sale of a large volume of central bank bills; and, on the external account, a more flexible exchange rate and reduced foreign exchange shortages (IMF 2023).

The turn to the IMF, something O'Neill had ruled out, was certainly a significant development. It required the replacement of O'Neill by Marape and also new top management at BPNG, prepared to move away from the foreign exchange rationing regime. Some progress has been made, but whether the IMF-backed reforms will succeed remains to be seen. Normally, when the IMF gets involved, there is a crisis and reforms have to be made. In the complacency of the quiet bust, there was neither an appetite nor even a public narrative in favour of important but difficult reforms.

The IMF program can also be questioned on technical grounds. Mopping up excess liquidity by remunerating the marginal central bank deposit will crowd out private sector lending. The IMF requirement that that BPNG return to having only a mandate for controlling inflation when formulating its monetary and exchange rate policy (8.3.4) ignores the fact that it was this sole focus on inflation that led to rationing and overvaluation in the first place.

All of these foreign official loans offered a lower interest rate than anything PNG could secure commercially abroad or at home. The 2018 USD500 million sovereign bond had a repayment period of 10 years and an interest rate of 8.4 per cent (IMF and IDA 2020, 4). The official loans by contrast have either low or very low interest rates, and typically have extended grace and/or repayment periods. Australia's 2020 AUD440 million loan was for 15 years, and, although interest rates have subsequently risen, at the time it was made, a 1.39 per cent interest rate (Australian Treasury 2020). Most of the official loans are also, for better or for worse, devoid of the onerous and controversial policy conditions of the nineties, staying away from contentious areas such as privatisation, with countries like Australia and Japan now providing budget support to PNG so that it does not turn to China. However, with international interest rates rising, and the somewhat more stringent conditionality of the IMF loan, the future of official foreign lending to PNG is unclear. Moreover, the more foreign borrowing PNG does, the more costly a devaluation becomes.

9

The turn to economic nationalism

After 40 years of independence, we have not gained control of our economy. We have not been able to fully drive the development agenda to achieve true self reliance as a nation. The vast majority of our people are greatly marginalised and are not engaged meaningfully in economic activities ... Our formal SME sector is crowded out by many foreign businesses after the removal of the reserved businesses.

—Extracts from the Small and Medium Enterprise Policy
(Ministry of Trade, Commerce and Industry 2016)

9.1 Economic policies

When Peter O'Neill took office in 2011, economic policy started to become more nationalistic and state-led (7.1.3). The shift was partial rather than complete, and often rhetorical rather than actual. Nevertheless, the changes, taken together, were significant. Marape took the rhetoric to a new level when he became prime minister in 2019 with his popular 'Take back PNG' slogan. We explore policy changes in the 2010s under five headings: state-owned enterprise and infrastructure policy, the push for reservations for national businesses, the re-emergence of protectionism, the promotion of national champions in the resource sector and the stalemate around land policy.

9.1.1 State-owned enterprise reform and infrastructure

There was little or no progress in state-owned enterprise (SOE) reform and no interest in privatisation. Many SOEs were plagued by frequent turnover of boards and CEOs, and by scandals, for example, relating to the National Development Bank, Kumul Minerals and the National Airports Corporation (*National* 2019, 2020; PNGi 2022). The financial position of most SOEs is poor and their arrears are significant (ADB 2022). The creation of a new SOE, Kumul Agriculture, in 2016, showed the appetite for state involvement in business. It immediately drew an adverse audit report in 2018. Another effort to limit political interference in the recruitment of boards and CEOs was made in 2021[1] as part of an ADB budget support program (8.3.5).

Perhaps the worst performing of PNG's SOEs was PNG Power, described as being in a 'crisis of governance' (Sandu et al. 2020). Three expatriate CEOs came and went from PNG Power between 2015 and 2021, while the utility's performance seemed to go from bad to worse, with what seemed to be growing blackouts, implacable opposition to any restructuring by the incumbent trade union and a worsening financial position, in part due to the government preventing any electricity tariff increases from 2013.

Electricity reliability and access remain major issues. Only about 15 per cent of the population has access to the grid (Pandey and Howes 2022, 170). In better news, an aid-supported, private sector initiative led to rapid sales of solar panels. Estimates of solar penetration (the ratio of households with a solar panel) range from 33 to 60 per cent (Pandey and Howes 2022, 169; IFC 2019), among the highest in the world.

B-Mobile, the state-owned mobile phone company (formerly part of PNG Telkom), proved completely unable to compete with Digicel, with neither a partial sale in 2008 to Hong Kong–based private equity firm GEMS, nor a subsequent injection of government funds helping. By 2015, Digicel had 1,100 towers and B-Mobile only 300 (Suwamaru 2020). B-Mobile has been reconsolidated into PNG Telkom, but without any boost to performance. A more positive development was a third mobile phone entrant in 2022, the Fijian company Amalgamated Telecom Holdings.

---

1   The Kumul Consolidated Holdings Authorisation (Amendment) Bill 2021.

Air Niugini was hit hard by the pandemic and by fuel shortages (linked to foreign exchange rationing) and its financial position is precarious (ADB 2022). Advances were, however, made in international and domestic connectivity. Funded by a Chinese EXIM Bank loan, Huawei started work in 2019 on the USD270 million Kumul Submarine Cable Network (KSCN) that connects many of PNG's coastal towns to the Asian internet transmission network via Jayapura on the other side of the Indonesian border. Australia, determined to prevent China from getting in first, provided AUD200 million of grant funding for the Coral Sea Cable from Sydney to Port Moresby and Honiara, Solomon Islands. This was completed in 2020, greatly increasing the capacity on that route. While these new projects are of great potential, various constraints need to be overcome: Digicel's de facto mobile monopoly has limited the extent to which cost savings are being passed on to consumers, the commercial viability of the KSCN is uncertain and there are technical problems hindering the utilisation of the new cable networks (Suwamaru 2020; Watson 2022; KCH 2021).

In 2003, with encouragement from the ADB, legislation had been passed to establish the National Roads Authority (NRA) and the PNG Road Fund, which the NRA would administer to maintain the country's national roads. Hopes at the time were high (McLay 2003); however, in 2016 a study found that the NRA had limited impact because of funding constraints, with the Road Fund constituting 'less than 1.5 per cent of total government spending on maintenance and rehabilitation of the national road network' (Dornan 2016, 452). The same study found a lack of clarity in the division of responsibility between the NRA and the Department of Works, traditionally responsible for road maintenance. The NRA repeatedly received qualified audit reports (Brown 2016). Meanwhile, the government itself reported in the 2013 budget that:

> Papua New Guinea's transport networks are failing. Major roads, including the crucially important Highlands Highway, have deteriorated alarmingly, raising the costs and reducing the availability of transport services. Most of the feeder roads are frequently impassable. Communities in coastal and mountainous areas that rely on sea and air transport are becoming more isolated because of deteriorating physical infrastructure. In all transport subsectors, the dilapidated state of infrastructure is largely the result of inadequate maintenance and poor management over a long period. Wharves, jetties and airstrips have fallen into disrepair and disuse.

Almost half of national roads and two thirds of provincial roads need rehabilitation or reconstruction before they can be properly maintained. (cited in Dornan 2016)

In 2020, the PNG government abolished the NRA and restructured the PNG Road Fund. It also launched the 'Connect PNG' road-building program (Leng 2022), which promises greater funding for road construction and maintenance.

A massive project, supported by an ADB loan of USD680 million, was launched in 2017 to rehabilitate the Highlands Highway, the nation's most important road, all the way from Lae to Mount Hagen. Encouragingly, given the problems with maintaining roads, the project will fund not only rehabilitation and upgrades, but also maintenance.

The operation of PNG's major Lae and Port Moresby ports was contracted out under a 25-year concession awarded in 2018 to the multinational ICTSI, with claimed benefits for performance, despite allegations of corruption (Robertson and Hui 2023) and incredibly high prices. An Independent Consumer & Competition Commission (ICCC) review found that ICTSI's return on capital exceeds 100 per cent in a single year (ICCC 2023; Howes and Kunda 2024).

9.1.2 Reservations for national businesses

PNG released a new policy for small and medium enterprises in 2016, the key feature of which was a reduction in the economic space available for foreign investors (Ministry of Trade, Commerce and Industry 2016). PNG has had a list of activities reserved for national enterprises since independence, but it had been pared back over the nineties as part of its structural adjustment reforms, and then again in 2005, leaving 'only a limited list of Cottage Business Activities' reserved for citizens (PWC 2016, 4). Under the new policy, all companies with a turnover of less than PGK10 million would need to be 100 per cent PNG owned, with a large number of sectors also reserved for fully PNG-owned firms (PWC 2016). The new policy generated debate in PNG (Nicholas 2016) and alarm among foreign businesses (Byrne 2017). In the end it proved too radical to implement. Legislation to implement the policy was drafted in 2019 but withdrawn after protest. Though a radical expansion of the reserved list retains some political support (PNG Facts 2021), in 2022 the Investment Promotion Authority released only a mildly expanded reserved list (*Post-Courier* 2022b).

9.1.3 Protectionism

During this period, the PNG government declined to sign the Pacific Agreement on Closer Economic Relations Plus treaty, which required signatories to gradually phase out tariffs on imports from other Pacific countries, Australia and New Zealand. PNG argued that it wanted a bilateral trade deal (Kisselpar 2016), but it also, perhaps, wanted the freedom to increase rather than reduce tariffs. Certainly the 2023 Medium Term Development Plan revealed a mercantilist outlook by projecting growing exports and declining imports (Mako and Howes 2024).

In 2015, the government issued a ban on several fresh fruit and vegetable imports from Australia to support PNG's own vegetable industry (Locke 2015). The ban was short lived, but a precursor of a major reversal in trade policy. In 2017, Deputy Prime Minister Charles Abel announced the suspension of the 20-year tariff reduction program in place since 1999 (7.1.2). In the 2018 budget, about 250 tariff lines were increased and 600 planned decreases abandoned. On average, the tariff increases were moderate (around 7 per cent) but there were some substantial increases. A 25 per cent tariff was imposed on various milk products, previously tariff free, to support PNG's first joint venture dairy enterprise, Ilimo Dairy Farm (Laveil 2019a). The 2019 budget included another 73 new and increased tariffs.

The increase in tariffs is unsurprising given the contraction in manufacturing over this period (8.2.2). A better policy would have been to tackle the underlying problems of exchange rate overvaluation and foreign exchange rationing (8.3.1).

The desire to expand domestic rice production has been a constant feature of post-independence policymaking. As Bourke et al. (2009, 168, 171) write:

> Since independence in 1975, plans for a domestic, import-replacement rice industry have been a feature of every government white paper on agriculture. Yet, since 1977, domestic rice production has never exceeded one per cent of the amount of rice imported … The most important reason that rice cultivation has not become significant in PNG is related to returns on people's labour. Returns to labour are higher in the production of root crops than in rice, both in terms of yield and food energy produced per hour worked [Bourke 2022]. Returns from growing coffee or cocoa are also higher than for growing rice in cash income per hour worked.

PNG's 2015 National Rice Policy promised a monopoly to a pioneer investor, and a USD2 billion foreign investment was announced the same year (Howes 2015b). It was not the first time that this particularly outrageous idea had appeared (Wrakuale 2012) and again it never got off the ground.

Protectionist policies over this period not only sought to keep imports out but also to encourage (or force) more downstream processing for export. A ban on log exports was announced in 2018 to take effect by 2020, the latest in a sequence of such commitments dating as far back as independence (7.1.3). Taxes on logs were increased in the 2017 budget (*RNZ* 2016) and again in the 2020, 2021 and 2022 budgets, before being cut in the 2024 one (Nanau 2020; Kuku 2023a). Logging volumes declined over this period, but analysis suggests a cessation of round log exports is unlikely any time soon (Figure B8; Filer 2022).

Domestic tuna processing had begun in the nineties (4.3.2). In addition to the two plants established in Madang (1994) and Wewak (2003), four more were set up in Lae: in 2006, 2013, 2015 and 2017 (Pacific Islands Forum Fisheries Agency 2021).[2] Onshore processing of tuna rose from 49,900 to 107,300 metric tonnes between 2010 and 2019, and employment rose from 7,100 to 12,500 over the same period (Ruaia, Gu'urau and Reid 2020).

The driver of this expansion is the ability of PNG to access the EU market duty free, escaping the standard 24 per cent tariff.[3] However, even with this concession, competition is tough (McQuillan 2017a), as reflected by the PNG government's decision to increase the import duty on canned tuna and other fish products from 10 to 25 per cent in January 2019.[4] Two canneries closed or reduced their operations in 2023, due to foreign exchange shortages among other factors (Giame 2023; Nangoi 2023).

PNG had incentivised the establishment of new plants via discounted license fees for ships to catch tuna at sea, but this meant that companies had an incentive to build rather than operate the plants. The introduction of a rebate was designed to increase plant utilisation. The rebate bill is over PGK100 million, making it an expensive job-creation scheme (*National* 2022; Katai

---

2   The 2015 plant was established for mackerel processing in 2012 and expanded production to include tuna in 2015.

3   This preference was first established under the Contonou Agreement between the ACP (African, Caribbean and Pacific) countries and the EU. When that expired in 2007, PNG and Fiji negotiated so-called 'interim' Economic Partnership Agreements.

4   Since 2014, the Philippines has also enjoyed duty-free access to the European Union (Canivel 2020).

2022). Even if we assume that all employment is due to the rebate, with employment of 12,500 workers, the annual subsidy per worker is about PGK7,000, roughly equal to their annual salary at the minimum wage.

PNG also benefited during this period from its participation in the Nauru Agreement, by which 10 Pacific nations agreed to collectively auction access to its fishing waters, resulting in a large increase in licensing fees, in the case of PNG from USD55 million in 2010 to USD133 million in 2019.

In 2019, the PNG parliament passed the Special Economic Zones Authority Act, the latest in a sequence of similar initiatives promising streamlined services and tax concessions. The new Act repealed the Industrial Centres Corporation Act of 1990 and the Free Trade Zones Act of 2000. Despite the poor track record of special economic zones in PNG in the past, Trade Minister Richard Maru called this 'probably the most important economic decision any government has made' (Myles 2023).

9.1.4 Resource sector policy

The push to give the state a more active role in the resource sector started in 2013 (7.1.3). There was more to come in subsequent years.

PNG had used its 18 per cent stake in Oil Search (gained in the late nineties, see 5.1.3) as collateral for a 2008 loan from an Abu Dhabi state-owned investment company to finance its equity share in the PNG LNG project. When the Abu Dhabi company decided in 2014 that it would exercise the option it had been given to retain those shares, Prime Minister O'Neill decided in the same year that PNG should rebuild its shareholding in Oil Search. An AUD1.2 billion loan was obtained from the Australian arm of the Swiss bank UBS to be taken out by Kumul Petroleum, to be paid back using PNG LNG dividends and to be used to buy 10 per cent of Oil Search. Treasurer Don Polye was opposed to the loan and was sacked as a result. The UBS loan was an expensive failure. The decision was taken to sell the newly acquired shares as early as 2015, but was not executed until after the 2017 elections (PNGi 2020). The loan, rationalised on the grounds of resource nationalism,[5] but lacking any clear justification and therefore giving rise

---

5   Oil Search (2019) said that the rationale for the loan was that 'the PNG Government wanted to maintain a shareholding in the country's biggest oil and gas company and the largest investor in-country'. O'Neill said at the time that: 'For the people not to own shares in their own company is completely out of mind for me to comprehend that people can even justify their argument' (Garrett 2014). The problem with this rationalisation is that the decision that PNG needed to hold shares in Oil Search was so quickly reversed.

to suspicion of corruption, was also costly for O'Neill. It caused national outrage, with protests and critiques around the loan's affordability and legality (Yala, Sanida and Mako 2014),[6] and led to a critical Ombudsman Commission (2018) report and, ultimately, a royal commission of inquiry. The latter described the deal as 'disastrous' and costed it at PGK902 million in fees and interest (GoPNG 2022, 1A–14, 15).

In the early 2000s, PNG had cut taxation rates in the resource sector, reducing corporate tax rates and abolishing the additional profits tax on new projects (4.3.2). Just over a decade later, the taxation regime was seen as too generous for mining and petroleum, and the 2017 budget reintroduced the additional profits tax (Department of Treasury 2016). It also removed the double deduction for exploration expenses (which had only been available in the mining sector). The same budget harmonised the treatment of petroleum and mineral projects, reducing the corporate tax rates on the former (harmonising them at 30 per cent), but making them also subject to the dividend withholding tax (now increased from 10 to 15 per cent) from which petroleum projects had previously been exempt (Department of Treasury 2016). The 2018 budget removed the tax deductibility on petroleum royalties (Department of Treasury 2017c).

Once James Marape took over as prime minister, radical reforms to the mining and petroleum regimes were tabled, including a move towards production-sharing arrangements—something the now mining minister Kerenga Kua had been arguing in favour of for a long time (Price 2012)—in which the key negotiating parameter would be the share of revenue going to government. This new approach would, it was envisaged, be administered by the two new national champions created in the previous decade (7.1.3): Kumul Petroleum and Kumul Mining (James 2019b). It was opposed by the PNG Chamber of Mining and Petroleum (2020), and, although a new bill was promised in 2020 to usher in the new regime,[7] the prime minister seemed to be less committed (*Business Advantage PNG* 2021a).

The Mining Amendment Act 2020 and the Oil and Gas Amendment Act 2020 were much more modest affairs, though they did continue the trend of building up national champions by allowing the government to

---

6   Although the loan was to be repaid by Kumul Petroleum, the company was still then being established and (perhaps for that reason) initially the loan was to the government, but outside of the normal budgetary approval process, thereby raising questions of legality.

7   The Organic Law on Papua New Guinea's Ownership and Development of Hydrocarbons and Minerals and the Commercialisation of State Businesses 2020 was drafted but not tabled.

preference state-owned entities when allocating prospective mining and petroleum sites (Merriam, Rowell and Kuman 2020; Leahy 2020). In 2021, Kumul Petroleum was awarded its first Petroleum Retention Licenses on various prospective gas fields, conveying the government's expectation that it should become an active developer of, rather than a passive investor in, resource projects (Kumul Petroleum 2021; Paul 2021).

All up, while PNG has long sought minority equity stakes in resource projects, and while not all recent plans have been implemented, developments starting in 2013 have resulted in the government taking a much more active stance in the resource sector, to the extent of it wanting its SOEs to become national champions and take the lead on extractive projects. This policy is certainly costly in terms of earnings foregone (8.3.2). Given weak governance and poor SOE performance, it is also highly risky.

This period also saw a continuation of earlier trends in relation to the greater localisation of resource project benefits, something that started in the nineties (4.3.2). One-third of the ownership of the Ok Tedi project, which had been nationalised in 2013 (7.1.3), was gifted to the provincial government of the region where the mine is located (the Western Province) and to landowners. As part of the negotiations around the extension of the Porgera gold mine 30-year lease (8.2.3), the royalty rate was increased from 2 to 3 per cent. The provincial government and landowners were together offered 15 per cent of the project's equity from PNG's new 51 per cent stake (given that the mine was already operating, PNG could extract a much better deal from the mine extension than from the original agreement). In 2022, the limit to which local investments could be made in lieu of tax payments through the tax credit system introduced in the early nineties (4.3.2) was increased from 1.25 to 2 per cent.

9.1.5 Land policy

A national land summit convened in 2005 had launched a push for voluntary customary land registration and leasing (7.1.4). This promising initiative floundered at the implementation phase. Problems included the complexities both of the new registration process and of customary ownership, as well as the weakness of the government machinery that was to administer the new regime. Several reviews of this land reform initiative (Duncan 2018; Kwapena 2021; Filer 2019a) indicate that, while there have been some positive developments, it is yet to deliver at scale. Filer (2019a, 76) writes:

By the end of 2016, the total area covered by land titles issued to land groups under the new legal regime was just over 100,000 hectares, about 0.2 per cent of PNG's total land area … [T]he 'bankability' of land titles granted to customary groups has turned out to be another illusion because the banks have refused to accept them as security for loans.

Another land summit was convened in 2019. This second summit criticised voluntary customary land registration for being 'long, cost[ly] and titles are not bankable' (Department of Lands and Physical Planning 2019). However, the summit failed to reach consensus on the way forward. With lease-leasebacks banned as a result of the land grab of the noughties (7.1.4) and voluntary registration not delivering, land reform was in the too-hard basket.

Also of interest from this period is the Land (Amendment) Bill of 2016 that would have prevented partially or fully foreign-owned companies and non-citizens from being granted state leases, and would have extinguished existing state leases to foreigners (Allens 2016). The draft never made it to parliament, but it is another symptom of the nationalist economic mood of the time.

9.2 Politics and governance

The politics of this period were dominated by Peter O'Neill, and by his successor as prime minister, James Marape. The country became increasingly litigious. New steps were taken to combat corruption, but with uncertain effect. This period was the first in which there was no change to decentralisation policy, but there was plenty of debate, and Bougainville voted almost unanimously for independence. More focus was given to violence against women and to the growing problem of sorcery-accusation-related violence. Geopolitics has not been a focus of this book, but PNG's geopolitical environment was transformed over this period.

9.2.1 Politics

The 2017 elections were worse than earlier elections. According to one report, the election was characterised by:

> widespread fraud and malpractice, including extensive vote rigging, coerced collective voting, and the hijacking and/or destruction of ballot boxes, political gifting and money politics which was qualitatively different to previous elections. (Haley and Zubrinich 2018, 92)

Two hundred and four election-related deaths were counted, double the number in 2002, previously thought of as the worst. One-third of voters said they were intimidated (Haley and Zubrinich 2018, 61). One long-time observer, Bill Standish, commented that 'popular democracy has been replaced by cynical manipulation by incumbents, their rivals and supporters alike' (Chandler 2018). No women at all were elected. Various proposals were once again (7.2.1) floated to reserve seats for women, but none got up (Sepoe 2021b).

The 2022 elections were described as 'disastrous' (Wood 2022; see also Wood, Laveil and Kabuni 2023). Two women were elected this time, and a third got up through a 2023 by-election.

Peter O'Neill served as prime minister from 2011 to mid-2019, making his tenure in PNG's top political position the second longest. When he first took power in 2011, albeit in controversial circumstances (7.2.1), he had a lot of support, not least because he brought a sense of energy and drive to the job that had been sorely lacking under Somare.[8] However, although he won the 2012 and 2017 elections, over time O'Neill lost support from both the public and from fellow members of parliament through a succession of polarising events: in 2014, the shutting down of the anti-corruption body Taskforce Sweep (9.2.3), the controversial and ill-fated UBS loan (9.1.4) and an unpopular attempt to amend the constitution to protect his position;[9] in 2016, UPNG student protests that ended in police shootings; and, throughout much of his rule, complicated legal manoeuvrings and personnel changes to avoid arrest (May 2022, Chapter 14). In the end, O'Neill finally resigned to avoid certain defeat in a vote of no confidence in June 2019.

O'Neill's eventual departure teaches us two things about PNG politics. First, PNG's egalitarian political culture will only tolerate the concentration of power in one person for so long. On his resignation from O'Neill's cabinet, Marape said that PNG was not a nation 'to be dominated by one

---

8   O'Neill himself said at the time: 'A lot of our people lost hope and trust that we leaders were capable of delivering. But now there is a generational change in the leadership, and people are expecting a big shift in the way we do business and manage the country. It's a time to hope again' (Callick 2012).
9   O'Neill got a series of amendments through parliament in 2013 to reduce the risks of being deposed (7.2.1); these were rejected by the Supreme Court in 2015. In 2014, he proposed a further constitutional amendment that would require that if a vote of no confidence was successful, then the new prime minister would have to come from the party with the largest number of seats in an election. However, this was widely opposed, including by Attorney General Kerenga Kua, who was sacked as a result, and it never got up (Cochrane 2014b).

person' (Nicholas 2019). O'Neill's fate was similar to that of Somare's in the eighties (3.2.1): his political longevity seemed to make him not less but more vulnerable. Second, it confirms our earlier argument that the resource boom was an aid to political stability (7.2.1). The end of the boom certainly undermined O'Neill's claim to power, and his repeated claims that his government was delivering prosperity rang increasingly hollow.

It is hard to see large policy differences between O'Neill and his successor, Marape. The latter has upped the rhetoric around economic nationalism and aspiration, including by committing to making PNG the world's richest black Christian nation by 2030 (12.5). Policies are similar between the two, except perhaps for Marape taking a harder line—or, rather, wanting to be seen as taking a harder line (8.2.3)—in relation to resource project negotiations, and a more realistic and transparent view in relation to the budget and the immediate health of the economy. The biggest difference is that Marape was willing to invite in the IMF (8.3.5), something O'Neill would not contemplate.

While O'Neill was defeated in 2019, he was down but not out. He was a driving force behind an almost successful bid to dislodge the government through a vote of no confidence in late 2019 and was the main contender against Marape for the position of prime minister at the 2022 elections, though, in the end, he was soundly defeated.

9.2.2 Public services

There was modest growth in government employment: by 8 per cent between 2015 and 2019 (Figure B16), the only years for which data are available. There was also significant growth in real wages paid to public servants (Howes 2020), a lagged effect from the boom. Payroll blowouts continued to be a problem throughout the period, with payments to civil servants regularly exceeding budgetary commitments. The worst example was in 2018, when employee compensation was budgeted at PGK4.1 billion but actuals revealed expenditure of PGK5.2 billion (Howes 2020). All in, the salary bill grew by 38 per cent after inflation between 2013 and 2019, while the real interest bill doubled. Salary and interest as a ratio of own revenue (revenue excluding aid) doubled, returning to and then exceeding its pre-boom high of 60 per cent in 2020 and 2021 before falling back to below 50 per cent due to the windfall revenue of 2022 (Figure 9.1).

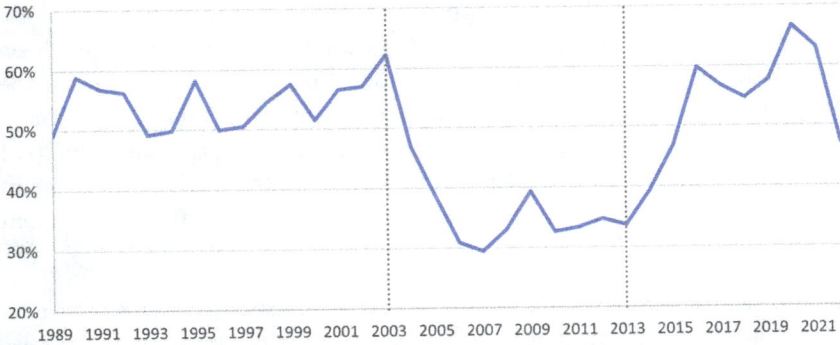

Figure 9.1: Salary and interest as a percentage of own revenue, 1989–2022
Note: Own revenue excludes foreign aid.
Source: PNG Economic Database.

The category of recurrent goods and services, that includes such essentials as drugs for hospitals and petrol for police cars, was crowded out. On a per person basis, this fell to PGK600 per person (in 2022 prices), not as low as the PGK400 reached in 2003, but still down from the PGK1,000-plus achieved in the eighties and during the boom (Figure 5.1).

A Public Expenditure and Financial Accountability assessment was carried out in 2016. PNG failed on 21 of 30 dimensions, making the country's public financial management the fourth worst of the 24 developing countries reviewed (Fellows and Leonardo 2016) and showing deterioration compared to earlier, similar assessments. Weaknesses exposed included poor control over budget execution, lack of bank reconciliations and lack of audit reports. One particular problem is the end-of-year expenditure rush. In 2020, 64 per cent of non-salary, non-interest expenditure was booked to the last quarter, and much of this was actually spent in the next year (Igara, Kamit and Howes 2021, 35).

Childhood immunisation rates rose over the nineties and stabilised over the noughties but fell precipitously over the tens, putting PNG in last spot in a global league table of immunisation rankings (Figure 10.6 and Table 10.14). This was likely due to a combination of funding cuts, the secular decline in the quality of rural health services and the increasing shift in political attention to constituency funding, which favours projects over services.

In the previous period, legislation had been passed in 2013 to sideline (for a second time) the Public Services Commission (PSC) in the selection of departmental heads, provincial administrators and heads of statutory authorities (7.2.2). The PSC appealed these changes, and in 2019 the Supreme Court ruled that proper legislative processes had not been followed, and that the legislation therefore was invalid. This returned the PSC to its central role in the appointment and termination of the contracts of the heads of departments given to it under 2003 legislation. The 2013 legislation had also increased the retirement age to 65. With its annulment, the retirement age was returned to 60 (Elapa 2019). In 2020, the retirement age was once again increased to 65.

This court challenge by the Public Services Commission, as well as O'Neill's own appeals to the court during his tenure as prime minister (9.2.1) are symptoms of PNG's shift towards a highly litigious society. Kama (2017) describes PNG as 'one of the most litigious societies in the world'. Many politicians go to court if they are unsuccessful at elections or to challenge parliamentary manoeuvres. But the recourse to the courts is widespread. 'Local landowners are well aware of their rights over land and highly litigious when they are aggrieved' (Macintyre and Foale 2004, 233).

The reliance on the courts helps keep the peace, but is also costly. May (2022, 211–12) notes the:

> increased costs to the government of maintaining the judicial system, a huge demand for compensation payments by the state and a substantial outsourcing by the state of legal services to private legal firms.

There is an enormous backlog of cases: about 25,000 before the National and Supreme Court in 2020 (*Post-Courier* 2020). Litigation in PNG is 'an expensive and drawn-out process, sometimes taking years for a decision to be handed down' (US State 2022).

The process often pits one part of government against another. In 2017, one of the ICCC commissioners complained that 'litigious SOEs' would often resort to the courts because their 'incentive is to "game" rather than "perform" in the public interest' (Manoka and Rodrigues 2013). The inquiry set up by the defence minister to investigate the Moti affair (7.2.6) was taken to the courts by both the prime minister and the defence secretary. Nelson (2007a, 9) comments:

> This is asking the courts to resolve what should be sorted out by the coalition politicians and their senior public servants. In most democracies it would be unthinkable for the courts to be engaged in such internecine detail.

A high level of litigation goes with a common failure of government institutions to go 'by the book', or what one commentator calls an 'indifference to law and procedures' (Nelson 2007a, 11). The public service commissioner was able to succeed in 2019 in his judicial bid to overturn the 2013 reforms to sideline the PSC because some of the legislation under question had been circulated two weeks prior to its tabling in parliament rather than the mandatory one month (Supreme Court 2019; Kolma 2019).

The frequent resort to the legal system also has a darker side. Some police are available for hire to the highest bidder: those who are powerful and hostile enough can now arrange for an arrest, regardless of the grounds (Howes 2018a, 2018b).

New authorities continued to be created, often with donor encouragement —for example, the National Energy Authority in 2021, established with support from USAID. There was little by way of rationalisation. The Insurance Act 1974 established the Office of Insurance Commissioner, which reports to the treasurer. Much later, the 2000 Life Insurance Act gave the job of regulating life insurance to the central bank. PNG, even though its insurance sector is small, may be the only country to regulate general and life insurance separately. BPNG (2007, 20) delicately commented on the 'difficulties in effectively regulating the insurance industry', given two different regulators and the 'difficulty in determining who regulates composite policies which contain characteristics of both life and general insurance'. The government's 2018–30 Financial Sector Development Strategy included a commitment to abolish the Office of Insurance Commissioner and give the job of regulating all insurance to BPNG, but nothing has been done so far by way of implementation.

9.2.3 Corruption

While these things are hard to measure, many claimed that corruption reached new heights under O'Neill. Former prime minister Mekere Morauta had retired from politics in 2012; he returned in 2017 on a mission 'to undo the damage of the past five years', in particular, to remove Peter O'Neill. He commented that 'corruption is on a scale never witnessed before' and noted 'the weakening, destruction and politicisation of institutions of state and systems and processes, a lack of respect for the rule of law, and the crushing of dissent' (Morauta 2017).

Certainly O'Neill embodied the merging of the business and political classes in PNG, a phenomenon apparent for decades (3.2.1). According to Institute of National Affairs head Paul Barker, with O'Neill as prime minister:

> there was no such thing as conflict of interest … His business enterprises were burgeoning. He was clearly spending a lot of his working hours advancing his business interests, rather than the government's interests. (McDonald 2022)

The anti-corruption body Task Force Sweep, established by O'Neill in 2011, was disbanded by him after the taskforce's investigations led, in mid-2014, to an arrest warrant being issued against the prime minister himself in relation to payments said to be authorised by him in relation to payments made for legal services not rendered, one of the previous period's massive scams (7.2.3). O'Neill challenged the arrest in court, sacked the police commissioner (Cochrane 2014a) and disbanded the task force. When he did so, he resurrected a commitment that goes back to the eighties to institute an anti-corruption commission (3.2.3). This was finally delivered on by his successor, James Marape, in 2020, when the legislation to establish the Independent Commission Against Corruption (ICAC) was unanimously passed. The Ombudsman Commission took the ICAC legislation to the Supreme Court saying that it was unconstitutional but lost the case. In July 2023, three foreigners were announced as ICAC commissioners. Unfortunately, the next year it was revealed they were accusing each other of corrupt behaviour (*Post-Courier* 2024).

In 2015, PNG passed the Anti-Money Laundering and Counter Terrorist Financing Act. This required banks to monitor the accounts of 'politically exposed persons', under the supervision of the newly established Financial Analysis and Supervision Unit (FASU), which was shifted from the police—where the Financial Intelligence Unit had been established in 2008—to the central bank. PNG had been placed on the international money laundering 'grey list' in 2014, but was removed in 2016 following passage of the Act. However, while FASU has been active, the lack of cases resulting from its investigations puts PNG at risk of once again being grey listed. A major focus of FASU is government spending, based on its own—completely unsubstantiated and certainly exaggerated—claim that 'approximately 25–50% of the government budget is misappropriated every year' (PNG FIU 2011). Cumbersome procedures to combat fraud are, as a result, imposed on banks. For example, contract payments require tender documentation, project proposal and proof that the relevant milestone has been met.

In 2018, a new National Procurement Commission was legislated and given responsibility for nearly all national procurement, including by government authorities. The theory is that central control would reduce corruption; the reality is long delays on critical projects (*LoopPNG* 2023).

These were the most significant of a number of anti-corruption initiatives, such as government corruption hot lines, joining of the international Extractive Industries Transparency Initiative, and legislation to protect whistleblowers and make unexplained wealth an offence under the Proceeds of Crime Act (UNODC 2022). These are all potentially positive developments, but their impact on the ground is more complex; the risk is that increasingly stringent procedures will add to delays but will not, in the end, reduce corruption and improve service delivery.

9.2.4 Decentralisation and Bougainville

This is the only one of our four periods in which there was no major policy shift on decentralisation. One was attempted but it was not seen through. As in earlier periods, there was no shortage of dissatisfaction with current arrangements. O'Neill commissioned a major policy review from the Constitutional and Law Reform Commission (CLRC), which reported in 2015, advising in favour of a new (third) Organic Law on Decentralisation that would:

> abolish local governments, relying instead on the DDAs [District Development Authorities, created in the noughties, see 7.2.4]. It would restore provincial elections, but the provincial MPs would remain as governors. And it would allow for more autonomy for those provinces who wanted it and were capable of exercising it. (Howes, Sause and Ugye 2022, 68)

However, these proposals were opposed by provincial MPs threatened by the restoration of provincial elections. Although the CLRC report was eventually endorsed by Marape's government in 2020, there appears to be a stalemate, and no legislation had been introduced as of the time of writing. The fact that a number of provincial governors have gone to the courts alleging that DDAs are unconstitutional (*Post-Courier* 2022a) is indicative of the divide between provincial and district (open) MPs.

Greater provincial autonomy remained a popular theme with governors, but, while a few memoranda of understanding were signed with select provinces (New Ireland, East New Britain, Enga), little has been done in practical terms to advance it. New Ireland put forward a charter of fiscal autonomy, under which it would become responsible for tax collection in the province, and amendments to the constitution to authorise the granting of autonomy to select provinces (Anis 2022); however, at the time of writing, these proposals remain just that.

Meanwhile, decentralisation via constituency funding has continued apace. Constituency funds had to be wound back following the end of the boom, but were still kept much higher than before the boom (Figure A1).

Bougainville voted overwhelmingly for independence in a non-binding 2019 referendum (with 97.7 per cent in favour). While Marape has taken a more conciliatory tone to Bougainville independence than O'Neill—who claimed that every PNG MP would vote against secession (Wiseman 2021)—he is still not supportive of it. Without national government support, the prospects for independence are remote (Carrick 2021).

9.2.5 Law and order

Much of what was true of the previous period—stabilisation of urban crime at a high level and growing concerns around heavily armed tribal warfare (7.2.5)—applies to this one as well. While violence was reduced in some parts of the Highlands, it increased in others. Main (2023b, 24) provides insight into the high level of violence when he writes, of one Highlands province, Hela, that:

> Land boundaries between clans is a highly contested affair, and conflict often breaks out between two individuals in a land dispute. Conflict between individuals can escalate, and those individuals can, in certain instances, each raise a small legion of supporters to assist them. These conflicts can be deadly, involving major gun battles and razing homes, schools, and any and all infrastructure associated with the opposing side. Disputes can take years or decades to resolve, and almost the entire landscape is haunted by either unresolved or active conflict. Political elites sometimes garner support by arming their supporters and assisting them in their disputes. Police, who have clan ties themselves, may sell ammunition and, sometimes, weaponry to their clansmen.

Hostage taking became a new risk for expatriates in parts of the Highlands, especially around Hela, home to the PNG LNG project (Main 2023a).

One remarkable feature of this period was the growth in the number of security guards. The total had grown slowly from 12,400 in 2006 to 16,800 in 2014 but then took off to reach 31,300 in 2018 (Walton and Dinnen 2020). One explanation for this growth trajectory, which hardly seems consistent with a growth slowdown, is that this is a count of guards working for licensed security companies, and that, over time, more companies have submitted to regulation. Given that there are fewer than 5,000 police, it is evident that, at least in urban areas, security has largely become a private matter.

Evidence that businesses were getting on top of crime came in 2017 in the latest of a series of business surveys. Similar surveys in 2002, 2007 and 2012 had all rated law and order as businesses' top concern, but in 2017 it was only their seventh (Figure 12.2). That said, the 'Black Wednesday' riots of 10 January 2024 in Port Moresby—catalysed by a police strike—saw widespread looting, arson, rapes and assault, and an estimated 22 deaths, and likely pushed insecurity back up the list of business concerns.

Moreover, it is not clear that crime has become less of a concern for the ordinary person. To the contrary, some provincial towns once thought of as relatively safe places came to be experienced by local residents as unsafe (Baroi 2023; Bungtabu 2023).

A positive feature of this period was the growing attention given to the deep problem of violence against women. This is not a new issue. PNG's Law Reform Commission published a series of reports in 1985 demonstrating the extent of the problem. There is no evidence that the incidence of violence against women is waning, indeed some say it is getting worse, but the growing attention to this problem from various non-government organisations, the police, business and politicians over this period was a welcome development.

Another problem that received increased attention was sorcery-accusation-related violence (SARV). The most comprehensive research has found that SARV is a 'a sustained and recurrent problem' in PNG, and that 'it is entering new geographical areas' (Forsyth et al. 2019, 4–5). The authors found that:

> SARV causes both immediate and long-term harm in multiple ways. Accusations without violence can be stigmatising and lead to social isolation and ongoing insecurity. Victims refer to it as a birthmark or scar that brands them for life … Physical violence against accused

sorcerers ranges from threats and tying up, to torture over multiple days and death ... It destroys social cohesion through eroding trust, and creates contexts in which suspicion and fear fester. (6–7)

They identify the underlying causes of SARV as:

a magical worldview in which the spirit world intervenes in the physical through human agency ... poverty ... inequality, including resentment about inequality ... declining education and health systems; polygamy; weak law and order; legal and moral pluralism; normalisation of violence ... and gender inequality. (9–10)

Proximate factors include 'land disputes, economic jealousy within the extended family, ongoing intra-clan feuds/revenge cycles, epidemics, food shortages, and election violence' and triggers 'most frequently involve a death (particularly of a child), a sickness, or a misfortune (money or goods disappearing, a business failing, etc.)' (9–10). While 'sorcery beliefs and violent practices' are 'entrenched and widespread' (32), so too are the actions of many individuals and organisations to prevent and respond to them (21–9).

9.2.6 Changing geopolitical environment

PNG's geopolitical environment changed dramatically over this period with the rise of China. By 2018, China was as important a destination for PNG exports as Australia and, while Australia remained the most important source of imports, China was catching up (Figure 9.2).

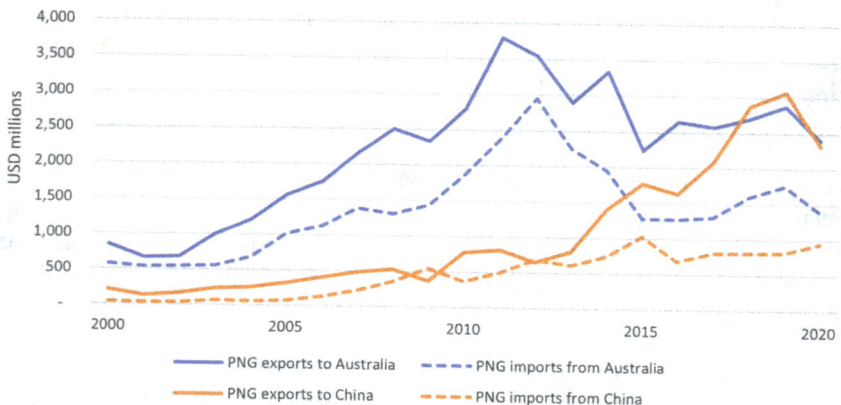

Figure 9.2: PNG exports to and imports from Australia and China, 2000–20
Source: Comtrade.

Investment from China grew in importance, as did the Chinese diaspora. The number of Chinese in PNG grew from only 5,000 in 2007 (including 3,000 of Chinese ethnicity born in PNG) to about 20,000 in 2020, mainly driven by new arrivals from China (Liu 2022). This is about double the number of Australians in PNG, which is estimated at about 10,000 (Australian Department of Foreign Affairs and Trade n.d.). Chin (2024, 89) has argued that the Chinese community 'were the biggest beneficiary of the sell-off of white businesses after Independence and after the dramatic fall in the value of the kina in the 1990s' and that new Chinese migrants have 'become the largest investors outside the oil and gas sectors'.

PNG signed up to Beijing's Belt and Road Initiative in 2018. While China has become an infrastructure financier, it has not become a major creditor. The more important role has been played by Chinese companies as infrastructure contractors on government- or multilateral-financed projects.

PNG has also benefited from Australia's greater generosity in its dealings with its former colony in response to fears about China, especially that it might seek to establish a military base. This has extended from providing an undersea cable free of charge (9.1.1), to providing massive and at times unconditional budget support (8.3.5). Other Western countries have also 'stepped up', including the United States, which in 2023 signed a new military agreement with PNG.

9.3 Conclusion

KK Kingston, founded in 1972 in Lae, is a household name in PNG and a leading producer of household goods, paper products and cooking oil. It employs some 800 staff. In 2015, the CEO was quoted as saying: 'It is increasingly difficult for businesses like KK Kingston to obtain foreign currency as and when we need it' (*Business Advantage PNG* 2015). In October 2016, the company announced it was laying off 10 per cent of its workforce. Michael Kingston, CEO and son of the company's founder, highlighted 'lower economic activities in the mining, petroleum, resources and other economic generating activities in the country' (Bailey 2016). Three years later, he commented on the mistakes made in the last boom in which, he says, Kingston 'over-invested in assets and capacity … and we took on too much debt in anticipation of sustained growth that didn't eventuate'. Now, by contrast, the company is 'avoiding additional investment, reducing debt and looking to eke out more efficiencies' (James 2019a).

The quiet bust was not a good period for PNG. Non-resource GDP growth was the lowest recorded for our four periods, and it was the only period in which formal sector employment consistently fell.

This period also stands out for very different macroeconomic outcomes compared to the other periods, including a record current account surplus and fiscal deficits, and record low imports and resource revenue (all controlling for GDP).

The bust was caused by a precipitous decline in revenue flowing to government from the resource sector that caught both government and businesses unaware. Businesses, finding themselves with excess capacity, went into retrenchment mode. A lack of new resource projects, higher costs due to a lagged Dutch disease and the pandemic intensified and elongated the downturn. The central bank made things worse by introducing foreign exchange rationing, and not allowing the exchange rate to adjust.

This abandonment of currency convertibility was the biggest policy change of the period. It compressed imports, encouraged fiscal profligacy, discouraged foreign investors, and induced rent-seeking to get to the front of the queue. Although it is an unusual strategy, PNG is not the only country to engage in foreign exchange rationing for a prolonged period. A 2020 study of Ethiopia, a relatively successful African economy, found that:

> the main binding constraint on the country's economic growth is the shortage of foreign exchange (forex). The forex shortage chokes output in nearly all sectors of Ethiopia's economy ... Stakeholder interviews repeatedly emphasized the time and opportunity costs associated with securing forex and the government's unpredictable prioritization and allocation of forex uses. (Deren and Motamed 2020, 6–7)

Much the same could be said about PNG. Recent reforms to reduce the extent of rationing (8.3.1) notwithstanding, rebuilding confidence in the kina will be difficult, as its prolonged non-convertibility has made it an undesirable currency to hold.

Economic nationalism was growing in PNG before the boom ended and the bust began, but the poor growth performance during the bust period no doubt added strength to the argument that something new was needed— that PNG is missing out if not being exploited, that tariffs need to be increased, that more sectors need to be reserved for national businesses and that national champions need to be created in the resource sector. However, most of these policies have been tried before in the eighties. The notion of national champions is new, but it seems neither affordable nor sensible. Indeed, such policies may worsen the investment climate. The saving grace is that the rhetoric has been more nationalistic than the actual policy, which has been tempered by pragmatism.

The quiet bust ended in 2022 with record-high commodity prices, increased resource revenue and, at last, higher growth. It is too early to say what period PNG is in now. At the time of writing, foreign exchange rationing has been reduced but not ended, and business leaders still speak of a lack of confidence (Esila 2023). The PNG economy is out of the bust, but not out of the woods.

Part V: Overview and conclusion

Fear not the past, learn from it, and let's move on and step up to the future!

—James Marape, in his maiden speech upon becoming prime minister in 2019 (*Business Advantage PNG* 2019)

Given its fortunate resource endowment, its early aspirations, and its generally sound beginnings, why has Papua New Guinea's economic performance been so disappointing, and what are its future prospects? (May [1997] 2001, 315)

10

Trends and patterns

What we thought should happen, has not happened ... We wanted to see our people healthy, educated and properly fed, like citizens of any sovereign nation in the world. My vision for Papua New Guineans was that they should be able to stand on their own two feet, to do business, as well as other meaningful activities in life, so that they could lead decent lives. Lives that were better than those of their ancestors.

—Minister for Foreign Affairs Michael Somare (2000, 125–7)

New resource projects have been developed. The oil palm and fresh food industries have developed. Small service industries have flourished not just in towns but all over the country ... There is growing Papua New Guinean ownership of business. A national entrepreneurial class is developing ... But in some areas Papua New Guinea has not done as well as it should. We have not made the most of our resources and our wealth ... We have not achieved sustained economic growth, the necessary basis for providing widespread, quality services to people, and for creating income-earning opportunities for our very large population of young people.

—Prime Minister Mekere Morauta (2000, 3)

10.1 Introduction

The economic history of PNG since independence is an important and absorbing story. The most recent histories were written before 2010 and are now out of date. The experience of another decade and a half adds new chapters to PNG's economic history and provides new perspectives on earlier periods.

This final part of the book brings the preceding four together. This chapter compares the four periods across various dimensions of economic performance. The next two link economic outcomes to policies and to institutions, respectively.

An important contribution of the book is the division of PNG's post-independence economic history into four parts, the eighties (1975–88), the nineties (1989–2003), the noughties (2004–13) and the tens (2014–22). The book so far has presented PNG's economic history chronologically, one period after another. This chapter provides a more explicit comparison between, and overview of, the four periods and also tries, at least cursorily, to fill in some of the gaps that remain. It starts with population, economic growth and employment. It then goes to the changing structure of the economy, commodity prices and the government resource take, which are key to any understanding of PNG growth. Subsequent sections examine the resource sector, agriculture, trade and the balance of payments, the financial sector, the exchange rate and inflation, fiscal outcomes and service delivery. We conclude with a summary comparison of the four periods, and an overall, internationally informed assessment.

10.2 Population, economic growth and employment

The more than tripling of PNG's population (Figure B1) is perhaps the biggest national change since independence. Data on PNG's population are weak, and the last reliable census was undertaken in 2001 (Connell 1997, 168; Bourke and Allen 2021). Such data as there are suggest population growth is rapid (Table 10.1), about equal to the average for Sub-Saharan Africa in recent years. Some claim that the population is higher than the figures traditionally used (and relied upon in this book). A UN Population Fund study claimed, using satellite data, that PNG's population was 17 million; the study's estimate was subsequently reduced in 2023 to 11.8 million and adopted by PNG's National Statistical Office (Kuku 2023b). It is possible that all early censuses were underestimates and/or that population growth has been higher than estimated over some or all of the post-independence period.

Table 10.1: Population over the four periods

	Eighties	Nineties	Noughties	Tens	1975–2022
Population (first and last year) (millions)	2.8, 3.8	3.9, 5.6	5.8, 7.3	7.5, 9.3	
Average population growth	2.4%	2.7%	2.7%	2.7%	2.6%

Note: The periods are defined as the eighties (1975–88), the nineties (1989–2003), the noughties (2004–13) and the tens (2014–22).
Source: PNG Economic Database.

In 1991, PNG launched a population policy. It aimed to increase contraceptive prevalence to 63 per cent by 2020. The 2016–18 Demographic and Health Survey revealed that just over one-third of married women aged 15–49 used contraceptives, despite the fact that nearly half said they wanted no more children. On average, in that survey, married women said they wanted three children, and married men 3.6, both well below the fertility rate of 4.4 (Pandey and Howes 2022). Only a few leaders have supported the idea that the fertility rate is a problem (e.g. Samana 1988). Although there have been two more population policies after the first, backing for family planning has never been strong (Connell 1997, 172–5). The still popular *Vision 2050* (National Strategic Plan Taskforce 2009) said that PNG's high population growth rate was acceptable and made no mention of the need to expand the use of contraception.

PNG is an extremely rural country. Official figures (World Bank Group n.d.-a) show that about 14 per cent of the population lives in urban areas, a share virtually unchanged from independence and the lowest of all countries in the world.

The number of non-citizen residents fell sharply from independence levels, with censuses recording 50,500 non-citizens in 1971, 32,760 in 1980 and 20,882 in 2011 (Nelson 2007b; NSO 2015).[1] The number has certainly risen more recently, with worker arrivals increasing (8.2.3) and an estimated 20,000 Chinese alone now resident in PNG (9.2.6).

---

1   Figures for other census years for the non-citizen population are 25,620 in 1990 and 19,235 in 2000 (Nelson 2007b).

GDP and non-resource GDP growth are close in the first two periods, and almost identical for the post-independence era as a whole, at 3 and 3.1 per cent, respectively (though not for exactly the same period, as non-resource GDP growth is only available from 1983). In the boom, non-resource GDP growth was, on average, 1 percentage point higher than GDP growth as rising commodity prices and PNG LNG construction stimulated output in the non-resource sector. During the quiet bust, non-resource GDP growth was only half of GDP growth, as, while PNG LNG exports boomed, resource revenue to government declined.

Table 10.2: Growth and employment — period averages

	Eighties	Nineties	Noughties	Tens	1976*–2022
GDP growth	1.5%	2.9%	4.5%	3.8%	3.0%
GDP growth volatility	2.5%	6.8%	3.2%	4.9%	4.9%
Non-resource GDP growth	1.3%	2.7%	5.6%	2.0%	3.1%
GDP per person growth	–1.0%	0.2%	1.7%	1.1%	0.4%
Non-resource GDP per person growth	–1.0%	0.0%	2.8%	–0.7%	0.4%
Employment growth	2.1%	0.6%	5.0%	–1.3%	1.5%

Notes: *GDP begins in 1976, employment in 1978 and non-resource GDP in 1983. Employment is only in the formal sector and excludes the public service. All these GDP growth rates are real (using the appropriate deflator). Volatility is measured by the standard deviation.
Source: PNG Economic Database.

Given the capital-intensive and enclave nature of the largely foreign-owned resource sector, non-resource GDP per person is our preferred measure of national economic activity and the closest thing we have in the book to a measure of average living standards. Growth in it was negative or zero in all periods except the boom, when it grew at an average of 2.8 per cent. The annual average growth for this variable for the post-independence period as a whole is just 0.4 per cent per year.

Formal sector employment (Figure B16) is another proxy for living standards. It it is also less than population growth, except in the third, boom period. The share of foreign workers in the total workforce is growing (8.2.3), and, if we take that into account, growth in the employment of nationals must be even slower.

Data on private sector wages are only available for the eighties, where there was a slight decline in average wages controlling for inflation (McGavin 1993, Table 3.6), and for this century (Blunch and Davies 2024). With wage deregulation and high inflation, real wages must have fallen sharply over the nineties. Adjusting for inflation, and depending on the estimation method used, private sector wages fell rapidly by an average of 7.6–8.6 per cent a year between 1999 and 2002, then grew rapidly during the boom years (7.9–8.4 per cent between 2003 and 2013), but then fell by 0.6–0.8 per cent a year on average from 2014 to 2018, the most recent year for which data are available (Blunch and Davies 2024).

Government salaries were protected in the eighties by indexation (McGavin 1993, Table 3.7), fell sharply in the nineties and then increased this century. Comparisons of average government salaries in the eighties and in the tens suggest very little change. McGavin reports an average government salary of PGK54,000 (converted into 2022 prices) for 1991 (McGavin 1993, Table 3.7), and more recent data give an average of PGK56,700 for 2019.[2]

Of course, these are imperfect measures, and we say more about the non-income dimensions of living standards later in this chapter (10.11) and about income inequality in the next (11.8). But, as per the Morauta quote with which this chapter began, only sustained economic growth can provide 'the material basis for achieving high levels of the basics of human wellbeing' (Pritchett 2022).

10.3 The structure of the economy

The growing importance of the resource sector relative to the rest of the economy (increasing resource dependency) is one of the biggest changes in PNG since independence (Figure B3). The average share of the resource sector in nominal GDP has increased in every period, from 10 per cent in the first, to 26 per cent in the last (Table 10.3). The agriculture, forestry and fishing sector makes up about a quarter of non-resource GDP (Figure B4). Manufacturing represents a small and declining share. Construction is the most rapidly growing sector, with growth during the boom doubling its share of non-resource GDP, which has stayed high since. Wholesale and retail trade, and transport have both become less important.

---

2   Combining the government payroll with the published number of government staff.

Table 10.3: The structure of the economy — period averages

	Eighties		Nineties		Noughties		Tens		1980*–2022	
	Growth	Share	Growth	Share	Growth	Share	Growth	Share	Growth	Share
Resource sector		10.4%	3.5%	16.8%	-0.6%	20.3%	11.8%	25.9%	5.1%	18.2%
Non-resource sectors (as share of non-resource GDP)										
Agriculture, forestry and fishing	1.6%	22.8%	2.9%	24.4%	3.3%	25.4%	2.1%	23.9%	2.6%	24.2%
Manufacturing	1.6%	4.4%	1.2%	4.0%	4.3%	3.1%	-0.5%	2.4%	1.6%	3.5%
Utilities	3.1%	0.7%	2.8%	0.9%	5.3%	1.3%	3.2%	1.4%	3.9%	1.0%
Construction	-3.2%	3.0%	7.9%	4.3%	10.2%	9.0%	-0.9%	9.1%	4.9%	6.1%
Wholesale and retail	5.0%	19.0%	0.5%	17.5%	4.2%	14.6%	1.5%	12.9%	2.3%	16.2%
Transport	6.3%	6.7%	-1.0%	6.8%	6.3%	3.4%	-0.6%	2.9%	1.8%	5.2%

Notes: *Shares start in 1980, and growth rates in 1983. Growth is adjusted for inflation using the appropriate deflator. First period resource sector growth is excluded as it is only from 1983 to 1988, from just before the opening of Ok Tedi to just before the closing of Panguna. It shows annual average growth of 10.1 per cent which is unrealistically high for the entire 1975–88 period.

Source: PNG Economic Database.

10.4 Commodity prices and exports

PNG is a commodity exporter, and its commodity exports have increased significantly since independence (Figure B5), from an average of 23 per cent of GDP in the first period to 32 per cent in the second to around 40 per cent in the third and fourth (Table 10.4). Moreover, PNG is increasingly a resource exporter, with the average share of resources in total commodity exports (Figure B6) increasing from 56 per cent in the first period to 84 per cent in the last. Fluctuations and trends in global commodity, and especially resource, prices are therefore fundamental to PNG's economic performance.

Table 10.4: Commodity prices and exports — period averages

	Eighties	Nineties	Noughties	Tens	1976*–2022
Commodity exports/GDP	22.9%	32.1%	39.5%	39.3%	32.5%
Share of resources in commodity exports	56.0%	72.1%	78.0%	83.9%	73.2%
Export price indices (2012 = 1)					
All commodities index					
Average	0.70	0.42	0.87	0.90	0.68
Growth	–2.5%	–1.4%	8.1%	2.2%	1.2%
Resource index					
Average	0.40	0.34	0.87	0.91	0.58
Growth	1.2%	–0.1%	9.8%	2.3%	2.3%
Non-resource index					
Average	1.76	0.78	0.86	0.85	1.08
Growth	–5.6%	–3.4%	2.6%	1.0%	–1.2%
Government resource take (ratio of government resource revenue to resource GDP)	16.6%	14.5%	22.9%	5.9%	15.1%

Note: *Government resource take starts in 1980.

Source: Index constructed by authors using price data from the World Bank and commodity data from PNG Economic Database (see Figure B12 for details).

Table 10.4 also summarises trends in our PNG commodity export price index (Figure B12). Resource and agricultural price indices have behaved differently. The non-resource commodity price index fell over the first two periods before only partially recovering in the third. This was especially damaging to growth in the first period when agricultural exports were almost as important as resource ones. The resource index was broadly flat in the first two periods, before rising sharply in the third, and, on average, even higher in the fourth, despite the dip in resource prices at the end of the boom. The all commodity price index fell from the eighties to the nineties but reached new highs in the noughties and tens.

The fact that commodity prices were falling over the first two periods helps explain their low growth. And the main reason for the acceleration of economic growth at the start of the third period is that commodity (specifically, resource) prices rose to a new high. Commodity price trends provide a less convincing explanation for the growth slowdown in the fourth period because the commodity price index stayed high; indeed, on average, it was higher in the fourth period than the third.

High resource prices are a necessary but not sufficient condition for economic growth in PNG. Prices have to be high in relation to resource projects that, if they yield high profits, yield high government revenue. We call these 'revenue-ready' projects (6.2.1). A variable that captures this is also shown in Table 10.4 (and Figure B26), namely the government resource take or the ratio of government resource revenue to resource GDP (Davies and Schröder 2022). This is about 50 per cent higher during the boom than in the earlier two periods. Although commodity prices stayed high in the fourth period, the government resource take plummeted in this period—down to 5.9 per cent, less than half of the post-independence average of 15.1 per cent—ending the boom and helping to explain the bust that followed.

10.5 The resource sector

Growth in the resource sector can be measured in different ways. We have already seen that, in real terms, the sector has grown at an annual average rate of 5.1 per cent since independence (Table 10.3). The information content of this estimate is limited, however, by the huge changes in composition of the resource bundle (Figures B10 and B11), and by its non-consideration of changing prices (Figure B14). As Table 10.5 shows, gold and copper were of roughly equal importance in the first period. Ok Tedi and Panguna produced both. In the nineties, gold production almost tripled as first Porgera and then Lihir came on line, whereas copper production stabilised as, although Ok Tedi expanded, Panguna was closed. Oil production started and peaked in the nineties, accounting for 30 per cent of resource exports in that period. Oil production halved in the noughties and halved again in the tens. Nickel and cobalt mining started in 2013–14 as did, more importantly, LNG production, which is now half of total resource exports. Gold is another third, and the remaining one-sixth is divided up between copper, nickel and cobalt, and oil.

Another way to measure growth in the resource sector is to value it in terms of domestic currency, adjusted for inflation (Figure B15). This is also shown in Table 10.5, which reveals that, adjusted for inflation, resource exports grew sixfold between the first and last period, again corresponding to an annual average growth rate of about 5 per cent. The real value of copper exports is about the same as at independence, but gold exports have almost increased fourfold, and petroleum exports, which were absent at independence, are now worth more than three times the value of all first period resource exports.

Table 10.5: Resource exports — period averages

	Eighties			Nineties			Noughties			Tens			1976*–2022		
	Volume	Share	Value	Volume	Share	Value	Volume	Share	Value	Volume	Share	Value	Volume	Share	Value
Gold	24	53%	2,851	56	46%	5,245	59	47%	8,842	61	33%	9,466	48	46%	6,228
Copper	179	47%	2,207	171	24%	2,541	167	28%	5,648	84	7%	2,067	159	29%	3,036
Nickel and cobalt	-	-	-	-	-	-	2	1%	88	31	6%	2,139	5	1%	438
Crude oil	-	-	-	22,674	30%	3,810	11,293	25%	4,786	6,366	5%	1,627	11,058	16%	2,601
LNG/ condensate	-	-	-	-	-	-	-	-	-	9,598	48%	15,467	1,493	7%	3,026
All resources		100%	5,060		100%	11,595		100%	19,364		100%	30,766		100%	15,330

Notes: *Shares and values start in 1977. Silver and alluvial gold are excluded as they are not available for all years. Volumes are in tonnes for gold, thousands of tonnes for copper, nickel and cobalt and thousands of barrels for oil and LNG/condensate. Values are measured in kina million in 2022 prices. Shares are measured by value.

Source: PNG Economic Database.

10.6 Agriculture

Growth in the value of agricultural commodity exports has been much slower than of resource exports (Figure B15 and Table 10.6).

Overall, production of traditional cash crops, other than palm oil, has stagnated or fallen (Figure B7). The production of copra, copra oil, rubber and tea has declined since independence, while that of coffee and cocoa has stagnated (Table 10.6). One reason traditional cash crops have not done well is that their purchasing power has fallen. Adjusting for inflation, in the last period, coffee and cocoa prices were less than one-half of their value in the first period (Figure B13). Nevertheless, these crops remain very important to PNG households. According to the 2016–18 Demographic and Household Survey, some 25 per cent of households grow coffee, 20 per cent cocoa and 16 per cent copra.

Palm oil, log exports and fish production have all grown rapidly (Figure B8), and between them now make up two-thirds of PNG's non-resource commodity exports (Figure B9). Non-traditional cash crops ('other agricultural products', such as vanilla) have also done well and make up another 10 per cent.

These bright spots have to be distinguished between. Despite rapid growth, log exports cannot be considered a success with only modest revenue for government and few local benefits. In the words of a World Bank (2004, 23) report:

> Logging has ... little long term beneficial impact on landowners, although they bear the environmental costs. Personal income is directed to immediate consumption, and community income tends to be squandered by so-called landowner companies who purport to represent the landowners. Whilst new large scale sustainable logging projects may offer the opportunity for landowners to receive a sustainable income, the level of income under current arrangements is generally too small to impact significantly on rural living standards. It is evident that in general landowners are not able to manage their affairs in the democratic way they are expected to with regard to their organization, and the management of cash flows from logging projects for long term benefits.

Table 10.6 assesses the aggregate success of non-resource commodity exports over time by measuring their kina value, adjusted for inflation. The fourth period average is 1.5 times the first period average, compared to six times for resource exports (Table 10.5).

Table 10.6: Non-resource commodity exports — period averages

	Eighties			Nineties			Noughties			Tens			1976*–2022		
	Volume	Share	Value	Volume	Share	Value	Volume	Share	Value	Volume	Share	Value	Volume	Share	Value
Cocoa	30,362	18%	72	34,980	8%	34	44,450	10%	521	33,978	6%	326	35,402	11%	480
Copra	90,292	8%	334	53,673	3%	128	22,560	1%	47	41,301	2%	91	55,940	4%	157
Copra oil	35,273	6%	227	38,700	4%	181	42,580	4%	206	15,676	1%	67	34,761	4%	176
Coffee	48,015	41%	1,544	64,053	24%	1,092	60,460	17%	923	46,987	10%	590	56,368	25%	1,075
Rubber	4,015	1%	40	3,440	1%	22	4,470	1%	51	3,056	0%	15	3,791	1%	32
Tea	6,500	3%	116	6,153	1%	55	5,500	1%	36	771	0%	4	5,294	1%	57
Cash crops (excl. palm oil)	214,458	77%	2,985	201,000	41%	1,828	180,020	32%	1,785	141,769	19%	1,093	191,557	46%	1,977
Palm oil	63,146	8%	321	238,173	17%	795	431,750	28%	1,532	582,368	28%	1,690	280,418	18%	1,007
Other agricultural products		0%	-		6%	255		10%	543		10%	593		6%	317
Marine products	-	0%	-	6	3%	116	52	9%	460	154	20%	1,215	39	6%	376
Logs/timber	908	15%	563	1,788	33%	1,544	2,732	22%	1,165	3,449	23%	1,303	2,025	24%	1,158
Total		100%	3,869		100%	4,538		100%	5,485		100%	5,893		100%	4,835

Notes: *Shares and values start in 1977; marine products start in 1990. Shares are measured by their value, and, in the case of timber, include other forest products (whereas only the volume of logs is recorded). Volumes are in tonnes except for logs, which are in thousand cubic metres. Values are measured in kina million in 2022 prices, adjusting nominal values by the CPI.

Source: PNG Economic Database.

There is a lack of data on food crops and *buai*, but no doubt their sale is very important and has grown (Bourke 2005b). The 2011 Census found that 66 per cent of rural households engage in the sale of food crops and cooked food, and that a stunning 44 per cent grow betel nut, up from only 8 per cent in 1990 (NSO 2015, 75). With more fresh food for sale, food markets have developed. Sharp (2019) notes several big changes: the rise of resellers (intermediaries) and of large-scale trading, more long-distance trading, more haggling and competitive behaviour, growth in the number of smaller ('corner') marketplaces, an increase in supply from commercial farming and the increased sale of store goods in fresh food markets.

Even less is known about subsistence agriculture, though research has repeatedly shown that those households exclusively reliant on subsistence are the worst off (Harvey and Heywood 1983), as cash crops allow households to improve the quality of their diet (Schmidt, Mueller and Rosenbach 2020). Around the time of independence, the theory of subsistence affluence held that rural households had enough to eat, giving rise to the idea that there was no poverty in PNG (2.2.4). However, more recent survey data indicate that both food poverty (Gibson 2014; Schmidt 2019) and hunger (Pandey and Howes 2021) are widespread phenomena in PNG. This remains a controversial claim (Bourke 2021), but internationally comparable data rank PNG the 15th most food insecure country in the world (Table 10.14). Whether or not quantities are sufficient, it has long been recognised that the quality of diets in PNG is low, with insufficient intake of protein and micronutrients (Heywood and Heywood 1990). Alarmingly, almost one in two children in PNG are stunted; this is the fourth-highest rate in the world (Hurney 2017).

ANU geographer Bryant Allen has been visiting the same villages, Tumam and Ngahmbole, near the town of Dreikikir in the province of East Sepik since 1971. After a 2016 visit, he wrote of these villages:

> Economically, they are stuck and seem likely to be stuck, for as long as can be foreseen. With the exception of very short-term boom prices for vanilla, the number of cocoa trees or vanilla vines that can be managed by individual families will never provide them with cash incomes that will allow them to build permanent houses, with electricity and running water. They will have to continue to grow most of their own food. They will not be able to afford to buy fertilisers … Reliable family planning is not available from the health centre, despite an expressed desire by men and women to reduce family sizes. There is never likely to be a local source of paid employment at Dreikikir that will enable most people to live in their villages but earn a cash income 'off the farm'. (Allen 2018, 115)

10.7 Trade and the balance of payments

Exports grew relative to the economy over the nineties and noughties, before falling over the tens due to lower resource prices and then picking up again as resource prices recovered (Table 10.7 and Figure B19). Imports grew over the first three periods, but collapsed in the fourth, where, as a share of GDP, they have fallen to three-quarters of the average for the post-independence period (Figure B19). The fourth period also stands out for its massive current account surplus, reflecting high exports being used to fund large capital repayments, especially related to the PNG LNG project, rather than imports. (Capital flows beyond those relating to foreign direct investment have always been limited in PNG. Superannuation funds are allowed to invest a portion of their funds offshore. The PNG stock market is illiquid, and only domestic financial institutions participate in the government bond market.)

Foreign exchange rationing, one of the causes of import compression, was used to protect foreign exchange reserves during the downturn of the fourth period (8.3.1). Foreign exchange reserves fell relative to imports from 4.5 months in 1976 to 2.3 in 1988 (Table 10.7), and were further run down in the second period leading to crisis (Figure B22). They recovered during the boom and were protected during the bust by rationing.

Table 10.7: Exports, imports, the current account balance (CAB) and foreign exchange (FX) reserves — period averages

	Eighties	Nineties	Noughties	Tens	1976–2022
Exports/GDP	28.5%	38.1%	44.4%	41.6%	37.5%
Imports/GDP	37.2%	37.4%	47.5%	28.3%	37.8%
CAB/GDP (average)	−4.8%	2.4%	−1.2%	13.6%	1.8%
FX/imports (months)	4.0	1.8	4.4	4.2	3.4
FX/imports (months) (first, last)	4.5, 2.3	2.4, 2.3	2.6, 3.7	4.6, 4.6	

Source: PNG Economic Database.

10.8 The financial sector

Commercial bank deposits have increased relative to the economy (Figure B32), with the peak (an average of 32 per cent of GDP) coming during the boom years of the noughties (Table 10.8). Private lending has been more constant at around 12 per cent of GDP. However, the period averages hide the volatility, with a collapse in private lending during the nineties (from 19 per cent in 1989 to 7 per cent in 2003), recovery during the boom (to a high of 17 per cent in 2013) and then another decline. Bank holdings of government debt have increased, but not enough to fully utilise available deposits. This has led to a situation of excess liquidity, which first became evident in the late nineties (Table 10.8 and Figure B36). In the final period, the banks parked more than one-fifth of their deposits at the central bank.

Table 10.8: The financial sector — period averages

	Eighties	Nineties	Noughties	Tens	1977*-2022
Deposits/GDP	17.1%	20.2%	31.5%	29.1%	23.6%
Deposits/GDP (first, last)	17.6%, 17.8%	19.9%, 14.7%	17.1%, 38.7%	33.1%, 27.8%	
Private lending/GDP	12.6%	12.8%	12.2%	12.4%	12.5%
Private lending/GDP (first, last)	6.8%, 16.2%	18.5%, 6.5%	6.0%, 17.1%	14.7%, 11.4%	
Government lending/GDP	2.6%	6.2%	8.4%	11.2%	6.7%
Share of comm. bank deposits at BPNG	5.0%	6.0%	13.4%	22.1%	12.3%
Interest rate spread	2.68	7.34	9.23	7.90	6.66
Number of bank branches	52	53	69	82	62
Number of bank agents (first, last)	298, 286	264, 87	87, 337	393, 589	

Notes: *The interest rate spread (the difference between the average lending and average deposit rate) and the number of bank branches and agents start in 1976. Data on agents missing for most of the noughties, so first and last year shown rather than average.

Source: PNG Economic Database.

The stability of the financial sector was threatened by political interference in the nineties. Tackling this was the signature success of the Morauta reforms. PNG's financial sector today is stable, but not supportive of economic growth. PNG's central bank governor noted at the start of the eighties that PNG's interest rates (on loans) were 'relatively low by international standards' (ToRobert 1982, 150). Today, they are, by the same standards, very high. Following deregulation of the banks in the eighties, deposit rates fell but lending rates stayed high, leading to interest rate spreads more than doubling (Table 10.8), and PNG's banks becoming among the most profitable in the world, which reflects the lack of competition in the sector.

Financial inclusion went backwards in the nineties with little growth in the number of bank branches, and a reduction in the number of bank agents, but has improved this century (8.2.2).

10.9 The exchange rate and inflation

Inflation has been moderate in PNG except in the second period during which it equalled almost 10 per cent, reflecting pass-through from the rapid depreciation (Table 10.9).

The kina was largely stable in the first period, depreciated precipitously in the second, recovered some of its value in the third and then lost that value in the fourth (Figure B31).

Table 10.9: The exchange rate and inflation — period averages

	Eighties	Nineties	Noughties	Tens	1975*–2022
USD/PGK (first and last)	1.26, 1.21	1.16, 0.28	0.31, 0.45	0.41, 0.28	
Nominal appreciation (against USD)	–0.3%	–9.3%	4.9%	–5.1%	–3.4%
Nominal appreciation (NEER)	0.4%	–4.9%	2.3%	–2.4%	–1.6%
Real appreciation (REER)	–1.7%	–2.1%	4.1%	0.3%	0.0%
REER (first and last)	133.2, 116.6	119.8, 85.1	87.9, 127	122.8, 130.8	
Inflation	6.4%	9.6%	4.4%	5.1%	6.8%
Relative inflation	–2.1%	2.8%	1.8%	2.8%	1.6%

Notes: *The REER (real effective exchange rate) starts in 1980 and the NEER (nominal effective exchange rate) in 1979. Both are indices with 2010 = 100. Inflation is measured from 1978. Relative inflation is REER–NEER.

Source: PNG Economic Database.

The real effective exchange rate (REER), which takes account both of movement in nominal exchange rates and differences between domestic and international inflation rates,[3] shows gradual depreciation in the first period,

---

3   The REER can also be defined as the ratio of the price of tradeables to non-tradeables. While data on this were collected in PNG, there is not a complete series.

more rapid depreciation in the second, but then an appreciation back to the level of independence during the third period and no change in the fourth period (Table 10.9). The REER in 2022 is remarkably close to the REER in 1980 (the first year for which data are available).

10.10 Fiscal outcomes

Revenue has been falling relative to GDP, except during the boom, where it was pushed up by a massive surge in resource revenue. It was 20 per cent on average during the first period and only 17 per cent in the last (Table 10.10), which reflects the sharp fall in foreign aid relative to GDP (Figure B25). The non-resource sector has become more heavily taxed over time (Figure B26), and, for the post-independence period as a whole, the government non-resource take (non-resource revenue relative to non-resource GDP) is slightly higher than the resource revenue rate (resource revenue relative to resource GDP) (Table 10.10).

Table 10.10: Government revenue, expenditure and borrowing — period averages

	Eighties	Nineties	Noughties	Tens	1976*–2022
Revenue/GDP	20.2%	19.3%	22.3%	17.0%	19.7%
Revenue growth	1.3%	0.4%	7.2%	0.5%	2.1%
Non-resource own revenue/GDP	12.0%	13.5%	14.2%	13.6%	13.2%
Resource revenue/GDP	1.7%	2.4%	4.9%	1.5%	2.5%
Aid/GDP	6.5%	3.4%	3.2%	1.9%	3.9%
Aid/revenue	32.3%	17.5%	14.2%	11.3%	19.7%
Aid growth	–5.3%	–0.4%	–2.5%	1.4%	–1.7%
A. Government non-resource take	14.1%	16.2%	17.7%	18.1%	16.5%
B. Government resource take	16.6%	14.5%	22.9%	5.9%	15.1%
B/A	1.18	0.89	1.29	0.33	0.91
Expenditure /GDP	21.9%	21.0%	22.1%	22.0%	21.7%
Expenditure growth	1.1%	0.4%	9.7%	0.6%	2.6%
Deficit/GDP	1.7%	1.7%	–0.1%	5.2%	2.0%
Interest/GDP	1.7%	2.6%	1.2%	2.2%	2.0%

	Eighties	Nineties	Noughties	Tens	1976*–2022
Debt (first, last)					
% GDP	17.3%, 24.1%	26.3%, 38.6%	37.3%, 24.9%	26.9%, 48.2%	
% domestic share of debt	25.2%, 20.6%	26.3%, 31.6%	39.1%, 72.1%	74.5%, 52.4%	

Notes: *Revenue and expenditure growth are adjusted for inflation and start in 1977. The government resource take is the ratio of resource revenue to resource GDP. The government non-resource take is the ratio of non-resource own revenue (excluding aid) to non-resource GDP.

Source: PNG Economic Database.

PNG ran modest fiscal deficits in the first two periods, surpluses in the third, and its largest deficits in the fourth (Figure B27). Deficits stayed large in the fourth period because foreign exchange rationing removed the risk that a high fiscal deficit would lead to a balance of payments crisis (8.3.1). Debt and interest payments have generally increased relative to GDP and revenue, though they fell during the boom (Figure B28). Government debt has been increasingly domestically financed, though there was a return to foreign funding of government debt in the last period (Figure B29).

Government expenditure, although it has bounced around year-to-year (Figure B23), has been remarkably constant over the four periods, with period averages restricted to the range of 21–22 per cent of GDP.

10.11 Service delivery

Public services have to be financed either by revenue or by borrowing, and their cost increases with the size of the population. Since government borrowing is limited, revenue per person, adjusted for inflation, is one measure of the capacity of the state to deliver public services. Despite a recovery in the third period, revenue per person has fallen significantly since independence (Figure B38 and Table 10.11). The fourth period revenue per person average is 80 per cent of the first period average.

Another measure is government recurrent goods and services per person. This removes salaries, interest and development spending from total expenditure, and focuses on the residual, which is the non-salary recurrent costs of running government. It includes expenditures on such items as drugs for hospitals, textbooks for schools and road maintenance. It is a particularly useful measure for PNG because it is net of salaries: real salaries fell over the nineties, but we do not know how much by. Data on this variable, shown in Figure 5.1, are not available for the first period. It collapsed over the nineties from PGK 1,208 in 1989 (2022 prices) to PGK367 in 2003, which is consistent with observations regarding a sharp decline in service delivery over that decade (5.2.2). Goods and services per person spending recovered during the boom to PGK1,074 (in 2013), but then collapsed again during the bust to PGK693 (in 2022).

These are all financial input measures. Long time series on non-financial inputs are limited, but one that is available is the number of medical doctors. This shows a fairly constant and very low ratio of doctors to patients. Another output variable for which a long time series is available is childhood immunisation (Figure B39). This shows improving levels in the first three periods followed by a rapid decline in the fourth.

Table 10.11: Service delivery indicators post-independence — period averages

	Eighties	Nineties	Noughties	Tens	1975*–2022*
Revenue per person	2,350	2,057	2,168	1,866	2,120
Goods and services per person (first and last)		1,208, 367	484, 1,074	1,018, 693	
Doctors per million	70	64	50	63	63
Immunisation rates (%)					
DPT	36.7	59.5	62.0	40.4	51.5
Hepb3		38.0	65.7	41.4	47.5
Measles	30.3	56.8	71.6	45.6	54.2

Notes: *Revenue per person is measured in 2022 kina and starts in 1977; goods and services per person are recurrent only, are measured in 2022 kina and start in 1989; data on doctors are up to 2021; the DPT (diphtheria, pertussis, tetanus) immunisation rate starts in 1980, measles in 1983 and Hepb3 in 1990. The immunisation rates are the percentage of children aged 12–23 months who have been vaccinated. See also the notes to Figure B39.

Source: PNG Economic Database.

More generally, although life expectancy in PNG has continued to improve and infant mortality has continued to decline over the post-independence period (as they have in nearly every country in the world), health services have worsened. Prior to independence, there were impressive improvements in PNG's health indicators (Hetzel 1974).[4] Up to the mid-eighties, it could

---

4   'Comparison between the two periods 1952–62 and 1962–67 shows a striking fall (54%) in deaths due to malaria, bacillary dysentery and tuberculosis' (Hetzel 1974, 216).

be said that the 'regime of public health in Papua Guinea is remarkable' (Denoon, Dugan and Marshall 1989, 5). But, writing two decades later, Thomason and Kase (2009, 117) recorded 'a slow but steady decline in the [health] services available to rural people'. A systematic study of health and education facilities between 2002 and 2012 found that 'PNG's primary schools have expanded rapidly over the last decade, but that fewer services are now provided by its health clinics' (Howes et al. 2014, v). In 2024, the deputy secretary of the Department of Health stated that public health indicators were at 'an all-time low' (*Islands Business* 2024). Meanwhile, non-communicable diseases (NCDs) have spread and today PNG has one of the highest rates of premature mortality from NCDs in the world (Table 10.14).

School enrolments have increased over the independence period. The share of 6–20 year olds in school increased from 37 per cent in 1996 to 50 per cent in 2006 and 65 per cent in 2016–18 (Pandey and Howes 2022, 171). However, while literacy has increased, the quality of education services provided has fallen. A Canadian husband and wife team who taught in PNG in 1972 recalled that the school they worked at—Kerevat National High School—'was in excellent condition and well run' and that the standard of education was high. Returning to the same school 38 years later (in 2010), they observed an:

> education system in failure ... rife with government corruption and plagued by inadequate funding, poor English skills of teachers, low curriculum standards, inappropriate assessment practices and a lack of teacher competence and professionalism. (Romanyshyn and Romanyshyn 2010, 1)

10.12 Summary period comparisons

Of the four periods, the third and fourth are opposites in terms of economic performance; the first and second are opposites with respect to volatility; and the fourth is the most unusual in terms of macroeconomic settings and outcomes.

The noughties were the best of times, and the tens were the worst (Figure 10.1). The noughties were a boom across multiple dimensions. This period stands out for its large, positive growth in economic outcomes, whether non-resource GDP, employment, tax revenue or commercial bank deposits. The fourth period stands out for its negative growth in formal private sector and SOE employment, real non-resource GDP per person growth and real deposits. Real revenue growth is only positive in the fourth period because of the rapid increase in resource revenue in 2022, which ended the bust. The fourth period has the worst growth performance in employment and deposits. Non-resource GDP per person growth is slightly worse in the first period, but the data for the latter are only from 1983 to 1988. The second period has marginally slower real revenue growth, again because of the rapid resource revenue growth of 2022.

The first and second periods are opposites in terms of volatility (Figure 10.2). The nineties were PNG's most volatile period, the eighties its least. The second period had the highest growth variability, the highest inflation and the most depreciation. The first period had the lowest growth volatility and the most currency stability. The first period had average rather than low inflation, but this is because of high average global inflation in these early years (Table 10.9).

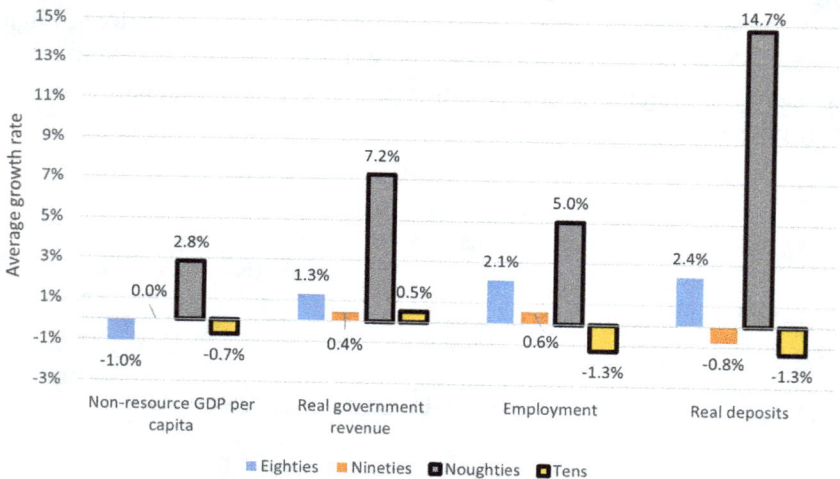

Figure 10.1: The best and worst of times—the noughties and the tens. An analysis using period average growth rates.

Notes: Non-resource GDP per person starts in 1983; government revenue in 1977; employment in 1978; and deposits in 1977. Appropriate deflators are used. Noughties and tens columns are highlighted to show their contrasting performance.

Source: PNG Economic Database.

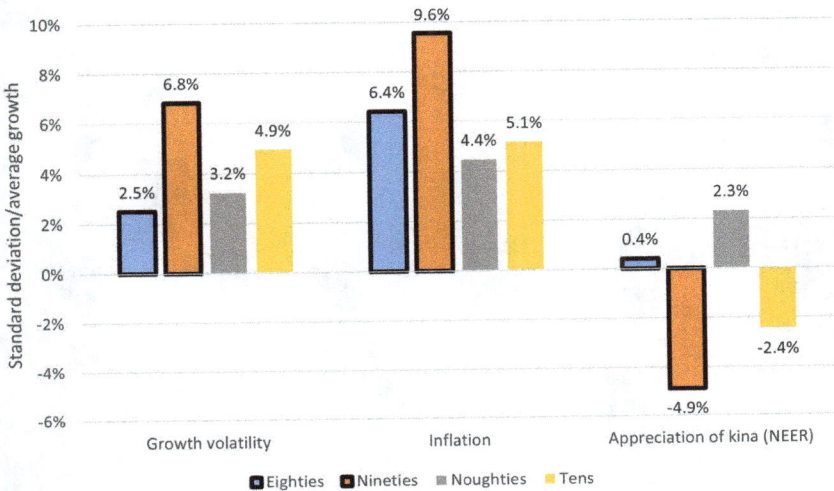

Figure 10.2: The most stable and volatile of times—the seventies/eighties and the nineties. An analysis based on growth volatility, inflation and depreciation

Notes: Growth volatility measured using standard deviation for real GDP. Inflation and nominal appreciation are average growth rates. GDP data start in 1976, inflation in 1977, nominal exchange rate data in 1975 and relative inflation in 1980. Eighties and nineties columns are highlighted to show their contrasting performance.

Source: PNG Economic Database.

Finally, on a number of macroeconomic variables, the fourth period is the most unusual or distinctive (Figure 10.3). It has (by far) the highest average fiscal deficit and current account balance (CAB), and the lowest average level of imports and resource revenue, all relative to GDP. These features are all related to this being the only period of currency inconvertibility. The low level of resource revenue put pressure on the kina, which the Bank of Papua New Guinea resisted by introducing foreign exchange rationing. This allowed the government to run high deficits without risking a balance of payments crisis. But it also compressed imports, contributing to the record current account surplus, though the primary reason for the latter was debt repayments from the PNG LNG project financed by LNG exports.

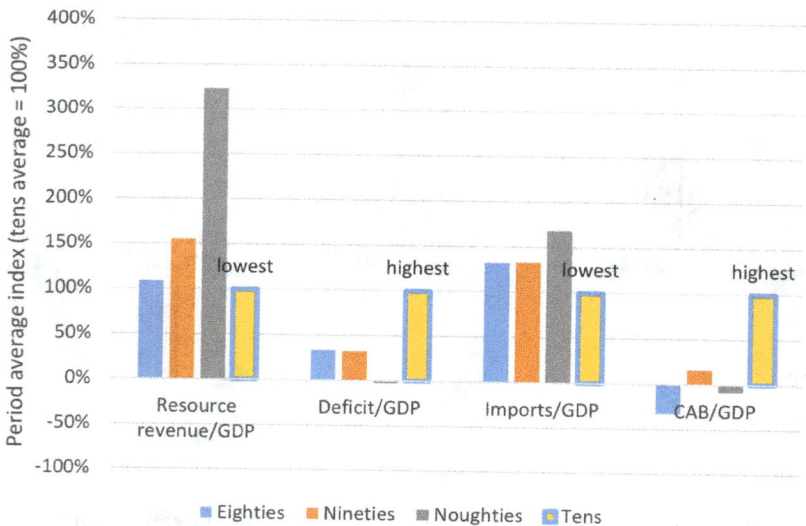

Figure 10.3: The most unusual of times—the tens. Index analysis, setting the average in the tens to 100%

Note: Variables start in 1976.

Source: PNG Economic Database.

We can learn a lot from these characterisations. One key lesson is that rapid growth in PNG is possible, but only if the conditions are right. These conditions include not only high commodity prices, but also 'revenue-ready' resource projects that ensure a high government resource take when resource prices are high (10.4). This combination was present in the noughties, but not in the other three periods. The first two had low and falling commodity prices, and the fourth had high commodity prices, but a low government resource take. Of course, there were also other reasons for low or high growth, including declining aid in the first two periods, the PNG LNG construction in the third, foreign exchange rationing in the fourth, and more generally the policy and institutional factors discussed in the next two chapters. That said, high commodity prices and revenue-ready resource projects emerge from this study as the best short-run predictors for rapid growth in PNG.

The noughties were a boom period worldwide. A natural group of comparator countries are the resource-rich countries of Sub-Saharan Africa. A World Bank study (Cust, Ballesteros and Zeufack 2022) defines the boom period for these countries as 2004–14 (very similar to our 2004–13) and looks at how these countries fared during, before (1993–2003) and after (2015–18) their boom, looking at both GDP and non-resource GDP. The results are shown in Table 10.12 with PNG added in.

Table 10.12: Pre-boom, boom and post-boom growth rates in Africa and PNG

	GDP avg. growth rate (%)			Non-resource GDP avg. growth rate (%)		
	Pre-boom	Boom	Post-boom	Pre-boom	Boom	Post-boom
Resource-rich Africa	4.6	5.4	2.7	4.5	5.8	2.5
Non-resource-rich Africa	2.9	4.2	3.8	3.2	3.5	3.2
PNG	2.9	4.5	3.8	2.7	5.6	2.0

Notes: For the African countries, pre-boom is 1993-2003, boom is 2004-14 and post-boom is 2015-18. For PNG, the dates are as per this book: 1989-2003, 2004-13 and 2014-22, respectively. There are 26 resource-rich African countries and 22 non-resource-rich ones. Resource-rich countries have at least 20 per cent of exports or 20 per cent of government revenue from the resource sector. PNG easily meets this criterion in terms of exports. All GDP growth rates are in constant prices, local currencies.

Source: African figures are for Sub-Saharan African countries only (Cust, Ballesteros and Zeufack 2022).

One of the main messages of the World Bank study is that, for resource-rich countries, 'the growth record was strong during the boom but collapsed once commodity prices fell' (Cust, Ballesteros and Zeufack 2022). This is true for PNG if we look at non-resource GDP. In the resource-rich African countries, non-resource growth fell from 5.8 per cent during the boom to 2.5 per cent after it. In PNG, the fall was even more dramatic, from 5.6 to 2.0 per cent. However, if we look at GDP growth, while growth halves in the African resource-rich countries after the boom (from 5.4 to 2.7 per cent), there is little decline in the PNG growth rate (just 4.5–3.8 per cent) due to the commencement of LNG exports in the post-boom era.

The World Bank study also finds that 'the resource boom did not equip resource-rich African countries with enough savings to sustain economic growth after the boom ended' (Cust, Ballesteros and Zeufack 2022, 50). PNG did not save enough during its boom either (6.3.1).

10.13 Overall assessment — an international perspective

While each period is quite distinctive, overall the post-independence development record has been disappointing. Writing in the late nineties, John Connell (1997, 317) concluded that 'neither consistent growth nor sustainable development have been achieved'. (These are the last words in the main text of his book.) Since then, average growth has improved slightly, but, for the post-independence era as a whole, non-resource GDP per person has only averaged 0.4 per cent per year, and formal sector employment growth only 1.5 per cent, well below the population growth rate.

How does PNG's growth and development experience post-independence look from an international perspective? PNG is a lower-middle-income country. Its 2022 GDP per capita is given by the World Bank as USD3,116 in current prices. The PNG government has itself held up Botswana and Malaysia as two other resource-rich countries whose growth record it aspires to emulate. Figure 10.4 updates a graph from the PNG government (GoPNG 2010). Clearly, PNG has been left behind by these two good performers, which at the time of PNG's independence were as poor or poorer than it, but which today are upper-middle-income countries.

Although this is a comparison favoured by the PNG government, it is not one that is fair to the country. The next graph (Figure 10.5) gives a good idea of the diversity of growth experiences around the world, especially among poorer countries. The vertical axis shows the long-term average growth rate over 40 years, from 1980 to 2020, for the nearly 150 countries for which these data are available. The horizontal axis shows their per person GDP in the base year, 1980. That the graph makes roughly the shape of a triangle indicates that poorer countries exhibit greater diversity in their growth performance than richer ones.

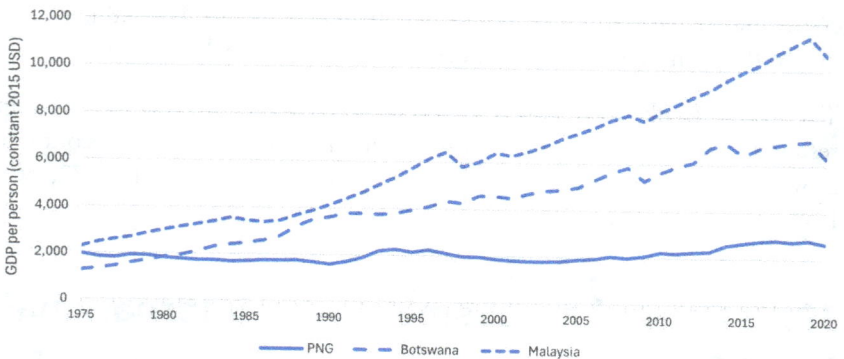

Figure 10.4: GDP per person in PNG, Botswana and Malaysia, 1975–2020
Source: World Development Indicators.

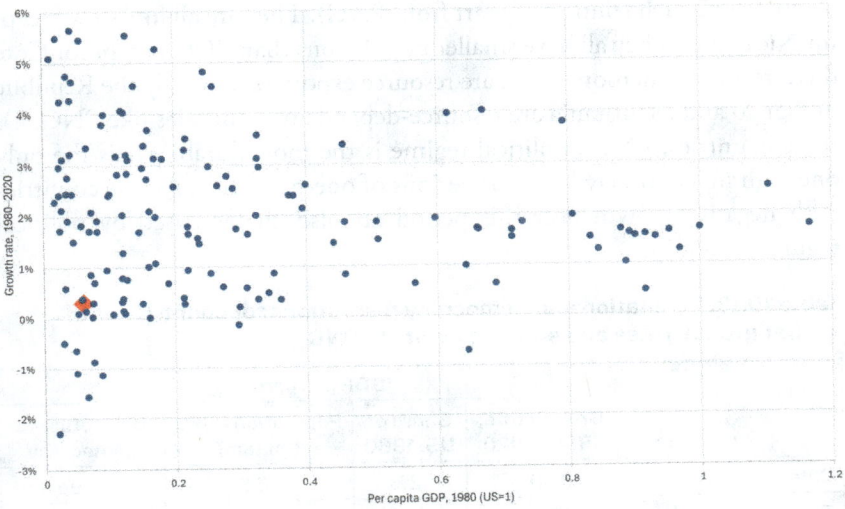

Figure 10.5: GDP per person in 1980 and GDP per person growth rate, 1980–2020, for a large number of countries, with PNG represented as a diamond

Note: PPPs used to calculate per person GDP. Horizontal axis truncated at 1.2.

Source: Calculated from PWT10 (Feenstra, Inklaar and Timmer 2015), except for PNG, on which see text below.

PNG is not included in the database from which this graph is constructed. However, in 1980, PNG's GDP per person was only 6 per cent of the US's using market exchange rates.[5] Therefore, on the horizontal axis, PNG would fall very much to the left-hand side, that is, as one of the poorest countries in the world in 1980. On the vertical axis, PNG's growth performance is by no means the worst in the world, but it is certainly towards the bottom end of the performance ranking. PNG's non-resource GDP average growth between 1983 (the first year for which this measure is available) and 2020 is 0.3 per cent in local currency, using constant prices. A handful of countries (eight) have done worse with negative growth. PNG has avoided that fate, but is in the next group of about a dozen poor countries with 0–0.5 per cent growth.

Table 10.13 zeroes in on these comparator countries. It shows those with starting GDP per person in 1980 of 20 per cent or less of the US's and subsequent average growth that is positive but no more than 0.5 per cent.

---

5   The graph uses purchasing power parities, but this gives a similar ratio for 1990, the first year for which these data are available.

There are 12 such countries (apart from PNG). They are all in Africa except for Nicaragua. They all have smaller populations than PNG except for Côte d'Ivoire and Cameroon. Some are resource exporters, but only the Republic of Congo and Mauritania are resource-dependent economies like PNG. Of these countries, PNG's political regime is the most durable. It is the only one with no coups, civil wars or periods of one-party rule. All the countries with negative growth over this period are also characterised by political regime instability.

Table 10.13: Population and democracy disruptions for countries with similar growth rates and starting points to PNG

	GDP per person			
	Growth rate, 1980–2020	Share of US, 1980	Population 2020 (million)	Disruption to democracy
Côte d'Ivoire	0.39%	12%	26.8	Coup
Togo	0.38%	6%	8.4	One-party rule
Congo	0.33%	12%	5.7	Coup
Liberia	0.30%	8%	5.1	Coup
Papua New Guinea	0.30%	6%	8.8	None
Nicaragua	0.29%	15%	6.8	Civil war
Sierra Leone	0.14%	6%	8.2	Civil war
Cameroon	0.14%	12%	26.5	One-party rule
Guinea-Bissau	0.10%	5%	2.0	Coup
Sao Tome & Principe	0.09%	12%	0.2	Coup
Comoros	0.08%	11%	0.8	Coup
Gambia	0.03%	7%	2.6	One-party rule
Mauritania	0.01%	16%	4.5	Coup

Notes: Countries selected from Figure 10.5 are those with a starting GDP relative to that of the US of 20 per cent or less and a long-term average per person growth rate of 0–0.5 per cent. The disruption to democracy variable shows one type of deviation from democracy, if any, the country experienced over the period.

Source: For first three variables, PWT10 (Feenstra, Inklaar and Timmer 2015) and World Development Indicators except for PNG growth and population, from the PNG Economic Database. Non-resource GDP per person growth used for PNG (1983–2020). Disruption to democracy from various sources.

Resource dependency is another interesting variable for international comparisons. PNG's resource dependency ratio (resource sector GDP to total GDP) has almost tripled over the post-independence period (Figure B3). According to UN data, it is the sixth most resource dependent, based on the same ratio (Howes and Leng 2023). A few resource-intensive economies are missing from this database, but the message is clear: PNG has become one of the most resource-dependent economies in the world. The fact that it ranks just above Saudi Arabia on this indicator speaks volumes.

We have already started a discussion of service delivery indicators in PNG from an international perspective (10.11). On some broad measures, PNG does not appear to do too badly. Life expectancy is estimated by the World Bank in 2021 at 65, just below the average for lower-middle-income countries (67). Adult literacy is estimated for 2010 (based on the 2011 Census) at 62 per cent, well below the lower-middle-income country average for that year of 73 per cent, but above the low-income average of 54 per cent. But there are a number of indicators where PNG does very poorly indeed. Table 10.14 provides data on international rankings for 14 indicators relating to education, health, household infrastructure, poverty and violence. PNG's ranking is the worst of all countries for which data are available (typically 100 or more) for immunisation and access to improved drinking water. It is a bottom-five country for universal health coverage, probability of premature death from NCDs, improved sanitation, grid connections, child stunting and households with children out of school. It is a bottom-10 country for rates of intimate partner violence, doctors per person and poverty. And it is a bottom-20 country for the share of households without an educated adult, severe food insecurity and the lack of a government monopoly over violence.

Table 10.14: PNG standard of living and service delivery indicators — international rankings

		Value (%)	Ranking (1 = worst)	No. countries ranked	Year	Source
Education						
1	Households with unenrolled children	41.8	5	88	2016–18	Baxi, Naidoo and Tandon (2024)
2	Households without educated adults	39.7	16	122	2016–18	Baxi, Naidoo and Tandon (2024)
Health						
3	Universal health service coverage	30	3	223	2021	WHO and World Bank (2023)
4	Probability of premature mortality from non-communicable diseases	36	4	183	2022	WHO (2022)

		Value (%)	Ranking (1 = worst)	No. countries ranked	Year	Source
5	Child immunisation rates	35.7	1	191	2019	Howes and Mambon (2021)
6	Doctors per million	63	7	193	2021	World Development Indicators
Household infrastructure						
7	No connection to the electricity grid	83.1	3	120	2016–18	Baxi, Naidoo and Tandon (2024)
8	No improved sanitation	88.0	4	99	2016–18	Baxi, Naidoo and Tandon (2024)
9	No improved drinking water	60.6	1	112	2016–18	Baxi, Naidoo and Tandon (2024)
Poverty and gender inequality						
10	Severe food insecurity	30.6	15	122	2016–18	Baxi, Naidoo and Tandon (2024)
11	Consumption below the poverty line	39.3	10	122	2016–18	Baxi, Naidoo and Tandon (2024)
12	Stunting in children under five years	49.5	4	132	2016	IFPRI (2016)
Violence						
13	Intimate partner violence	31.0	6	177	2018	GIWPS and PRIO (2023)
14	State monopoly over violence	N/A	11–17	137	2022	Bertelsmann Stiftung (n.d.)

Notes: 1. At least one school-age child up to the age of Grade 8 is not at school. 2. No adult in the household (at age of Grade 9 or above) has completed primary education. 3. Combines 14 indicators of health service coverage. 4. Probability of dying between age 30 and 70 from cardiovascular disease, diabetes, cancer or chronic respiratory disease. 5. Average (value and ranking) for three childhood immunisations: DPT, Hep3 and measles; the variable is measured as percentage of 12–23 month olds immunised. 6. Data are from 2021 or latest available year. 8. Neither flushed toilet leading to a piped sewer system or septic tank nor composting toilet. 9. Drinking water sourced from a pipe, borehole or protected well. 10. Households answer yes to seven or more of the standard eight Food and Agriculture Organization food insecurity questions. 11. Household imputed to be poor based on non-monetary indicators in the 2016–18 DHS based on relationship between monetary poverty and the same indicators in the PNG 2009 Household Income and Expenditure Survey. 12. Stunting is the percentage of children under five years of age whose height for age is below two standard deviations from the median of the WHO Child Growth Standards. 13. Intimate partner violence is the percentage of ever-partnered women who experienced physical or sexual violence committed by their intimate partners in the preceding 12 months. 14. PNG scores a 4 on a scale out of 10 with six other countries in the Bertelsmann Stiftung Transformation Index ranking for 2022 on the state's monopoly on the use of force, which indicates that the 'state's monopoly on the use of force is established only in key parts of the country. Large areas of the country are controlled by guerrillas, paramilitaries or clans' (BTI 2022).

Source: See table. All the Baxi, Naidoo and Tandon (2024) sources rely on data from the PNG 2016–18 Demographic and Health Survey (DHS) and compare these results to DHS findings from other countries.

For at least some of these indicators, the very low rankings are the result of relative or absolute decline in PNG's performance, and so cannot be said simply to be the product of the country's difficult geography.

For example, in 1975, the ratio of doctors to population put PNG 43rd from the bottom in a global ranking of countries, and at about the average ratio for the 'least developed' country grouping, about 85 per million. Over time, most countries have been better serviced by doctors. But PNG has gone backwards. The 2019 figure for PNG is 63 per million, seventh from the bottom, and just a quarter of the average for least developed countries.

Likewise, PNG was an above-average performer for immunisation, but whereas the average low-income and lower-middle-income country has seen its immunisation record consistently improve, PNG has seen a massive slide in performance. Figure 10.6 illustrates using the vaccine for measles.

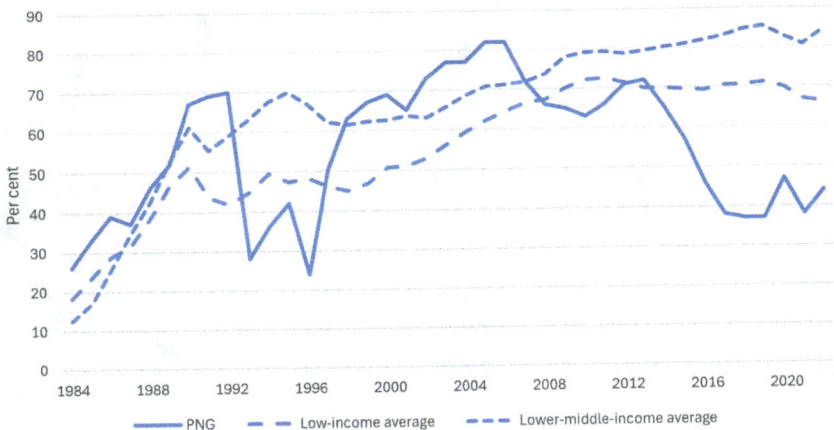

Figure 10.6: Immunisation rates for measles—PNG, low-income and lower-middle-income countries 1984–2022

Notes: The rate is the percentage of children aged 12–23 months who have been vaccinated.

Source: World Development Indicators.

In summary, PNG has enjoyed an unusual level of political regime stability, but its growth and development performance has nevertheless been disappointing, both relative to expectations at independence and from an international perspective. Growth has been slow, the economy has become much more resource dependent, and some important indicators of living standards and service delivery are alarmingly low and, in some cases, have fallen, either relatively or absolutely.

11

Economic policies

The essential point above all is that exchange rate policy, budget policy, minimum wages policy and many other things were in there together. Newcomers to Papua New Guinea often have difficulty in understanding one or other aspect of our policies, particularly in regard to the exchange rate. The beginning of wisdom for them is to grasp that the policies must be seen as a whole.

—Prime Minister Julius Chan (1982, 11)

11.1 Introduction

It would be a mistake to think we can find a close correlation over the four periods between variations in growth performance and variations in policies and institutions. The previous chapter brought out the critical importance of both commodity prices and the responsiveness of the government resource take to commodity prices as critical short-term drivers of growth (10.12). Nevertheless, both policies and institutions clearly also matter for economic growth, and they are the subject of these last two chapters.

Economic policies show as much variation in PNG's post-independence years as economic outcomes. In this book, we have tried to bring new insights and challenge some of the orthodoxies regarding the history of economic policymaking in PNG since independence. This chapter integrates our findings over the four periods in relation to the economic policies of PNG's post-independence journey. It examines macroeconomic, including fiscal, policies; the rise and fall of the Washington Consensus; the large changes in resource sector policies; the persistent but restrained use of industrial policy;

the contentious and ultimately too-difficult issue of land policy; the benign neglect of the informal economy, which has come to the country's rescue; and the retreat from equality.

11.2 Macroeconomic policy challenges

Overall, PNG has not yet been able to find a durable macroeconomic policy stance to support both growth and stability.

The seventies and eighties are often presented as a golden age from the perspective of macroeconomic stability (Chand and Yala 2005). Macroeconomic outcomes were indeed largely positive in these early years. However, this period was also one in which macroeconomic problems were being stored up for the future. First, low growth itself made it harder to support macroeconomic stability. As the self-styled 'revolutionary' (expansionary) budget of 1993 showed (4.4.1), slow growth meant that there were no prizes for being responsible and generated pressure to do something different, even if irresponsible. Second, declining foreign exchange reserves through the seventies and eighties meant that it would be increasingly difficult to avoid a balance of payments crisis and/or a devaluation. Foreign exchange reserves were four or five months of imports up to 1980, but fell to three months by 1981, and only two months by 1988 (Figure B22).

The macroeconomic instability of the nineties (4.4.1) is often explained in terms of high deficits, but the greater reliance on domestic financing and the reduction in foreign aid, especially in the form of budget support, were also important contributory factors. In addition, there was less margin for error given the low level of foreign exchange reserves with which the period started. Monetary policy, which had helped manage demand in the eighties, became ineffective in the nineties. Declining confidence did not help either. Given all this, and kina convertibility, it is not surprising that there were two balance of payments crises in the nineties.

The Achilles heel of the boom period was fiscal policy (6.3.1). The abolition of the Mineral Resources Stabilisation Fund (MRSF) in 1999 was understandable but unfortunate (4.4.3). In hindsight, it would have been better to leave the MRSF in place. Even wiping out its balance and starting again under the same rules would have been better than abolishing the MRSF altogether. The absence of the MRSF meant that there was no mechanism in place to put aside the massive influx in resource revenues that occurred in the earlier years of the boom. Rather, excess funds were put into short-term trust funds, already earmarked for expenditure in particular sectors. Most was spent as early as 2009, and by the time the bust came very little was left in the trust funds (Figure B30). To make matters worse, the government started to borrow heavily in 2013, before the boom had ended.

While it was inevitable that a bust would follow the boom, it is harder to explain why the bust lasted as long as it did. We have explained this in terms of an array of negative factors and costly policy choices (8.3 and 9.1), in particular the introduction of foreign exchange rationing.

Looking at the last half century as a whole, there have been five major changes in fiscal and macroeconomic settings since independence.

First, the exchange rate regime moved from fixed (or at least a no-devaluation stance) to pegged over the eighties (2.3.3), to floating in 1994 (4.4.2) and then back to pegged two decades later in 2014 (8.3.1).

Second, currency convertibility on the current account was the bedrock of economic policy from independence, but was abandoned in 2014 in favour of rationing foreign exchange (8.3.1 and 9.3).

Third, wage indexation (in the formal sector, and full or substantial) was present from independence to 1992 (3.1.2) but abandoned thereafter with the deregulation of the urban labour market (5.1.1). Today, adjusting for inflation, the urban minimum wage is less than one-third of its value at independence, adjusting for inflation, and no longer out of line with comparator countries (Howes, Mambon and Samof 2022) (Figure B18).

Fourth, there have been two major changes in fiscal policy. The use of convertibility as a fiscal constraint was discarded in 2014 and replaced, unsuccessfully, by legislative constraints on borrowing (8.3.3). Also, PNG went into independence with a mechanism, the MRSF, to smooth and save resource revenues (2.3.1), but scrapped it in 1999 due to fiscal stress (4.4.3). Despite repeated efforts, including legislation in 2012 and then again 2015 for a sovereign wealth fund (SWF), a successor mechanism has not been made operational (7.1.3).

Fifth, monetary policy instruments have become ineffective due to the emergence of excess liquidity (4.4.4). With commercial banks holding up to a quarter of their deposits with the central bank or in cash, there is no need for them to borrow from the latter. The minimum liquid asset ratio (MLAR) had worked in the eighties to tighten or loosen monetary policy

(2.3.2), but it lost its potency as banks turned to government bonds (4.4.4), thereby exceeding whatever level the MLAR was set at. The Kina Facility Rate, introduced at the turn of the century—is ineffectual due to excess liquidity (8.3.4).

Unfortunately, most of these changes have been in the wrong direction. Wage deregulation is the honourable exception: it has made the economy more flexible and macroeconomic management easier. Whether moving to a floating exchange rate was a good idea can be debated. The loss of monetary policy effectiveness is obviously unfortunate. And trying to manage the economy without any sort of savings or smoothing mechanism is surely mistaken in an economy as volatile as PNG.

The biggest mistake was the abandonment of current account convertibility. Very few countries ration foreign exchange in relation to current account transactions. Why did PNG turn to rationing in 2014 and persist with it for so long? There are a variety of reasons (8.3.1), but the most fundamental is that foreign exchange rationing seemed to guarantee PNG macroeconomic stability (no balance of payments crisis, limited depreciation, moderate inflation). Given that monetary policy had become ineffective, and that fiscal discipline could not be assumed, this was an attractive proposition. No-one wanted a repeat of the nineties. However, while rationing has succeeded in bringing about stability, the price has been too high in terms of foregone growth and development. Moreover, the minimisation of depreciation by rationing is why the real exchange rate is back at its eighties' level. It was overvalued then (2.3.3), and it is overvalued now.

The challenge for PNG macroeconomic policy is to support stability without sacrificing growth. For this, currency convertibility needs to be reintroduced. It will not be easy to restore confidence in the kina. But PNG signed up to convertibility when it joined the IMF in 1975 (under article VIII of the IMF's articles of agreement). The Bank of Papua New Guinea (BPNG), which manages the exchange rate regime, should be constrained by this international commitment, as it was up to 2000.

Reintroducing convertibility would be good for growth but would add to risk. It would put the onus back on the politicians to limit borrowing to avoid a balance of payments crisis. This threat did not work in the nineties, but it is a risk that must be taken. No country has become prosperous under a regime of foreign exchange rationing. Trade and foreign investment are both critical to PNG and neither will flourish (apart from large, ring-fenced resource projects) until convertibility is reintroduced. While the next boom may make foreign exchange rationing unnecessary for some time, unless there is a strong commitment to convertibility, rationing is likely to reappear in the next bust.

Reintroducing a savings or smoothing mechanism at this stage is purely a matter of political will, since the necessary legislation has long been in place, sitting idle. However, one can question whether a separate SWF, held apart from BPNG reserves, is sensible, or would only add to risk. An alternative would be to bring back the MRSF, which was held as part of the central bank's reserves.

The problem of monetary policy ineffectiveness will not be easy to solve, given the non-competitive nature of PNG's banking sector and high spreads. One solution, favoured by the IMF (2023), is to remunerate deposits held at the central bank using the policy rate. However, apart from the cost, this would make banks even more reluctant to lend. A more structural, but also more difficult, solution is to increase the demand for loans by reducing interest rates and/or improving the investment climate.

Finally, whatever policy reforms follow, there is a need to re-establish credibility. Throughout the period of the quiet bust, the existence of foreign exchange rationing was frequently denied by the central bank, and the exchange rate was still often said to be floating, where clearly it was not. While recent bank statements are much franker (Howes 2023), central bank credibility was harmed as a result. Government credibility has also been damaged by non-implementation of its 2015 SWF legislation. Macroeconomic policy credibility and predictability would be helped if government and its agencies abided by existing rules and communicated transparently.

11.3 The rise and fall of the Washington Consensus

Papua New Guinea went to independence with a highly regulated economy and unrealistically high growth expectations (3.1.1). Growth performance disappointed, but there was little by way of economic reform in the eighties with the important exception of the deregulation of the financial sector (3.1.2).

The nineties was a period of radical reform, with the slashing of the country's minimum wage, price liberalisation, the introduction of a less regulated regime for foreign investment, tariff reductions, some privatisation and financial sector reform (5.1).

Some of these reforms were homegrown. Others reflected external pressures. All of them were consistent with the 'Washington Consensus' thinking that dominated globally in the nineties (Williamson 1990). The Washington Consensus emphasised privatisation, liberalisation, foreign investment and deregulation: exactly the sorts of reforms that PNG pursued over the nineties.

Over time, however, support for the Washington Consensus has lost ground in PNG. In the third and fourth periods, there was less economic reform in general, and what there was was nationalistic and interventionist in nature. Privatisation has been replaced as a reform objective by an expansion in the scope and number of state-owned enterprises, and a push to give these enterprises a more active role in the resource sector in particular (11.4). As part of this nationalistic policy turn, there has also recently been more support for the protection of domestic businesses, whether by expanded reservation lists or by increased tariffs (9.1.2 and 9.1.3).

The Washington Consensus also emphasised the importance of 'competitive exchange rates' (Williamson 1990), something endorsed by subsequent consensus growth 'recipes' (Commission on Growth and Development 2008). PNG's shift to foreign exchange rationing (8.3.1) and consequent exchange rate overvaluation is another rejection of the Washington Consensus.

A variety of factors explain the demise of the Washington Consensus in PNG. Support for it has fallen worldwide. The rise of China and other Asian economies has led many to conclude, rightly or wrongly, that free markets are overrated. This has been the case in PNG, where many point to Malaysia, in particular, as the role model that PNG should emulate.

It should also be admitted that, as in many other countries (World Bank 2005), growth did not increase in PNG after the introduction of Washington Consensus reforms. Some of the reforms may not have been suitable for PNG since, without competition, liberalisation can be counterproductive. Consider the financial sector. Its deregulation came as early as the eighties, but interest spreads in PNG are now among the highest in the world (4.3.3). Has financial sector deregulation actually helped PNG? Or does the sector need to be re-regulated? There is no guarantee that regulation would be a success, but the experience of the financial sector and the concentrated nature of several sectors of the PNG economy should give us pause before automatically supporting deregulation in the PNG context. Moreover, even if and when the reforms were suitable, their impact was undermined by other deviations from the Washington Consensus playbook (e.g. poor macroeconomic management) or by factors beyond it, such as increasing crime. The reforms delivered in the nineties, such as tariff and indirect tax reforms, were not the most important for the quality of the PNG investment climate. Other institutional constraints are far more binding on growth (12.2) but more difficult for politicians to act on. Understandably, PNG's politicians look for levers to pull that are within their reach. Constraints such as high levels of crime and a poorly functioning land market are difficult, so far too difficult, for government to address, but the drag on growth they result in leads to solutions being sought elsewhere—in recent years, through economic nationalism.

Finally, it seems likely that a more interventionist approach is attractive to PNG's politicians, given their weak ideological allegiances, and their many business links and aspirations. It also no doubt seems reasonable to PNG's politicians to blame excessive external influence if not exploitation for their country's economic woes. This helps explain why, in this sense, the noughties was a return to the days of independence, when there was also a strong mood of economic nationalism (3.1.1).

11.4 Resource policy — big changes and questions

The resource sector is the best documented part of the PNG economy, with the written record including fascinating accounts of individual mines by those involved with them, including Panguna (Quodling 1991), Ok Tedi (Jackson 1993) and Mount Kare (Henton and Flower 2007).

In fact, the resource sector often gets too much attention; however, there is no denying its growing importance. Resource sector policy has undergone four major changes.

First, the emphasis at independence on maximising the yield of resource projects for the central government has given way to a policy of maximising the yield for PNG more broadly, defined to include the central government, the provincial government and landowners (4.3.2). This reflects the lesson learnt that, while, by law, subsoil assets belong to the state, in practice, the consent of landowners and other local stakeholders is required for any resource project to commence and continue.

The share expected to go to the provincial government and especially landowners has grown manyfold. Royalties, which are split between these two groups, have increased; corporate tax can now be spent locally through income tax credits; provincial and local infrastructure grants are also expected as part of project negotiations; the provincial government and landowners are now also expected to be equity owners, with minimum equity stakes granted free of charge, and potentially more available at cost; and landowners are given preferential employment and business opportunities.

The changes are dramatic. Landowners only got royalties worth 0.06 per cent of sales from PNG's first mine; now they typically get 1 per cent of sales in royalties, a 16-fold increase. When Bougainville leader Paul Lapun tried to secure that first modest amount in royalties from Panguna back in 1966, his amendment was defeated the first time it was put to the House of Assembly on the grounds that, in the word of one senior administrator, it was 'parochial and relate[d] to the importance of the village and tribe, but disregard[ed] the importance of the country' (Woolford 1976, 32). Things looked very different once the power of landowners to disrupt mining operations became clear.

This policy shift has worked well in preventing any mines being shut down by landowners after the first, Panguna. There is a convincing argument that the closure of Panguna was not:

> 'uniquely Bougainvillian', but should at most be regarded as an extreme case of a recurrent problem in the relationship between mining communities, landowning communities, and the remarkably fragmented and disorganised 'state' of Papua New Guinea. (Filer 1992, 116)

If so, then avoiding 'another Panguna' is no mean feat.

At the same time, it is also an expensive policy for the central government. One study showed that in 2009 the Porgera gold mine paid PGK59 million to landowners in dividends, royalties and compensation, almost one-third of the PGK200 million to the central government in various taxes (Johnson 2012).

Moreover, how much benefit this greater sharing has been to the provincial governments and landowners who have been the recipients of it is a matter for debate. Local communities benefit from infrastructure, the provision of health services and employment opportunities. At the same time, the changes can be disruptive. Project areas attract migrants, whose arrival can further boost the local economy, but also give rise to social tensions. Landowner companies operate as sub-contractors to resource companies. Some do well and have expanded their operations, while others have major governance problems.

Benefits are normally distributed very unequally, which has:

> created a sharp conflict amongst the haves and have-nots. While compensation funds have led to an increase in consumption, individuals have made little provision for the future, such as investing in their children's education, and collective living standards have not improved. (World Bank 2004, 21)

They are also often wasted, with royalties commonly used:

> to settle outstanding debts, incurred as a consequence of their taking on new wives and having to pay bridal wealth, or having pigs slaughtered on 'credit' for bridal or mortuary feasts or traditional compensation purposes. (Koyama 2004, 25)

The same critic (Koyama 2004) points to the intensive and wasteful dissipation of rents through litigation and leadership contestation, and the unlawful and unfair sharing of benefits, often shrouded in a lack of transparency. Mako (2023) writes about the 'local resource curse' in relation to the Porgera gold mine. An earlier study on the same mine found 'the impact of large amounts of cash, especially in the form of compensation payments, had a negative impact on women' (Filer 1999, 6) and noted local women's concerns around 'a breakdown in law and order (especially the increase in rape and police violence)' (Bonnell 1999, 53). Porgera has experienced a '"new polygamy", whereby the number of wives a man may marry appears to have increased exponentially' (Johnson 2010, 20). One estimate is that 60–70 per cent of Porgera men have more than one wife, with 'many having between 3 and 6 wives, plus a few with 16+' (Johnson 2010, 20).

There was a move in the context of the PNG LNG project to give landowner benefits to individuals rather than groups (as is done for the Ok Tedi project). While this would certainly have improved the equity of royalty distribution, Filer (2019b, 47) recalls that neither the government nor the developers were prepared to invest in the census required, and, moreover, that the proposal:

> did not appeal to the more idealistic national stakeholders, especially members of the legal fraternity, who thought it would undermine the integrity of customary social groups, and was equally unappealing to those 'prominent leaders' who wanted to control the distribution of landowner benefits.

The second major change in resource policy has been the alternate tightening and relaxing of the fiscal regime. It was tightened in the run-up to independence through the renegotiation of the Bougainville Panguna mine agreement, when the resource rental or super-profits tax was introduced (2.2.3). But it was then relaxed just before the boom began, including by abolishing the super-profits tax (4.3.2), and then tightened once the boom had ended, including by reintroducing the same tax (9.1.4).

The decline in resource revenues during the bust (8.3.2) has led many to conclude that PNG's resource revenue regime is too lax. But the analysis has not yet been undertaken to fully explain this trend. A comprehensive review concluded that mining tax rates are comparable with those of other countries (Bogan et al. 2014). Despite PNG belonging to the Extractive Transparency Industries Initiative, which publishes annual reports on revenue flows from various resource projects to the government, there remains, for many projects, a lack of transparency about the ratio of taxes to profits (2.2.3).

Third, PNG has always favoured taking a minority equity share in large resource projects. The policy has pros and cons, the main pro being that it makes the state a beneficiary of any tax minimisation; the main con being the risks involved and the difficulty of raising the funds. The policy has been pursued haphazardly, with stakes being sold over the nineties in response to fiscal stress or to finance stakes in other projects. The change in this area has been the push in the last two periods to create national champions: state-owned companies that will not only hold minority stakes in existing resource projects but also accumulate revenue to hold minority, or even majority, stakes in future projects, and potentially operate those projects or decide who will (7.1.3 and 9.1.4). This reflects growing resource nationalism, a trend that began in the nineties (4.3.2) and has intensified each decade since. Given governance weaknesses, it is a high-risk strategy.

Fourth and last, resource sector policy has become more complex and uncertain. Proposals circulate, with strong political backing, to fundamentally alter the policy regime by handing ownership of all subsoil assets to landowners (7.1.4), and to move away from a profit-sharing to a production-sharing set up (9.1.4). The distribution of benefits from any one resource project between central government, provincial government and landowners is ultimately the outcome of negotiations. Negotiations are extensive, and projects are more likely to end up in the courts. PNG was rated the fifth from the bottom in terms of its resource sector policy climate according to a recent global survey of resource companies (Mejía and Aliakbari 2022).

Overall, resource sector policy can be judged a success in terms of the growth rate of the sector (above 5 per cent per year on average—Table 10.3), but a failure set against the sensible goal at independence to support large resource projects 'not for any direct benefit they can bring, but for the financial support that they can provide for progress towards other national goals' (2.2.3). For the post-independence era as a whole, the government has obtained much less financial support from the resource sector than from the non-resource sector. Moreover, the resource sector is actually slightly less heavily taxed than the non-resource sector: for the post-independence period, the ratio of resource revenue to resource sector output is, on average, 91 per cent of the ratio of (own) non-resource revenue to non-resource output (Table 10.10).[1]

PNG is certainly unusual in this regard. The IMF defines a country as resource rich if it derives at least 20 per cent of either its exports or of government revenue (excluding aid) from the resource sector (Thomas and Trevino 2013). PNG is one of the most resource-rich countries in the world on the former criterion (Table 10.4), but not resource rich at all on the latter criterion (with resource revenue only contributing, on average, 16 per cent of own revenue). This book has suggested several reasons why the PNG government is unable to derive more revenue from the resource sector, including a greater share for other national stakeholders (provincial governments and landowners), and, recently, retention of dividends off-budget by national champions. However, these arguments fall well short of a full explanation. Finding one is a matter of urgency, as the facts need to be settled before current resource sector policy is either maintained or

---

1   Income tax from the resource sector is excluded from the government resource take as our interest is in how much resource profits are taxed.

jettisoned. Greater transparency will be required from companies to relate tax paid to profits and to understand why, when the former is low, taxable profits are not higher.

11.5 Downstream processing and import substitution — pursued in moderation

Getting the PNG economy more engaged with downstream processing— oil refining, tuna canning, timber milling—has been an objective since independence, as has import substitution (sugar, rice and cement). These are natural goals for a commodity exporter, but difficult ones to realise. We have discussed the main individual initiatives in earlier chapters and now conclude our treatment of this topic with some general remarks.

First, this is an area in which rhetoric has outstripped policy. PNG has repeatedly threatened/promised to ban the exports of unprocessed logs, but has never followed through, instead constantly extending self-imposed deadlines (9.1.3). Various projects to grow rice, and to ban or limit rice imports, have been proposed but not actually implemented. That realism has prevailed is good, but it has been at a cost to credibility.

Second, where the rhetoric has been accompanied by policy, results have largely been modest. The most successful downstream processing effort in terms of employment has been tuna processing (canning), but this has been by the government effectively paying the equivalent of the sector's wage bill (9.1.3). It would be hard to endorse such an extravagant policy. In other cases, results have been disappointing. Despite granting a 10-year ban on sugar imports to pioneer domestic producer Ramu Sugar in the 1980s (2.2.2), PNG now imports about half its sugar. The Napa Napa oil refinery commenced production in 2004, with the intention of giving it a monopoly, but PNG in fact imports a significant share of its refined oil needs (ICCC 2016).

A range of natural difficulties has hindered the promotion of downstream processing: for example, a high diversity of trees makes timber processing more difficult and indigenous sugar diseases have threatened commercial sugar production. More systemic problems have also had an impact, including the high cost of doing business in PNG, and, in recent years, the overvalued exchange rate and difficulties of getting hold of foreign exchange for projects that are reliant on foreign inputs.

Third, while their benefits have often disappointed, the costs of these industrial policies have also been contained by the liberalisation of the nineties, which reduced tariffs across the board, and by adoption of a pragmatic approach. To take the two examples given above: the ban on imports that protected Ramu Sugar for a decade has been replaced by a much more modest 30 per cent tariff (ICCC 2019a); and when the Napa Napa oil refinery first ran into production difficulties in 2007, the 30-year import ban on refined oil products that protected it was set aside (ICCC 2019b).

Industrial policy was not mentioned in the original Washington Consensus document. The use of such policies might be said to run contrary to the emphasis of the Consensus on liberalisation and deregulation. One might equally argue, however, that the Consensus allows for some industrial policy, as long as it is not excessive. In any case, there is no doubt the commendable goals of more downstream processing and manufacturing will continue to be pursued in PNG. Hopefully, the country's pragmatic approach will continue to contain the costs of such policies. For, without better fundamentals, the objective of diversifying the economy away from the resource sector will make little progress.

11.6 The land stalemate

Expensive, difficult and insecure access to land has been recognised as an important constraint on growth since independence (3.1.5). In 1984, Finance Minister John Kaputin (1984, 12) referred to it as a major but not insurmountable constraint to growth. Subsequent events have proved him right on the first point, but wrong on the second.

Property rights are stronger in relation to land that has been alienated from its traditionally customary ownership, but such land is scarce and therefore expensive, its administration often inept and corrupt, and its ownership still subject to claims from customary owners (Filer 2014). Some argue that customary land arrangements are conducive to smallholder agricultural growth.[2] However, at least outside of smallholder agriculture, there is no debate that reforms to customary land are necessary to promote development. Filer (2019a, 84) writes of the 'incompatibility of customary social institutions with the operation of a capitalist economy that includes a land market'.

---

2   For the two sides of this argument, see Bourke (2005a) and Holzknecht (2003), on one side, and Curtin (2003) on the other.

Major disagreement exists in relation to the type of reforms that are needed. Cooter (1991) classified the possible reforms into various types. The first are collective in nature: these aim to facilitate the commercial transaction of group-owned land. Cooter calls this a 'socialist fantasy' arguing that clans cannot be organised into legal structures. The second are individualistic in nature and aim to replace group (customary) by individual (freehold) ownership. Cooter call this a 'capitalist fantasy' and writes that 'freehold ownership goes against custom and usage in PNG to such an extent that conversion inevitably creates misunderstandings and disputes' (Cooter 1991, 780).

The PNG government, supported by a number of PNG and Australian consultants and academics (Fingleton 2004; Yala 2010b), has pursued the collective approach. Two variants of this have been attempted: the lease-leaseback approach (from the seventies, see 3.1.5) and voluntary customary land registration (from the noughties, see 9.1.5). Neither has been successful. The former was abused and suspended, and the latter has been little used. Neither has unlocked financing for landowners.

The individualistic approach has been supported by a small number of mainly Australian economists on the grounds that it is the only known basis for development (Gosarevski, Hughes and Windybank 2004). It has been tried in PNG through the longstanding Land (Tenure Conversion) Act, but this approach was written off as a failure by the colonial administration even before independence (Fingleton 1981, 214) and has hardly been used since. Even if it is conceded that, in customary society, use rights often rest with households (Lea 2023), given what Filer (2014, 82) calls 'the national ideology of landownership', a constituent part of which is that 'customary groups of landowners are the basic building blocks of national society', it is simply unrealistic to expect the individualist approach to land reform to succeed.[3]

Cooter recommended a third, case law approach that would involve relying on decisions under the Land Disputes Settlement Act with the aim of allowing:

---

3   Freehold titles acquired through the land tenure conversion process are also largely unbankable (Kimas 2010, 35).

customary law to evolve and produce its own answer to the question of ownership. Under this proposal, Parliament would remain neutral on the question of individual vs. clan ownership. Instead of a centralized decision, land courts would let custom take its course and enforce the changes that evolve. (Cooter 1991, 792)

Unfortunately, this approach, even if viable at the time it was suggested, is no longer credible. While many land disputes come to courts, and the courts play a useful, clarificatory role, for example, in denying customary claims to alienated land, PNG's land dispute mediation and settlement system has weakened since independence (Oliver and Fingleton 2008). It 'has become orphaned by the institutional ambiguities surrounding the devolution of functions to the provinces and subsequent reforms to national departments and agencies' (Allen and Monson 2014, 3).

Land reform is, therefore, at a stalemate. The growth of the informal land market has been noted by commentators since at least the eighties (3.1.5), and, for the foreseeable future, informal land transactions will dominate in PNG.

Port Moresby's settlement population is estimated to have grown twice as fast as the city's overall population (Chand and Yala 2008, 91), and roughly equal numbers are now estimated to live in suburbs and settlements. Surveys in the noughties showed that settlements were:

> full of entrepreneurial activity. Services available ranged from tucker shops, billiard tables, hairdressing services, repair shops and trade stores to illegal activities such as bootlegging. Permanent structures, some with septic toilets, television antennae and electricity generators, were discovered as was a commercial complex valued by the proprietor at K300,000 built on land with no formal title in the name of the investor. For the most part, settlements were accessible only to residents—strangers were not welcome within them. (Chand and Yala 2008, 94)

Of course, there are concerns, as in any informal market, with the integrity of these transactions:

> In some circumstances, the buyers or tenants cannot be sure that what they have purchased or rented is in fact customary land, and if it is, whether it has not already been informally sold or leased to someone else. (Filer 2019a, 83)

Rooney (2017) gives a fascinating case study that is instructive of the complexities involved.

Given the lack of security that informal land transactions provide, and their word-of-mouth nature, it is not surprising that individual settlements tend to be dominated by particular ethnic (tribal) groups (Chand and Yala 2005; Rooney 2017). This cannot be good for social integration. Already, ethnic conflict is no longer an exclusively rural phenomenon.

Despite these downsides, given the impasse that land reform has come to, there is simply no alternative to reliance on informal land markets, especially for housing. These markets were given a boost by the boom, which greatly increased both employment opportunities and property prices (6.2.2). A survey in Port Moresby by Gouy et al. (2010) of advertised property prices in 2010 found the average lease to be PGK9,300 per month. While rents were significantly lower in the cheapest of the three formal or suburban zones studied (at PGK2,900), they were *much* cheaper outside of the formal sector, in a settlement (either on customary land or on alienated land without title) where average rent was only PGK326.[4] The almost tenfold difference between settlement and cheap formal sector accommodation is striking, and explains the demand for settlement land.

That said, there are some things informal transactions cannot do. The Markham-Ramu valley is estimated to have 405,000 hectares of arable land. Only 59,000 hectares is given over to commercial farming and another 16,000 hectares is used by smallholders (IFC 2021), leaving 330,000 hectares of land suitable for agriculture unfarmed. Most of the valley is grass, as it has been for centuries. There are various constraints to the region's development, but the biggest is the difficulty of securing and retaining access to land for commercial agriculture. An earlier estimate for the country as a whole is that, of the 11.8 million hectares of land suitable for cultivation, only 3 million hectares is 'actually currently in the food production cycle (that is, land currently in food production plus vegetation regrowth)' (Saunders 1993, 11). The difficulties of registering customary land for commercial use are illustrated by Schwoerer (2022), while the difficulties of running a business on land that was once customarily owned are readily apparent in the book on the Ramu Sugar project by Errington and Gewertz (2004).

---

4   Settlements were not surveyed, so this figure is based on 'anecdotal evidence from the real estate agents' surveyed (Gouy et al. 2010, 18).

There is no easy way forward. Commendable efforts continue to bring customary land into the formal market. However, weak and under-resourced land administration—'corrupt, inefficient and dysfunctional' (Yala 2010a, 3)—is a binding constraint, its weakness evident from the early 1980s.[5] Voluntary land registration and the lease-leaseback schemes would have worked better with a stronger bureaucracy. But bad governance trumps good policy.

11.7 The informal economy — benign neglect

The importance of informal or unregulated ways of doing business to PNG's land markets is evident from the previous section. If land transactions were only made in accordance with the law, urban land markets would cease to exist for all but the best resourced. It is not only land markets where PNG's informal economy has come to the rescue. The percentage of the employed population in wage employment (a proxy for the formal sector) fell from 15.1 per cent in 1980 to 11.3 per cent in 2011 (NSO 2015, 60), the year of the last census, and in urban areas from 85.5 per cent to 53.4 per cent. By 2011, 32 per cent of urban households were engaged in the sale of *buai* (betel nut) or mustard (the two go together), and 29 per cent in the sale of fresh or cooked food (NSO 2015, 75)—the two leading informal activities. There is also evidence that, unlike pre-deregulation (McGavin 1991), some informal workers now earn more than some wage earners (Samof 2023).

PNG's informal economy is still relatively weak compared to its Asian neighbours or even many African countries: one example is the lack of a widespread black market for foreign exchange. Nevertheless, any evaluation of the informal economy today has to take into account its inauspicious beginnings and the many challenges it has faced.

At independence the informal economy was virtually non-existent outside of agriculture. Various factors account for this, including subsistence affluence (2.2.4), the absence of trading prior to colonisation, and the negative attitude to urbanisation on the part of the coloniser and, subsequently, PNG's elite (Conroy 2020). Outside of agriculture, urban centres are needed for the

---

5   'It is unfortunate that the Department of Lands is administratively weak. Its weakness seems to be due at least in part to shortages of staff, inexperience, lack of training and the fact that the procedures which must be followed are in many cases cumbersome. The department has a large backlog of transactions waiting to be processed, and its inefficiency is further reflected in long delays in completing transactions or failure to complete them at all' (Goodman, Lepani and Morawetz 1985, 122).

informal economy to flourish. But in PNG, urban centres were meant to be areas for formal employment only, as places not to settle but only to take up wage labour, intended for men, not their families (11.8).

Another barrier to the informal economy at independence was the excessive level of regulation the economy was subject to under Australian standards (3.1.3). The regulatory impulse persists to this day with periodic bans in Port Moresby and other cities on *buai*, cooked food and street sales (Wenogo 2022; Mirr 2022); daily harassment by police and city rangers (Kavan 2010, 358); and new regulatory architectures, such as embodied in the 2004 Informal Sector Development and Control Act. In the end, however, attempts at regulation and control are typically short lived and ineffectual. This is one benefit of the state being weak: wrongheaded initiatives are no more likely to succeed than well-justified ones. While there are legitimate concerns around health and hygiene, people have to make a living. There is no safety net to fall back on, and voters deprived of their livelihoods are unlikely to re-elect their incumbent MP. Finally, there is also, and opposing the regulatory impulse, a contrary tradition in PNG going back to the pre-independence Faber Report and the Eight-Point Plan that is much more positively inclined to informal economic activity (3.1.1; Conroy 2020). This tradition has led to little by way of positive support for the informal economy, but it has encouraged a disposition on the part of the state of benign neglect towards it, and that has supported its growth.

The informal economy has also benefited from expatriate participation. Many immigrants from mainland China, who have arrived in large numbers over the last two decades (9.2.6), have become small traders, operating outside the formal sector, some even running 'kai bars' (small takeaway food bars), even though these are on the reserved list for nationals (Chin 2024, 88).

Of course, the informal economy is held back by the same policy constraints of weak law and order and poor infrastructure that afflict the formal economy. Why the former has grown faster than the latter is an interesting question. In the case of land, the formal path is simply closed. Informal enterprises pay no corporate tax and their employees pay no income tax: both are relatively high in PNG by world standards. Goods sold in the informal market attract no sales tax. The advantages of joining the formal economy to get a respectable international profile are also minimal in PNG given that exporting is almost exclusively the domain of commodity producers. It may also be that the more robust growth of the informal economy reflects its low starting point at independence and that the informal economy suits PNG's conditions and culture.

Whatever the reason, we should be grateful that the regulatory impulse, though not extinguished, has been kept in check with regards to the informal economy, and that a de facto policy of benign neglect has, in general, prevailed. In many ways, the informal economy has come to PNG's rescue. Without it, the country's overall economic performance would have been much worse.

11.8 The retreat from equality

Equality was an extremely important rhetorical principle at independence (3.1.1). The Eight-Point Plan PNG took to independence promised a 'more equal distribution of economic benefits including a move toward equalising incomes' and 'a rapid increase in the equal and active participation of women in both the economy and social activity'. Most egalitarians argue for the reduction rather than the elimination of inequality. But, around the time of independence in PNG, a utopian egalitarianism prevailed, at least rhetorically. As Deputy Prime Minister Paias Wingti put it in 1981 at one of the annual Waigani Seminars:

> As we promised in our election campaign, we are determined to eliminate all imbalances. Let's face it, there are still many in our society. They include rural versus urban, educated versus illiterate, rich versus poor. None of them is healthy, and the gaps between them must be narrowed and finally removed. (Wingti 1985, 16–17)[6]

In subsequent decades, equality has featured much less prominently in government policy statements. The current prime minister likes to talk of creating a nation in which 'no-one is left behind'. However, growth and employment have become the priority, rather than, as Finance Minister Julius Chan graphically put it in 1992, 'the ramblings and wafflings from self-proclaimed philosophers who continue to want everyone to be equal' (Chan 1992, 24). The 2009 *Vision 2050* aspiration is for a 'smart, wise, fair, healthy and happy society by 2050' that is 'wealthy and safe'. 'Fair' is a long way from 'equal'. There is virtually no formal social safety net. Whereas

---

6   Wingti goes on to a long discussion on the importance of gender equality.

Somare in 1974 undertook to restrict the building of new hospitals in urban areas to 'give priority to the neglected rural areas' (Somare 1974, 14); now, even though rural health care has deteriorated, the government wants to build 'modern world class' hospitals in all 22 provinces (PNG Facts 2020).

Meanwhile, if we look at the data, PNG is now one of the most unequal countries in the Asia-Pacific region (ADB 2012b). The official measure for the Gini coefficient is 41.9 per cent, based on a 2009 survey (World Bank Group n.d.-b). Ironically, donors, who once worried that PNG was placing too much emphasis on equity, now ask the government to reduce inequality (ADB 2012b).

PNG's high level of inequality is not hard to explain. Its resource dependency (ratio of resource sector to GDP) is one of the highest in the world (Howes and Leng 2023), but its official urban share of 14 per cent makes it the least urbanised country in the world (10.2). Together, these facts make PNG one of the most dualistic countries in the world.

On urbanisation, there is a strand in PNG policy that goes back to well before independence that has wanted to minimise rural–urban migration or 'urban drift' as it is called. The desire to keep as many as possible in the countryside was shared by both PNG's colonial ruler and by the PNG elite. Australia wanted to 'secure village life' (from the title of MacWilliam 2013) and was 'hostile to the emergence of a committed indigenous urban workforce' (Conroy 2023, 5). In 1969, the House of Assembly passed a motion portraying 'urbanisation as a threat to village life and as a cause of unemployment', and asking the administration 'to reintroduce restrictions on movements to towns except where employment was assured or for short visits' (cited in MacWilliam 2013, 213). There were similar motions in 1964, 1971 and 1973 (Conroy 2023, 243). Vagrancy was a crime under colonial role. The Vagrancy Act of 1977 made it a crime once again, but was ruled unconstitutional (3.2.5). Official attitudes have remained unchanged. In 1991, Finance Minister Paul Pora said: 'Our young people must realise the importance and opportunities of working on the land and avoid the temptation to drift to the cities where high expectations have only led to disappointment and despair' (Pora 1991, 46). In 2023, Prime Minster James Marape told the youth of PNG: 'Do not come to Port Moresby or Lae' (PNG Facts 2023).[7] PNG's success at restraining urban drift—as indicated

---

7   When commercial advertising was first introduced onto radio by the National Broadcasting Commission, 'this was limited to urban areas as it was feared that commercials would raise the expectations of rural people by showing them the 'bright lights' of the towns' (Goodman et al. 1985, 163).

by its very low urban share—is the result neither of this sort of official discouragement nor of improved rural living conditions but rather of a lack of urban opportunity.

We lack the data to say whether inequality has increased in PNG. However, it is hard to believe that it has decreased. Gewertz and Errington (1999) documented the growing differentiation between an 'elite middle class' (those in waged jobs) and the 'grass roots' majority (those in rural areas and in urban settlements). With the fall in the minimum wage (Figure B18), Cox (2014) has argued that there is now a third class, the 'working poor' who are waged but nevertheless struggling.

Even in the early days, the commitment to equality was more rhetorical than substantive. In particular, the large increases to the urban minimum wage in the run-up to independence were sharply at odds with such a commitment (3.1.1). From this same perspective, the sharp reduction in the urban minimum wage over the nineties (5.1.1 and Figure B18) must be regarded as a victory for national equity. However, the recent overvaluation of the exchange rate (8.3.1), like a high minimum wage, is a form of urban bias, as it benefits urban dwellers (food purchasers) and disadvantages rural ones (food producers).

Government expenditure can promote or undermine equality. There has always been a focus on rural development since independence (3.1.4). And since most members of parliament serve rural constituencies, the growth in MP funding (Figure A1) is to the benefit of rural areas. Nevertheless, the assessment that 'the actual allocation of resources remains heavily biased toward urban areas' (McKillop, Bourke and Kambori 2009, 59) continues to be reasonable, and perhaps inevitable, given limited budget spending capacity and the demands of urban areas for roads, policing and basic services.

One area where there has been at least some progress is in relation to equality between men and women. A study of PNG's schools and health facilities found that:

> In 2002, only 13 per cent of primary school principals were females. In 2012, it was 27 per cent, more than double. The number of female teachers also increased sharply: from 27 to 55 per cent. (Howes et al. 2014)

Women are active participants in PNG's informal economy, which is where the great majority of nationals work. For example, the share of market vendors who are women has increased and is now above 80 per cent

(Sharp, Busse and Bourke 2022). This progress notwithstanding, PNG is still a long way from equal participation, with limited contraception access (10.2) and violence against women providing two of the most insurmountable barriers. On the latter, PNG has the sixth-highest rate of intimate partner violence in the world (Table 10.14). The share of women in a polygynous relationship grew from 14 per cent in 1996 to 18 per cent in 2016–18 (Pandey and Howes 2022, 179). Women who earn more than their husband are at increased risk of violence (Smith 2024). PNG's very low level of political representation—depending on the parliamentary term, either the lowest in the world, or one of the lowest—both reflects the country's extreme level of gender disparity and helps perpetuate it.

11.9 Conclusion

When thinking about economic policy in Papua New Guinea, the question naturally arises as to whether the country suffers from the resource curse, that is, whether its resource endowments have actually hindered rather than helped development. While it is impossible to say whether PNG would be better off without its subsoil assets, one can certainly say that its endowments have been, at best, a mixed blessing. In the next chapter, we look at how resource dependency might be linked to weak institutions (12.4). Economic symptoms of a resource curse, sometimes called Dutch disease, include an overvalued exchange rate and a high-cost economy, both of which have certainly been in evidence in independent PNG (3.1.3 and 7.3). That said, it would be a mistake to reduce the PNG economic story to one of the resource curse; things are much more complex than that.

Managing the PNG economy is an intrinsically difficult task for (at least) five reasons. First, as a small, open, resource-dependent economy, the PNG economy is prone to numerous shocks, which makes forward planning very difficult. A boom was anticipated in the early eighties, but did not eventuate at all (2.2.1). The boom of the early nineties was much shorter than expected. The long boom of the noughties was completely unexpected, as was the bust of the tens. Second, the economy is highly monopolistic, which has the implication that standard liberalising policies may not be welfare improving. Deregulation may backfire due to limited competition. Third, even sensible policies have risks. Currency non-convertibility is very damaging for growth and encourages fiscal profligacy. It would be sensible to reintroduce convertibility, yet such a reform may, if it does not induce adequate fiscal discipline, lead to a balance of payments crisis, as it did, twice, in the nineties. Fourth, economic reforms may have a limited return because other constraints are binding and cannot be addressed, such as insecurity. Fifth, some of the reforms needed are technically demanding. One can smooth resource revenue to government using a formula, but PNG also gets a revenue boost from the construction of resource projects, and these non-resource-revenue booms are much difficult to smooth. Everyone knows that land reforms are important, but no-one knows which land reforms will work.

Moreover, managing the PNG economy is more difficult now than at independence, for another two reasons. First, stability seems to have become the most important organising economic principle in PNG. Instability hurts confidence but, looking back on PNG's history (and international experience), more stability means less reform. Second, there is a lack of consensus around economic reform. There is a reaction against policies and reforms supported in the nineties, with less support for Washington Consensus–type reforms, and more for nationalistic policies. At the same time, the stalling of various reform proposals in recent years, for example to greatly expand the reservation list, and to rewrite the country's resource policies, shows that there is much disagreement about the direction the country should take. The result is often drift.

Thus there are many difficulties for any would-be Papua New Guinean reformer, but nevertheless reform is needed. We have already indicated our priorities for macroeconomic reform: a return to currency convertibility on the current account, the reintroduction of a revenue smoothing mechanism and the restoration of credibility. On the microeconomic front, policies that promote competition and market entry should be encouraged, but regulatory approaches should not be discarded without careful analysis and may need to be introduced where competition is weak. Clampdowns on the informal economy should be avoided. A better understanding is urgently needed of the failure of the national government to accrue more revenue from the resource sector. And there should be a return to the emphasis at independence on equality, including gender equality, with a special focus on improving the country's appalling vaccination and nutrition indicators (Table 10.14).

These reforms are needed for higher growth and better development. Whether or not they will be undertaken depends on deeper institutional factors, to which we now turn.

12

Institutional underpinnings

[It will help to have] honest, competent leaders, but leadership alone is not sufficient. Lying at the root of the problem is the breakdown of the structure, systems and processes of government. As a result, good leaders are imprisoned by this fractured, corrupt system. Unless steps are taken to repair and reform the system and processes of government, to rebuild the capacity of the public sector, good leaders will achieve and change little.

—Former prime minister Mekere Morauta (2012a)

12.1 Introduction

Most of the existing analysis of economic outcomes in PNG has been directed to the assessment of economic policy, as the previous chapter was. Policy settings are important for growth but ignoring broader issues of governance is unhelpful. In their analysis of the forestry sector, Daniel and Sims (1986, 76) drew attention to the tendency of the government to enter into agreement with 'inexperienced companies', but left that odd preference unexplained, rather than linking it to corruption as it surely was.

Likewise, the analysis of the previous chapter takes us some way in explaining PNG's economic performance but leaves many questions unanswered. Why has the quality of macroeconomic policy deteriorated since independence? Why did the reforms of the nineties not give a more sustained boost to growth? To dig deeper, we need a more institutional analysis.

The idea that explanations for economic growth performance should be sought in the sphere of institutions is by now accepted wisdom. In 1983, one economist concluded his survey of growth in developing countries with the remark that 'the single most important explanatory variable' that explains the difference between faster and slower growing countries is 'political organisation and the administrative competence of government' (Reynolds 1983, 975). Since then, many economists have elaborated on this theme.

'Institutions' is not an easy word to define. An institution need not be an organisation, but to say, as some do, that institutions are just the rules of the game is to give too broad a definition, one that would encompass cultural and social explanations of economic outcomes as well. Institutions clearly include political arrangements; they include the way in which the rule of law is exercised, and the degree to which security is provided to citizens and their property; and they include basic economic arrangements, such as the degree to which a country relies on markets or central planning. We dealt with the last in the previous chapter. Our focus in this chapter is on the former two: the interaction between PNG politics and development, and the interaction with insecurity.

We start by summarising our findings so far in relation to institutions. We then go in search of theories that link these findings to economic performance. Thus armed, we set forth our institutional explanation of PNG's growth and development performance.

12.2 Post-independence institutional trends

Each of the preceding four parts of this book provided an account of key institutional developments in the relevant period (3.2, 5.2, 7.2 and 9.2). In this section, we bring together and summarise our various findings under the headings of politics, government effectiveness, and law and order. We also turn to survey data to understand the importance of institutional constraints on growth in PNG.

12.2.1 Hyper-politics

Five defining characteristics of PNG politics have become prominent.

First, there is the 'progressive primacy of politics in post-colonial PNG' (Dinnen 1998, 58), as becoming a member of parliament has come to be seen as 'the fastest road to wealth, power and influence' (Ketan 2000, 245). Democracy suited PNG. Over time, extraordinarily large numbers have come to stand for national elections; leaders in all other fields have wanted to become politicians. Seeking power through elections has become not only more popular but also more legitimate over time. In a country in which no group is large enough to mount a serious claim to national power by methods other than the ballot box, success at elections has become universally accepted as the main way in which power should be obtained and challenged.

Second, and contributing to the primacy of politics, the business and the political classes have merged into a 'politician-businessman ruling class' (Hegarty and King 1998, 356). Politicians and their parties have entered business to offset the costs of campaigning, to secure political success and in pursuit of wealth. Businessmen—and a few businesswomen—have entered politics in pursuit of power.

Third, politics is both clientelist and precarious. Elections are decided on local issues and networks, and often involve competition and conflict between different local groups. Kabuni et al. (2022) note that, according to the relevant international index for it, PNG is the fifth most clientelist polity in the world. But being a local patron is not easy. Politicians have struggled to be re-elected: normally only about half are.

Fourth, there has emerged since 1978 a constant jostling for power among MPs, who have sought not only to represent their electorate but to rise up the political ladder, to become a minister and, if possible, prime minister. To make such efforts, unconstrained by party allegiances or ideological differences, has come to be regarded as a normal part of any MP's role.[1] This has resulted in frequent attempts to hold votes of no confidence and change the prime minister. These efforts have been less successful this century than last, but they have been no less vigorously pursued.

---

1   When deputy prime minister Sam Basil tried to bring down James Marape's government at the end of 2020 (shortly after it had passed the protected 18-month period), he told one newspaper, after he failed, and had been given back his deputy prime minister position: 'This is all political. We are simply doing our job.' Marape graciously responded. 'These sorts of things happen. Every party leader when the opportunity (to become) PM presents itself, has the right to make a bid for it. It didn't happen (this time) and the next best available option is deputy and it's still vacant' (Tarawa 2020).

Fifth, election quality has fallen over time and, in some parts of the country, elections have become increasingly violent (5.2.1 and 9.2.1). Local groups use extra-parliamentary means to achieve their goals, in particular, threats of violence to extract compensation (5.2.5).

Various labels have been attached to PNG politics by political scientists: Wood (2018) describes PNG politics as clientelist, Steeves (1996) as 'unbounded' and May (2003a) as 'disorderly'. Fraenkel (2014) writes that Melanesian politics is 'incessantly fleeting, precarious and contested'. One useful summary label might be 'hyper-political': politics in PNG is hyper (very) local, popular, intense and insecure.

PNG's culture of hyper-politics has been broadly supportive of political regime stability, somewhat supportive of democracy and barely supportive of development. While PNG politics has been, at different times, more or less stable—as measured by prime ministerial tenure, more in the seventies, noughties and tens, and less in the eighties and nineties—its regime stability has been second to none, at least at the national level. A political regime (form of government) lasts on average for only one or two decades in a developing country (Cox, North and Weingast 2019). Even if we include rich countries, a democracy only lasts for just over 20 years on average (Knutsen and Nygard 2015). But such is the buy-in to it that PNG's political system has lasted half a century (since home rule in 1972), with only very minor changes. Every now and then a major political reform is mooted, such as a shift to a presidential system or the introduction of a second house of parliament. But no major national shift has happened to date. If one does, it will be through an orderly system of constitutional reform. Notwithstanding, or perhaps as illustrated by, the Sandline affair (5.2.1), unconstitutional change such as a coup or a move to one-party rule or comprehensive state capture by one faction of the elite is highly unlikely. There is too much commitment by the elite to the current system, and other power sources are too fragmented to make a grab for power, for example through the army (Mietzner and Farrelly 2013).

The qualifications to this verdict of regime stability are all at the sub-national level: major changes have taken place with respect to the way provinces, districts and local areas are governed, and, of course, there is the conflict and secessionist push in Bougainville. That said, PNG's national regime stability is striking, and, among the slow growers of the world, unique (Table 10.13).

Turning to the impact of hyper-politics on democracy, PNG has been rated by international indices for about the last two decades as a partial rather than a full democracy (Figure A2) because of the many problems with its elections. Politicians are committed to the idea that MPs should be elected and should decide on who governs the country, but not necessarily to all the rules of democracy.[2]

Apart from the positive effect of supporting regime stability, hyper-politics has been bad for economic development. Politicians have developed short time horizons and have been distracted from matters of state and a focus on the public interest by constant power struggles and their extensive business interests (3.2.1). The poor quality of elections surely reduces the quality of MPs elected, as those more likely to cheat are more likely to win. MPs are barely constrained by the national interest. At best, MPs need to show local results to be re-elected, but even that link appears weak. Once elected, they do their own thing. Prime ministers cannot impose much discipline or ministers may defect to the opposition, taking backbenchers with them. Votes of no confidence are regarded as a matter solely for MPs not for citizens.[3] In combination with the fact that prime ministerial incumbents are now highly likely to be returned at election time (7.2.1), this means that voters are effectively disenfranchised when it comes to deciding who will lead the country. More broadly, the system, as it has evolved, without strong parties, means that voters are unable to punish ineffective governments or reward effective ones, let alone vote for particular policies.

12.2.2 Government effectiveness

Shortly after independence PNG was adjudged to have 'an effective set of institutions for economic and financial management' (World Bank 1978, 5). However, by the nineties, PNG was diagnosed as a weak state (Hegarty 1989; May [1997] 2001b). Now it consistently features in both the World Bank's and the Asian Development Bank's lists of fragile states.[4] 'Weak' is a better word than 'fragile', since the latter means prone to collapse, and PNG's state seems much more stable than that. A weak state is one that is

2   The more positive conclusion of Reilly (2000) that PNG's extreme ethnic fragmentation supports its democratic set-up needs to be qualified thus some two decades on.

3   Iambakey Okuk, reflecting on one of the many votes of no confidence he supported, said: 'The voters have no rights at the moment. Once elected, the MP must decide what is best for his career' (cited in Denoon 2005, 184).

4   PNG escaped from these lists during its boom years, but in hindsight was being rewarded for good economic times rather than an improvement in state capability.

unable to act in a united and coherent way to implement national policies, whether good or bad. There are no cases of weak states supporting growth for a sustained period of time. Rather, as the World Bank's Commission on Growth and Development (2008, 26) put it, sustained rapid growth needs 'committed, credible and capable governments'. PNG's weak state also helps to explain its inability to contain the uprising in Bougainville and to enforce the rules of electoral democracy.

Some object to describing the PNG state as weak on nationalistic grounds (McKenna, Morona and Samgay 2021), but many domestic critics and citizens support this label. Martin (2015, 230) writes, on the basis of his extensive fieldwork, of 'the widespread, if not universal feeling that was expressed to me around the Gazelle Peninsula [in East New Britain] that the Papua New Guinea state had indeed been a failure', commenting also that 'most of the expressions of failure come from grassroots villagers, whereas as most of the claims of partial success or justification for failure come from political elites'.

Others object to 'weakness' as a label on the grounds of over-simplification (Nelson 2006). It is indeed difficult to summarise so complex an institution as PNG's government:

> with its individuals and institutions of combative vigour; its many predatory [and, it should be added, at least some well-intentioned] elected and career officers; its inefficiencies and indifference to written and unwritten laws … a government of several hierarchies and shifting alliances. (Nelson 2007a, 13)

But try we must, and 'weak' seems like an apt summary.

International indices of governance, for what they are worth, support the claim that government effectiveness has fallen in PNG over time. The Worldwide Governance Indicators government effectiveness measure is available from 1996. Between that year and 2022, PNG's percentile ranking fell from the 44th percentile of countries (from the bottom) to the 22nd (Figure 12.1). The broadly steady rankings between 2005 and 2015 probably reflect the boom effect: the economy doing better made people think government was more effective.[5]

---

5   Teskey et al. (2021, 15) make the contrary argument that 'governance in PNG over the long-term is improving, yet at a very slow rate'. Their first year is 2004, before the boom was evident, and at the end of a period of despair in PNG's national life. This may influence their conclusion.

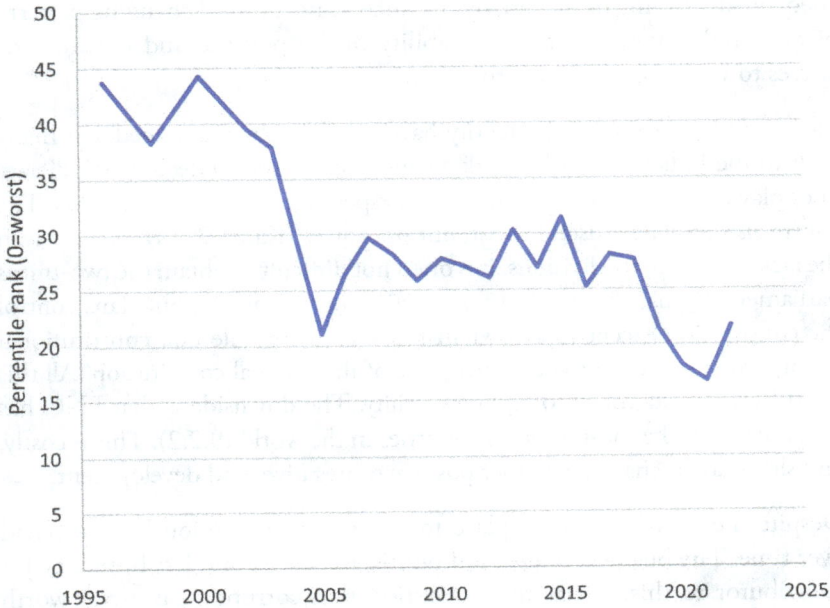

Figure 12.1: PNG's ranking on the Worldwide Governance Indicators effective government index, 1996–2022

Note: Biannual data till 2002.

Source: World Bank Group (n.d.-c).

A measured assessment would note that the reach of the PNG state has always been limited (Nelson 2009) and that there are some bright spots. The Morauta financial sector reforms (5.1.3) gave an enduring boost to the governance of the financial sector. But the overall direction of governance travel has been negative.

State weakness manifests itself in the public service, with an 'inability of many government departments and agencies to carry out basic functions' (Nelson 2006, 17), whether due to a lack of incentives, confusion, inertia or infighting. Both the public service and state-owned enterprises suffer from the lack of a strong development orientation emanating from the country's hyper-politics, and no technocracy has emerged strong enough to ensure such an orientation. The public sector was stymied early on by rapid localisation and then by austerity, and, as early as 1990, was 'perhaps the greatest recipient of criticism in PNG' (Turner 1990, 124). Since then its effectiveness has been undermined by the creation of new agencies without

STRUGGLE, REFORM, BOOM AND BUST: PART 5

adequate defunding of the old, by the uncertainty around changing patterns of decentralisation, and by the inability of the political and bureaucratic classes to work together constructively.

Judicial independence and integrity have been largely maintained and many look to the judiciary as a bulwark against chaos. And, indeed, the judiciary does play a vital dispute-settlement role, especially for the political class. The courts also provide a useful constraint on power (Kama 2024). Since, given the lack of fixed party divisions, it is often not difficult to obtain the two-thirds parliamentary majority needed for constitutional change, politicians control the constitution except to the extent that the courts rule that constitutional changes are inconsistent with other parts of the original constitution. All this contributes substantially to regime stability. The downside is that PNG has become one of the most litigious countries in the world (9.2.2). This is costly, and slows down change, whether positive or negative, and development.

Despite the measures put in place to control it, corruption has worsened over time. The business interests of politicians have doubtless been a major contributor to this, as has the perception that corruption is a risk worth taking. PNG is now ranked 128th out of 180 countries on the Transparency Index (TI) corruption perception index. The extent to which corruption is a constraint on development is debated. Some, including many businesses (Figure 12.2), see it as one of PNG's main problems. Others note that corruption in PNG differs little from levels seen in Asia, and yet Asia has done so much better: Bangladesh, for example, actually sits below PNG on the TI index, and yet has a much stronger development record.

An obvious inference from the above observation is that the key difference between PNG and Asia is not corruption, but state weakness. And yet it may also be the case that corruption may matter more in PNG because the state matters more, especially given resource dependency. Corruption may also be more damaging in PNG more because it is so uncoordinated (Olson 1993). Corruption also contributes to the low level of trust and high transaction costs that now permeate government. Politicians are not trusted to hire bureaucratic leaders in the national interest; therefore, cumbersome and restrictive procedures have been put in place to constrain hiring and firing practices (5.2.2). Politicians and departments are not trusted to spend their budgets with probity, so the central bank requires commercial banks to check whether proper procedures have been followed before releasing funds, and a central body has been established to run all procurement, resulting in enormous delays (9.2.3).

12. INSTITUTIONAL UNDERPINNINGS

Decentralisation and regional autonomy are unfinished business for PNG. Shortly after independence, the country embarked on a radical plan of decentralisation involving the creation of elected provincial assemblies to which extensive powers were given. But in the nineties, these were abandoned and provincial powers were given instead to national MPs, mainly provincial ones, to exercise in their provinces. In the noughties, there was an emphasis on fiscal decentralisation, with the increases in funds going both to provinces and to districts. The latter increases were the largest and were under the control of district (as against provincial) MPs. In the fourth and final period, there was a lot of debate but no resolution on the future of decentralisation in PNG. It is impossible to predict with confidence either the future of decentralisation in general or of the status of Bougainville in particular. The lack of a settled sub-national distribution of power is a clear constraint on state effectiveness.

12.2.3 Law and order

Law and order, or the lack of it, has been a pressing problem for PNG for most of its independent years. In 1979, tribal violence led to a state of emergency being declared in the Highlands, and, in 1985, urban crime to a state of emergency for Port Moresby. In his 1991 book, noted commentator Sean Dorney nominated law and order as the biggest problem PNG would face in the coming decade, and he was right. All forms of violence seemed to worsen over the nineties. Levantis (2000b, 1), who undertook pioneering research in this field, talked of PNG's 'crime catastrophe', calling it PNG's 'most serious social and economic problem' and writing of 'its profound consequences for the legitimacy and integrity of property rights and personal rights'. Globally, PNG is rated as a bottom-20 country when it comes to the state's monopoly on the use of force (Table 10.14).

Incidents of tribal violence have increased and they have become more deadly due to the spread of weapons, criminal gangs and self-styled warlords in some provinces. Urban crime may have plateaued in PNG's bigger cities, but at a very high level by global standards (Levantis 2000b), and it may still be increasing in smaller towns. Claims for compensation or other payments backed by threats of violence are common. Violence against women is at very high levels by global standards—though at least is now gaining more attention—and sorcery-related violence seems to be spreading (11.8).

It is often commented that PNG has very few police by international standards. 'At 1:1,145, the current police-to-population ratio is significantly lower than the UN recommended level of 1:450' (Walton and Dinnen

277

2022, 93). But are more police the answer? In 2004, the then police minister said that 'the greatest fear that our people have is not the criminals but it's the police' (Denoon 2005, 178). In 2020, the new occupant of the same position admitted to a 'rampant culture of police ill-discipline and brutality' (Doherty 2020).

Lack of employment contributes to PNG's crime problem, but criminality is the resort not only of the powerless and the marginalised, but also of the powerful and the well connected, both in government and in the private sector (*RNZ* 2015a; Walton and Dinnen 2022). Marxist criminologist Kristian Lasslett has done more than anyone to investigate the criminal end of political elite behaviour in PNG. His conclusion is that:

> Formally speaking, Papua New Guinea boasts an impressive range of laws, regulatory mechanisms, institutional structures and policies, which have been designed to ... balance economic growth, social need and environmental management. However, behind this formal edifice is an informal regime ... typified by clientelism, corruption and fraud—which has permeated key institutions. (Lasslett 2018, 57)

In summary, 'law and order challenges in Papua New Guinea are intractable. Levels of crime and violence are high and are a major obstacle to economic development' (Haywood-Jones 2016).

12.2.4 The importance of institutional constraints

It is difficult to tease out the importance of various institutional and policy constraints on PNG's investment climate, but some insight can be gained by looking at the five-yearly surveys of businesses carried out by the PNG think tank the Institute of National Affairs, in collaboration with the ADB, in 2002, 2007, 2012 and 2017. One hundred and eighty-seven firms were surveyed in 2017, 136 in 2012 (Holden, Barker and Goie 2017), 243 in 2007 and a similar number in 2002 (ADB and INA 2008, 1). The surveys cover both large and small businesses, and ask them about constraints to their success or, put differently, their views on the investment climate. Figure 12.2 shows the top 10 constraints, rated on a 6-point scale, where a higher score indicates a bigger constraint.[6] The 10 variables are ordered by their average score, and the data labels show the rankings among the 10. On average, the top three constraints are institutional: law and order,

---

6   The 2017 survey uses a 4-point scale and is rescaled. In 2017, 'foreign exchange access' was asked about separately from 'exchange rates'. The latter was the third-ranked constraint, the former the top. In the figure, the former is used for the 2017 rating and score.

corruption and political uncertainty. The next three relate to infrastructure: transport, electricity and telecoms. Of the remaining bottom four, one is skills shortages and the other three relate to macroeconomic policy: the exchange rate, inflation and interest rates.

Exchange rates—really, foreign exchange shortages (see Footnote 6)—were rated as the top concern in 2017 (and in other surveys in other years around that time, see Figure 8.4): economic policy does matter. But overall, by this admittedly imperfect measure of the importance of institutional settings, the ones that matter are the ones that we have focused on in this book, and they matter more than economic policies.

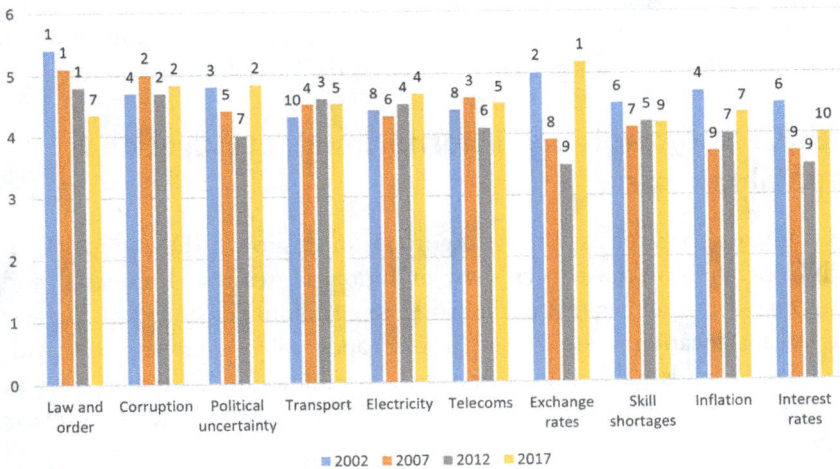

Figure 12.2: Constraints to business, 2002–17

Notes: Data labels are rankings (with 1 the worst); columns are scores out of 6 (with a higher number indicating a more acute constraint). The variables are ordered by their average ranking over the four surveys.

Source: ADB and INA (2008), INA (2013), Holden, Barker and Goie (2017).

It is striking that the top constraint in three out of the four surveys is law and order. It was also ranked the top concern by a considerable margin in 1982 (3.2.5) and 1996 (5.2.5) surveys of businesses, though these surveys had a different format and cannot easily be compared with the more recent ones. Given that law and order was the top-ranked concern of businesses for at least three decades (1982–2012), it is encouraging that the figure shows that the problem is becoming less serious and was no longer the top-ranked constraint by 2017. This may mean that crime has stabilised or even reduced, that businesses have learnt to live with crime and pay for protection, and/or that other problems have got worse.

A recent study of the attitudes of PNG citizens (urban and rural) showed that law and order was also their top concern (Baptiste et al. 2022). When the residents of five villages were asked to identify two 'problems for PNG' (not from a menu), the only two responses nominated by at least half the respondents were 'stealing' and 'fights' (Baptiste et al. 2022, Figure 4.4).

12.3 Growth determinants

There is an extensive global literature on the deep determinants of growth (Rodrik 2003). Institutional explanations of growth stress the importance of politics and security. These are our main interest, but we begin with a brief examination of other explanations—geographical, international, cultural and social—for growth in PNG, or the lack of it.

12.3.1 Geographical, international, cultural and social factors

A country's geography is clearly important for its growth (Diamond 1997). PNG neighbours the poorest part of Indonesia (eastern Indonesia) and was one of the last regions in the world to be colonised. Both facts suggest it lacks a locational advantage. PNG's topography is unforgiving, with its many islands hard to integrate, and its mountainous terrain prone to landslides and home to many remote and separate communities. Large parts of the country are malarial. While some of PNG's land is very fertile, much is mountainous or swampy and therefore unsuitable for agriculture. Allen, Bourke and Gibson (2005, 202) write that:

> Less than 1 per cent of the total land area is classified as 'very high quality land' and almost 60 per cent is classified as 'low' or 'very low' quality land. Poor quality land is higher, steeper, has higher rainfall, floods more often, is cloudier and has less fertile soils than better quality land.

At the same time, some aspects of PNG's geography are more favourable for development, including its rich resource base of minerals, petroleum, timber and fish.

International factors are also relevant. Shortly after independence, dependency theorists started blaming international capital for the country's woes (Mortimer, Kenneth and Amarshi 1979), a zero-sum critique of globalisation that was criticised at the time (Garnaut 1980; Gupta 1992) and is hard to take seriously four decades on given how well many countries have done precisely by integrating themselves into the global economy (Commission on Growth and Development 2008).[7]

Aspects of Australia's colonial management are a more legitimate target for criticism, particularly the low levels of education and high levels of economic regulation it left behind (Daniel and Sims 1986). Australia's White Australia policy kept Papua New Guineans in PNG, leading to a high level of isolation.[8] Papua New Guineans were never welcome in Australia. When the White Australia policy was abandoned over the 1960s and 1970s, it was replaced by a skilled migration regime that was equally successful at keeping Papua New Guineans at home. According to the latest census, Papua New Guineans are only Australia's 82nd-largest ethnic group. The lack of access to Australia helps explain why PNG's share of remittances in GDP is one of the lowest in the world, and why there is so little migration out of the country, to the detriment of its human capital and the free flow of ideas.

In relation to PNG's colonial heritage, one might also complain that the artificial boundaries drawn by PNG's first colonial powers—England and Germany—are at the root of the unresolved issue of Bougainville's status within PNG (Denoon 2000), and all the conflict and destruction that part of PNG has seen since independence (5.2.4).[9]

Some blame foreign aid for making PNG's problems worse, arguing that, because aid flows 'bias the economy against the private sector, they undercut employment and growth and lead to corruption' (Hughes 2003, 1). High levels of foreign aid in the early years of independence may have pushed up costs. And it is certainly true that aid has sometimes been unhelpful— for example, contributing to an excessive reliance on corporate plans and workshops—but it is hard to see it as a fundamental negative. Multilateral and some bilateral donors supported the reforms of the nineties (5.1.4), and

7   The most economically successful countries, the Commission on Growth and Development (2008, 21) argued, 'have fully exploited the world economy'.
8   The difficulties Papuans and New Guineans had travelling to Australia was a common source of criticism during colonial times (Kiki 1968, 178–9).
9   'Geographically and ethnically it [Bougainville] belongs with the British Solomon Islands Protectorate rather than with New Guinea' (Woolford 1976, 29). One friction between Bougainville and the rest of PNG has related to skin colour. Bougainvilleans (like many in Solomon Islands) are black-skinned, and often refer to other Papua New Guineans as 'red skins'. Bougainville is also physically much closer to Solomon Islands than the rest of PNG. Early agitation around the political status of Bougainville canvassed the option that it should be part of Solomon Islands rather than PNG (Denoon 2000, 172, 178). See also Regan and Griffin (2005).

some individual aid projects have been beneficial. More generally though, the PNG case casts serious doubt on the argument that aid can significantly change a country's development trajectory, whether for better or worse.

Some aspects of PNG culture seem conducive to development, such as a high level of entrepreneurialism. Finney's (1973, x–xi) research led him to emphasise 'how readily New Guineans accept economic innovations' and to argue 'that traditional values and institutions were positive assets rather than liabilities in the adoption of cash cropping and commerce'.[10]

Others cultural aspects seem less favourable for development, such as beliefs in sorcery;[11] preferences for consumption, distribution and communal activity over work, accumulation and commercial enterprise;[12] and pressures to put traditional obligations to kin above modern obligations to state law (Ekeh 1975; May 1997). PNG cultural traditions have likely contributed to its hyper-politics and insecurity (12.4). Allen (1983, 215) makes the very interesting remark that the concept of subversion had no place in traditional PNG culture. By this he presumably meant that regime change was never a goal; rather, all the focus was on who would hold or take power within the existing regime. This may help to explain why the population seems so tolerant of its political leaders, and why mass protests are very rare. The low esteem in which women are held—with high levels of polygamy, and violence against women widely accepted—is a drag on development and results in continuing rapid population growth. Most fundamentally, perhaps, the country has had to confront and adapt to markets and modernity in a very short time span. Prior to colonisation, Melanesian society was characterised by 'the absence of specialised trading and intermediary functions' (Conroy 2023, 34). Even the

---

10   Finney's research was of Goroka. He writes: 'The motivation necessary for economic growth was present in the traditional setting, but the economic factors were missing until contact with the outside world supplied the cash crops, technology, monetary system, and marketing channels that made it possible for the Gorokans to earn money and start their own enterprises' (Finney 1973, 22). See Epstein (1968) for a similar analysis of the Tolai of East New Britain.

11   Of a group of landowners, the Mari, whose land is used for the Ramu sugar project (2.2.2), it has been written that 'a sizeable number of Mari, perhaps all, still believe that to accumulate is to evoke jealousy: they are convinced that to rise above the rest attracts the attention of sorcerers. Thus, although virtually all Mari see development as a good thing, and virtually all agree that solid, permanent-material houses are an important aspect of development, few people are willing or able to build such houses' (Errington and Gewertz 2004, 190).

12   This relates back to subsistence affluence. In the words of the *Black Harvest* filmmaker about the Western Highlands people he got to know well: 'While they might lack material possessions, the Ganiga were by and large economically self-sufficient: their houses were built out of local bush materials, their food gardens—tended primarily by women—supplied most of their daily needs. Consequently, they were able to put most of their energy into themselves—personal and clan relations and so on—rather than into economic production in the Western sense' (Connolly 2005, 80). See also Kiki (1968, 77).

most developed of PNG's pre-colonial markets—those of the Tolai in what is now East New Britain—'were only comparable with the least advanced rural markets in pre-colonial West Africa' (Conroy 2023, 46).

Turning to social factors, ethnolinguistic fragmentation has been shown to be a constraint on development internationally, and PNG's level is world leading (1.2.1). Easterly and Levine (1997, 1241) explain Africa's 'growth tragedy' by reference to ethnic diversity, arguing that 'interest group polarization leads to rent-seeking behaviour and reduces the consensus for public goods'. Consistent with this international analysis, many reference PNG's traditional social structures—its strong micro-societies, as Bizhan and Gorea (2022) refer to them. Traditional affiliations remain strong, though, as Nelson (2006, 6) has written:

> there is less consciousness of the radical changes that have been taking place in traditional systems. Some continue to serve their communities well, but in many villages when people regret the breakdown in law and order they are talking of the failure of the system that thirty years ago ensured law and order for most of the people for most of the time.[13]

While cultural and social factors are clearly important, both for better and for worse, some want to go further and make them the primary explanation of PNG's failure to develop more quickly. May (2003b, 154; 2022, 71), has argued that PNG suffers from 'a poorly developed sense of national identity' and that citizens therefore 'see the state as the source of things', something to plunder rather than contribute to. Such claims are hard to assess. One survey of university students in fact shows a high degree of nationalist sentiment (Feeny, Leach and Scambary 2012). And, while many in PNG clearly do see the state as a source of benefits,[14] it is rational to want to get more from government, and hardly something specific to Papua New Guinea.

Political scientist Francis Fukuyama, who has written specifically on PNG, gives primacy to social factors, writing, in accordance with the arguments of Migdal (1988), that:

13 Reilly (2004) claimed to find a negative link between ethnic fragmentation and development at the provincial level in PNG.
14 The anecdote that concludes Chapter 3 is consistent with this argument (3.3). So is the fact that, after Somare was deposed as prime minister by O'Neill in 2011, he sued the state and in 2015 won PGK2 million in an out-of-court settlement (Cochrane 2015), money that would otherwise have been available for government programs.

The sources of state weakness in Papua New Guinea lie in the country's social structure and culture. The extreme ethnolinguistic fragmentation of the country is noted by every observer of PNG, and is obviously the root cause of the failure to generate strong collective action at a national level. It is not just that the society is fragmented; the underlying social groups are very strong and cohesive compared to traditional social structures in other developing societies. The acid of modernization that has dissolved traditional social structures and driven millions of people to from countryside to cities or abroad in much of Latin America and Africa is much less evident in PNG. (Fukuyama 2007, 9)

Fukuyama is correct that PNG has a weak state and that this is deeply damaging for the country's development prospects. But recall that PNG did not go to independence with a weak state. Why the PNG state has become weak needs to be explained. To do so, we need to engage with institutional theories of development. The next two subsections introduce critical concepts and arguments that are built upon in the rest of the chapter.

12.3.2 Political theories of development

Acemoglu and Robinson (2012, 430) foreground political factors in explaining economic outcomes. They cast their argument in terms of extractive and inclusive institutions, and contend that growth cannot be sustained indefinitely under politically extractive institutions, which they define as those that 'concentrate power in the hands of the few'. Perhaps PNG's political institutions are, despite being semi-democratic, extractive, but Acemoglu and Robinson's theory predicts high growth under such a set up for some period before it runs out of steam. After all, economic growth should be in the interest of the elite; it is only when countries approach high-income levels that, the authors argue, non-inclusive political set-ups become unstable and unable to support the churning and innovation that economic growth requires at higher levels of development. That does not match the PNG case, where growth has been low from the start. More recent work by Acemoglu and Robinson (2019) explains state weakness in terms of the elite's fear of social mobilisation that state strength and therefore development could give rise to, but this presupposes a unity of purpose among the elite that certainly does not fit the PNG case.

A more helpful approach for PNG references political settlements or elite bargains. The World Bank (2017) *World Development Report* categorised elite bargains into two sorts: rules-based, which were good for development, and deals-based, which were not. PNG evidence provides little support for this theory. Its political settlement is rules-based. There are clear and well-respected—even if only partially democratic—rules for assuming, retaining and transferring political power. These rules have ensured regime stability and, for most of the time, have prevented violence from getting out of hand—that is, degenerating into coups or civil war. This in turn has helped prevent state, and economic, collapse. However, PNG politics has not otherwise been supportive of economic growth (3.2.1). Not all rules-based bargains are equally good for development.

Dercon (2022) takes an altogether different approach to elite bargain theory. He neglects entirely whether the bargain is rules-based or not, emphasising instead the importance of the elite coming together, agreeing to set aside their differences and promote development—that is, making a development bargain. Clearly no such development bargain has been able to take hold in PNG, and we need to explain why.

12.3.3 Insecurity

Institutional explanations for growth have often and long emphasised the importance of law and order or security for development. Adam Smith (1762, 5) wrote that:

> The first and chief design of every system of government is to maintain justice: to prevent the members of society from encroaching on one another's property, or seizing what is not their own. The design here is to give each one the secure and peaceable possession of his own property.

Providing security for property rights was one of the few institutional reforms to make it into the Washington Consensus's 10-point policy recipe (Williamson 1990). The extensive discussion of the need for and attempts at land reform in this book suggest these are salient references for PNG.[15]

Security is not only about land. Also important is the security of produce and, even more so, of the person. Rodrik (2003, 10) has argued that 'institutions that provide dependable property rights, manage conflict, maintain law and order, and align economic incentives with social costs and benefits are the foundation of long-term growth'. PNG has had variable success in aligning

---

15   In this book, land reform has been discussed under the heading of economic policy; however, any system of property rights constitutes an institution, so we could have equally presented the topic under the 'politics and governance' heading.

economic incentives with social costs and benefits, but has not been able to build institutions that fulfil the first three security-related tasks that Rodrik says are foundational for growth.

There is also the link between violence and the quality of governance more broadly. Indeed, the 'limited access order' theoretical framework of North, Wallis and Weingast (2010) puts the inability of the state to exercise a monopoly over the use of violence at the heart of their explanation of poor governance. The more the state lacks a monopoly of violence, the more important the capacity for violence is as a source of non-state power, and the more likely the state, rather than providing a level playing field for all or 'open access' as the authors put it, will be dominated by those with such a capacity.

12.4 An institutional explanation

To summarise the preceding two subsections, an institutional explanation of PNG's growth performance should explain why its politics has not been supportive of development and examine the detrimental impact of insecurity on development. In this section, we link PNG's hyper-politics and its insecurity to its weak but stable state and low growth.

We begin with political factors. As Kölln (2015, 593) puts it, 'parties save politics from becoming a dispersed and even possibly a contradictory set of actions'. In PNG, because of weak parties, politics is dispersed and contradictory. Going further, we have argued that politics in PNG is characterised not only by clientelism, but also by other characteristics, such as the strong pull of politics, a merging of the business and political classes, and a constant, precarious and sometimes violent struggle for power, and have called this bundle of characteristics 'hyper-politics' (12.2.1). The result, we have argued, is a political elite that is only lightly constrained by the interests of the disempowered masses, and that often acts on the basis of short-term, local and private interests, rather than pursuing long-term, national, broad-based development.

Hyper-politics has weakened the state. It has done this by preventing the formation of a development bargain, or a coalition around the sustained pursuit of long-term national objectives, such as strengthening the state. The priority given instead to short-term, local and private issues has become reflected in the way the state operates, and undermined its capacity to take tough policy decisions and act in the national interest.

Former prime minister Peter O'Neill has been quoted as saying that Papua New Guinea 'has too much politics and not enough good government' (Ives 2004, 92). One can go further and say that PNG has not enough good government *because* it has too much politics.

Given the damage that politics does to PNG's economic performance, it is natural to talk about the PNG elite in critical terms. It has been described as predatory (Namorong 2014), and kleptocratic (Garnaut 2000), and there is certainly a poor alignment of interests between the elite and the masses. Founding prime minister Somare himself commented in 1988 that:

> This country is not pulling together in the desired direction … The political leadership is headed in one direction—towards reaping wealth and status for themselves—while the masses are stuck with the problems of increased crime, unemployment, urban drift and sub-standard health and education services. (cited in Hegarty 1989, 11)[16]

But as critical as one might want to be about the elite, we should also recognise that it is itself trapped by the weak state it has helped to create. This is the meaning of the quotation from Mekere Morauta with which this chapter began. There are good leaders in PNG. But even those who want to pursue national goals find that they cannot as a result of state weakness, and that they cannot fix the state. This, in turn, makes them take their national responsibilities less seriously, inducing a greater focus on other priorities, such as local and business interests and the pursuit of power. Thus, a weak state is not only the product of PNG's hyper-politics but also a cause. The disempowerment of the ordinary Papua New Guinean is both the direct (due to predatory behaviour) and indirect (via the weak state) outcome of the country's hyper-politics.

PNG's hyper-politics is an important part but not the whole story of PNG's development difficulties. Another institutional constraint on development that is important in the PNG context is insecurity (12.3.3). This has two aspects: the poor law and order situation, and the insecurity of property rights.

The severity of the former as a constraint on development is self-evident, starting with the fact the poor law and order is itself a form of under-development—an intrinsic bad. A lack of physical security impinges on the daily life of ordinary people, especially women. PNG's law and order situation has been rated by business as their top-ranked constraint for most of the post-independence period (12.2.3).

---

16   On the very Papua New Guinean fear of urban drift, see Section 11.8.

Turning to the latter, the importance of insecure property rights has long been recognised as an important constraint to growth in PNG. Land in PNG is expensive, difficult to access and/or insecure for a range of commercial activities and livelihoods (11.6). Household surveys indicate that land is by far the leading cause of disputes in rural areas, and, even though its lead is less, in urban areas (NSO n.d., Table 8.1). Not long after independence, Trebilcock (1983, 228) wrote that:

> unless some break-through can be achieved in customary land law reform, existing land tenure arrangements will continue to constitute perhaps the major brake on the economic development of Papua New Guinea.

Land policy reforms have been attempted, but the task is complex. It is not surprising that such reforms have failed to deliver the institutional prize of secure property rights (11.6).

One cause of insecurity in PNG is a weak state. As things stand, the police contribute to as well as deter violence. A more capable state would bring greater clarity to competing customary ownership claims and greater protection to property rights. But insecurity also weakens the state by making it more difficult for the state to fulfil its fundamental function of acquiring—or enabling to be acquired—land for development, and, more generally, by stripping it of its monopoly of violence.

Insecurity and hyper-politics reinforce each other. Indeed they overlap: with violent electoral competition the norm in some parts of the country, with politicians often violating the law for private ends and with local groups making threats to extract resources from the state backed by violence (Strathern 1993). The insertion of violence into the political process further marginalises policies from the political process and makes politics more about the distribution of resources between different local groups. It normalises, and is normalised by, insecurity.

It is not just that growth is low, but that it is increasingly resource dependent (Figure B3). The various constraints to broad-based growth—hyper-politics, insecurity, a weak state—are less constraining of big, ring-fenced resource projects. While positive impacts of resource growth are evident in PNG, there are also negative feedbacks. An increasingly resource-dependent economy is one in which a weak state becomes ever more important as a distributor of economic rents,[17] and perhaps weaker as it is distracted from, or reluctant to take on, other policy challenges. It is also one that is even more prone to conflict. Growing resource dependency is another force that increases the importance of traditional groupings and rent-seeking to the detriment of development. Specifically, it has, to return to sources used earlier, helped to make landowners PNG's 'most powerful pressure group' (Saffu 1998f, 486) and given rise to the dominant belief that 'customary groups of landowners are the basic building blocks of national society' (Filer 2014, 82). All of this has made land reform more difficult, and claims for compensation more likely, and not only in the resource sector. This subset of feedback loops constitutes Papua New Guinea's institutional resource curse (Murshed 2018).

Another set of feedback loops is from low growth and resource dependency to hyper-politics and violence. Low growth boosts the relative importance of the state and of traditional groupings, and thus of politics, broadly defined, as a source of economic opportunity. Low growth also reinforces the social status quo, whereas more rapid growth would shake things up and perhaps give rise to new, larger-scale social formations from which stronger political parties could arise (Wood 2023). On low growth leading to violence,[18] in 1962, Australian academic and leading PNG adviser John Crawford wrote of the dire consequences of a premature reduction in Australian aid. Perhaps Australian aid was cut too quickly, but today his remarks can be read as prescient with regard to the consequences of low growth more generally:[19]

> Capital for investment would be insufficient, necessary imports could not be financed, and even the present limited medical and educational services would be curtailed. In these circumstances there would be a marked reversion to tribalism and fragmentation of Papua New Guinea society. Lacking, however, would be the relative stability of the old self-subsistence order—for the taste for change has now been cultivated. Disorder would be the ruling state of affairs. (Crawford 1962, 65)

It would be a gross exaggeration to say that disorder is the ruling state of affairs in Papua New Guinea, but less of one to say that insecurity is.

---

17 'Lack of alternative sources of comparable wealth have contributed directly to the centrality of the state as the single most important controller of resources in modern PNG' (Dinnen 1998, 58).
18 See also Levantis (2000a) who argues that the high wages going into independence encouraged rural–urban migration and then, when insufficient jobs eventuated, crime.
19 A micro confirmation to this macro prediction can be found in Zimmer-Tamakoshi (1997).

Finally, why, given these negative forces, has the PNG state not collapsed? Why is growth still positive? The tenuous grip any ruling party or faction has on power prevents complete state capture, and thus reduces the risk of conflict and collapse. The inability of any one group to dominate by seizing power has ensured a commitment by the elite to the rules of the game, which induces regime stability (12.2.1), which in turn provides a basis for investor confidence and helps to contain violence. The many different directions in which the state is pulled by the many who exercise power means that the state is both stable and weak.

Figure 12.3 provides a summary of our argument, which is that PNG's hyper-politics and insecurity both lead to and are reinforced by a weak but stable state and low and increasingly resource-dependent growth. We can call it a hyper-political, insecurity trap.

The figure, and this section, is far from a complete explanation of the deep determinants of PNG's economic performance, but may be useful in showing how factors stressed by the institutional scholars of growth—politics and insecurity—have influenced development outcomes in the country.

For a full explanation, one would need to integrate the relevant geographical, international, social and cultural factors (12.3.1). That would be a formidable task, though these links are no doubt important: politics and low growth enhance the salience of ethnicity, for example. For our purposes, however, it is sufficient to be reassured that the characteristics we focus on, namely hyper-politics and insecurity, are not themselves completely explicable in terms of low growth and a weak state but are at least partly due to other factors. This is a low bar to jump. The country's extreme ethnic fragmentation, as well as the emphasis on achieving status and prestige in Melanesian culture (Conroy 1982, 83), has surely contributed to PNG's hyper-politics.[20] Group ownership of land would make the management of property rights difficult no matter how capable the state. And 'violent conflict has a strong cultural basis in PNG, as the use of violence is seen as a legitimate means of expressing grievances' (Lakhani and Willman 2014a, 3).[21]

---

20   Views on the extent of the influence of culture on PNG politics are, in fact, divided. Wood (2016) provides a survey and argues convincingly for an intermediate position. Ketan (2000) gives the most instructive and fascinating account from the Mt Hagen area of how traditional arenas of competition and cooperation have been incorporated into modern politics.

21   In his memoir, one of PNG's first politicians, Albert Maori Kiki (1968), wrote about the precolonial 'state of perpetual war' (18) and preoccupation with violent payback (5, 15).

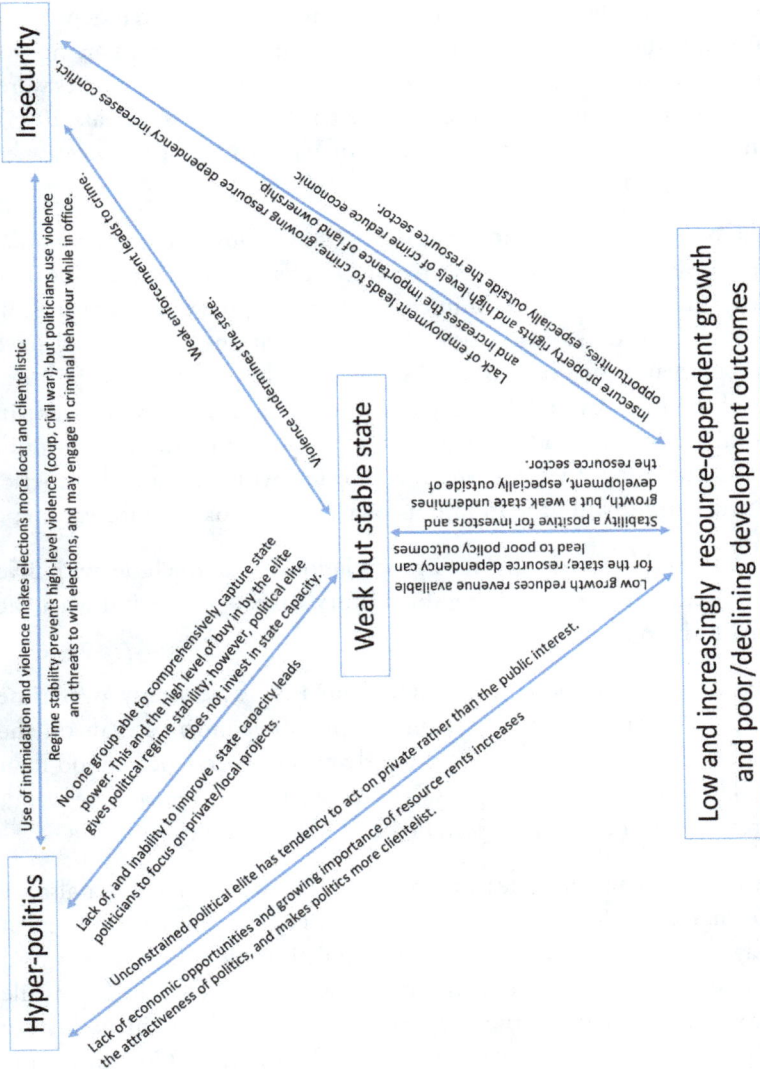

Figure 12.3: A political economy model of PNG — the hyper-political, insecurity trap

Source: Authors.

Insecurity

Hyper-politics

Weak but stable state

Low and increasingly resource-dependent growth and poor/declining development outcomes

Use of intimidation and violence makes elections more local and clientelistic.

Regime stability prevents high-level violence (coup, civil war); but politicians use violence and threats to win elections, and may engage in criminal behaviour while in office.

Weak enforcement leads to crime.

Violence undermines the state.

Lack of employment leads to crime; growing resource dependency increases conflict.

Insecure property rights and high levels of crime reduce economic opportunities, especially outside the resource sector.

No one group able to comprehensively capture state power. This and the high level of buy in by the elite gives political regime stability; however, political elite does not invest in state capacity.

Lack of, and inability to improve, state capacity leads politicians to focus on private/local projects.

Unconstrained political elite has tendency to act on private rather than the public interest.

Lack of economic opportunities and growing importance of resource rents increases the attractiveness of politics, and makes politics more clientelist.

Stability a positive for investors and growth, but a weak state undermines development, especially outside of the resource sector.

Low growth reduces revenue available for the state; resource dependency can lead to poor policy outcomes

12.5 Final reflections

We have argued in this concluding chapter that PNG is in a trap, in which hyper-politics and insecurity combine to produce, and are reinforced by, a weak but stable state, and low and increasingly resource-dependent growth. While the picture painted is not an optimistic one, traps are not for ever. Today's prosperous democracies with their strong political parties were, in the nineteenth century, clientelist (Shefter 1973; Stokes et al. 2013). Over an even longer period, the countries of Western Europe have escaped a centuries-long conflict trap.

Traps can be escaped given enough time, but how? Our institutional model is illuminating, but it does not give rise to concrete recommendations. If it is difficult to confidently recommend economic policy reforms (11.9), it is impossible to do so in relation to institutional ones. Those that have been proposed and tried have often disappointed, for example, the political reforms of the nineties (5.2.1). May (2001a, 16) says that development in PNG would require 'a fundamental shift in patterns of political behaviour'. Advice to secure property rights and reduce crime would be equally generic. Papua New Guinea will have to find its own institutional way forward.

Rather than ending with any recommendations, we conclude with five general reflections on what writing this history has taught us, and what the future might hold.

First, the reduction in academic material on PNG's economy over time is striking. There is more material on the pre-independence than on the independence period, and more on the early pre-independence period than the late. This volume is itself a partial corrective to this unfortunate trend, but there is much more to be researched and written about.

Second, while much can be learnt from PNG's history, much can also be learnt from international comparisons. Yes, PNG is unusual, unique in some ways. It is the world's most ethnolinguistically diverse country and the most rural, as well as one of the most resource dependent. But while every economy is different, there is also much PNG shares in its history with other countries. The rise and fall of the Washington Consensus, the difficult period of the eighties and the boom of the noughties, the adoption of foreign exchange rationing, clientelism—these are all international phenomena. We have tried to use these comparisons in our history, but much more could be done to understand PNG's economy and its challenges in an international context.

Third, development in PNG is much more difficult than it was at first, and is still, often understood to be. Recall Michael Somare's words at independence, quoted at the start of Chapter 2, that it would be up to PNG to decide how much development it wanted, and the assumption of the influential Faber Report at independence of annual growth in excess of 7–9 per cent (3.1.1). The reality has been very different, but in many ways the optimism remains. *Vision 2050*, published in 2009, articulated the aim of placing PNG among the 50 countries with highest Human Development Index (HDI) by 2050. In 2010, PNG was placed 159th out of 189 countries on the HDI index: as of 2021, it is 156th (UNDP Human Development Reports n.d.).

In 2008, the then deputy prime minister expressed his aspiration that PNG could become the 'richest black nation' in the world (Temu 2010, 110). Non-resource GDP per capita—our best measure of living standards—was only 12 per cent higher in 2019 than in 2008, but that did not stop the current prime minister doubling down on that earlier commitment. James Marape said when he took power in 2019 that he wanted PNG to be the 'richest black Christian nation' on earth by 2030 (Laveil 2019b).

Business media websites, international banks and development partners reinforce this excessive optimism or boosterism. During the boom, PNG was referred to as a 'Pacific tiger economy' (Callick 2012); it clearly was no such thing. During the bust, *Business Advantage PNG* said that hosting APEC in 2018 would transform the country (McQuillan 2017b); it did not.

The reality is that development in PNG has got more difficult since independence, not easier. Barriers to growth have increased more than they have been reduced. Optimism and hope are important, but not helpful if disconnected from reality.

Fourth, the prophets of collapse have also not seen their predictions vindicated. On the left, Marxist scholars Thompson and MacWilliam (1992, 193–4) argued in the early nineties that the 'collapse of the social formation … was probable' in the short term.[22] On the right, Windybank and

---

22   The two authors had some disagreements, and this view was one put forward by Thompson.

Manning (2003, summary) argued a decade later that the PNG government was on the brink of 'collapse'.[23] This pessimism has been as misplaced as the optimism of PNG's boosters. Independent PNG 'has shown a remarkable capacity for surviving crises' (Ketan 2000, 321). This undermines the credibility of predictions of general collapse, such as the outbreak of a civil war or a coup or a mass exodus. The pessimists also underestimate what our model stresses: the high level of buy-in to the PNG state by the political class, and the stability that this delivers (12.2.1). Precisely because the PNG state is one in which 'power is diffused' it is also one that 'continues to function ... despite many "grabs at the wheel"' (Hegarty 1989, 14). This is why 'the PNG state is far from collapsing' (Ketan 2000, 322).

That collapse is not imminent does not mean that it will never be a risk in the future. Moreover, not collapsing is not the same as progress, and, in fact, is consistent with regress. While economic growth has been slow rather than negative, many indicators of living standards place PNG at or close to the global bottom (Table 10.14). Government effectiveness is in decline (Figure 12.1). A recent survey of University of Papua New Guinea students found that an overwhelming majority thought the country was heading in the wrong direction (Samof and Howes 2024).

Fifth, in assessing the country's prospects too much weight is still given to the country's resource potential. As recently as 2020, the IMF (2020, 1) wrote that 'Papua New Guinea's longer-term outlook remains positive, largely reflecting the likelihood of major resource sector projects'. There are a number of reasons why this is misleading (11.4). First, these projects are ever more complex and controversial and are less likely to, and take longer to, come to fruition. Second, existing resource projects are depleted over time, and there are a limited number of potential new projects. As shown in the introductory chapter, PNG's non-renewable resource endowments are just not large enough on a per capita basis—one-sixteenth the size of Australia's, for example (Figure 1.4)—to be transformational. Third, more resource projects mean a stronger resource curse, both economic (11.9) and institutional (12.4). And converting resource revenue into development is a difficult task for a weak state. Fourth, PNG has experienced reasonable resource sector growth since independence (Table 10.5), yet overall growth has been slow. Manning (1999, 15) commented that 'Papua New Guinea ... enjoyed an unprecedented flow of riches from mineral and petroleum finds

---

23   For other instances of PNG crisis-mongering, see the references in Standish (1999, footnote 4).

during the 1990s'. It did not help much then, and there is no guarantee or even likelihood that it will in the future. If more resource sector projects were the answer, PNG's problems would have been solved. PNG's long-term outlook depends on the quality of its policies and above all its institutions, rather than on the resource projects it is able to negotiate.

Beyond these general points, divining what the future holds for PNG is a task we leave for others. The nation is young and has embarked on a long journey. Whatever happens, the next half century in Papua New Guinea's post-independence economic history will surely be as difficult to predict and as interesting as the first.

Annex A: Political tables and figures

Table A1: PNG prime ministers, 1975–2024

Name	Term of office			Party
	Took office (reason)	**Left office**	**Time in office**	
Michael Somare	16 September 1975 (Independence)	11 March 1980	4.48 years	Pangu Pati
Julius Chan	11 March 1980 (Vote of no confidence)	2 August 1982	2.39 years	People's Progress Party
Michael Somare	2 August 1982 (General election)	21 November 1985	3.3 years	Pangu Pati
Paias Wingti	21 November 1985 (Vote of no confidence)	4 July 1988	2.62 years	People's Democratic Movement
Rabbie Namaliu	4 July 1988 (Vote of no confidence)	17 July 1992	4.04 years	Pangu Pati
Paias Wingti	17 July 1992 (General election)	30 August 1994	2.12 years	People's Democratic Movement
Julius Chan[1]	30 August 1994 (Resignation of previous prime minister)	22 July 1997	2.71 years	People's Progress Party
Bill Skate	22 July 1997 (General election)	14 July 1999	1.98 years	People's National Congress

---

1   Julius Chan stood down between 27 March and 2 June 1997 during the Sandline inquiry, during which time John Giheno was acting prime minister.

Name	Term of office			Party
	Took office (reason)	Left office	Time in office	
Mekere Morauta	14 July 1999 (Resignation of previous prime minister)	5 August 2002	3.06 years	People's Democratic Movement
Michael Somare	5 August 2002 (General election)	4 April 2011[2]	8.40 years	National Alliance Party
Peter O'Neill	2 August 2011 (Parliament declared prime minister's position to be vacant as Somare in long-term hospital stay; this was disputed by the courts, but O'Neill won the 2012 elections)	29 May 2019	7.82 years	People's National Congress
James Marape	30 May 2019 (Resignation of previous prime minister)	Incumbent	Still in office as of end of 2024	Pangu Pati

Source: Authors' research.

Table A2: Trends in Papua New Guinea elections, 1977–2022

Year	Average number of candidates per seat	Mean winner vote shares	Percentage of incumbents returned	Percentage of independents competing	Party with most seats (% seats)	Number of females elected
1977	8	35%	39%	No data	28%	3
1982	10	31%	52%	41%	47%	1
1987	14	26%	52%	67%	24%	0
1992	15	23%	46%	74%	18%	0
1997	22	20%	51%	73%	15%	2
2002	26	20%	26%	43%	17%	1
2007	25	33%	46%	No data	25%	1
2012	31	32%	44%	64%	24%	3
2017	30	34%	49%	57%	26%	0
2022	31	Unknown	62%	No data	33%	2

Notes: From 2007 onwards, limited preferential voting has been used, which has pushed up the mean winner voter share. There were 109 seats until the 2012 elections, and then 111 until the 2022 elections, and then 118.

Source: Wood (2017), Laveil (2021), Saffu (1988), Howes, Kabuni et al. (2022).

2   Sam Abal was acting PM from 12 December 2010 to 17 January 2011 while Somare was facing Leadership Tribunal charges (7.2.3), and then again from 4 April 2011 due to the latter's ill-health.

Table A3: Women in parliament

Name	Period in parliament	Party
Nahau Rooney	1977–87	Pangu/People's Democratic Movement/Independent
Waliyato Clowes	1977–82	United Party/National Party/Papua Besena/Papuan Alliance
Josephine Abaijah	1972–82, 1997–2002	Papua Besena
Dame Carol Kidu	1997–2012	Independent
Delilah Gore	2012–17	Triumph Heritage Empowerment/People's National Congress
Loujaya Kouza	2012–17	Triumph Heritage Empowerment
Julie Soso	2012–17	Triumph Heritage Empowerment/People's National Congress
Kessy Sewang	2022–	People's First Party/People's Transformation Party
Rufina Peter	2022–	People's National Congress
Francesca Semoso	2023–	Pangu

Source: Development Policy Centre (n.d.).

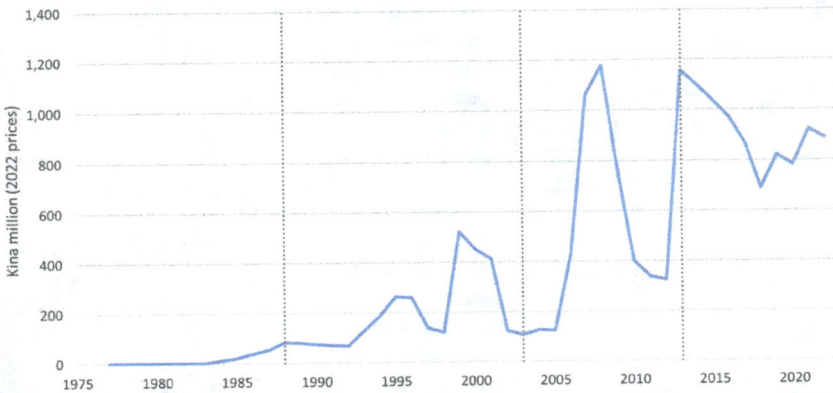

Figure A1: Constituency funding (adjusted for inflation), 1977–2022

Notes: Figures are actuals. Only district (open) MP funding included (such as the District Support Improvement Program).

Source: PNG Economic Database.

The provision of funding to be spent under the direction of MPs goes back to the eighties, increased in the nineties, and really took off in the boom years of the noughties. Due to fiscal constraints, it fell somewhat over the tens.

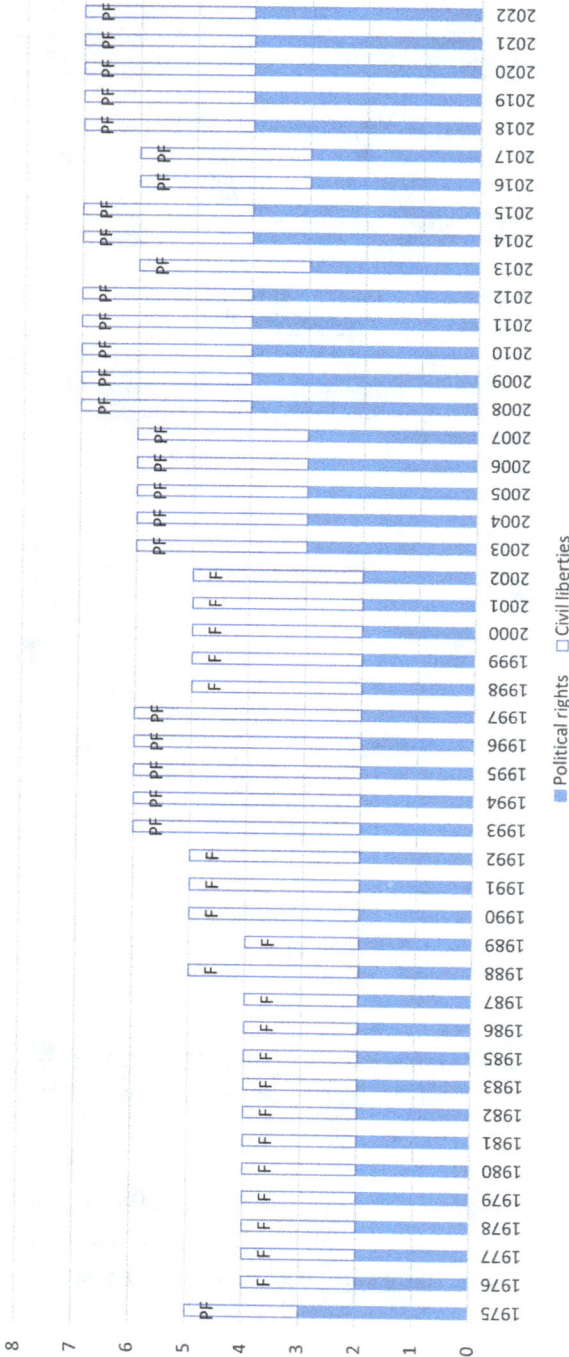

Figure A2: Freedom House ratings for PNG, 1975–2022

Notes: Both political rights and civil liberties are rated on a scale of 1–7 (where 1 is the highest). Based on both scores, countries are rated as free (F), partly free (PF) or not free. PNG was rated as free from independence to 1992 and then again from 1998 to 2002. Since 2002, as well as between 1993 and 1997, it has been rated as 'partly free'. The decline in rating is due to, first, a higher (worse) civil liberties score, and, then, a worse political rights score. V-Dem (the Varieties of Democracy Project) permanently downgraded PNG from an electoral democracy to a partial democracy ('electoral autocracy') in 2007.

Source: Freedom House (n.d.).

Annex B:
Economic figures

List of figures

Unless otherwise indicated, these figures are drawn from the PNG Economic Database (devpolicy.org/pngeconomic/). The database, as well as Howes, Fox et al. (2022), can be consulted for further information on underlying sources and definitions.

Most of the graphs are divided into the four periods that provide the basis for the book's analysis: the seventies and eighties (1975–88), the nineties (1989–2003), the noughties (2004–13) and the tens (2014–22).

Population

Based on rough estimates—PNG's last reliable census was in 2001—PNG's population has more than tripled since independence, from 2.8 million in 1975 to 9.3 million in 2022 (Figure B1). Other estimates put the PNG population at above 10 million. According to our estimates, PNG gained some 250,000 citizens in 2022—9 per cent of the population at the time of independence.

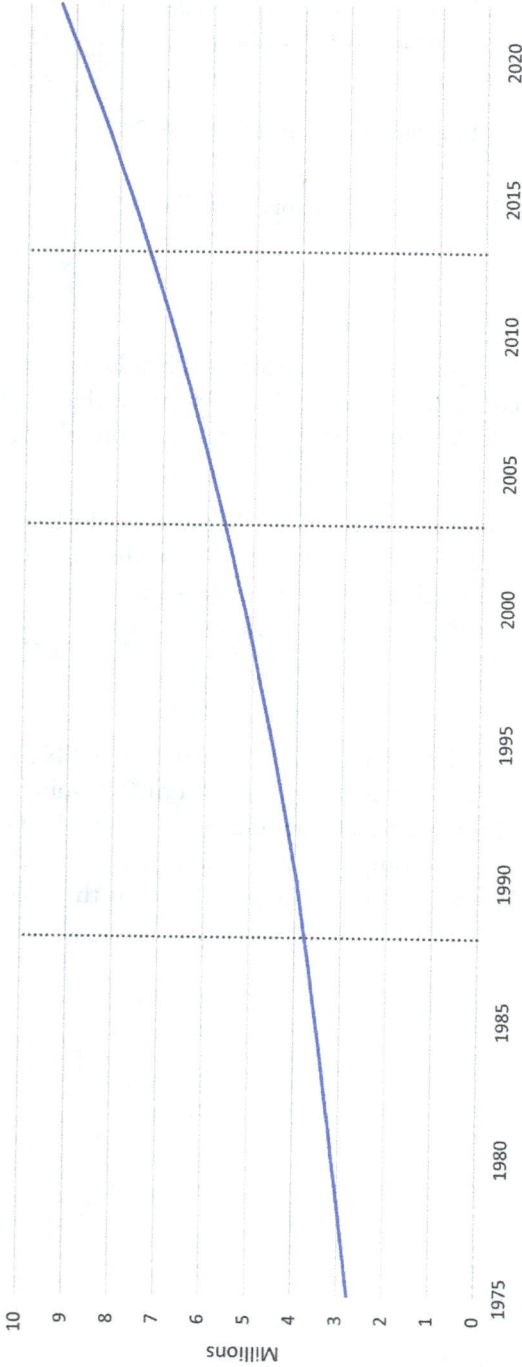

Figure B1: Population, 1975–2022

Source: Annual figures interpolated from Bourke and Allen's (2021) decadal medium-case estimates.

GDP and non-resource GDP

The volatility of PNG's growth is evident, especially when the resource sector is included (Figure B2). GDP and non-resource GDP per person are shown in Figure 1.2.

The PNG economy has become increasingly resource dependent (Figure B3). The resource (mining and petroleum) sector (sometimes called the mineral sector in PNG) made up as little as 6 per cent of PNG's GDP in 1984, a year of low copper prices. Since then, resource dependency has fluctuated due to the opening and closing of large mines and wells and changing commodity prices. But the trend has clearly been upwards, and in 2022 resource dependency reached an all-time high of 32 per cent.

The structure of the non-resource sector is quite stable (Figure B4). The agricultural share is normally between 20 and 25 per cent of non-resource GDP. Manufacturing, wholesale and retail, and transport shares are slightly declining, and construction is increasing.

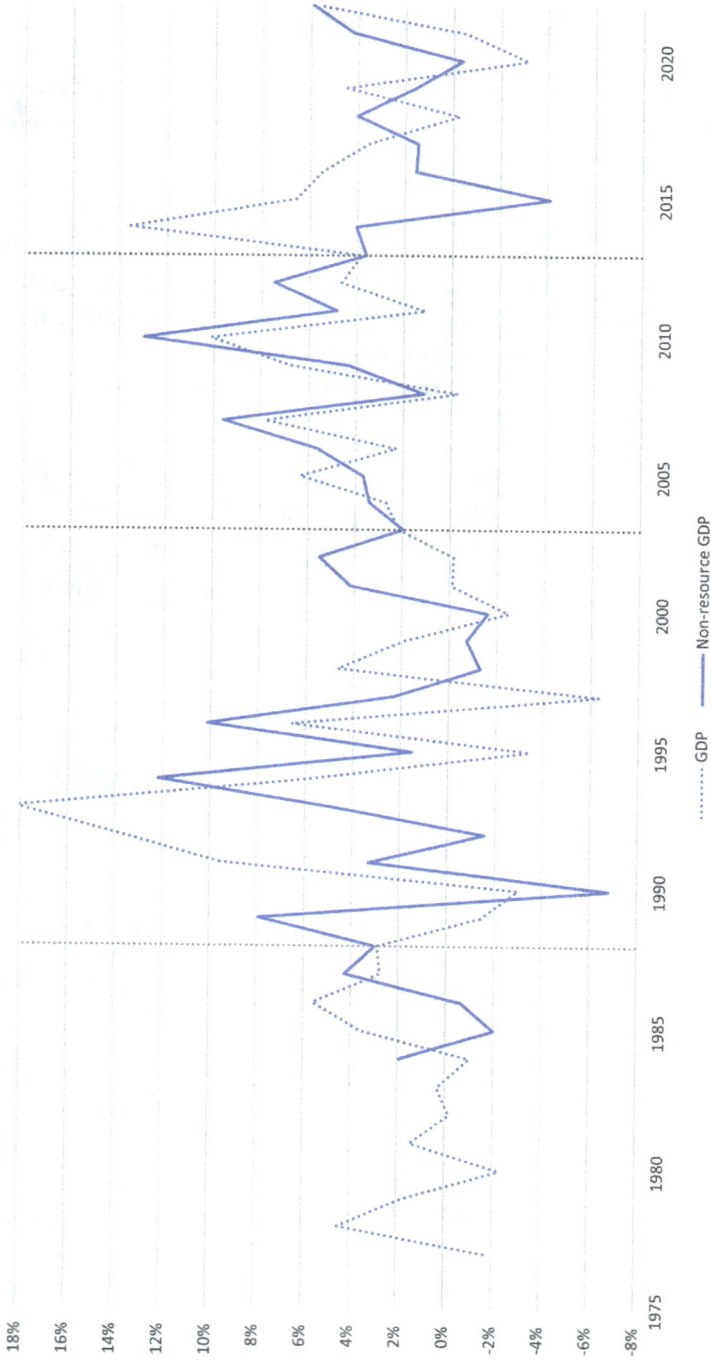

Figure B2: GDP and non-resource GDP growth, 1976–2022 (kina, constant prices)

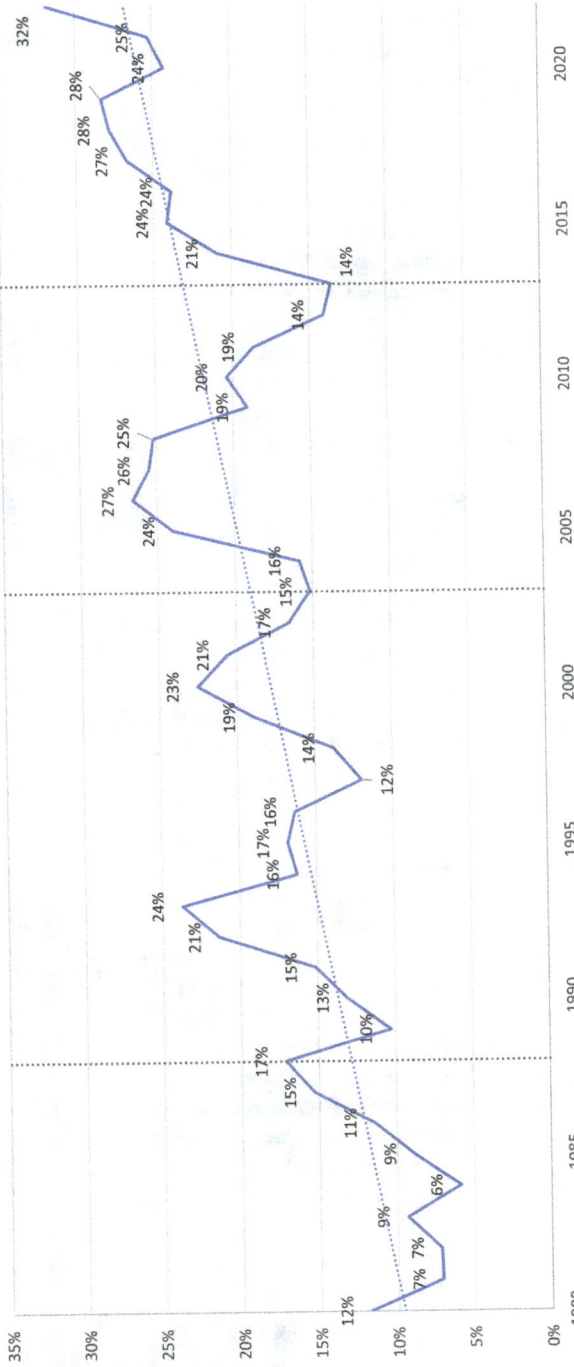

Figure B3: Resource dependency, 1980–2022

Notes: The percentage share of resources (value-added [output minus intermediate inputs] in the resource sector) in total GDP, both measured in current prices. Trendline added.

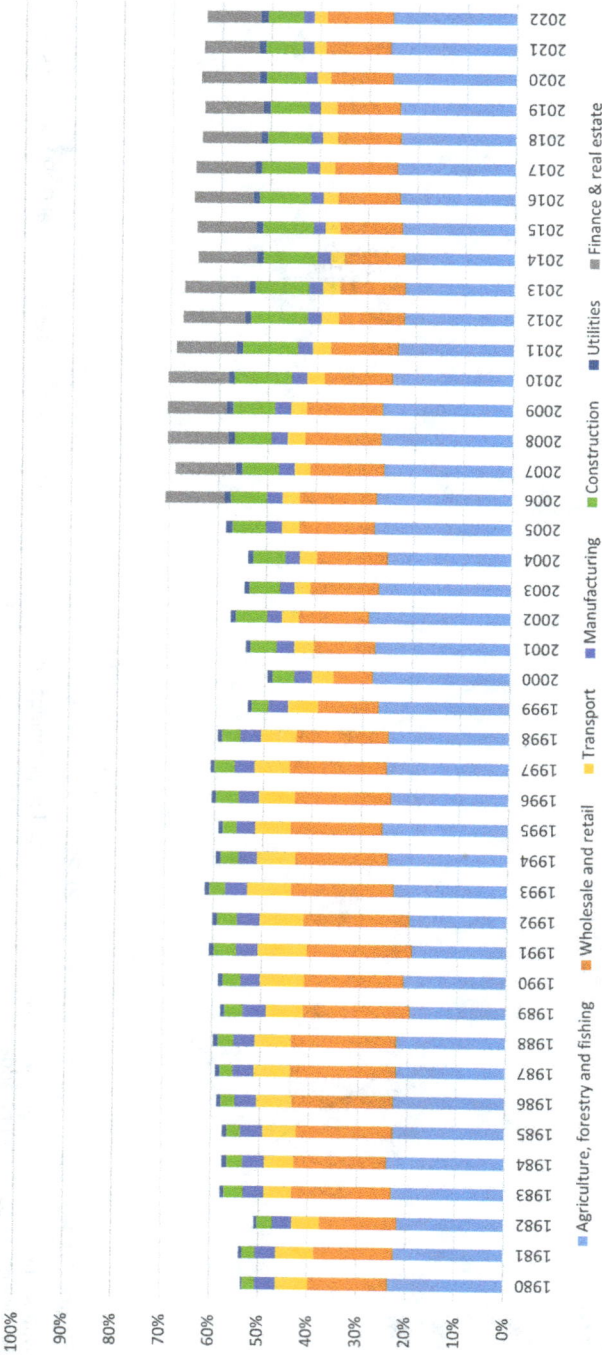

Figure B4: Sectoral composition of non-resource GDP, 1980–2022

Notes: All variables are measured in current prices. The finance and real estate series is unreliable before 2006.

Commodity production, values and prices

The PNG economy relies heavily and increasingly on commodity, and especially resource, exports (Figure B5). The ratio of commodity exports to GDP has increased since independence, from around 25 per cent in the late seventies to a peak of 49 per cent in 2006—the height of the resource boom. Thereafter, commodity exports to GDP dropped, returning almost to independence levels in 2013, but then they recovered due to the commencement of LNG production.

At independence, resource (mineral and petroleum) exports made up half of all commodity exports (Figure B6). Over time, the former have come to dominate PNG's commodity exports, reaching over 80 per cent for most years since 2005, and, recently, sometimes close to 90 per cent.

The performance of traditional cash crops (other than palm oil) has been dismal (Figure B7). None of the crops shows a positive growth trajectory.

The export performance of marine products, logs and especially palm oil has been impressive (Figure B8).

At independence, PNG non-resource commodity exports were dominated by coffee, cocoa and copra, which made up more than 80 per cent (Figure B9). Coffee alone was half. In 2022, these three traditional crops made up less than 20 per cent.

Gold and copper have been exported since independence (Figure B10). Gold is the stand-out performer, with production more than tripling by volume since independence, though falling in recent years due to the temporary closure of Porgera. Copper production is now only at half the level of independence. Oil exports began in 1992, peaked by volume the following year and have fallen ever since. Cobalt and nickel started in 2012 and LNG in 2014.

Copper once dominated PNG's exports by value, but not anymore (Figure B11). Gold has remained an important export, and LNG has become the most important one. Oil became the most important export in the nineties but is unimportant now.

After the coffee and cocoa boom that followed independence, the eighties and nineties were a period of commodity price stagnation or decline (Figure B12). Then everything changed. Resources prices rocketed upwards to well above their level at independence. They declined somewhat in the tens, but then increased again in 2022 with the Ukraine war. Non-resource commodity prices have fallen compared to their levels at independence. However, because resources increasingly dominate commodity production, the overall commodity price index has increased to record levels.

Coffee and cocoa prices have fallen by more than half relative to inflation compared to independence (Figure B13). Palm oil and logs have done better, though log prices have fallen from their high of the mid-nineties.

The domestic purchasing power of PNG's resource exports has improved over time (Figure B14). Resource prices all peaked during the boom period; they largely recovered over the course of the bust. (The price of gas is not shown but is linked to the price of oil.)

Adjusting for inflation, agricultural exports show no growth since independence (Figure B15). Timber and marine product exports have grown but remain small in absolute size. Resource exports have grown in fits and starts but overall strongly, from PGK4 billion in 1976 to PGK43 billion in 2022 (in 2022 prices).

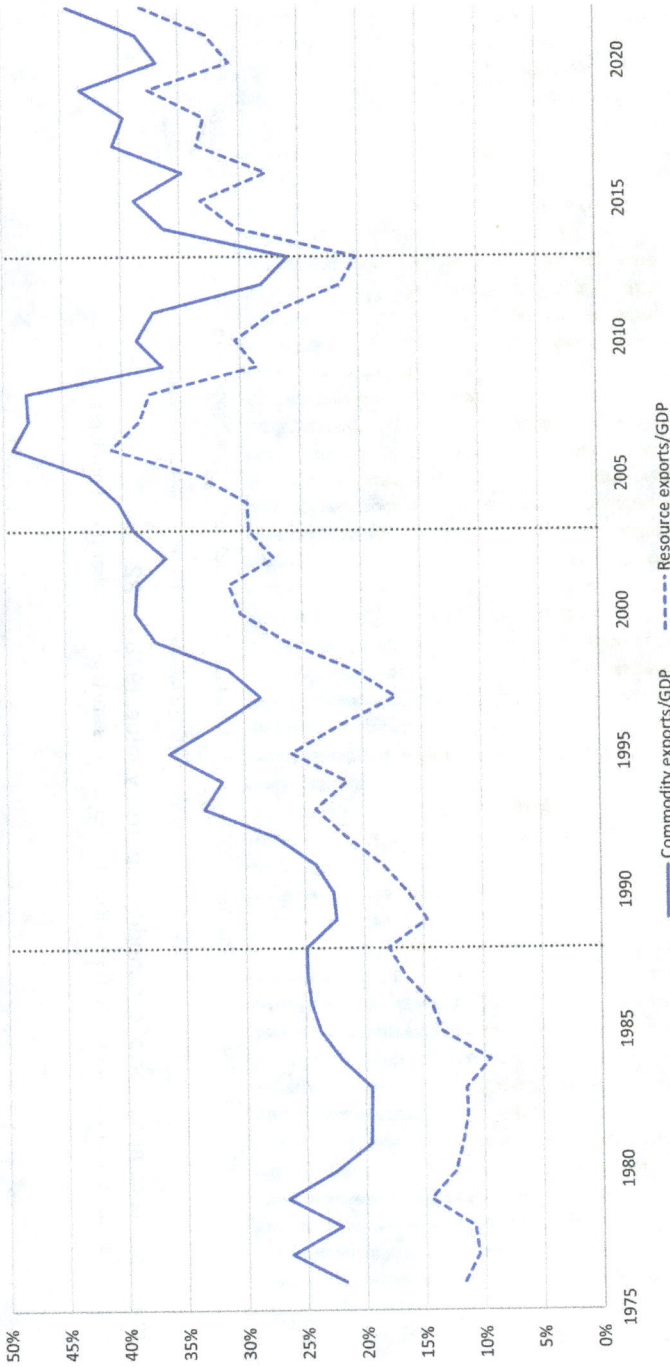

Figure B5: Commodity and resource exports as a percentage of GDP, 1976–2022

Notes: Both variables are measured in current prices. Commodity exports include resource (mining and petroleum) exports, and agricultural cash crops, timber and marine products.

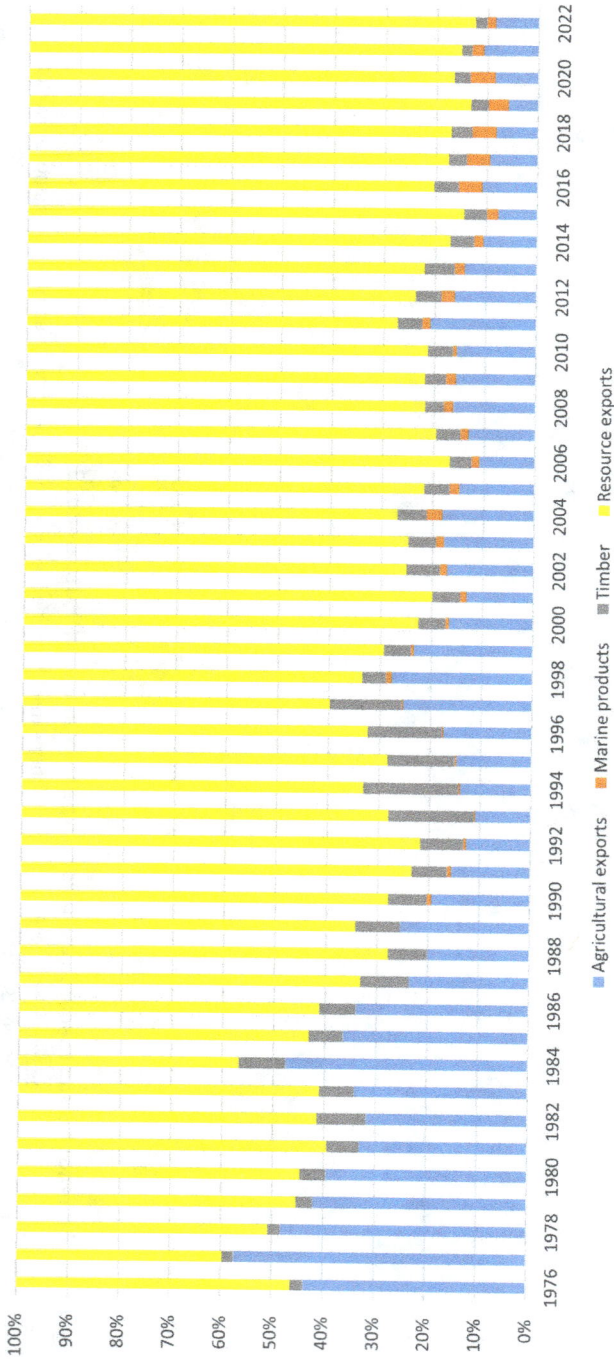

Figure B6: The composition of commodity exports by value, 1976–2022

Notes: All variables are measured in current prices. Timber exports are logs and other forest products.

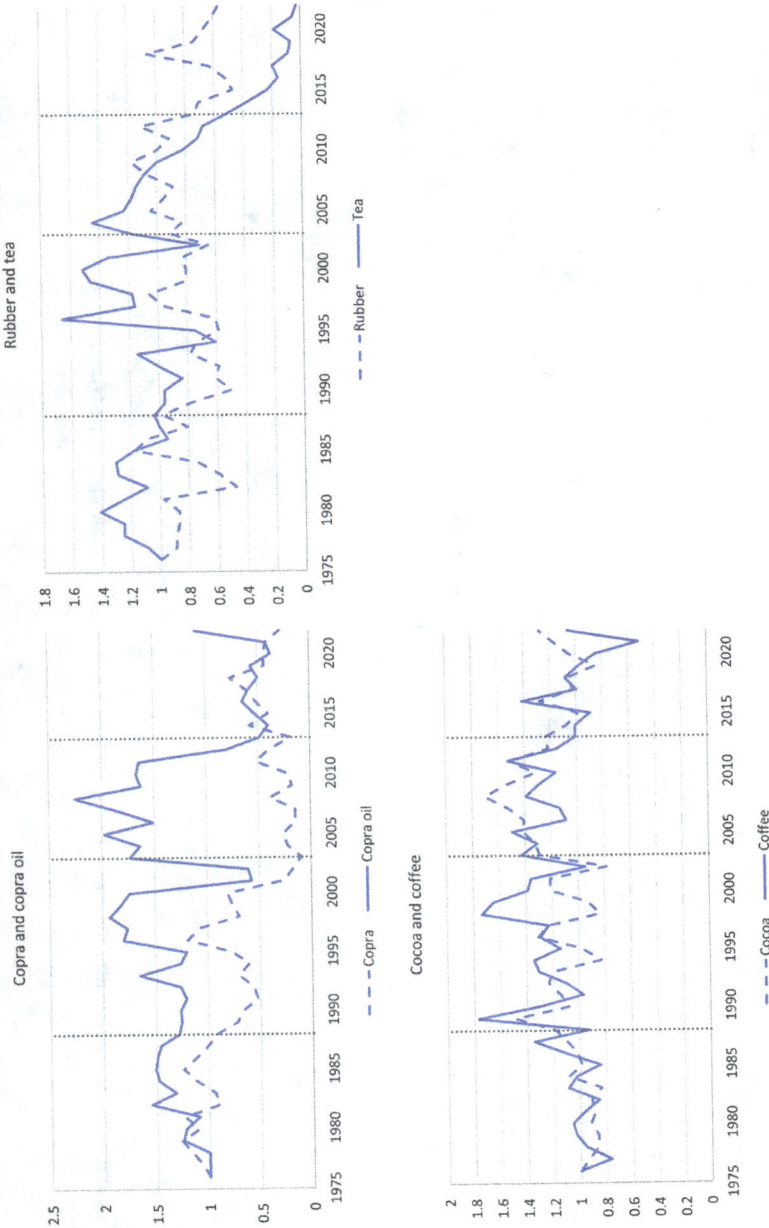

Figure B7: Export volume indices of cash crops, 1976–2022

Notes: Indices set equal to unity in 1976.

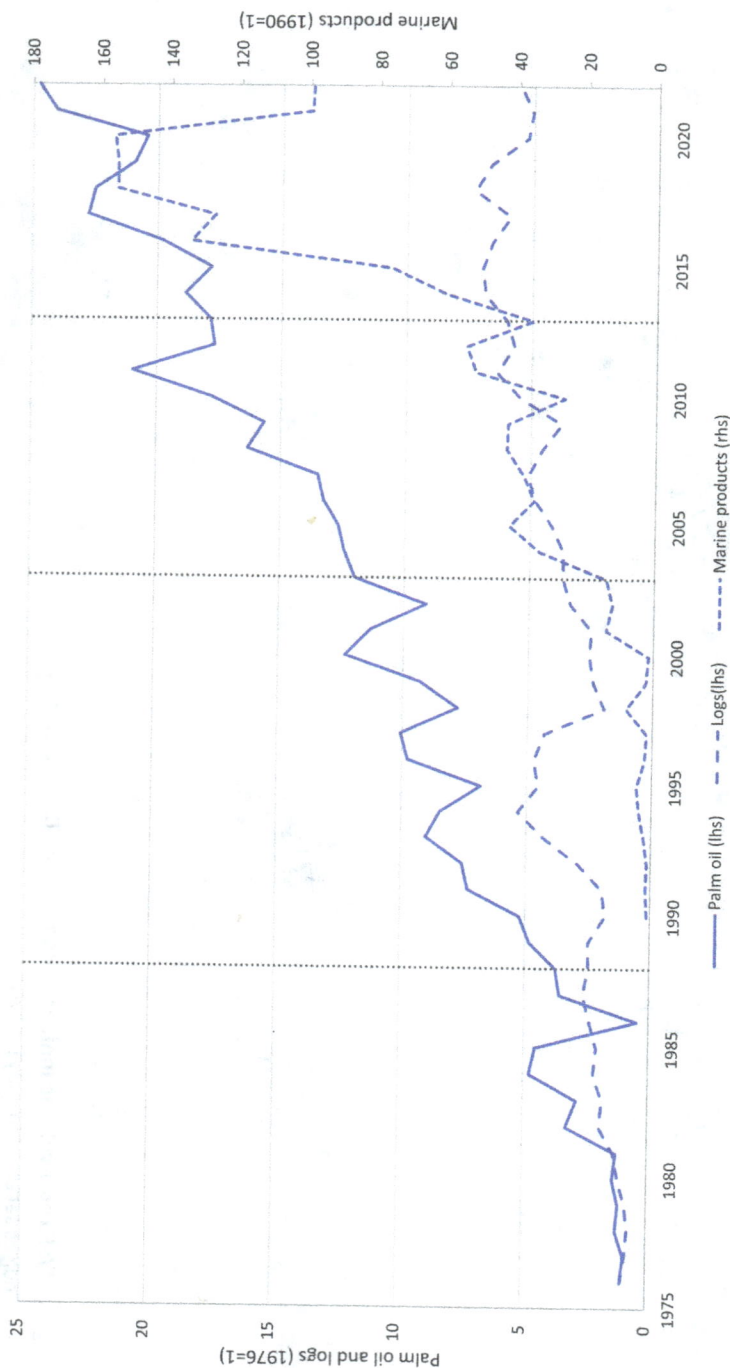

Figure B8: Export volume indices of marine products, palm oil and logs, 1976–2022

Notes: Indices set equal to unity in 1976 for palm oil and logs, and in 1990 for marine products.

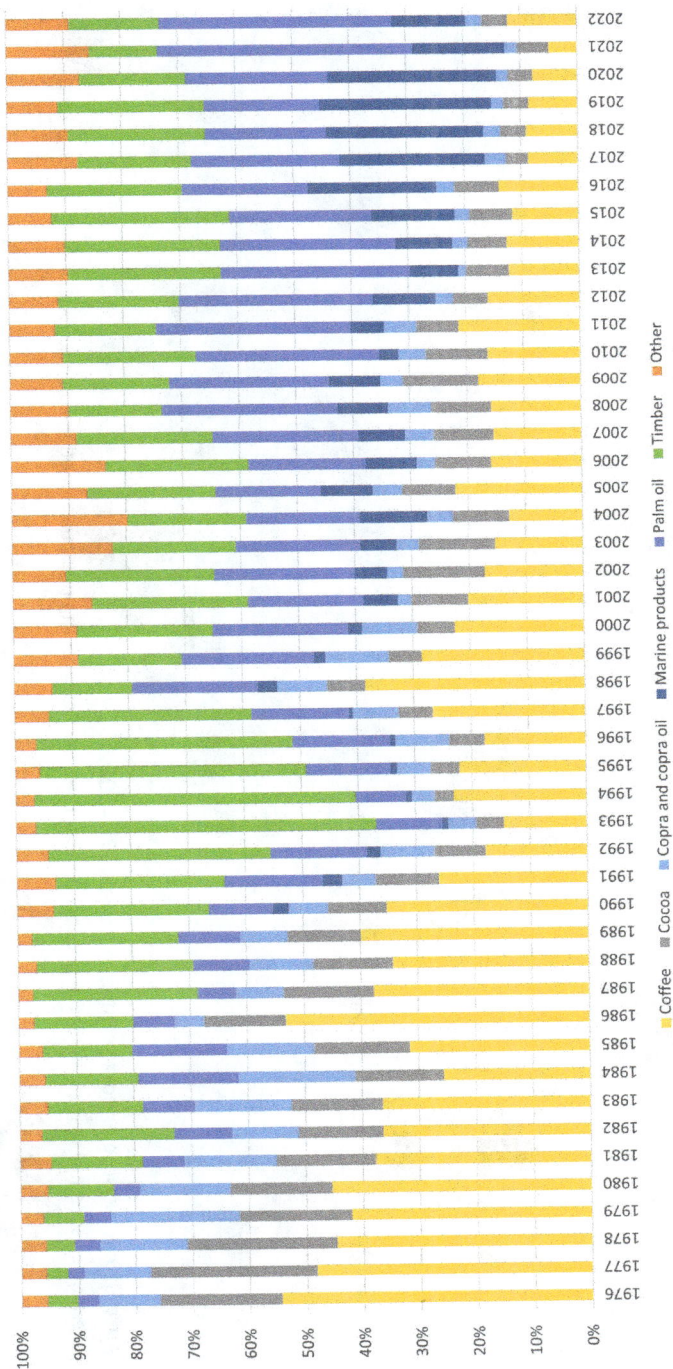

Figure B9: Composition of non-resource commodity exports by value, 1976–2022

Notes: Current prices are used for all variables. Timber exports are logs and other forest products. Other includes tea, rubber and other agricultural products.

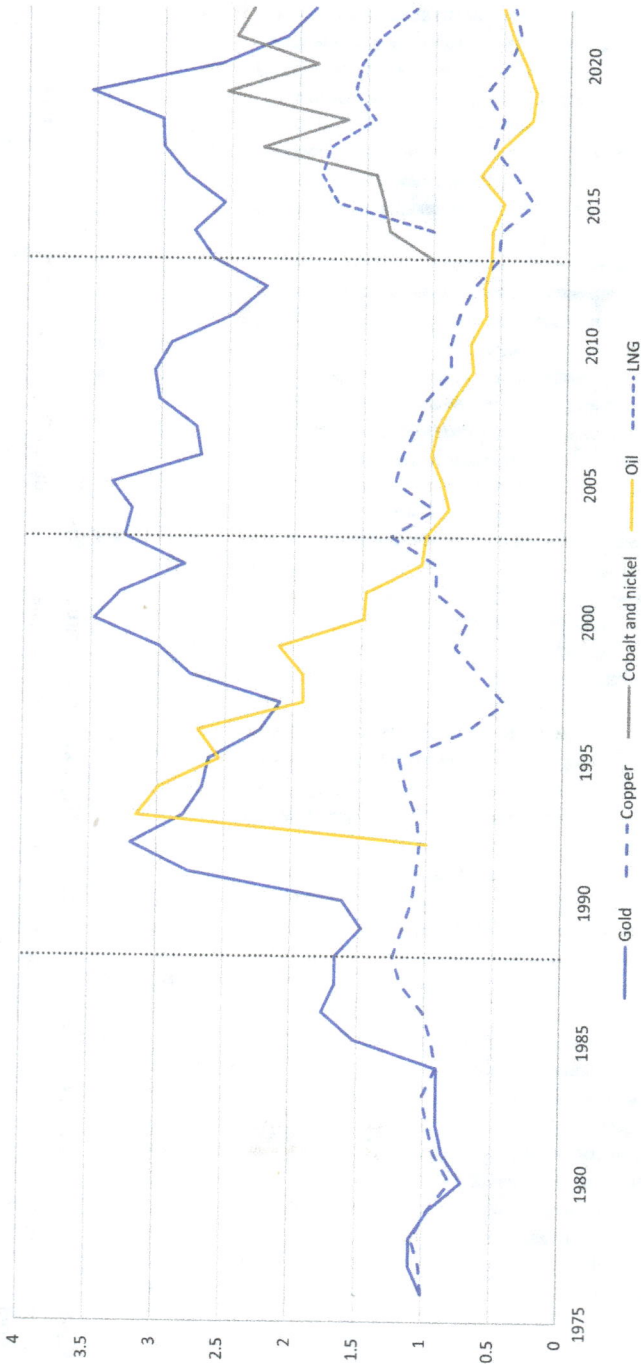

Figure B10: Resource export volume indices, 1976–2022

Notes: Indices set equal to unity in 1976 for copper and gold and the first year of production for other commodities.

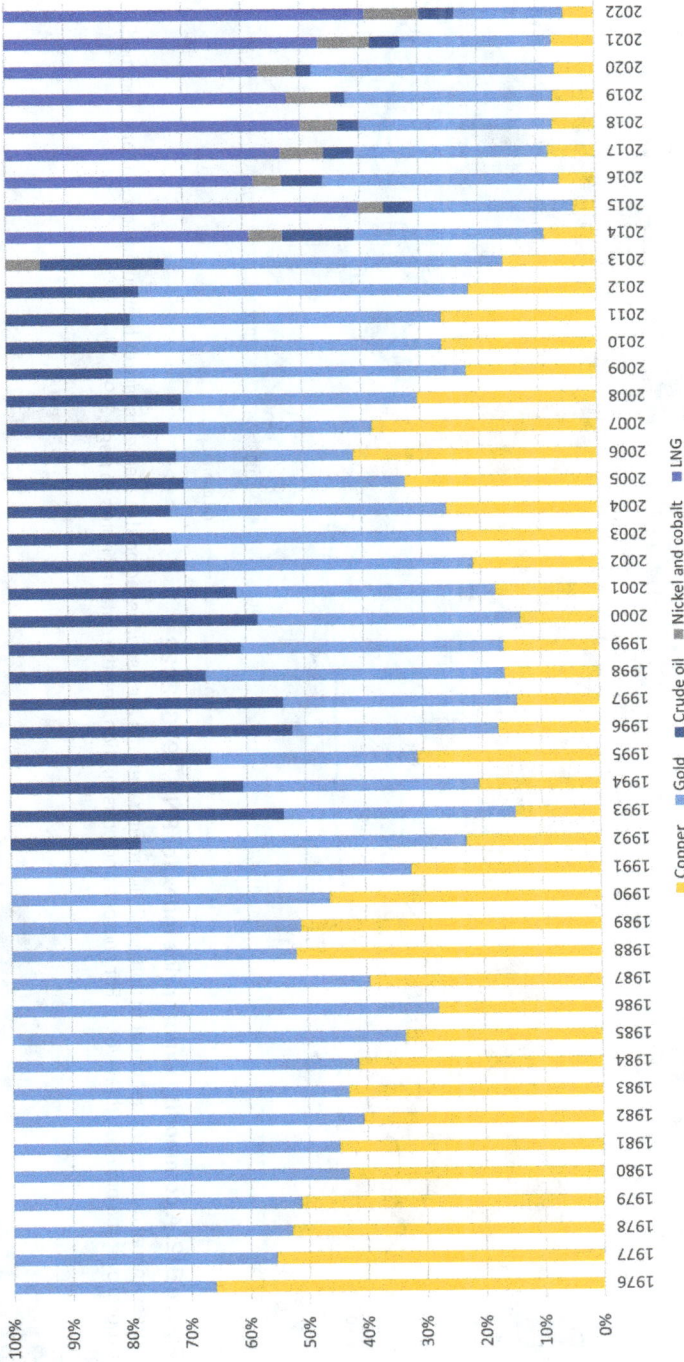

Figure B11: Composition of resource commodity exports by value, 1976–2022

Notes: Current prices are used for all variables. Silver and alluvial gold are included with gold.

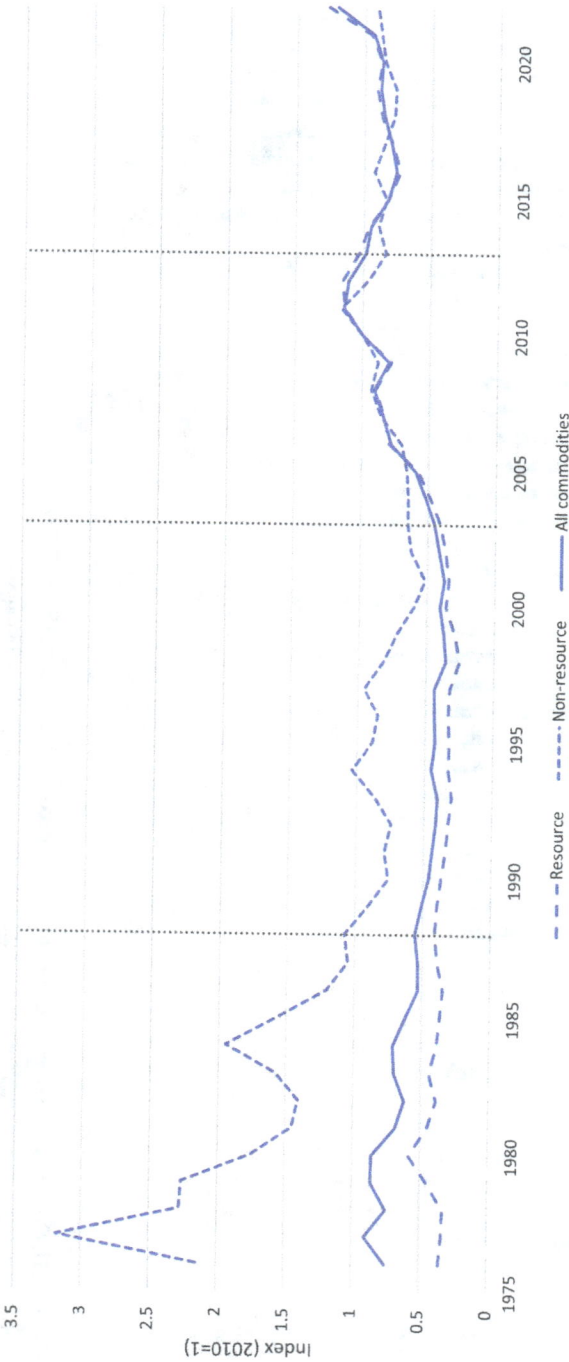

Figure B12: A commodity export price index for PNG, 1976–2022

Notes: Annual data; index set equal to unity in 2010; rolling weights are used, based on the average share of that commodity in total commodity exports over the previous three years. For sources and construction, see the detailed notes on page 319.

This commodity price index is constructed using the method of Gruss and Kebhaj (2019). The IMF commodity price index produced using this method for PNG is out of date and does not give a separate index for resource and non-resource commodities.

Weights are commodity export values (current price, kina). Rolling weights are used with the average of previous three years (t-1 to t-3) as the weights. For the first one to three years, the weights are, respectively, the current year, the current and previous year, and the current and previous two years.

Prices are from the World Bank commodity price data (August 2023), expressed in real 2010 US dollars, for the following commodities:

- copra and copra oil: Coconut oil ($/mt)
- cocoa: cocoa ($/kg)
- coffee: coffee Arabica ($/kg)
- palm oil: palm oil ($/mt)
- rubber: rubber RSS3 ($/kg)
- tea: tea, avg three auctions ($/kg)
- marine products: fish meal ($/mt)
- logs: logs, Malaysian ($/cubic metre)
- gold: gold ($/troy oz)
- copper: copper ($/mt)
- nickel and cobalt: nickel ($/mt) (the cobalt price is not included in the World Bank data set)
- crude oil: crude oil, average ($/bbl)
- condensate/LNG: liquefied natural gas, Japan ($/mmbtu).

Commodity data are obtained from the PNG Economic Database, in turn sourced from the Bank of Papua New Guinea (BPNG). Silver is excluded because silver and alluvial gold are grouped together in BPNG data, and not available for all years.

To calculate each index, natural log differences of the price are obtained for each commodity and multiplied by the relevant weight. The different components of the index are summed, and the exponent taken. The first year (1976) is set equal to unity, and subsequent years are defined as the previous year times the exponent of the summed log index. The index is then rebased to 2010. Resource, non-resource and all commodity price indices are thus calculated.

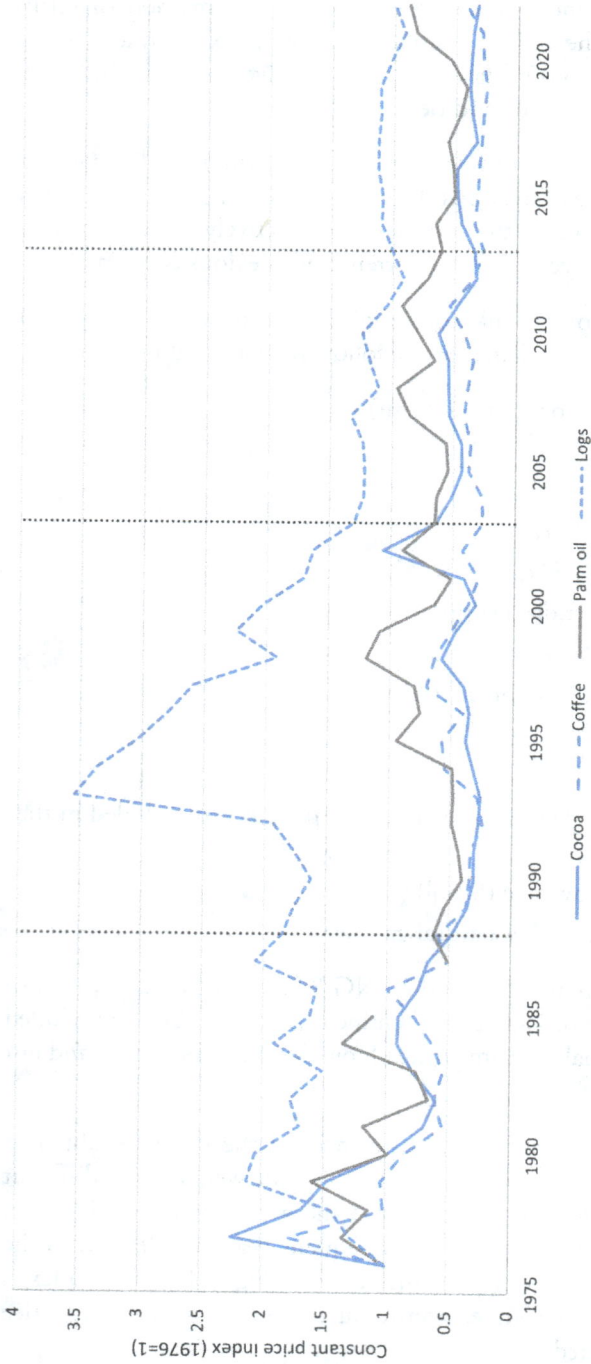

Figure B13: Inflation-adjusted price indices of some important non-resource commodities, 1976–2022

Notes: Indices derived from unit value data calculated by dividing commodity export values by commodity export volumes and then adjusting by CPI. Indices set equal to unity in 1976. These can be thought of as indices of the domestic purchasing power of agricultural commodities.

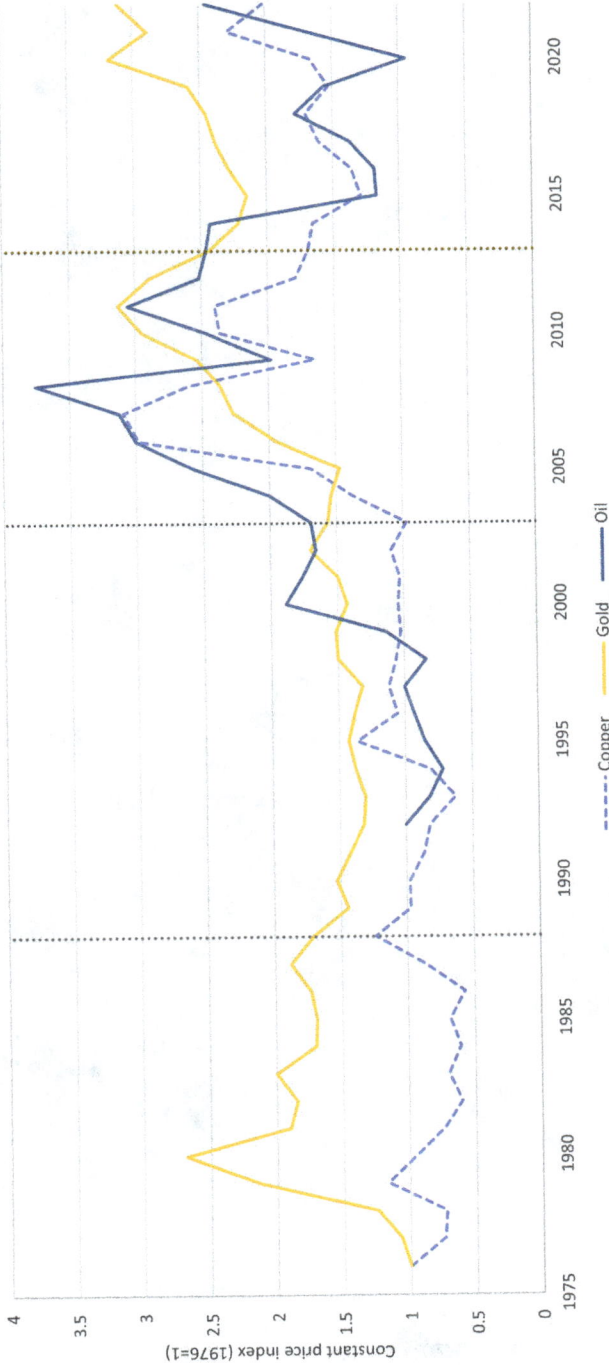

Figure B14: Inflation-adjusted price indices of some important resource commodities, 1976–2022

Notes: Indices derived from unit value data calculated by dividing commodity export values by commodity export volumes and then adjusting by CPI. Indices set equal to unity in 1976, except for 1992 for oil (first year of production). These can be thought of as indices of the domestic purchasing power of resource commodities.

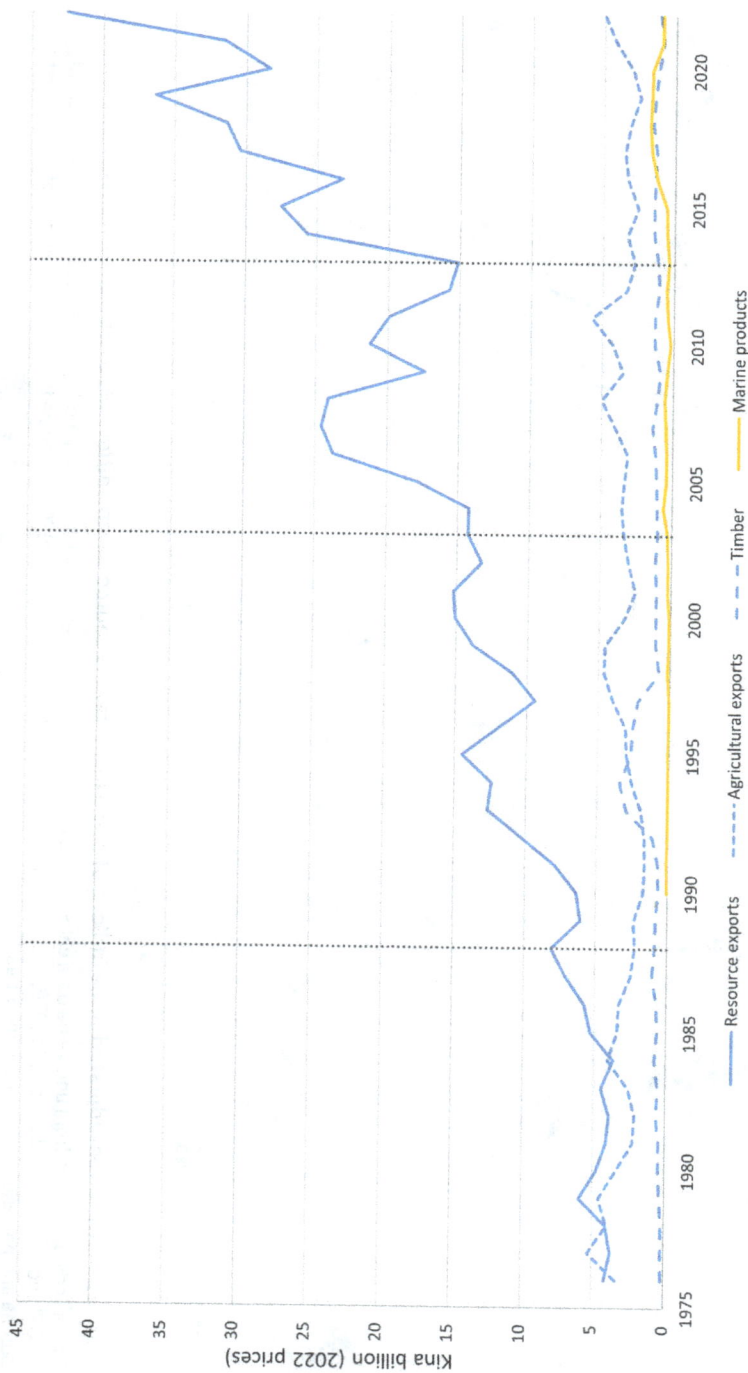

Figure B15: The value of resource, agricultural, timber and marine exports (kina billion, constant prices), 1976–2022

Employment

Formal sector employment, both private and public, is mainly flat until the end of the nineties (Figure B16). Employment in the private sector (also including state-owned enterprises or SOEs) increased rapidly in the noughties but has fallen since the boom ended. Overall, one sees a decline in the employment/population ratio, from 6 per cent just after independence to 4.5 per cent in 2019.

Plantation agriculture and manufacturing are more important employers than the resource sector (Figure B17).

The urban minimum wage was doubled just before independence (Figure B18). The urban minimum wage stayed high due to indexation, but in 1992 a separate minimum wage for urban workers was done away with, and replaced by a new, unified minimum wage (existing workers were grandfathered). There was no real increase until 2005. Even today, the urban worker on a minimum wage earns a third of what they did at independence.

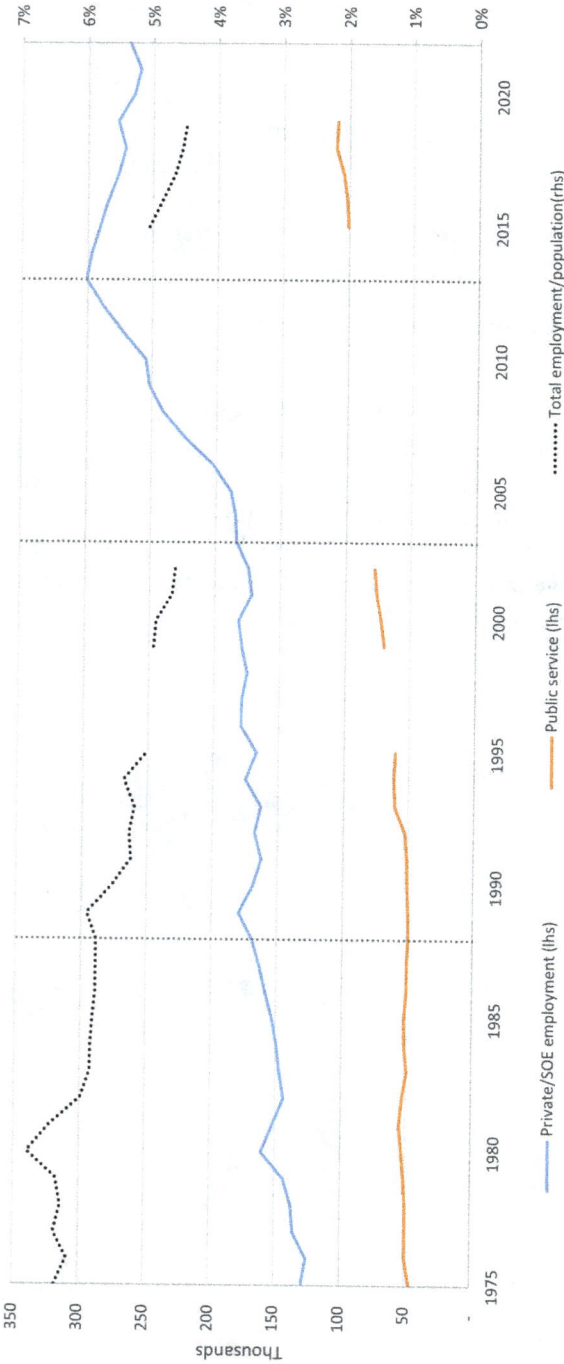

Figure B16: Formal sector employment, totals and population percentage, 1975–2022

Notes: Public service time series is incomplete.

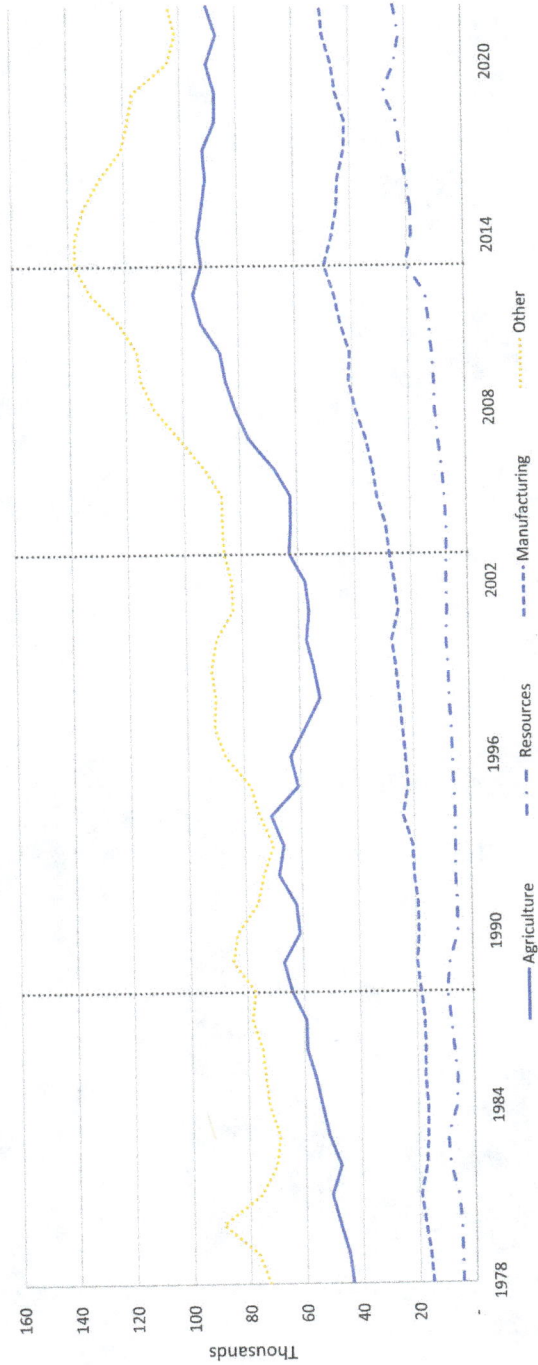

Figure B17: Formal employment by sector, 1978–2022

Notes: Only private sector and SOE employment are shown, so 'other' excludes public servants.

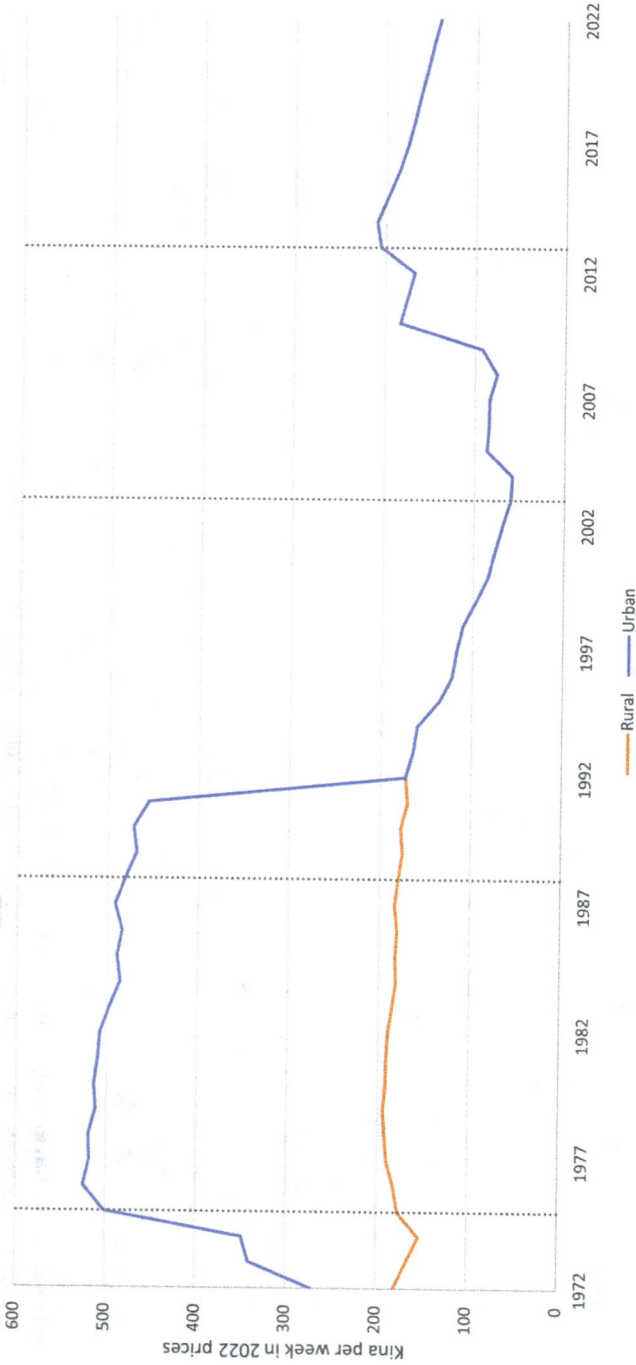

Figure B18: Urban and rural minimum weekly wage (kina per week in 2022 prices), 1972–2022

Notes: CPI is used to convert from current to constant prices.

Balance of payments and the exchange rate

More often than not, PNG has run current account surpluses, with notable exceptions in the eighties and late noughties (Figure B19). Foreign exchange rationing in the fourth period pushed imports below 30 per cent. Meanwhile, the current account surplus reached a record high of around 15 per cent due to booming resource exports and offshore revenue repatriation.

Under the 'hard kina' policy that PNG took to independence, the kina was fixed, first against the Australian dollar, and then against a bundle of currencies (Figure B20). The kina was depreciated against the US dollar by 10 per cent after the Panguna mine closed in 1989, and then floated in 1994, after which it plummeted in value. There was marked appreciation against the US dollar during the resource boom due to the heavy inflow of US dollars, and then a controlled gradual depreciation from 2014 onwards when the floating regime was done away with and replaced by a peg.

The real effective exchange rate (REER) declined during the first two periods, rapidly when it was floated in the second (Figure B21). It recovered its value during the resource boom and has maintained that value ever since due to the shift to a pegged regime, supported by foreign exchange rationing. In 1980, the REER was 1.33. In 2022, it was 1.31.

Foreign exchange (FX) reserves relative to imports declined rapidly from the time of independence to the first balance of payments crisis of 1994 (Figure B22). After a second crisis in 1999, they picked up again and have stayed healthy even since the boom ended as a result of foreign exchange rationing.

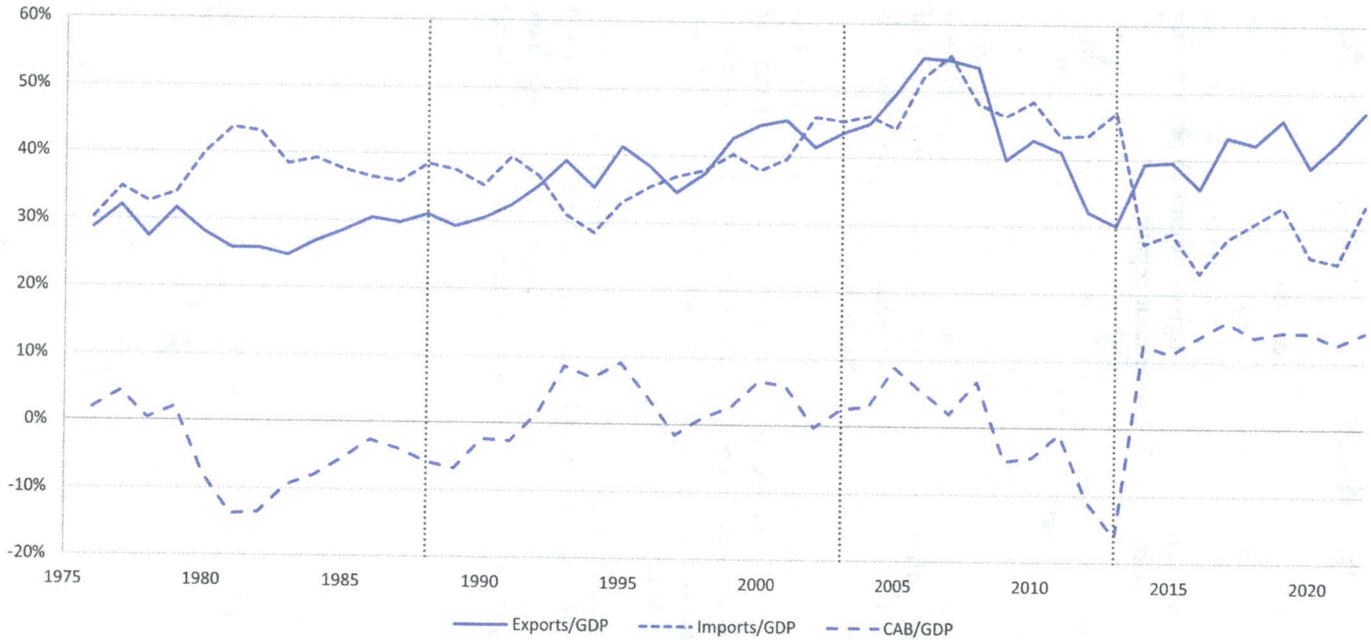

Figure B19: Exports, imports and the current account balance (% GDP), 1976–2022

Notes: CAB is the current account balance. Due to official transfers (aid), the CAB is sometimes positive even if imports exceed exports.

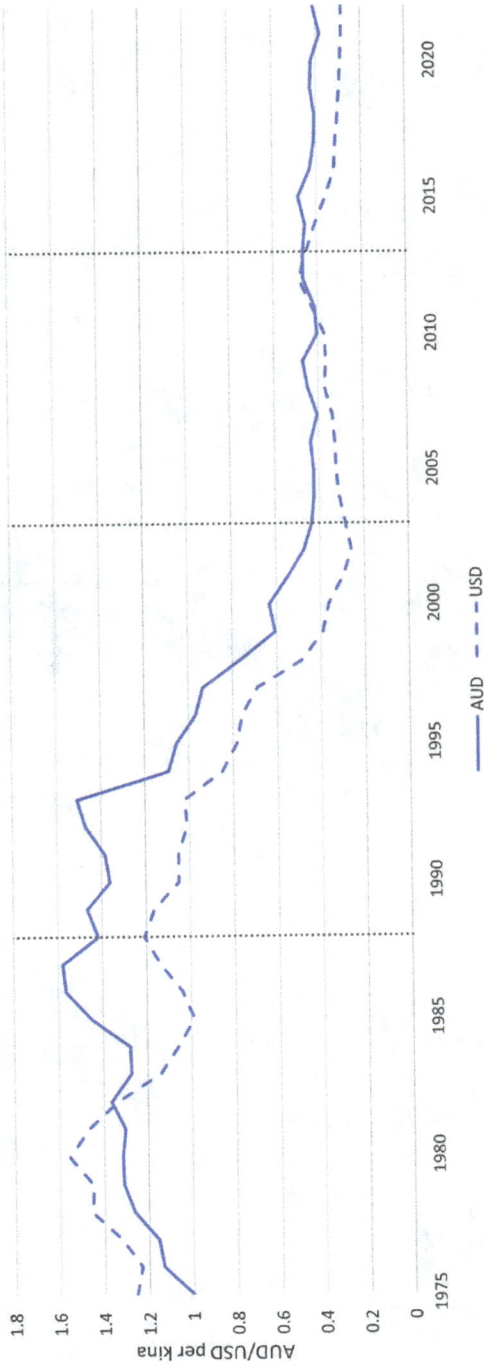

Figure B20: The PGK–AUD and PGK–USD exchange rates, 1975–2022

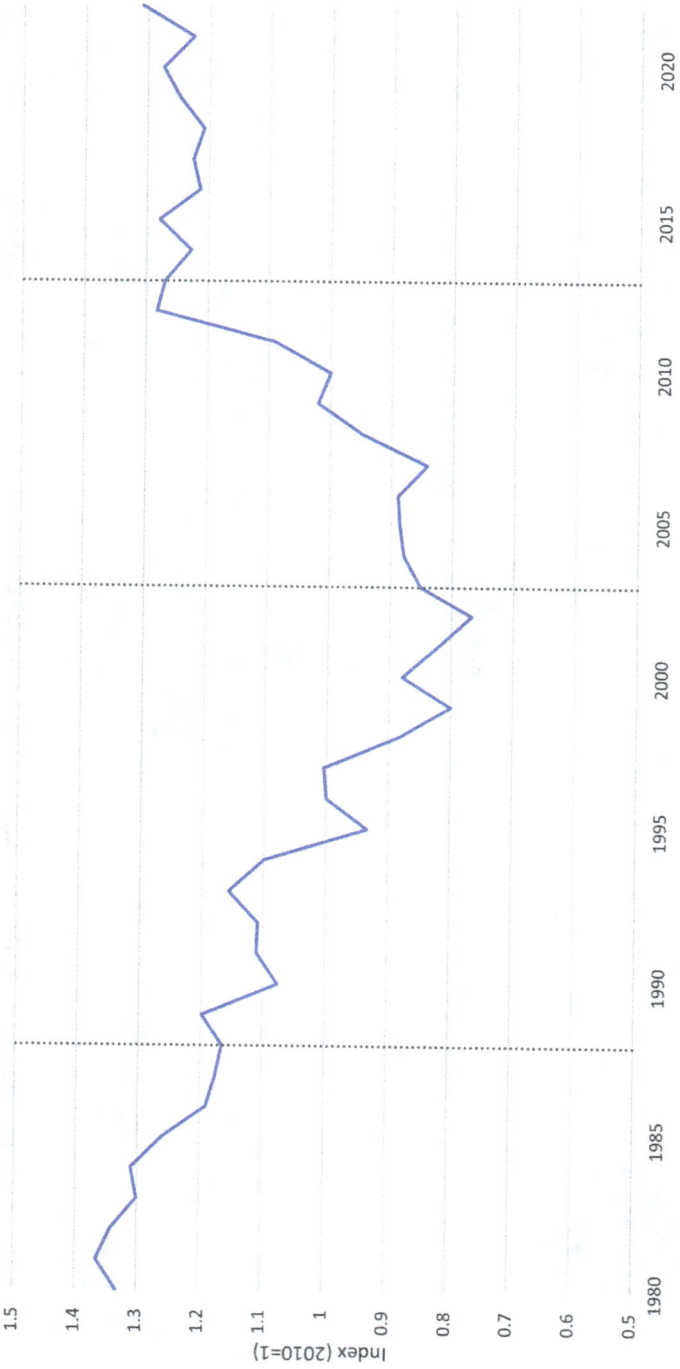

Figure B21: Real effective exchange rate index, 1980–2022

Notes: Index set equal to unity in 2010.

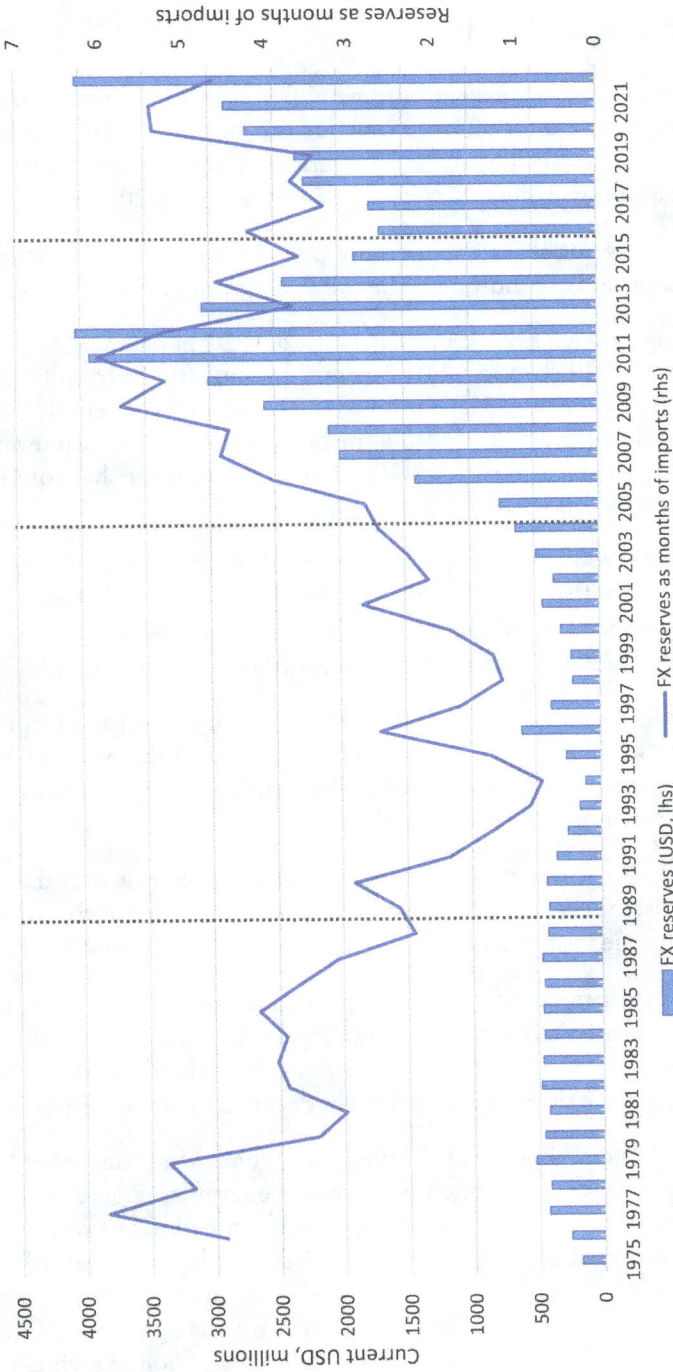

Figure B22: Foreign exchange reserves, 1975–2022

Fiscal outcomes

Both revenue and expenditure are highly volatile (Figure B23). Expenditure averages just under 22 per cent for the entire post-independence period. Revenue averaged about 20 per cent until the last period, in which it fell precipitously, falling to as low as 15 per cent in 2020.

Adjusting for inflation, the only period that has shown rapid growth in revenue and expenditure is the third (boom) period (Figure B24).

Foreign aid fell from about 7 per cent of GDP at independence to just 2 per cent in 2020 (Figure B25). Resource revenue increased from an average of about 2 per cent of GDP prior to the boom to 5 per cent during the boom but fell to 1.5 per cent during the bust. Non-resource own revenue also fell during the bust relative to GDP, but is still a higher share of GDP than at independence.

Resource revenue as a share of resource GDP is highly volatile, reaching above 30 per cent five times, and falling to below 5 per cent eight times (Figure B26). Its sustained low value during the bust is evident. Non-resource own revenue is less volatile and has gradually grown relative to non-resource GDP.

Throughout most of PNG's economic history, PNG has run mild budget deficits (Figure B27). During the early years of the resource boom it ran some sizeable surpluses, but the later years of the boom and the subsequent bust saw a number of large deficits.

The PNG government's debt and interest burden rose over the eighties and nineties, then fell during the early years of the boom, but then returned during the bust to equal or exceed earlier highs (Figure B28).

For the first decade after independence, about 25 per cent of PNG's government debt was domestic (Figure B29). By the mid-nineties that figure had reached 50 per cent, and, by 2012, around 70 per cent. During the bust, the share of domestic debt declined to about 50 per cent.

The Mineral Resources Stabilisation Fund was established just before independence to stabilise PNG's resource revenue (Figure B30). It built up a balance of 7 per cent of GDP by the late nineties, but was then abolished due to overall fiscal stress. It was replaced in the early years of the resource boom by a set of ad hoc trust funds, which were quickly built up, and then quickly depleted. Today, although a sovereign wealth fund has been legislated, PNG has no resource revenue stabilisation or savings mechanism.

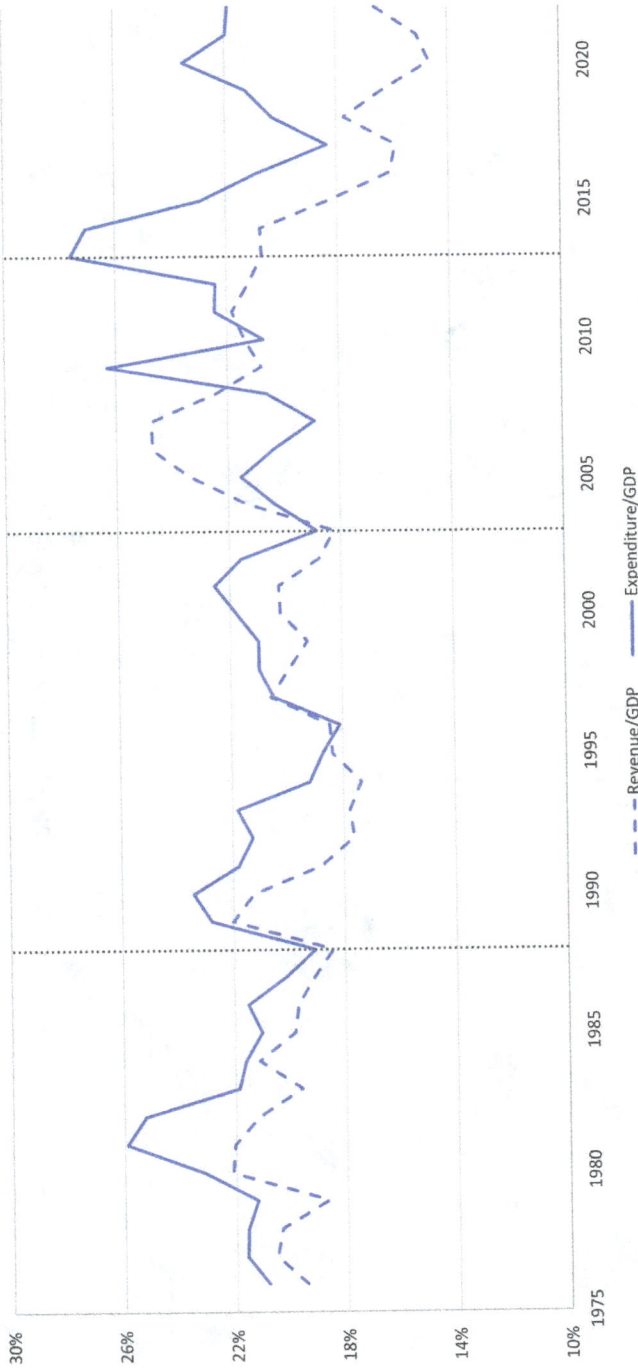

Figure B23: Revenue and expenditure (% GDP), 1976–2022

Legend: - - - Revenue/GDP   ——— Expenditure/GDP

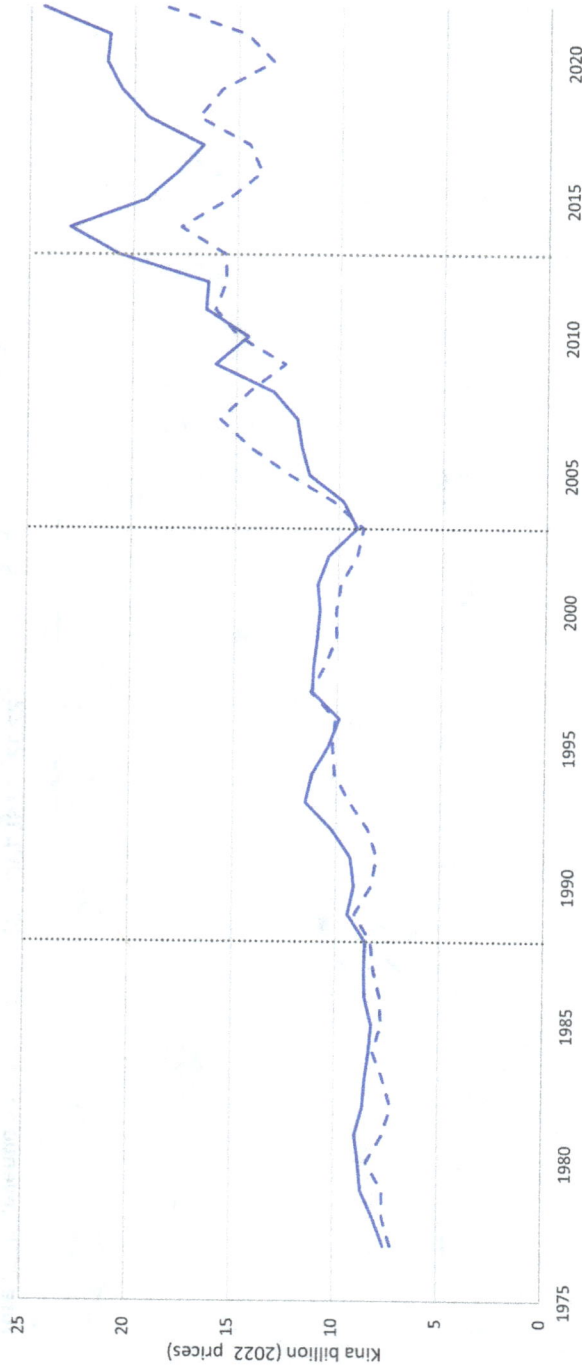

Figure B24: Revenue and expenditure, 1976–2022 (kina billion in 2022 prices)

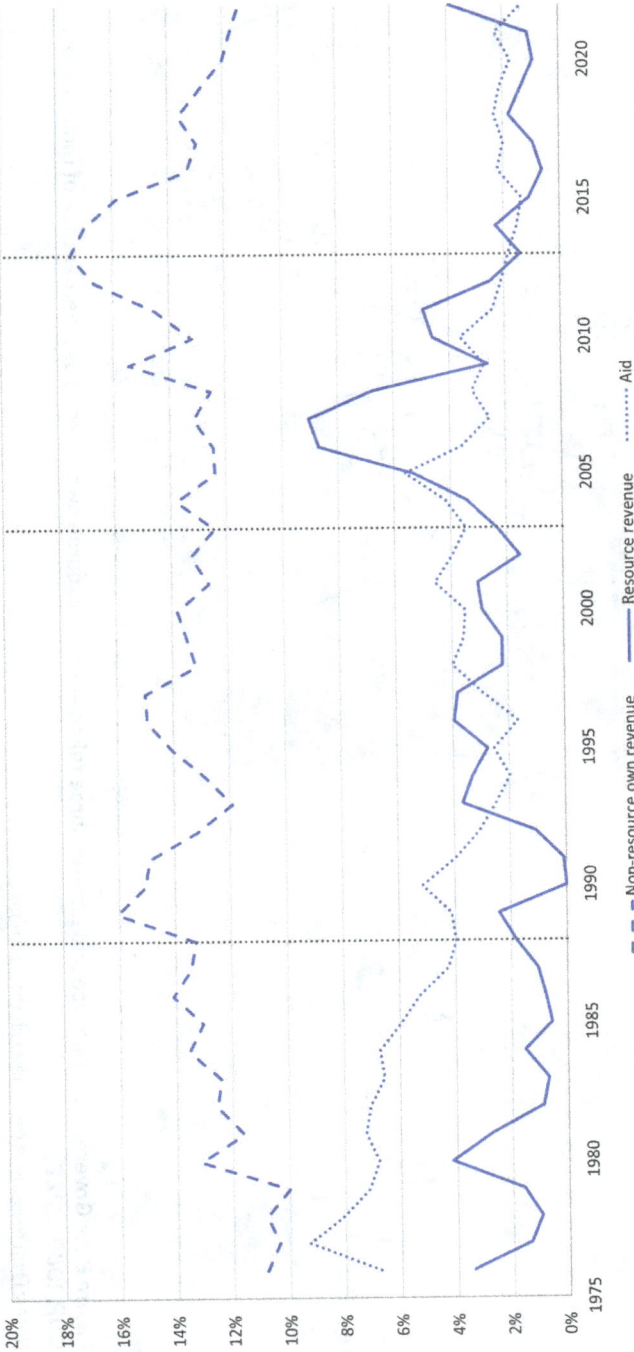

Figure B25: Non-resource own revenue, resource revenue and aid (% GDP), 1976–2022

Notes: Own revenue is revenue excluding foreign aid.

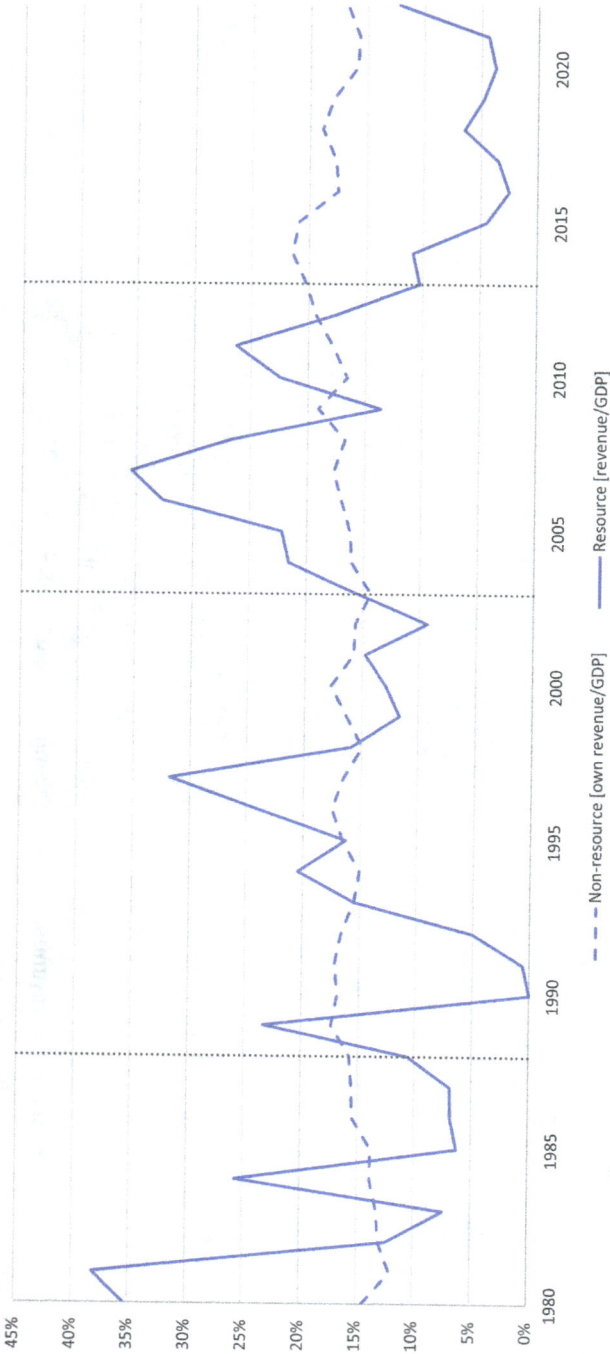

Figure B26: Government resource and non-resource takes—(non-)resource own revenue as a percentage of (non-) resource GDP, 1980–2022

Notes: Own revenue is revenue excluding foreign aid.

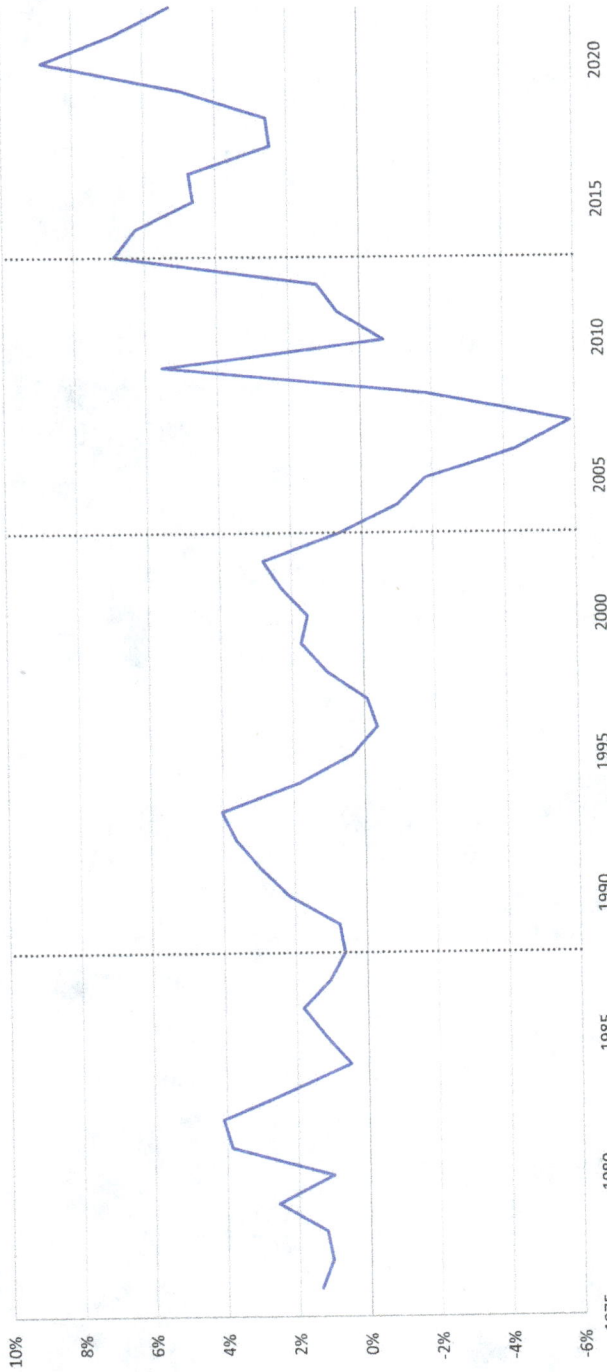

Figure B27: Deficit/GDP (%), 1976–2022

Notes: A negative deficit is a surplus.

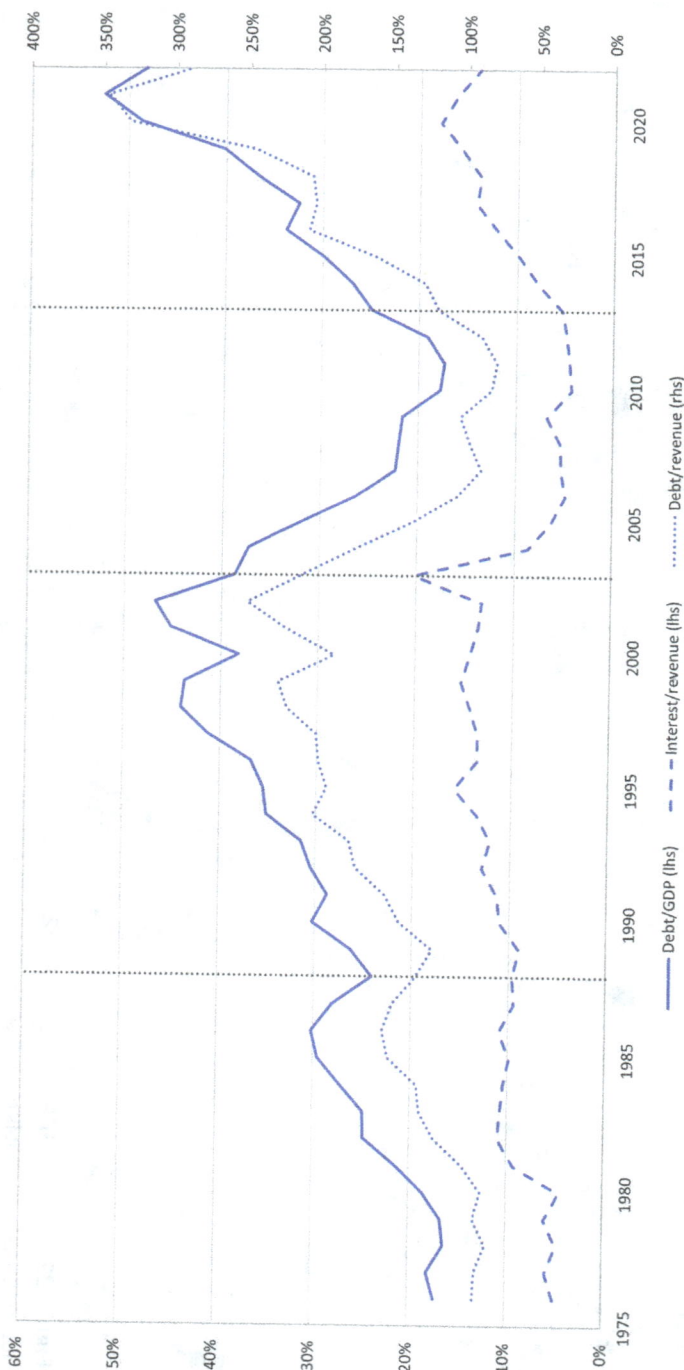

Figure B28: Debt/GDP, debt/revenue and interest/revenue (%), 1976–2022

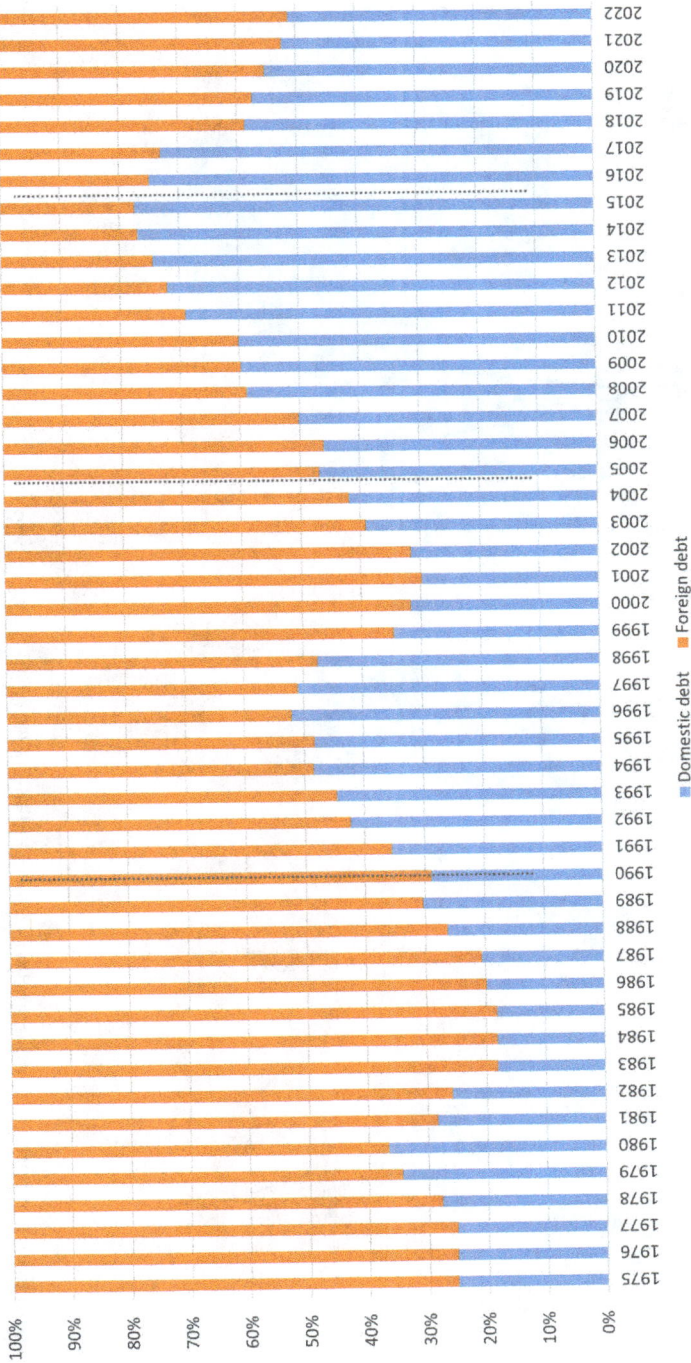

Figure B29: Domestic and foreign debt as percentages of the total, 1975–2022

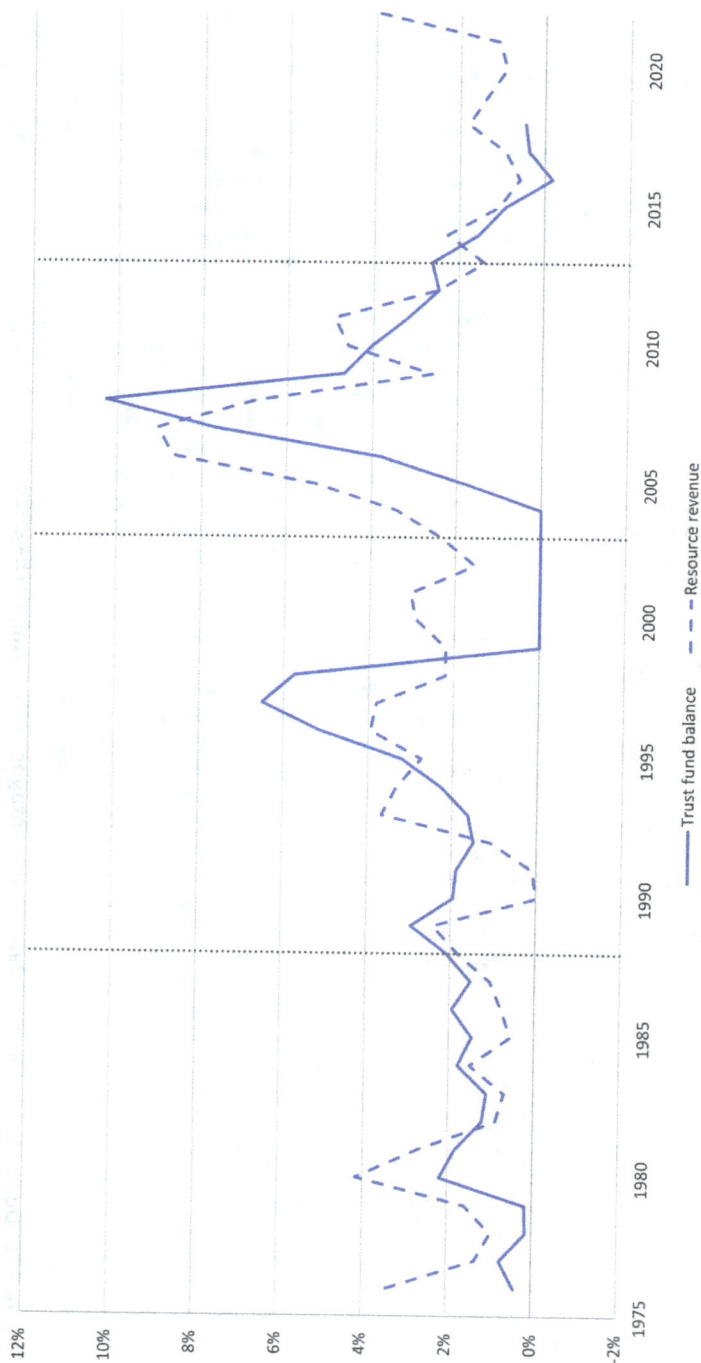

Figure B30: Resource revenues and trust fund balances (% GDP), 1976–2022

Notes: Trust fund balances only to 2018. After that a consistent series is not available. However, the data that are available indicate that trust fund balances have been kept small since 2018.

Monetary policy and banking

Inflation has generally been moderate in PNG (Figure B31). However, it did noticeably increase in the nineties due to rapid currency depreciation and perhaps central bank deficit financing (Figure B35).

Since independence, deposits held by the commercial banking sector have almost doubled in size relative to GDP (Figure B32). Private sector loans, which increased relative to GDP in the first period, fell following the Bougainville crisis, recovered during the boom, but then fell during the subsequent bust. Lending to the government has become as important for the banks as lending to the private sector.

The actual liquid asset ratio and the statutory minimum liquid asset ratio (set by BPNG) generally moved in a parallel motion throughout the eighties and early nineties (Figure B33), indicating that the Bank of Papua New Guinea (BNPG) was successful at influencing the behaviour of banks. The divergence in these values from the mid-nineties onwards—due to increased purchase by banks of government bonds—indicates the opposite situation. In the late nineties, BPNG introduced a cash reserve requirement (Figure B40) and in 2010 it abandoned the minimum liquid asset ratio.

Between around 1990 and 2013 (following deregulation), the average deposit rate was on a downwards trajectory, declining to close to zero (Figure B34). The increase in the spread between the average lending rate and the average deposit rate is because lending rates have not fallen by nearly as much as the deposit rates. The KFR or policy rate has no influence on lending rates due to excess liquidity (Figure B36).

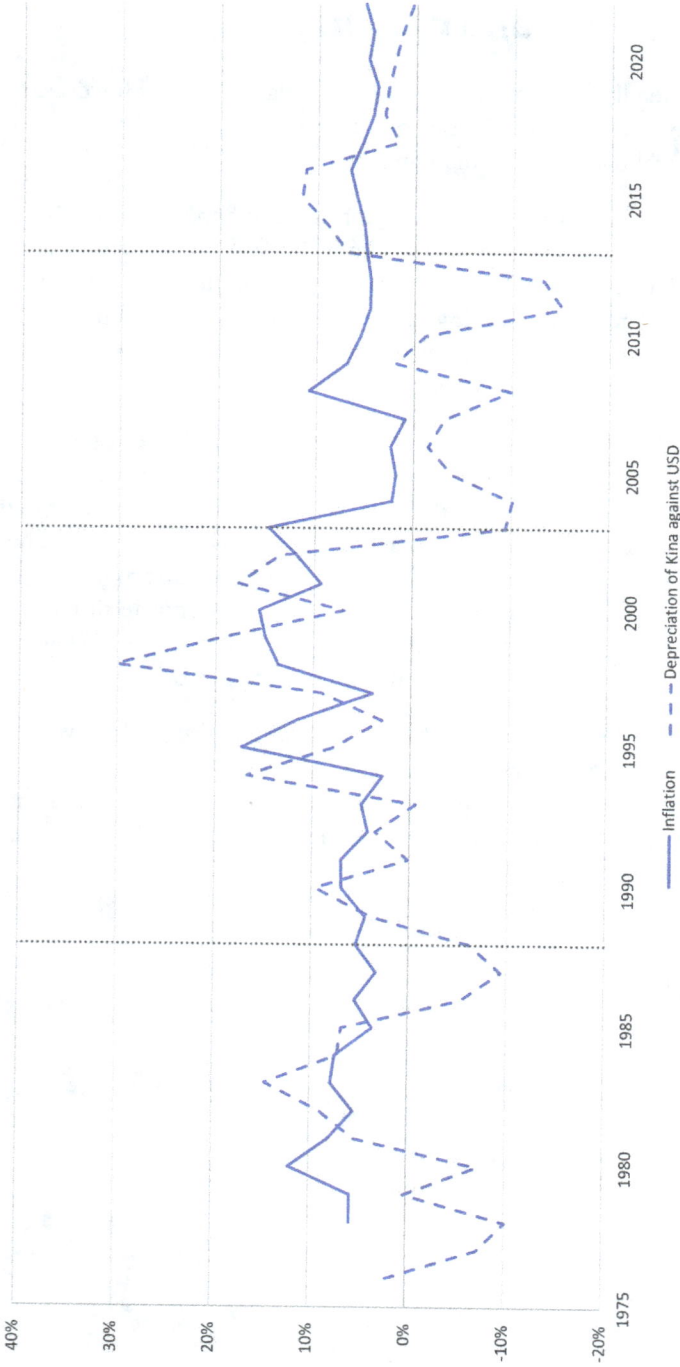

Figure B31: Inflation and currency depreciation, 1976–2022

Inflation — — Depreciation of Kina against USD

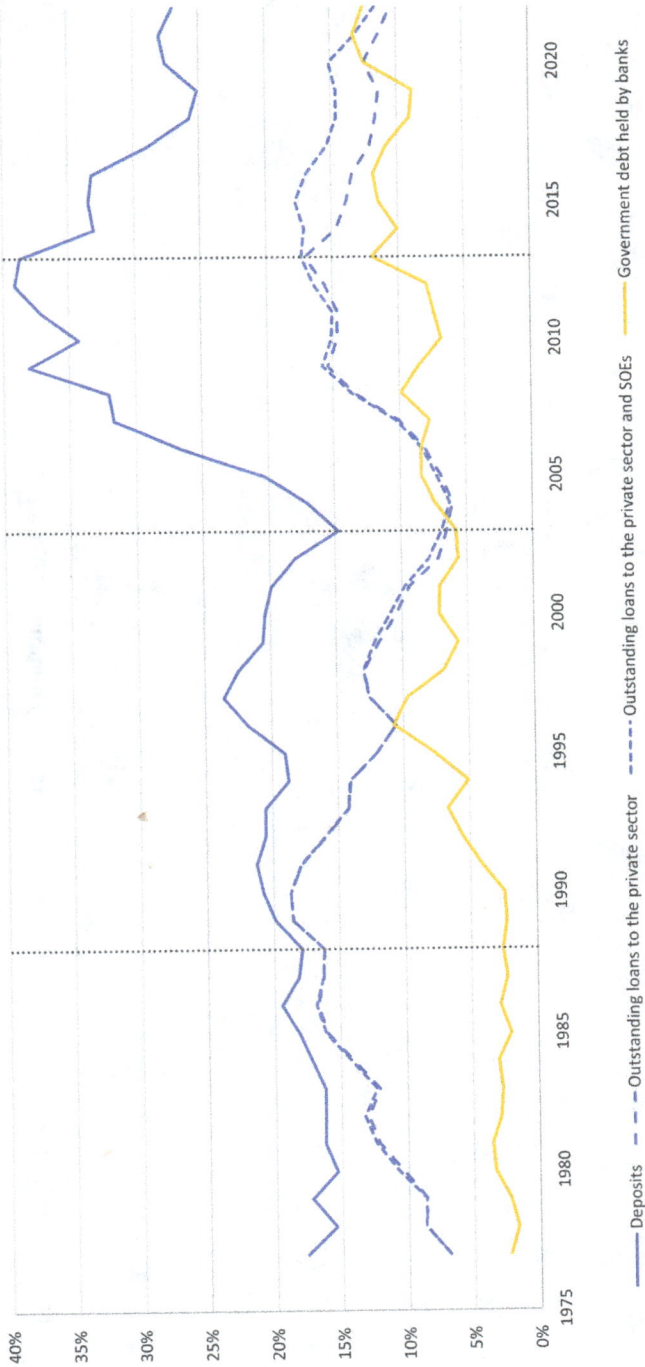

Figure B32: Deposit and lending ratios (% GDP), 1977–2022

Legend: Deposits — Outstanding loans to the private sector — Outstanding loans to the private sector and SOEs — Government debt held by banks

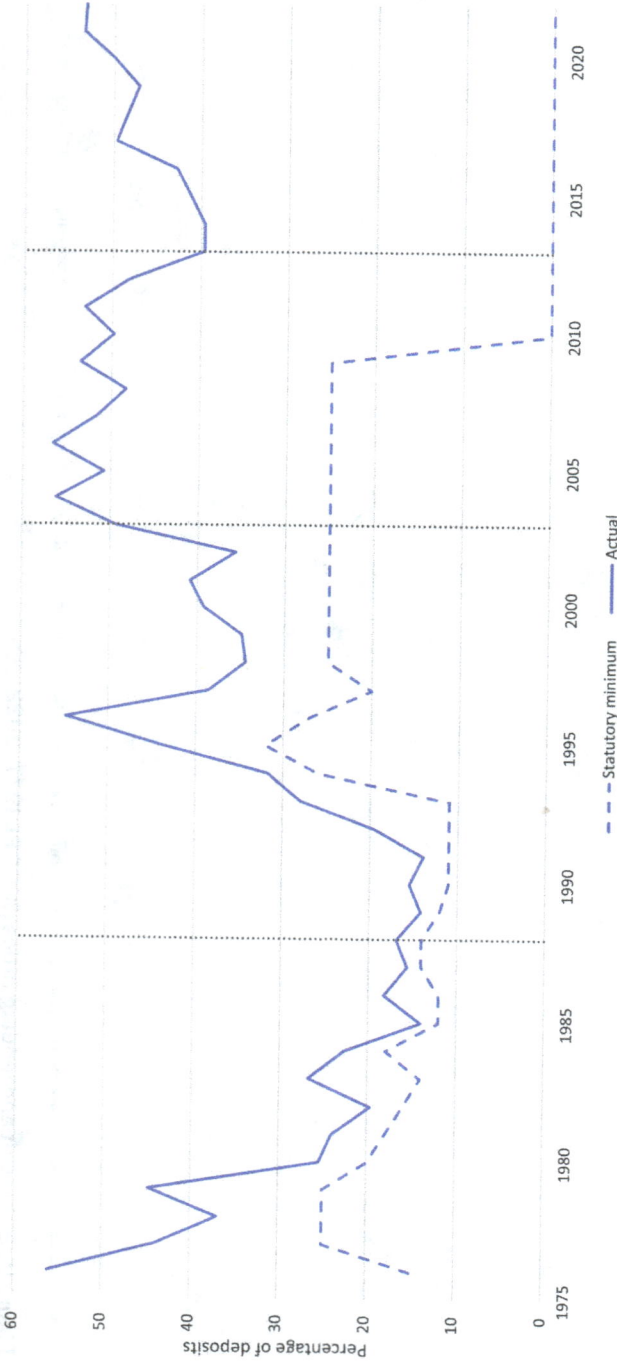

Figure B33: Banks' liquid asset ratios—actual and statutory minimum, 1976–2022

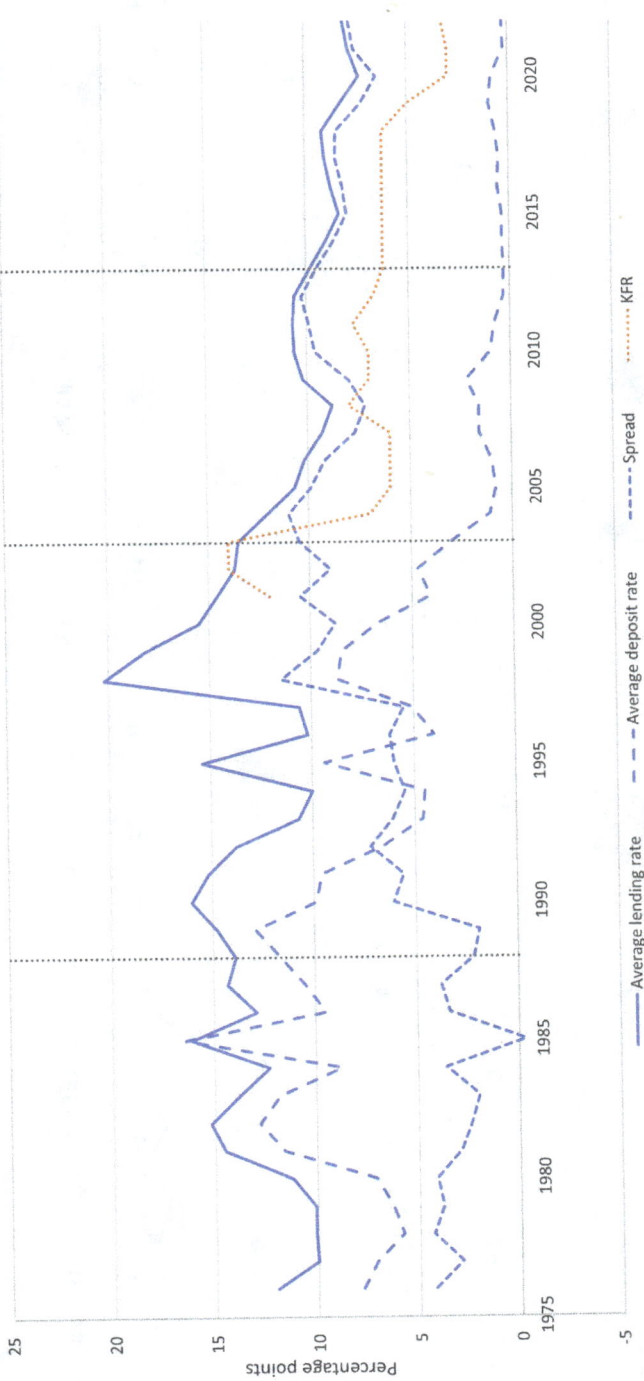

Figure B34: Weighted average lending and deposit rates and spread, 1976–2022, and Kina Facility Rate, 2001–22

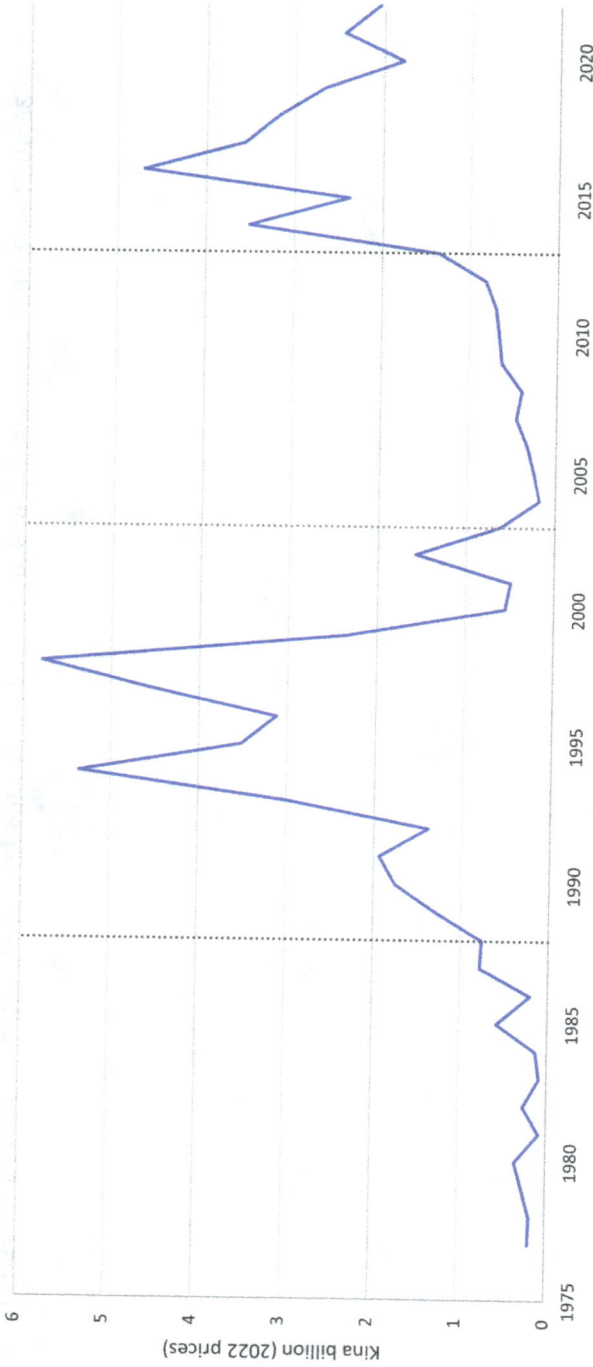

Figure B35: BPNG holdings of government debt adjusted for inflation, 1977–2022 (kina billion, constant prices)

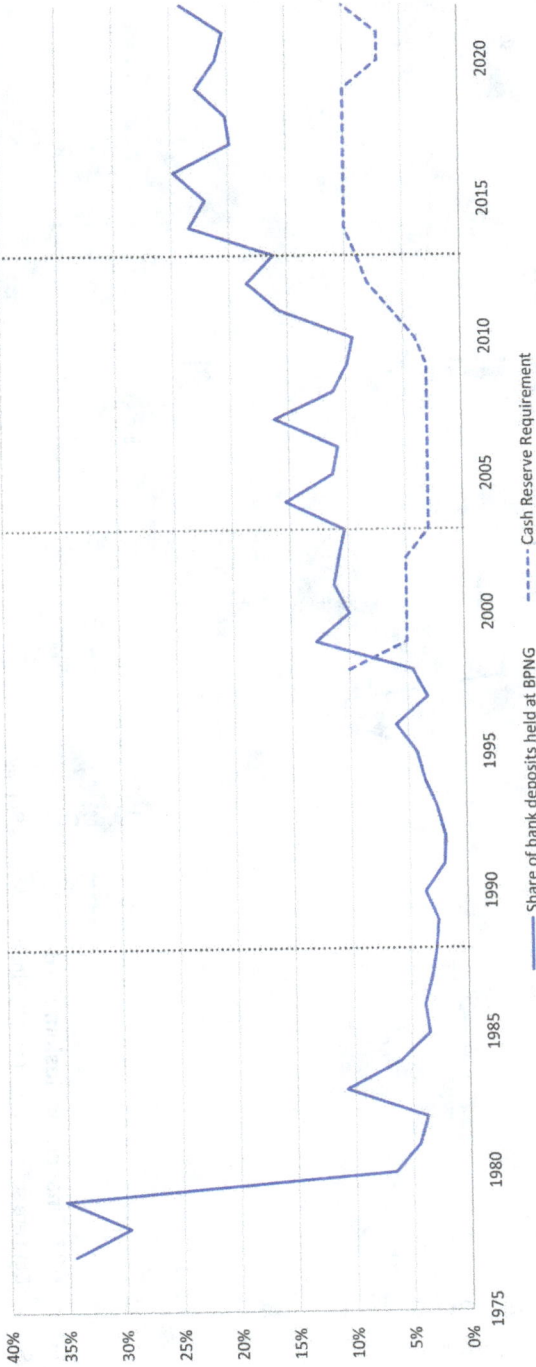

Figure B36: Share of commercial bank deposits held at BPNG and in cash, 1977–2022, and cash reserve requirement, 1998–2022

Note: Cash held by commercial banks is included as well as their deposits at BPNG for historical reasons, since the two variables are combined in BPNG (2007). Over time, cash is a declining ratio of the two variables combined, 11 per cent for the last four years.

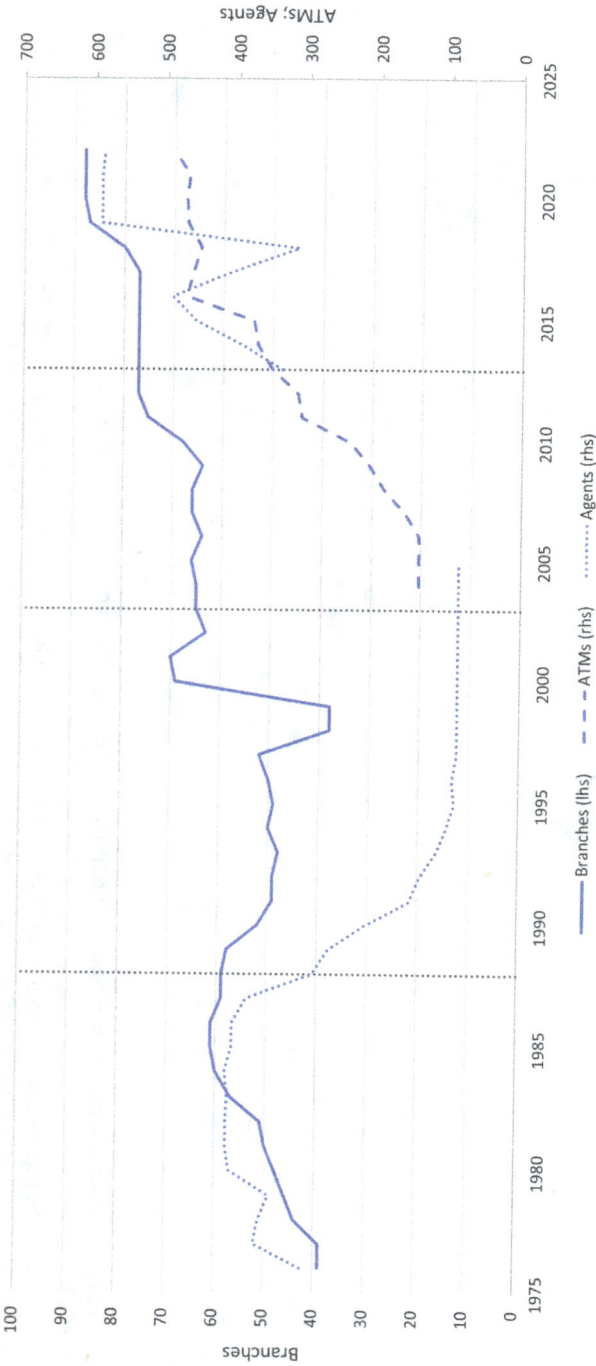

Figure B37: Financial inclusion, 1976–2021

Source: Data are sourced from the IMF Financial Access Survey.

Monetary policy and banking (cont.)

Deficit financing emerged as a feature of the mid- and late nineties (Figure B35). It was then banned by the Central Banking Act of 2000, but nevertheless re-emerged between 2014 and 2016.

The excess liquidity at independence did not last long (Figure B36). However, it re-emerged in the late nineties and has got worse since. In 1998, BPNG introduced a minimum cash reserve requirement (CRR) of 10 per cent. It was reduced to 5 per cent the following year, but the share of deposits held by the commercial banks at BPNG stayed between 10 and 15 per cent, and then increased above 15 per cent during the late boom years, and above 20 per cent during the bust, so that even when the CRR was increased in the second half of the boom, it had no effect.

The number of bank branches has risen, but not kept up with population growth (Figure B37). The number of bank agents has fallen and then risen. ATMs are now in the country, but the number is no longer growing.

Service delivery

Adjusting for both inflation and population, government revenue is significantly lower today than at independence (Figure B38). Expenditure has recovered since its collapse in the nineties, but not revenue, which in 2020 on a per person basis was at its lowest level ever.

Vaccination rates rose over the eighties and were mainly stable or rising in the nineties and noughties, but fell sharply in the tens (Figure B39). In 2019, according to World Bank data, PNG had the lowest immunisation rates in the world (Table 10.14). The number of doctors has struggled to keep pace with population growth and is now one of the lowest in the world.

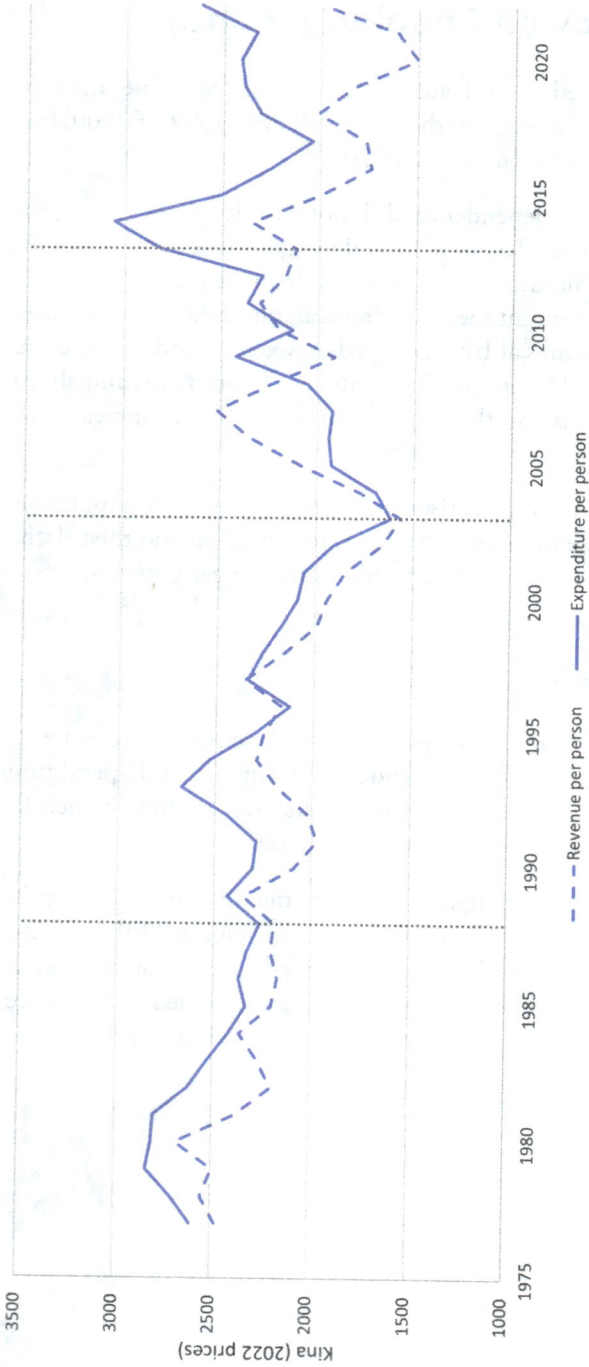

Figure B38: Government revenue and expenditure per person, 1976–2022 (kina in 2022 prices)

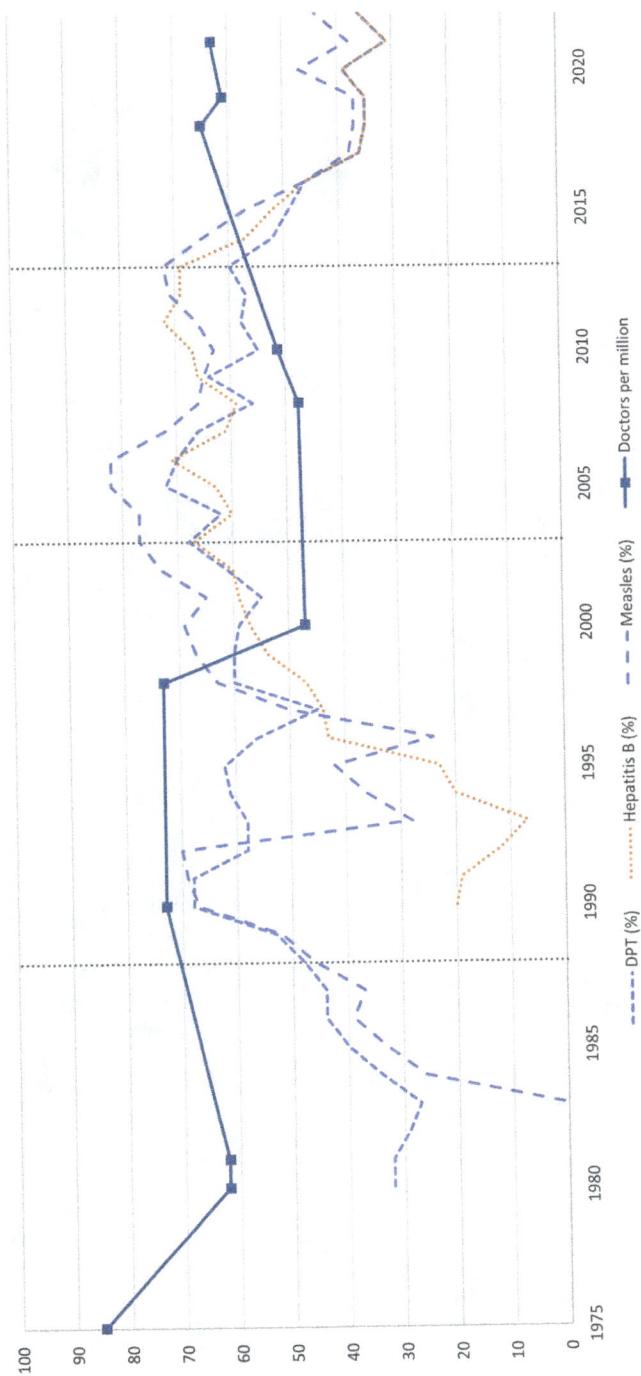

Figure B39: Immunisation rates, 1980–2022, and doctors per million, 1975–2021

Notes: The rates are the percentage of children aged 12–23 months who have been fully vaccinated. DPT is diphtheria, pertussis (or whooping cough) and tetanus; it requires three vaccine doses. Three doses of the Hepatitis B vaccine are also required, but only one for measles.

Annex C:
Resource projects

Table C1: PNG's main resource projects, 1969–2024

Project	Province	Resource	Construction commenced	Production commenced	Production ceased	Capital investment costs (kina m)	Capital investment/GDP
(A) Opened							
Panguna	Autonomous Region of Bougainville	Gold/silver/copper	1969	1972	1989	660	Unknown
Panguna was established by Bougainville Copper Ltd (BCL) — a subsidiary of Rio Tinto. At its inception, the national government of PNG held 19 per cent of BCL's shares. The mine was closed in 1989 due to conflict and has not been reopened. In 2016, Rio Tinto transferred its 53.8% shareholdings in BCL for distribution to the Autonomous Bougainville Government (36.4%) and the national PNG government (36.4%, which includes the original 19%). BCL is listed, and the remaining shares are held by a range of parties.							
Ok Tedi	Western	Gold/silver/copper	1981	1984	Still active	990	39%
At its inception, the shares of Ok Tedi Mining Company Ltd (OTML) were distributed between BHP (30%), Amoco (30%), German companies (20%) and the State of Papua New Guinea (20%). BHP increased its shareholdings, but in 2002 withdrew from the mine as a consequence of the Ok Tedi environmental disaster and consequent legal action and transferred its majority shareholding (52%) to the newly created, self-governing PNG Sustainable Development Program (SDP). After the transfer, project shareholding was as follows: SDP (52%), the State of Papua New Guinea (30%) and Inmet Mining Corporation (18%). Inmet was subsequently bought out. In 2013, the PNG government nationalised the mine — two-thirds (67%) of OTML shares are now owned by the national government, and the remaining one-third by the provincial government and landowners.							
Misima	Milne Bay	Gold/silver	1988	1989	2004	206	4%
At its inception, the mine was a joint venture between Placer Dome Inc (80%) and the PNG state-owned Orogen Minerals Ltd (20%). Since its closure in 2004, ownership of the mine has gone through multiple hands, but none were able to reopen the mine. Currently, Kingston Resources Limited owns the mine.							

Project	Province	Resource	Construction commenced	Production commenced	Production ceased	Capital investment costs (kina m)	Capital investment/GDP
Porgera	Enga	Gold/silver	1989	1990	See text	1,000	22%
The Porgera Joint Venture's original shareholders were Placer Dome (30%), Highlands Pacific (30%), Renison Goldfields Consolidated (30%) and the PNG government (10%). Placer Dome went on to gain more shares at the expense of its other partners, eventually becoming the major shareholder. There were then a number of negotiations, mergers and acquisitions, including efforts by the PNG government to increase its ownership. As of 2020, Barrick Niugini Limited (BNL) owned 95% of Porgera. It was the operator of the mine and a 50/50 joint venture between Barrick Gold and Zijin Mining. The remaining 5% was shared equally by the Enga Provincial Government and Porgera landowners. In 2020, the government of PNG announced it would not renew BNL's 30-year mining lease, and that the mine would be run by the state-owned Kumul Mining. This decision was challenged domestically and internationally. Following negotiations, it was agreed that 51% of shares would be owned by PNG stakeholders (36% national government, 15% provincial government and landowners), and the other 49% would be retained by BNL, which would continue as the operator. The mine reopened in 2024.							
Hides	Hela	Gas	1990	1991	Still active	199	4%
The Hides gas field was discovered by BP, which relinquished its interest to ExxonMobil – the developer and operator of the gas fields. The majority of gas production from the Hides field is directed toward the PNG LNG project (see below for more detail). However, a small proportion of gas production was dedicated to the earlier-established Hides Gas-to-Electricity Project – operated and entirely owned by Santos – which provides electricity to the Porgera gold mine.							
Kutubu Petroleum	Southern Highlands	Oil	1991	1992	Still active	1,190	22%
The Kutubu project was operated by Chevron Niugini – a local subsidiary of Chevron – until 2003. In 2003, Santos acquired Chevron Niugini and took over operations. Santos is the majority shareholder (60.05%); landowners have a minority share through Petroleum Resources Kutubu (6.75%).							
Wapolu	Milne Bay	Gold/silver	1994	1995	1997	12	0%
Owned by Crater Gold Mining when the mine was in operation. Currently, Adyton is trying to reopen the mine.							
Tolukuma	Central	Gold/silver	1995	1996	2018	45	0%
The Tolokuma mine has gone through multiple owners. Dome Resources developed the mine and started production in 1995. In 2000, DRDGOLD Ltd acquired Dome Resources and the Tolokuma mine. In 2006 Emperor Mines acquired the mine, which was then sold to Petromin in 2008, which then sold it to Asidokona Mining Resources in 2015. In 2018, the National Court ordered a liquidation. In 2022, Lole Mining Limited was granted a mining lease for the Tolukuma mine.							

Project	Province	Resource	Construction commenced	Production commenced	Production ceased	Capital investment costs (kina m)	Capital investment/GDP
Lihir	New Ireland	Gold/silver	1995	1997	Still active	1,147	12%
	The Lihir project was owned by Lihir Gold Limited (LGL), which consisted of many different shareholders – none of them with a commanding interest. One of the influential shareholders of LGL was Rio Tinto, which established and owned the Lihir Management Company to develop and operate the mine for LGL. In 2005, Rio Tinto divested its interest in the Lihir Management Company and its operations were then incorporated into LGL. In 2010, LGL was acquired by Newcrest and became a 100% owned subsidiary company of Newcrest, which was itself acquired by Newmont in 2023. At one point, PNG national and provincial government and landowners held 30% of Lihir shares (through MRL); this was reduced over time, eventually to zero; however, most of the landowner share was reinvested in a diversified portfolio by MRL Capital.						
Gobe main	Gulf/Southern Highlands	Oil	1997	1998	Still active	213	2%
	Gobe main is operated by Santos. Ownership interests are as follows: Santos (10%), ExxonMobil (14.5%), Merlin Petroleum Company (JX Nippon) (73.5%) and Petroleum Resource Gobe Ltd (2%), the last representing landowners.						
SE Gobe	Southern Highlands	Oil	1997	1998	Still active	524	5%
	South East Gobe is operated by Santos. Ownership interests are as follows: Santos (22.3%), ExxonMobil (7.7%), Merlin Petroleum Company (JX Nippon) (39.1%), Barracuda Ltd (Santos) (7.5%), Petroleum Resources Gobe Ltd (2%) on behalf of landowners and Kumul Petroleum (21.4%) on behalf of the national government.						
Moran	Hela Province	Oil	1997	1998	Still active		
	The Moran project comprises three license areas: petroleum development licence (PDL) 2, PDL 5 and PDL 6. It is operated by Santos. The interests are as follow: Santos (49.5%), ExxonMobil (26.8%), Merlin Petroleum Company (JX Nippon) (8.3%), Kumul Petroleum (11.3%) and landowners (4.1%).						
Kainantu Gold	Eastern Highlands	Gold	2004	2006	Still active	127.7	1%
	The mine was first developed by Highlands Pacific but was sold to Barrick Gold in 2007. Production stopped in 2009. In 2014 the mine was bought by K92 Mining, a Canadian company, and was restarted in 2016.						

Project	Province	Resource	Construction commenced	Production commenced	Production ceased	Capital investment costs (kina m)	Capital investment/GDP
Hidden Valley	Morobe	Gold	2005	2007	Still active	757.6	3%
	Hidden Valley was originally built and owned by Harmony Gold; in 2008, Newcrest Mining bought into the project and formed the Morobe Mining Joint venture — a 50/50 split between Harmony and Newcrest; however, in 2020, 100% ownership reverted to Harmony Gold.						
Simberi Gold	New Ireland	Gold	2006	2007	Still active	51.2	0%
	Allied Gold originally opened and operated the mine. In 2012, Allied Gold ceased to exist after it merged with St Barbara — the new owner of the mine.						
Ramu Nickel and Cobalt	Madang	Nickel/cobalt	2006	2008	Still active	2,539.4	10%
	The Ramu Nickel project is a joint venture between China Metallurgical Construction (85%), which is the operator, MRDC (6.44%) on behalf of the provincial and local governments, and Highlands Pacific (8.56%). In 2019, Cobalt 27, now Nickel 28, acquired Highlands Pacific and its interest in this project.						
South-East Mananda Oil	Hela	Oil	2006	2006	Closed		
	The project operator was Oil Search (72.3%) in partnership with Merlin Petroleum (19.8%) and Petroleum Resources Kutubu (7.9%) on behalf of landowners.						
Sinivet Gold	East New Britain	Gold	2008	2012	Closed		
	A very small gold mine, operated by Canadian miner New Guinea Gold; abandoned after protests from landowners and operating license not renewed; shrouded in environmental controversy.						
PNG LNG	Hela/Southern Highlands/ Gulf/Central	Gas	2010	2014	Still active	51,630	133%
	ExxonMobil is the operator of PNG LNG and holds a 33.2% interest. The other joint venture partners are Santos (39.9%), Kumul Petroleum (19.4%) on behalf of the national government, JX Nippon Oil and Gas Exploration (4.7%) and MRDC (2.8%) on behalf of the provincial government and landowners.						

(B) Prospective

Note: Only major prospective projects shown. The PNG government is expected to exercise its right to buy a minority equity share in these projects.

Project	Province	Resource	Construction commenced	Production commenced	Production ceased	Capital investment costs (kina m)	Capital investment/GDP
Wafi-Golpu	Morobe	Gold/copper					
Newmont and Harmony Gold currently each own 50% of the Wafi-Golpu Project.							
Papua LNG	Gulf	Gas					
The main co-owners of Papua LNG are TotalEnergies (40.1%), ExxonMobil (36.5%) and Santos (22.8%). In July 2022, TotalEnergies announced the commencement of upstream front-end engineering and design studies.							
P'nyang	Western	Gas					
Will be operated by ExxonMobil. Currently, ExxonMobil has a 49 % interest in P'nyang, while Santos has 38.5% and JX Nippon has 12.5%.							
Pasca A	Western	Offshore gas					
To be operated and partly owned by Twinza Oil.							
Frieda River	East Sepik	Gold/copper					
Owned by PanAust (80%) and Highlands Pacific (20%).							

Notes: Updated from BPNG (2007) using a range of sources. Capital investment costs are in nominal terms, and are divided by GDP in the first year of construction to get capital investment/GDP. Oil Search was acquired by Santos in 2021; the only interest by Santos in an existing project prior to that acquisition was its 13.5 per cent share in PNG LNG. The very small but longstanding Edie Creek Mining Lease in Morobe is excluded.

References

Abaijah, J. and E. Wright. 1991. *A Thousand Coloured Dreams*. Mount Waverley: Dellasta Pacific.

ABC News. 2002. *Four Corners*. Pacific Joker, 24 June. tapatalk.com/groups/pacificjoker/abc-transcript-of-the-four-corners-program-for-tho-t13611.html.

Acemoglu, D. and J. Robinson. 2012. *Why Nations Fail: The Origins of Power, Prosperity, and Poverty*. New York: Random House.

Acemoglu, D. and J. Robinson. 2019. *The Narrow Corridor: States, Societies and the Fate of Liberty*. London: Viking.

ACIL Tasman. 2009. 'PNG LNG Economic Impact Study'. ACIL Tasman. scribd.com/document/118394202/Acil-Tasman-Impact-Study-Revision-01.

ADB (Asian Development Bank). 2012a. *Finding Balance: Benchmarking the Performance of State-Owned Enterprises in Papua New Guinea*. Asian Development Bank. www.adb.org/sites/default/files/publication/29776/png-critical-development-constraints.pdf.

ADB. 2012b. *Papua New Guinea: Critical Development Constraints*. Asian Development Bank. www.adb.org/sites/default/files/publication/29988/finding-balance-benchmarking-performance.pdf.

ADB. 2014. *Finding Balance 2014: Benchmarking the Performance of State-Owned Enterprises in Island Countries*. Asian Development Bank. www.adb.org/sites/default/files/publication/42836/finding-balance-2014.pdf.

ADB. 2018. 'Proposed Programmatic Approach, Policy-Based Loan for Subprogram 1, and Project Loans Papua New Guinea: Health Services Sector Development Program'. Report and Recommendation of the president to the Board of Directors, Asian Development Bank.

ADB. 2020. 'Proposed Programmatic Approach and Policy-Based Loan for Subprogram 1 Papua New Guinea: State-Owned Enterprises Reform Program'. Report and Recommendation of the president to the Board of Directors, Asian Development Bank.

ADB. 2021. '$150 Million ADB Loan to Support SOE Service Delivery in PNG'. *Asian Development Bank*, 10 December. adb.org/news/150-million-adb-loan-support-soe-service-delivery-png.

ADB. 2022. 'Proposed Policy-Based Loan for Subprogram 3 Papua New Guinea: State-Owned Enterprises Reform Program'. November. adb.org/sites/default/files/project-documents/53424/53424-003-rrp-en.pdf.

ADB and INA (Institute of National Affairs). 2008. *The Challenges of Doing Business in Papua New Guinea*. Asian Development Bank. adb.org/sites/default/files/publication/29738/png-business-environment-survey.pdf.

AIDAB (Australian International Development Assistance Bureau). 1990. *Papua New Guinea: Economic Situation and Outlook*. International Development Issues, no. 11.

AIDAB. 1991. *Papua New Guinea: Economic Situation and Outlook*. International Development Issues, no. 16.

AIDAB. 1992. *The Papua New Guinea Economy: Prospects for Recovery, Reform and Sustained Growth*. International Development Issues, no. 27.

AIDAB, 1993. *The Papua New Guinea Economy: Prospects for Sectoral Development and Broad-Based Growth*. International Development Issues, no. 30.

AIDAB. 1994. *Papua New Guinea: The Role of Government in Economic Development*. International Development Issues, no. 33.

Albaniel, R. 2016. 'IFC Approves K967.7M Loan'. *Post-Courier*, 2 May. postcourier.com.pg/ifc-approves-k967-7m-loan/.

Allen, B. 1983. 'Paradise Lost? Rural Development in an Export-Led Economy: The Case of Papua New Guinea'. In *Rural Development and the State*, edited by D. Lea and D. Chaudri, 215–40. London: Methuen.

Allen, B. 2018. 'An "Infinite Pause" at Dreikikir? Forty Years of Change in Rural Papua New Guinea'. In *Change and Continuity in the Pacific: Revisiting the Region*, edited by J. Connell and H. Lee, 102–17. London: Routledge. doi.org/10.4324/9781315188645-7.

Allen, B. and R. Bourke. 2001. 'The 1997 Drought and Frost in PNG: Overview and Policy Implications'. In *Food Security for Papua New Guinea,* edited by B. Allen, R. Bourke and J. Salisbury, 155–63. Lae: Australian Centre for International Agriculture Research.

Allen, B., R. Bourke and J. Gibson. 2005. 'Poor Rural Places in Papua New Guinea'. *Asia Pacific Viewpoint* 46 (2): 201–17. doi.org/10.1111/j.1467-8373.2005. 00274.x.

Allen, M. and R. Monson. 2014. 'Land and Conflict in Papua New Guinea: The Role of Land Mediation'. *Security Challenges* 10 (2): 1–14.

Allens. 2016. 'Proposed Amendments to the PNG Land Act'. *Allens,* 3 May. allens. com.au/insights-news/insights/2016/05/proposed-amendments-to-the-png-land-act/.

Alpers, P. 2005. *Gun-Running in Papua New Guinea: From Arrows to Assault Weapons in the Southern Highlands.* Geneva: Small Arms Survey.

Alpers, P. 2008. 'Papua New Guinea: Small Numbers, Big Fuss, Real Results'. *Contemporary Security Policy* 29(1): 151–74. doi.org/10.1080/1352326080199 4451.

Anderson, K. and M. Bosworth. 2009. *Reforming Trade Policy in Papua New Guinea and the Pacific Islands.* Adelaide: University of Adelaide Press (first published in 2000 by the Institute of National Affairs and the Centre for International Economic Studies).

Anis, P. 2022. 'A Proposed Autonomy Model'. Paper presented at the National Conference on Autonomy and Decentralisation, 16–17 February. pngnri.org/ images/ADRP/PPT_Presentations/18_Anis_ppt.pdf.

Antonio, W., M. Wagi and L. Kari. 2010. 'Incorporated Land Groups'. In *The Genesis of the Papua New Guinea Land Reform Program: Selected Papers from the 2005 National Land Summit,* edited by C. Yala, 61–7. Boroko: The National Research Institute.

ANU TV. 2013. 'PNG Budget Forum 2013: Hon Don Polye, PNG Minister for Treasury'. YouTube, 4 March. youtube.com/watch?v=ABdd4EJakbQ.

Auditor-General (Auditor-General's Office of Papua New Guinea). 2014. *Performance Audit on the Management and Reporting of Trust Accounts: A Report Examining the Extent of Trust Accounts in Use within the Government of Papua New Guinea.* Auditor-General Office of Papua New Guinea. pngiportal.org/directory/ ago2014f-pdf.

AusAID. 1995. *Papua New Guinea: Improving the Investment Climate*. International Development Issues, no. 39.

AusAID. 1996. *The Economy of Papua New Guinea*. International Development Issues, no. 46.

AusAID. 1997. *Economic Survey of Papua New Guinea*. International Development Issues.

AusAID. 1998. *Papua New Guinea: Coping with Shocks and Achieving Broad-Based Development*. International Development Issues, no. 52.

AusAID. 2000. *The Economy of Papua New Guinea: Macroeconomic Policies, Implications for Growth and Development in the Informal Sector, 1999 Report*. International Development Issues, no. 53.

Australian Department of Foreign Affairs and Trade. n.d. 'Australia-Papua New Guinea Engagement'. Accessed 21 September 2023. Australian Government. dfat.gov.au/geo/papua-new-guinea/australia-papua-new-guinea-engagement.

Australian Treasury. 2004. 'Putting the Enhanced Cooperation Package to the Test— a Response'. *Pacific Economic Bulletin* 19 (1): 76–9.

Australian Treasury. 2020. *National Interest Statement: 2020 Loan Agreement between the Commonwealth of Australia and the Independent State of Papua New Guinea*. 17 December. Australian Government. treasury.gov.au/publication/p2020-136 751.

Australian Treasury. 2022. *National Interest Statement: Loan Agreement between the Commonwealth of Australia and the Independent State of Papua New Guinea*. 14 February. Australian Government. treasury.gov.au/publication/p2022-247810.

Australian Treasury. 2023. *National Interest Statement: 2022 Loan Agreement between the Commonwealth of Australia and the Independent State of Papua New Guinea*. 9 February. Australian Government. treasury.gov.au/publication/p2023-360908.

Australian Treasury. 2024. *National Interest Statement: 2023 Loan Agreement between the Commonwealth of Australia and the Independent State of Papua New Guinea*. 8 February. Australian Government. treasury.gov.au/publication/p2024-490108.

Australian Treasury. 2025. *National Interest Statement: 2024 Loan Agreement between the Commonwealth of Australia and the Independent State of Papua New Guinea*. 4 February. Australian Government. treasury.gov.au/publication/p2025-622411.

Badui Owa, J. 2021. 'Landowners Affected by Wafi-Golpu Project Delay'. EMTV, 2 June. emtv.com.pg/landowners-affected-by-wafi-golpu-project-delay/.

Bailey, J. 2016. 'KK Kingston Layoff Workers'. *Post Courier*, 20 October. postcourier.com.pg/kk-kingston-layoff-workers/.

Bakani, L. 2010. 'Address by Governor, Mr Loi Bakani at the Farewell Function of the Outgoing Governor, Sir Wilson L Kamit, CBE'. Bank of Papua New Guinea. bankpng.gov.pg/speech/address-by-governor-mr-loi-bakani-at-the-farewell-function-of-the-outgoing-governor-sir-wilson-l-kamit-cbe/ (site discontinued).

Baker, L. 2005. 'Political Integrity in Papua New Guinea and the Search for Stability'. *Pacific Economic Bulletin* 20 (1): 98–117.

Ballard, J. 1981. 'Reforming the Bureaucratic Heritage'. In *Policy Making in a New State: Papua New Guinea 1972–1977*, edited by J. Ballard, 75–94. St Lucia: University of Queensland Press.

Banks, G. 2001. *Papua New Guinea: Baseline Study*. Mining, Minerals and Sustainable Development, report no. 180. International Institute for Environment and Development and World Business Council for Sustainable Development. researchgate.net/publication/265553794_Papua_New_Guinea_Baseline_Study.

Banks, G. and C. Ballard, eds. 1997. *The Ok Tedi Settlement: Issues, Outcomes and Implications*. Canberra: ANU.

Baptiste, L., L. Yamarak, H. Sarvassy, et al. 2022. *PNG Voices: Listening to Australia's Closest Neighbour, Papua New Guinean Perspectives on Australia and the World*. Whitlam Institute.

Barcham. 2002. 'The Politics of Reform: The Failure of PNG's 1995 Structural Adjustment Program'. *Revue Juridique Polynésienne* 2: 193–212.

Baroi, M. 2023. 'Protest Against Crime'. *The National*, 31 July. thenational.com.pg/protest-against-crime/.

Basil, S. 2019. 'Treasurer's Statement: "January to May 2019—Fiscal Position"'. Government of Papua New Guinea, 26 June. treasury.gov.pg/html/speeches/files/2019/Treasurer's%20Speech%20on%20State%20of%20Economy.pdf.

Batten, A. 2008. 'On the Brink of Success—Papua New Guinea's Economic Revival'. *East Asia Forum*, 31 July. eastasiaforum.org/2008/07/31/on-the-brink-of-success-papua-new-guineas-economic-revival/.

Batten, A. 2010a. 'Foreign Aid, Government Behaviour, and Fiscal Policy in Papua New Guinea'. *Asian-Pacific Economic Literature* 24 (2): 142–60.

Batten, A. 2010b. 'Papua New Guinea's Development Success Depends on Learning from Its Past'. *East Asia Forum*, 8 January. eastasiaforum.org/2010/01/08/papua-new-guineas-development-success-depends-on-learning-from-its-past/.

Batten, A. 2012. 'Growing the Future, but Can Government Manage the Risks? PNG's 2013 Budget'. *Devpolicy Blog*, 12 December. devpolicy.org/growing-the-future-but-can-government-manage-the-risks-pngs-2013-budget-20121212/.

Batten, A., J. Gouy and R. Duncan. 2009. 'Papua New Guinea Economic Survey: From Boom to Gloom?' *Pacific Economic Bulletin* 24 (1): 1–26.

Baxi, P., D. Naidoo and S. Tandon. 2024. 'How Much of Economic Growth Trickles Down to the Population in Resource-Rich Countries? Evidence from Papua New Guinea.', Policy Research Working Paper no. 10798, World Bank Group.

Bertelsmann Stiftung. n.d. 'BTI Transformation Index'. Accessed 19 September 2024. atlas.bti-project.org/.

Biggs, P. 2007. 'The Financial Sector in Papua New Guinea—a Good Case of Reform'. *Economic Round-Up*, 73–94.

Bird, N., A. Wells, F. Helden and R. Turia. 2007. *The Current Legal and Institutional Framework of the Forest Sector in Papua New Guinea*. Overseas Development Institute.

Bizhan, N. and E. Gorea. 2022. 'A Weak State and Strong Microsocieties in Papua New Guinea'. In *State Fragility: Case Studies and Comparisons*, edited by N. Bizhan, 221–46. London: Routledge. doi.org/10.4324/9781003297697-7.

Bizhan, N. and S. Howes. 2024. 'Papua New Guinea's Public Services Commission since Independence: Sidelined Or Strengthened'. Development Policy Centre Discussion Paper no. 109. doi.org/10.2139/ssrn.4775491.

Blades, J. 2011. 'Who Owns Papua New Guinea's Resource Boom?' *Guardian*, 12 October. theguardian.com/society/2011/oct/14/papua-new-guinea-resources-boom.

Blunch, N-H. and M. Davies. 2024. 'Real Wage Growth in Papua New Guinea over Three Decades'. *Asia and the Pacific Policy Studies* 12 (1). doi.org/10.1002/app5.70001.

Bogan, N., D. Sode, J. Crittin, J. Lohberge and A. Tauvasa. 2014. 'Papua New Guinea Taxation Review (2013–2015): Issues Paper No.1: Mining and Petroleum Taxation'. Committee of the Taxation Review. businessadvantagepng.com/wp-content/uploads/2014/04/Issues-Paper-1-MPT.pdf.

Bonnell, S. 1999. 'Social Change in the Porgera Valley'. In *Dilemmas of Development: The Social and Economic Impact of the Porgera Gold Mine, 1989–1994*, edited by C. Filer, 19–87. Canberra: Australian National University Press.

Booth, A. 1995. 'Development Challenges in a Poor Pacific Economy: The Case of Papua New Guinea'. *Pacific Affairs* 68 (2): 207–30. doi.org/10.2307/2761368.

Bourke, R. 2005a. 'Agricultural Production and Customary Land in Papua New Guinea'. In *Privatising Land in the Pacific: A Defence of Customary Tenures*, edited by J. Fingleton, 6–15. Discussion Paper no. 80, Australia Institute.

Bourke, R. 2005b. 'Marketed Fresh Food: A Successful Part of the Papua New Guinea Economy'. *Development Bulletin*, no. 67: 22–4.

Bourke, R. M. 2009. 'History of Agriculture in Papua New Guinea'. In *Food and Agriculture in Papua New Guinea*, edited by R. M. Bourke and T. Harwood, 10–26. Canberra: ANU E Press. doi.org/10.22459/FAPNG.08.2009.

Bourke, R. M. 2021. 'PNG: Not Such a Hungry Country'. *Devpolicy Blog*, 18 June. devpolicy.org/png-not-such-a-hungry-country-20210618/.

Bourke, R. M. 2022. 'Returns on Labour Inputs to Smallholder for Cash Crops in Papua New Guinea'. Development Policy Centre Policy Brief no. 23. devpolicy. org/publications/policy_briefs/PB23-Returns-on-labour-inputs-for-cash-crops-in-PNG-2022.pdf.

Bourke, R. M. and B. Allen. 2021. 'Estimating the Population of Papua New Guinea in 2020'. Development Policy Centre Discussion Paper no. 90. doi.org/10.2139/ssrn.3770356.

Bourke, R. M., J. Gibson, A. Quartermain, K. Barclay, B. Allen and J. Kennedy. 2009. 'Food Production, Consumption and Imports'. In *Food and Agriculture in Papua New Guinea*, edited by R. M. Bourke and T. Harwood, 129–92. Canberra: ANU E Press. doi.org/10.22459/FAPNG.08.2009.02.

BPNG (Bank of Papua New Guinea). 2007. *Money and Banking in Papua New Guinea*. Carlton: Melbourne University Publishing.

Brown, A. 2016. 'Reporting Issues Challenging the National Roads Authority of Papua New Guinea: The Case for Using Local Indigenous Mechanisms'. *Public Money & Management* 36 (2): 97–103. doi.org/10.1080/09540962.2016.111 8931.

Brunton, B. 1992. 'The Struggle for the Oil Pipeline in Papua New Guinea'. National Research Institute Discussion Paper no. 68. pngnri.org/images/Publications_Archive/NRI_DP68.pdf.

BTI (Bertelsmann Stiftung Transformation Index). 2022. *Codebook for Country Assessments*. bti-project.org/fileadmin/api/content/en/downloads/codebooks/BTI2022_Codebook.pdf.

Bungtabu, P. 2023. 'Walk to Fight against Crime in Province'. *Post-Courier*, 2 February. postcourier.com.pg/walk-to-fight-against-crime-in-province/.

Burke, K. 2007. 'Phone Company Issues Raised with PNG Govt'. *The Sydney Morning Herald*, 3 September. www.smh.com.au/world/phone-company-issue-raised-with-png-govt-20070903-wvj.html.

Burton, J. and G. Banks. 2020. 'The Porgera Mine in PNG: Some Background'. *Devpolicy Blog*, 7 May. devpolicy.org/the-porgera-mine-in-png-some-background-20200507-2/.

Business Advantage PNG. 2015. '"One Building at a Time": Papua New Guinea's KK Kingston Prepares for Next Wave after Consolidation'. 30 June. businessadvantagepng.com/one-building-at-a-time-papua-new-guineas-k-k-kingston-prepares-for-next-wave-after-consolidation/.

Business Advantage PNG. 2019. 'Opinion: "The Richest Black Christian Nation on Earth"', 30 May. businessadvantagepng.com/opinion-the-richest-black-christian-nation-on-earth/.

Business Advantage PNG. 2021a. 'Marape Moves to Reassure Papua New Guinea's Mining and Petroleum Industry'. 7 June. businessadvantagepng.com/marape-moves-to-reassure-papua-new-guineas-mining-and-petroleum-industry/.

Business Advantage PNG. 2021b. 'Papua New Guinea's P'nyang LNG Project: What We Know So Far'. 13 October. businessadvantagepng.com/papua-new-guineas-pnyang-lng-project-what-we-know-so-far/.

Byrne, S. 2017. 'Australian Companies Optimistic about Investing in Papua New Guinea but Reserve List Poses a Threat, Say Business Council Executives'. *Business Advantage PNG*, 25 July. businessadvantagepng.com/australian-companies-optimistic-about-investing-in-papua-new-guinea-but-reserve-list-poses-a-threat-say-business-council-executives/.

Callick, R. 1993. 'Tough Decisions Ahead'. *Australian Financial Review*, 20 September. afr.com/politics/tough-decisions-ahead-19930920-k5lhq.

Callick, R. 1997. 'The Papua New Guinea Elections'. *Pacific Economic Bulletin* 12 (2): 110–14. openresearch-repository.anu.edu.au/bitstream/1885/157494/1/122_papua.pdf.

Callick, R. 2011. 'Miners in Shock as PNG Plans to Put Landowners in Charge of Resources'. *The Australian*, 19 August.

Callick, R. 2012. 'Leader with a Difference: Peter O'Neill's New Path for PNG'. *The Australian*, 3 September. www.pngattitude.com/2012/09/leader-with-a-difference-peter-oneills-new-path-for-png.html.

Canivel, R. 2020. 'Tuna Exports to EU in Peril'. *Philippine Daily Inquirer*, 23 September. business.inquirer.net/307933/tuna-exports-to-eu-in-peril.

Carrick, D. 2021. 'Bougainville Independence Talks Underway. And Are Judges Too Lenient When Sentencing Sex Offenders?' *Law Report*, ABC, 6 July. abc.net.au/radionational/programs/lawreport/bougainville-independence-and-report-judges-sentencing/13401970.

Chan, J. 1982. 'Papua New Guinea's Post-Independence Economic Development'. Keynote Address. In *Post-Independence Economic Development of Papua New Guinea*, edited by P. Dahanayake, 3–11. Boroko: Institute of Applied Social and Economic Research.

Chan, J. 1992. *Statement on Economic Development Policies to the Fifth National Parliament*. 11 August. Government of PNG.

Chan, J. 2010. 'Evolving Democracy, National Currency and Autonomy'. In *Living History and Evolving Democracy*, edited by I. Maddocks and E. Wolfers, with contribution from R. Crocombe, 216–28. Port Moresby: University of Papua New Guinea Press.

Chan, J. 2016. *Playing the Game: Life and Politics in Papua New Guinea*. St Lucia: University of Queensland Press.

Chand, S. 2004. 'Papua New Guinea Economic Survey: Transforming Good Luck into Policies for Long-Term Growth'. *Pacific Economic Bulletin* 19 (1): 1–17.

Chand, S. 2009. 'Overview'. In *Papua New Guinea's Development Performance 1975–2008*, edited by L. Duncan and T. Webster, 1–18. Boroko: The National Research Institute.

Chand, S. 2015. 'Papua New Guinea Sovereign Wealth Fund: The Efficacy of the Withdrawal Formula'. National Research Institute Issue Paper no. 17. pngnri.org/images/Publications/Issues_paper_17_PNGs_SWF_the_efficacy_of_the_withdrawal_formula_final1.pdf.

Chand, S. 2017. 'Registration and Release of Customary-Land for Private Enterprise: Lessons from Papua New Guinea'. *Land Use Policy* 61: 413–19. doi.org/10.1016/j.landusepol.2016.11.039.

Chand, S. and C. Yala. 2005. 'Economic Policy Making in Papua New Guinea'. National Research Institute Discussion Paper no. 101. pngnri.org/images/Publications/NRI_DP_101.pdf.

Chand, S. and C. Yala. 2008. 'Informal Land Systems within Urban Settlements in Honiara and Port Moresby'. In *Making Land Work: Volume Two: Case Studies on Customary Land and Development in the Pacific*, 85–106. Canberra: AusAID. Commonwealth of Australia. dfat.gov.au/sites/default/files/MLW_VolumeTwo_Bookmarked.pdf.

Chandler, J. 2018. 'Unprecedented Violence and Fraud "Hijacked" 2017 PNG Election—Report'. *Guardian*, 30 October. theguardian.com/world/2018/oct/30/unprecedented-violence-and-hijacked-2017-png-election-report.

Chin, J. 2002. 'Papua New Guinea in 2001: Election Fever Begins'. *Asian Survey* 42 (1): 150–5. doi.org/10.1525/as.2002.42.1.150.

Chin, J. 2005. 'Papua New Guinea in 2004: Recolonisation, Somare's Staying Power, and a Slight Economic Recovery'. *Asian Survey* 45 (1): 191–5. doi.org/10.1525/as.2005.45.1.191.

Chin, J. 2024. 'The Rise and Rise of China: Contemporary Chinese Community in PNG (2010–2020)'. In *The Chinese in Papua New Guinea: Past, Present and Future*, edited by A. Hayes, R. Henry and M. Wood, 87–113. Canberra: ANU Press. doi.org/10.22459/CPNG.2024.04.

Chowdhury, M. B. 2018. *Resources Booms and Macroeconomic Adjustments in Developing Countries*. London: Routledge (first published 2004). doi.org/10.4324/9781351150163.

Clifford, W., L. Morauta and B. Stuart. 1984. *Law and Order in Papua New Guinea: Report and Recommendations*. Port Moresby: Institute of National Affairs.

Cochrane, G. 1986. *Reforming National Institutions for Economic Development*. Boulder: Avalon Publishing.

Cochrane, L. 2014a. 'Papua New Guinea Prime Minister Peter O'Neill Axes Anti-Corruption Taskforce Sweep'. *ABC News*, 18 June. abc.net.au/news/2014-06-18/an-png-pm-axes-anti-corruption-task-force-sweep/5533400.

Cochrane, L. 2014b. 'The Rapid Unravelling of Papua New Guinea's Political Stability'. *ABC News*, 21 June. abc.net.au/news/2014-06-21/the-rapid-unraveling-of-pngs-political-stability/5541082.

Cochrane, L. 2015. 'PNG's Ousted Prime Minister Michael Somare Paid Almost $1 Million for "Illegal Removal"', *ABC News*, 12 August. abc.net.au/news/2015-08-12/png-ousted-prime-minister-paid-1-million-for-ilegal-removal/6690936.

Commission on Growth and Development. 2008. *The Growth Report: Strategies for Sustained Growth and Inclusive Development*. World Bank Group. openknowledge.worldbank.org/handle/10986/6507.

Connell, J. 1997. *Papua New Guinea: The Struggle for Development*. London: Routledge.

Connolly, B. 2005. *Making 'Black Harvest': Warfare, Film-Making and Living Dangerously in the Highlands of Papua New Guinea*. Sydney: ABC Books.

Conroy, J. 1976. *Education, Employment and Migration in Papua New Guinea*. Canberra: Development Studies Centre, ANU.

Conroy, J. 1980. 'Aid from the Recipient's Viewpoint: Disturbing Possibilities for Papua New Guinea'. *Australian Outlook* 34 (2). Republished in *Essays on the Development Experience in Papua New Guinea*, edited by J. Conroy, 89–102. Boroko: Institute of Applied Social and Economic Research. doi.org/10.1080/10357718008444705.

Conroy, J., ed. 1982. *Essays on the Development Experience in Papua New Guinea*. Boroko: Institute of Applied Social and Economic Research.

Conroy, J. 2020. *The Informal Economy in Development: Evidence from German, British and Australian New Guinea*. Canberra: Development Policy Centre, ANU.

Conroy, J. 2023. *Exchange and Markets in Early Economic Development: Informal Economy in the Three New Guineas*. New York: Berghahn Books. doi.org/10.1515/9781800739697.

Conroy, J. and R. Curtain. 1978. 'Circular Migration and the Emergence of Permanent Urban Populations'. In *Essays on the Development Experience in Papua New Guinea*, edited by J. Conroy, 29–48. Boroko: Institute of Applied Social and Economic Research.

Cooter, R. 1991. 'Inventing Market Property: The Land Courts of Papua New Guinea'. *Law & Society Review* 25 (4): 759–802.

Corden, R. 1982. 'Obstacles to the Development of Secondary Industry in Post-Independence Papua New Guinea'. In *Post-Independence Economic Development of Papua New Guinea*, edited by P. Dahanayake, 133–5. Boroko: Institute of Applied Social and Economic Research.

Cox, G., D. North and B. Weingast. 2019. 'The violence trap: a political-economic approach to the problems of development'. *Journal of Public Finance and Public Choice* 34 (1): 3–19.

Cox, J. 2014. '"Grassroots", "Elites" and the New "Working Class" of Papua New Guinea'. SSGM in Brief no. 2014/6, ANU. openresearch-repository.anu.edu.au/server/api/core/bitstreams/57a20baa-19d3-4869-8731-952ef1b542f8/content.

Crawford, J. 1962. 'Emerging Issues in New Guinea'. In *The Independence of Papua-New Guinea: What Are the Pre-Requisites? Four Lectures Presented under the Auspices of the Public Lectures Committee of the Australian National University*, edited by D. Bettison, E. Fisk, F. West and J. Crawford, 60–78. Sydney: Angus and Robertson.

Curtin, T. 2000. 'A New Dawn for Papua New Guinea's Economy?' *Pacific Economic Bulletin* 15 (2): 1–35.

Curtin, T. 2003. 'Scarcity amidst Plenty: The Economics of Land Tenure in Papua New Guinea'. In 'Land Registration in Papua New Guinea: Competing Perspectives'. SSGM Discussion Paper no. 2003/1.

Cust, J., A. Ballesteros and A. Zeufack. 2022. 'The Dog That Didn't Bark: The Missed Opportunity of Africa's Resource Boom'. Policy Research Working Paper 10120, World Bank Group. documents.worldbank.org/en/publication/documents-reports/documentdetail/099250407062241649/idu0b75f6a280775e041420816b0734e6d9ed810.

Cust, J. and D. Mihalyi. 2017. 'The Presource Curse'. *Finance and Development*, December: 36–40. imf.org/external/pubs/ft/fandd/2017/12/pdf/cust.pdf.

Daniel, P. and R. Sims. 1986. *Foreign Investment in Papua New Guinea: Policies and Practices*. Canberra: National Centre for Development Studies, ANU.

Davies, M. 2021. 'The Path to Kina Convertibility: Study of the Foreign Exchange Market of Papua New Guinea'. Discussion Paper no. 120, Institute of National Affairs.

Davies, M. and M. Schröder. 2022. 'A Simple Model of Internal and External Balance for Resource-Rich Developing Countries'. ADB Economics Working Paper no. 660. doi.org/10.22617/WPS220222-2.

Davis, M. 1995. 'PNG Royalties Rise in Spite of Criticism'. *Financial Review*, 20 March.

Denoon, D. 2000. *Getting under the Skin: The Bougainville Copper Agreement and the Creation of the Panguna Mine*. Carlton: Melbourne University Press.

Denoon, D. 2005. *A Trial Separation: Australia and the Decolonisation of Papua New Guinea*. Canberra: ANU E Press.

Denoon, D., K. Dugan and L. Marshall. 1989. *Public Health in Papua New Guinea: Medical Possibility and Social Constraint, 1884–1984*. Cambridge: Cambridge University Press. doi.org/10.1017/CBO9780511563447.

Department of Lands and Physical Planning. 2019. 'National Land Summit 2019'. 4 September. Government of Papua New Guinea, dlpp.gov.pg/news/press-release/national-land-summit-2019.

Department of Mining. 2003. *Information Booklet 2003*. Government of Papua New Guinea. www.bougainville-copper.eu/mediapool/59/599247/data/PNG_mininginfo_2003.pdf.

Department of National Planning and Monitoring. 2010. *Papua New Guinea Development Strategic Plan*. Government of Papua New Guinea.

Department of Petroleum and Energy. 2005. *Petroleum Policy Handbook*. November. Government of Papua New Guinea.

Department of Treasury. 1992. *1993 National Budget, Volume 1: Economic and Development Policies*. Government of Papua New Guinea.

Department of Treasury. 2005. 'Medium Term Fiscal Strategy 2002–2007'. Government of Papua New Guinea. www.treasury.gov.pg/wp-content/uploads/2023/11/Medium-Term-Fiscal-Strategy-2002-2007.pdf.

Department of Treasury. 2008. 'Medium Term Fiscal Strategy 2008–2012'. Government of Papua New Guinea. www.treasury.gov.pg/wp-content/uploads/2023/11/Medium-Term-Fiscal-Strategy-2008-2012.pdf.

Department of Treasury. 2016. *2017 National Budget: Volume 1: Economic and Development Policies*. Government of Papua New Guinea. treasury.gov.pg/budget/annual-budgets/2017-annual-budget/.

Department of Treasury. 2017a. 'Medium Term Fiscal Strategy 2018–2022'. Government of Papua New Guinea. www.treasury.gov.pg/wp-content/uploads/2023/11/Medium-Term-Fiscal-Strategy-2018-2022.pdf.

Department of Treasury. 2017b. 'Medium Term Revenue Strategy 2018–2022'. Government of Papua New Guinea. www.treasury.gov.pg/wp-content/uploads/2023/11/Medium-Term-Revenue-Strategy-2018-2022.pdf.

Department of Treasury. 2017c. *2018 National Budget: Volume 1: Economic and Development Policies*. Government of Papua New Guinea. treasury.gov.pg/budget/annual-budgets/2018-annual-budget/.

Dercon, S. 2022. *Gambling on Development: Why Some Countries Win and Others Lose*. London: Hurst.

Deren, B. and M. Motamed. 2020. *Ethiopia Constraints Analysis Report*. Millennium Challenge Corporation and Government of Ethiopia. assets.mcc.gov/content/uploads/Ethiopia-CA.2020-3.pdf.

Development Policy Centre. n.d. *PNG Elections Database*. The Australian National University. devpolicy.crawford.anu.edu.au/png-project/png-election-database.

Diamond, J. 1997. *Guns, Germs and Steel: The Fates of Human Societies*. New York: Norton.

Dinnen, S. 1995a. 'Papua New Guinea in 1994—the Most Turbulent Year?' *Current Issues in Criminal Justice* 6 (3): 395–407. doi.org/10.1080/10345329.1995. 12036670.

Dinnen, S. 1995b. 'Law, Order and the State in Papua New Guinea'. SSGM Discussion Paper no. 97/1. openresearch-repository.anu.edu.au/server/api/core/ bitstreams/7a1e68df-0573-4260-bb90-459fe57d8d32/content.

Dinnen, S. 1998. 'In Weakness and Strength—State, Societies and Order in Papua New Guinea'. In *Weak and Strong States in Asia-Pacific Societies*, edited by P. Dauvergne, 38–59. Sydney: Allen & Unwin.

Dinnen, S., D. Porter and C. Sage. 2010. 'Conflict in Melanesia: Themes and Lessons'. World Bank Group World Development Report 2011 Background Paper. documents1.worldbank.org/curated/en/970751468144280744/pdf/620 250WP0Confl0BOX0361475B00PUBLIC0.pdf.

Doherty, B. 2020. 'Papua New Guinea Police Accused of Gun Running and Drug Smuggling by Own Minister'. *Guardian*, 18 September. theguardian.com/ world/2020/sep/18/papua-new-guinea-police-accused-of-gun-running-and-drug-smuggling-by-own-minister.

Donigi, P. 2010. *Lifting the Veil that Shrouds Papua New Guinea*. PNG: UA Business Brokerage Ltd.

Dornan, M. 2016. 'The Political Economy of Road Management Reform: Papua New Guinea's National Road Fund'. *Asia & the Pacific Policy Studies* 3 (3): 443–57. doi.org/10.1002/app5.142.

Dorney, S. 1991. *Papua New Guinea—People, Politics, and History since 1975*. 2nd ed. Sydney: Random House.

Dorney, S. 1998. *The Sandline Affair: Politics and Mercenaries and the Bougainville Crisis*. Sydney: ABC Books.

Duncan, R. 2002. 'Structural Adjustment Programs: The Roles of the IMF and the World Bank'. Kumul Scholars International Conference Paper, ANU. openresearch-repository.anu.edu.au/bitstream/1885/40598/3/KSI02-3.pdf.

Duncan, R., ed. 2011. *The Political Economy of Economic Reform in the Pacific*. Metro Manila: Asian Development Bank.

Duncan, R. 2018. 'Land Reform in Papua New Guinea: Securing Individual Title to Customary Owned Land'. *Policy: A Journal of Public Policy and Ideas* 34 (1): 15–20.

Duncan, R. and C. Banga. 2018. 'Solutions to Poor Service Delivery in Papua New Guinea'. *Asia & the Pacific Policy Studies* 5 (3): 495–507. doi.org/10.1002/app5.260.

Duncan, R. and T. Lawson. 1997. 'Cost structures in Papua New Guinea'. Discussion Paper no. 69, Institute of National Affairs.

Duncan, R. and I. Temu. 1995. 'The Need for Fiscal Discipline'. *Pacific Economic Bulletin* 10 (1): 14–18.

Duncan, R., R. Warner and I. Temu. 1995. *Papua New Guinea: Improving the Investment Climate*. Canberra: Australian Agency for International Development.

Easterly, W. and R. Levine. 1997. 'Africa's Growth Tragedy: Policies and Ethnic Divisions'. *Quarterly Journal of Economics* 112 (4): 1203–50. doi.org/10.1162/003355300555466.

Ekeh, P. 1975. 'Colonialism and the Two Publics in Africa: A Theoretical Statement'. *Comparative Studies in Society and History* 17 (1): 91–112.

Elapa, J. 2019. 'Retirement Age Is 60'. *The National*, 23 May. thenational.com.pg/retirement-age-is-60/.

Epstein, S. 1968. *Capitalism, Primitive and Modern: Some Aspects of Tolai Economic Growth*. Canberra: Australian National University Press.

Errington, F. and D. Gewertz. 2004. *Yali's Question: Sugar, Culture & History*. Chicago: University of Chicago Press.

Esila, P. 2021. 'Japan Gives K1bil Low-Interest Loan'. *The National*, 1 February. thenational.com.pg/japan-gives-k1bil-low-interest-loan/.

Esila, P. 2023. 'Consumer Confidence Low: Clough'. *The National*, 19 September. thenational.com.pg/consumer-confidence-low-clough/.

Eves, R. 2008. 'Cultivating Christian Civil Society: Fundamentalist Christianity, Politics and Governance in Papua New Guinea'. SSGM Discussion Paper no. 2008/8. openresearch-repository.anu.edu.au/bitstream/1885/10049/1/Eves_CultivatingChristian2008.pdf.

Faber, M., A. McFarquhar, J. Hart and J. Diddens. 1973. *A Report on Development Strategies for Papua New Guinea*. Prepared by the Overseas Development Group of the University of East Anglia for the World Bank as executive agency for the UNDP. Office of the Chief Minister, Government of Papua New Guinea.

Fallon, J. 2017. 'State-Owned Enterprises in Papua New Guinea: Public Policies and Performance'. National Research Institute Discussion Paper no. 152. pngnri.org/images/Publications/Discussion_Paper_152_Fallon-SOEs.pdf.

Feenstra, R., R. Inklaar and M. Timmer. 2015. 'The Next Generation of the Penn World Table'. *American Economic Review* 105 (10): 3150–82. doi.org/10.1257/aer.20130954.

Feeny, S., M. Leach and J. Scambary. 2012. 'Measuring Attitudes to National Identity and Nation-Building in Papua New Guinea'. *Political Science* 64 (2): 121–44. doi.org/10.1177/0032318712466762.

Fellows, D. and J. Leonardo. 2016. 'Poor Financial Management in PNG: Can It Be Turned around?' *Devpolicy Blog*, 12 January. devpolicy.org/pngs-financial-management-can-it-be-turned-around-20160112/.

Filer, C. 1992. 'The Escalation of Disintegration and the Reinvention of Authority'. In *The Bougainville Crisis: 1991 Update*, edited by M. Spriggs and D. Denoon, 112–40. Canberra: Department of Political and Social Change, Research School of Pacific Studies, ANU.

Filer, C. 1999. 'Introduction'. In *Dilemmas of Development: The Social and Economic Impact of the Porgera Gold Mine, 1989–1994*, edited by C. Filer, 1–18. Canberra: Australian National University Press.

Filer, C. 2011. 'The Political Construction of a Land Grab in Papua New Guinea'. Resources, Environment and Development (READ) Pacific Discussion Paper Series no. 1, ANU.

Filer, C. 2014. 'The Double Movement of Immovable Property Rights in Papua New Guinea'. *Journal of Pacific History* 49 (1): 76–94. doi.org/10.1080/00223344.2013.876158.

Filer, C. 2017. 'The Formation of a Land Grab Policy Network in Papua New Guinea'. In *Kastom, Property and Ideology: Land Transformations in Melanesia*, edited by S. McDonnell, M. Allen and C. Filer, 169–203. Canberra: ANU Press. doi.org/10.22459/KPI.03.2017.06.

Filer, C. 2019a. 'Two Steps Forward, Two Steps Back: The Mobilisation of Customary Land in Papua New Guinea'. Development Policy Centre Discussion Paper no. 86. doi.org/10.2139/ssrn.3502585.

Filer, C. 2019b. 'Methods in the Madness: The "Landowner Problem" in the PNG LNG Project'. Development Policy Centre Discussion Paper no. 76. doi.org/10.2139/ssrn.3332826.

Filer, C. 2022. 'Will PNG Really Stop Log Exports in 2025? Part Two'. *Devpolicy Blog*, 21 November. devpolicy.org/will-png-really-stop-log-exports-in-2025-part-two-20221119/.

Filer, C., N. Dubash and K. Kalit. 2000. *Thin Green Line: World Bank Leverage and Policy Reform in Papua New Guinea*. Boroko: National Research Institute.

Filer, C., J. Gabriel and M. Allen. 2020. 'How PNG Lost US$120 Million and the Future of Deep-Sea Mining'. *Devpolicy Blog*, 28 April. devpolicy.org/how-png-lost-us120-million-and-the-future-of-deep-sea-mining-20200428/.

Filer, C. and B. Imbun. 2009. 'A Short History of Mineral Development Policies in Papua New Guinea, 1972–2002'. In *Policy Making and Implementation: Studies from Papua New Guinea*, edited by R. May, 75–116. Canberra: ANU E Press. doi.org/10.22459/PMI.09.2009.06.

Filer, C. with J. Numapo. 2017. 'The Political Ramifications of Papua New Guinea's Commission of Inquiry'. In *Kastom, Property and Ideology: Land Transformations in Melanesia*, edited by S. McDonnell, M. Allen and C. Filer, 251–82. Canberra: ANU Press. doi.org/10.22459/KPI.03.2017.08.

Fingleton, J. 1981. 'Policy-Making on Lands'. In *Policy Making in a New State: Papua New Guinea 1972–1977*, edited by J. Ballard, 212–37. St Lucia: University of Queensland Press.

Fingleton, J. 2004. 'Is Papua New Guinea Viable without Customary Land Groups?' *Pacific Economic Bulletin* 19 (2): 96–103.

Finney, B. 1973. *Big-Men and Business: Entrepreneurship and Economic Growth in the New Guinea Highlands*. Honolulu: University Press of Hawaii.

Fisk, E. 1971. 'Labour Absorption Capacity of Subsistence Agriculture'. *Economic Record* 47 (3): 366–78. doi.org/10.1111/j.1475-4932.1971.tb02646.x.

Fitzpatrick, P. 1980. *Law and State in Papua New Guinea*. London: Academic Press.

Flanagan, P. and L. Fletcher. 2018. *Double or Nothing: The Broken Economic Policies of PNG LNG*. Jubilee Australia. jubileeaustralia.org/storage/app/uploads/public/5fb/8c7/0b4/5fb8c70b40558371250118.pdf.

Forsyth, M., P. Gibbs, F. Hukula, J. Putt, L. Munau and I. Losoncz. 2019. 'Ten Preliminary Findings Concerning Sorcery Accusation-Related Violence in Papua New Guinea'. Development Policy Centre Discussion Paper no. 80. doi.org/10.2139/ssrn.3360817.

Fox, L. 2010. 'Protesters March against Anti-Corruption Changes in PNG'. *ABC News*, 4 May.

Fox, L. 2012. 'Corrupt "Mobocracy" Undermining PNG Democracy'. *ABC News*, 11 May. abc.net.au/news/2012-05-11/png-corruption-widespread/4004694.

Fox, L. 2020. 'PNG Landowners Take Legal Action to Stop Chinese-Owned Mine Dumping Waste into the Sea'. *ABC Radio*, 7 February. abc.net.au/radio-australia/programs/pacificbeat/png-landowners-sue-chinese-owned-mine/11942160.

Fox, R. and M. Schröder. 2017. 'After Papua New Guinea's Resource Boom: Is the Kina Overvalued?' *Asia and the Pacific Policy Studies* 5 (1): 65–76. doi.org/10.1002/app5.205.

Fraenkel, J. 2004. 'Electoral Engineering in Papua New Guinea: Lessons from Fiji and Elsewhere'. *Pacific Economic Bulletin* 19 (1): 122–33.

Fraenkel, J. 2014. 'The Hidden Order in Melanesian "Disorderly Democracy"'. Paper prepared for 'How Representative Is Representative Democracy?' Australasian Study of Parliament Group New South Wales Chapter 2014 Annual Conference. aspg.org.au/wp-content/uploads/2017/08/Session-1-Prof.-Jon-Fraenkel-The-Hidden-Order-in-Melanesian-Disorderly-Democracy.pdf.

Freedom House. n.d. 'Country and Territory Ratings and Statuses FIW 1973–2023'. Accessed 20 September 2024. freedomhouse.org/sites/default/files/2023-02/Country_and_Territory_Ratings_and_Statuses_FIW_1973-2023%20.xlsx.

Fukuyama, F. 2007. 'Governance Reform in Papua New Guinea'. World Bank. documents1.worldbank.org/curated/en/426851468145477761/text/686490E SW0P11400in0Papua0New0Guinea.txt.

Garnaut, J. 2015. 'PNG: More to Australia than Just Another Point on a Star'. *Sydney Morning Herald*, 13 August. smh.com.au/opinion/png-much-more-to-australia-than-just-another-point-on-a-star-20150813-giy7jr.html.

Garnaut, R. 1980. 'The Neo-Marxist Paradigm in Papua New Guinea'. *Australian Journal of Politics & History* 26 (3): 447–52. doi.org/10.1111/j.1467-8497.1980.tb00544.x.

Garnaut, R. 1981. 'The Framework of Economic Policy-Making'. In *Policy Making in a New State: Papua New Guinea 1972–1977*, edited by J. Ballard, 157–211. St Lucia: University of Queensland Press.

Garnaut, R. 2000. 'The First 25 Years of Searching for Development'. *Pacific Economic Bulletin* 15 (2): 9–36.

Garnaut, R. and A. Clunies-Ross. 1979. 'The Neutrality of the Resource Rent Tax'. *Economic Record* 55 (3): 193–201. doi.org/10.1111/j.1475-4932.1979.tb02221.x.

Garnaut, R., P. Baxter and A. Krueger. 1984. *Exchange Rate and Macroeconomic Policy in Independent Papua New Guinea*. Canberra: Development Studies Centre, ANU.

Garrett, J. 2014. 'Oil Search Share Purchase a Good Investment for Papua New Guinea, PM Peter O'Neill Says'. *ABC News*, 22 May. abc.net.au/news/2014-05-22/png-pm-oil-search-purchase/5470278.

Gelu, A. 2005. 'The Failure of the Organic Law on the Integrity of Political Parties and Candidates (OLIPPAC)'. *Pacific Economic Bulletin* 20 (1): 83–97.

Gewertz, D. and F. Errington. 1999. *Emerging Class in Papua New Guinea: The Telling of Difference*. Cambridge: Cambridge University Press. doi.org/10.1017/CBO9780511606120.

Giame, Z. 2023. 'Cannery Closes, 5000 Out of Work'. *The National*, 20 June. thenational.com.pg/cannery-closes-5000-out-of-work/.

Gibson, J. 2014. 'Two Decades of Poverty in Papua New Guinea'. Paper presented to the PNG Update, UPNG, 12 June. devpolicy.org/presentations/2014-PNG-Update/Day-1/Two-decades-of-poverty-in-PNG_John-Gibson.pdf.

GIWPS (Georgetown Institute for Women, Peace and Security) and PRIO (Peace Research Institute Oslo). 2023. 'Women, Peace, and Security Index 2023/24'. Washington, DC: GIWPS and PRIO. giwps.georgetown.edu/wp-content/uploads/2023/10/WPS-Index-full-report.pdf.

Good, K. 1979. 'The Formation of the Educated Petty Bourgeoisie'. In *Development and Dependency: The Political Economy of Papua New Guinea*, edited by R. Mortimer, G. Kenneth and A. Amarshi, 152–8. Oxford: Oxford University Press.

Good, K. 1986. *Papua New Guinea: A False Economy*. London: Anti-Slavery Society.

Goodman, R., C. Lepani and D. Morawetz. 1985. *The Economy of Papua New Guinea: An Independent Review*. Canberra: National Centre for Development Studies, ANU.

GoPNG (Government of Papua New Guinea). 2002. *The Commission of Inquiry into the National Provident Fund: Final Report*. s3-eu-west-1.amazonaws.com/downloads.pngiportal.org/documents/COINPF2002.pdf.

GoPNG. 2004. *The Medium Term Development Strategy: 2005–2010, 'Our Plan for Economic and Social Advancement'*. pacific-data.sprep.org/dataset/papua-new-guinea-medium-term-development-strategy-2005-2010-our-plan-economic-and-social.

GoPNG. 2009. *The Commission of Inquiry Generally into the Department of Finance: Final Report*. transparencypng.org.pg/wp-content/uploads/2022/03/Department-of-Finance-Commission-of-Inquiry-Final-Report.pdf.

GoPNG. 2010. *Papua New Guinea Development Strategic Plan, 2010–2030*. Department of National Planning and Monitoring.

GoPNG. 2022. *Royal Commission of Inquiry into Processes and Procedures Followed by the Government of Papua New Guinea into Obtaining the Off-Shore Loan from the Union Bank of Switzerland and Related Transactions: Volume 1A.* downloads.pngi portal.org.s3.amazonaws.com/UBSCOI_2022_Ch1_Ch8/UBSCOI_2022_Ch1_Ch8.pdf.

Gosarevski, S., H. Hughes and S. Windybank. 2004. 'Is Papua New Guinea Viable *with* Customary Land Ownership?' *Pacific Economic Bulletin* 19 (3): 133–6.

Gouy, J. n.d. 'NEFC Analysis of Vertical Fiscal Balance and Revenue Trends'. Unpublished Powerpoint presentation.

Gouy, J., J. Kapa, A. Mokae and T. Levantis. 2010. 'Parting with the Past: Is Papua New Guinea Poised to Begin a New Chapter towards Development?' *Pacific Economic Bulletin* 25 (1): 1–23.

Gregory, C. 1982. *Gifts and Commodities.* London: Academic Press.

Gridneff, I. 2010. 'PNG Govt Turns Blowtorch on Garnaut & BHP'. *PNG Attitude*, 20 October. www.pngattitude.com/2010/10/png-govt-turns-blowtorch-on-garnaut-bhp.html.

Gridneff, I. 2011. 'PNG's Somare Suspended from Office'. *The Sydney Morning Herald*, 24 March. smh.com.au/world/pngs-somare-suspended-from-office-20110324-1c8bf.html.

Griffin, J. 1998. 'July–December 1975'. In *A Papua New Guinea Political Chronicle 1967–1991*, edited by C. Moore and M. Kooyman, 247–70. London: C. Hurst.

Griffin, J., H. Nelson and S. Firth. 1979. *Papua New Guinea: A Political History.* Richmond: Heinemann Educational Australia.

Gruss, B. and S. Kebhaj. 2019. 'Commodity Terms of Trade: A New Database'. IMF Working Paper no. 2019/021. doi.org/10.2139/ssrn.3333745.

Guest, J. 1987. 'Problems in Managing the Mineral Resources Stabilisation Fund'. *BPNG Quarterly Economic Bulletin* 15 (2): 17–24.

Gumoi, M. 1993. 'An Evaluation of the Effectiveness and Relevance of the Commodity Price Stabilisation Schemes in Papua New Guinea'. National Research Institute Discussion Paper no. 74.

Gupta, D. 1992. *Political Economy of Growth and Stagnation in Papua New Guinea.* Port Moresby: University of Papua New Guinea Press.

Haley, N. and R. Muggah. 2006. 'Jumping the Gun? Reflections on Armed Violence in Papua New Guinea'. *African Security Review* 15 (2): 38–56. doi.org/10.1080/10246029.2006.9627400.

Haley, N. and K. Zubrinich. 2018. *2017 Papua New Guinea General Elections— Election Observation Report*. Canberra: Department of Pacific Affairs, ANU.

Hangatt, R. and C. Momoi. 2011. 'A New Path for Development Policy in Papua New Guinea'. *Devpolicy Blog*, 17 April. devpolicy.org/a-new-path-for-development-policy-in-papua-new-guinea20110417/.

Harriman, B. 2021. 'Major PNG Gas Project Gets Greenlight but Landowners Want Issues Resolved'. *ABC Radio*, 15 February. abc.net.au/radio-australia/programs/pacificbeat/major-png-gas-project-gets-greenlight/13154964.

Harvey, P. and P. Heywood. 1983. 'Twenty-Five Years of Dietary Change in Simbu Province, Papua New Guinea'. *Ecology of Food and Nutrition* 13 (1): 27–35. doi.org/10.1080/03670244.1983.9990729.

Havieta, C. 1995. *1995 Budget Speech*. Government of Papua New Guinea.

Haywood-Jones, J. 2016. 'The Future of Papua New Guinea: Old Challenges for New Leaders'. *Lowy Institute*, 11 March. lowyinstitute.org/publications/future-papua-new-guinea-old-challenges-new-leaders.

Hegarty, D. 1983. 'The 1977 National Elections in Papua New Guinea: An Overview'. In *Electoral Politics in Papua New Guinea: Studies on the 1977 National Elections*, edited by D. Hegarty, 1–17. Port Moresby: University of Papua New Guinea Press.

Hegarty, D. 1989. 'Papua New Guinea in 1988: Political Crossroads?' Strategic and Defence Studies Working Paper no. 177, ANU. babel.hathitrust.org/cgi/pt?id=uc1.31822004936209&seq=3.

Hegarty, D. 1998a. 'May–August 1974'. In *A Papua New Guinea Political Chronicle 1967–1991*, edited by C. Moore and M. Kooyman, 220–6. London: C. Hurst.

Hegarty, D. 1998b. 'July–December 1976'. In *A Papua New Guinea Political Chronicle 1967–1991*, edited by C. Moore and M. Kooyman, 286–93. London: C. Hurst.

Hegarty, D. 1998c. 'January–June 1977'. In *A Papua New Guinea Political Chronicle 1967–1991*, edited by C. Moore and M. Kooyman, 294–307. London: C. Hurst.

Hegarty, D. 1998d. 'January–June 1978'. In *A Papua New Guinea Political Chronicle 1967–1991*, edited by C. Moore and M. Kooyman, 316–20. London: C. Hurst.

Hegarty, D. 1998e. 'July–December 1978'. In *A Papua New Guinea Political Chronicle 1967– 1991*, edited by C. Moore and M. Kooyman, 321–9. London: C. Hurst.

Hegarty, D. 1998f. 'January–December 1980'. In *A Papua New Guinea Political Chronicle 1967–1991*, edited by C. Moore and M. Kooyman, 338–46. London: C. Hurst.

Hegarty, D. and P. King. 1998. 'January–June 1982'. In *A Papua New Guinea Political Chronicle 1967–1991*, edited by C. Moore and M. Kooyman, 355–61. London: C. Hurst.

Henton, D. and A. Flower. 2007. *Mount Kare Gold Rush: Papua New Guinea 1988–1994*. Cotton Tree: Mt Kare Gold Rush.

Hetzel, B. 1974. *Health and Australian Society*. Ringwood: Pelican.

Heywood, P. and A. Heywood. 1990. 'Protein-Energy Malnutrition in Papua New Guinea: Its Functional Significance'. In *Child Nutrition in South East Asia*, edited H. Visser and J. Bindels, 141–8. Dordrecht: Springer. doi.org/10.1007/978-94-009-1996-9_10.

Holden, P., P. Barker and S. Goie. 2017. 'Being Heard: The Results of the 2017 Survey of Businesses in Papua New Guinea'. Discussion Paper no. 105, Institute of National Affairs.

Holzknecht, H. 2003. 'Customary Land Tenure Systems: Resilient, Appropriate and Productive'. In 'Land Registration in Papua New Guinea: Competing Perspectives'. SSGM Discussion Paper no. 2003/1. openresearch-repository.anu.edu.au/server/api/core/bitstreams/b7b9cdc6-6ed9-4fa1-882b-0cdf6617b225/content.

Howell, B., P. Pertus and R. Sofe. 2018. 'From Design to Action: Papua New Guinea's Latest State-Owned Enterprise Policy'. *Asia Pacific Journal of Public Administration* 40 (4): 260–9. doi.org/10.1080/23276665.2018.1555933.

Howes, S. 2015a. 'Shifting In-Line in Papua New Guinea'. *Devpolicy Blog*, 6 August. devpolicy.org/shifting-in-line-in-png-20150806/.

Howes, S. 2015b. 'What Is Happening to Rice Policy in PNG?' *Devpolicy Blog*, 30 October. devpolicy.org/what-is-happening-to-rice-policy-in-png-20151030/.

Howes, S. 2018a. 'Papua New Guinea Loses another Vice Chancellor'. *Devpolicy Blog*, 20 August. devpolicy.org/papua-new-guinea-loses-another-vice-chancellor-20180820-2/.

Howes, S. 2018b. 'Albert Schram's Arrest'. *Devpolicy Blog*, 13 May. devpolicy.org/albert-schrams-arrest-20180513/.

Howes, S. 2020. 'PNG's Salary Bill Problem'. *Devpolicy Blog*, 8 September. devpolicy.org/pngs-salary-bill-problem-20200908/.

Howes, S. 2022. 'PNG's Stuck Exchange Rate'. *Devpolicy Blog*, 10 May. devpolicy.org/pngs-stuck-exchange-rate-20220510/.

Howes, S. 2023. 'BPNG Changes Tack, But Will It Follow Through?'. *Devpolicy Blog*, 8 September. devpolicy.org/bpng-changes-tack-but-will-it-follow-through -20230908/.

Howes, S. 2024. 'May, Ekeh and Migdal: Revisiting Ron May's Early Diagnosis of Papua New Guinea as a Weak State'. Mimeo.

Howes, S., R. Fox, M. Laveil, L. Mckenzie, A. Gudapati and D. Sum. 2022. 'PNG's Economic Trajectory: The Long View'. In *Papua New Guinea: Government, Economy, and Society*, edited by S. Howes and L. Pillai, 125–62. Canberra: ANU Press. doi.org/10.22459/PNG.2022.05.

Howes, S. and M. Kabuni. 2022. 'Prime Ministerial Incumbency Bias in PNG'. *Devpolicy Blog*, 2 May. devpolicy.org/prime-ministerial-incumbency-bias-in-png-20220502.

Howes, S., M. Kabuni, M. Laveil et al. 2022. '2022 PNG Election Results: Nine Findings'. *Devpolicy Blog*, 26 August. devpolicy.org/2022-png-election-results-nine-findings-20220826/.

Howes, S and B. Kunda. 2024. 'AIFFP Oblivious to Excessive PNG Port Charges'. *Devpolicy Blog*, 8 April. devpolicy.org/aiffp-oblivious-to-excessive-png-port-charges-20240408/.

Howes, S., R. Fox, M. Laveil, B. Nguyen and D. Sum. 2019. '2019 Papua New Guinea Economic Survey'. *Asia & the Pacific Policy Studies* 6 (3): 271–89. doi.org/10.1002/app5.287.

Howes, S. and A. Leng. 2023. 'PNG as Resource Dependent as Saudi Arabia'. *Devpolicy Blog*, 16 February. devpolicy.org/png-as-resource-dependent-as-saudi-arabia-20231216/.

Howes, S. and A. Mako. 2023a. 'ANZ's Stubborn Optimism on the PNG Economy'. *Devpolicy Blog*, 20 April. devpolicy.org/anz-stubborn-optimism-on-png-economy-20230420/.

Howes, S. and A. Mako. 2023b. 'Doubling of PNG MP Funds a Bad Move'. *Devpolicy Blog*, 7 February. devpolicy.org/doubling-of-png-mp-funds-a-bad-move-20230207/.

Howes, S., A. Mako, A. Swan, G. Walton, T. Webster and C. Wiltshire. 2014. *A Lost Decade? Service Delivery and Reforms in Papua New Guinea 2002–2012*. The National Research Institute and the Development Policy Centre. devpolicy.org/publications/reports/PEPE/PEPE_A_lost_decade_FULL_REPORT.pdf.

Howes, S. and K. Mambon. 2021. 'PNG's Plummeting Vaccination Rates: Now the Lowest in the World?' *Devpolicy Blog*, 30 August. devpolicy.org/pngs-plummeting-vaccination-rates-now-lowest-in-world-20210830/.

Howes, S., K. Mambon and K. Samof. 2022. 'PNG's Minimum Wage'. *Devpolicy Blog*, 28 September. devpolicy.org/pngs-minimum-wage-20220928/.

Howes, S. and L. Pillai, eds. 2022. *Papua New Guinea: Government, Economy and Society*. Canberra: ANU Press. doi.org/10.22459/PNG.2022.

Howes, S., L. Sause and L. Ugyel. 2022. 'Decentralisation: A Political Analysis'. In *Papua New Guinea: Government, Economy, and Society*, edited by S. Howes and L. Pillai, 57–86. Canberra: ANU Press. doi.org/10.22459/PNG.2022.03.

Howie-Willis. I. 1980. *A Thousand Graduates: Conflict in University Development in Papua New Guinea, 1961–1976*. Canberra: ANU.

Hoy, C. and R. Toth. 2020. 'Taking Financial Access to Remote and Insecure Areas: Impacts of a Comprehensive Financial Inclusion Intervention in Papua New Guinea'. Development Policy Centre Discussion Paper no. 89. doi.org/10.2139/ssrn.3718809.

Hughes, H. 2003. 'Aid Has Failed the Pacific'. *Issue Analysis*, The Centre for Independent Studies, no. 33. cis.org.au/wp-content/uploads/2015/07/ia33.pdf.

Hurney, M. 2017. 'Short Changed: The Cost of Child Undernutrition in Papua New Guinea'. *Devpolicy Blog*, 24 August. devpolicy.org/short-changed-cost-child-undernutrition-papua-new-guinea-20170824/.

Human Rights Centre. 2020. *After the Mine: Living with Rio Tinto's Deadly Legacy*. Human Rights Centre.

Iangalio, M. 1995. *1995 Budget Reply*. Government of Papua New Guinea.

ICCC (Independent Consumer & Competition Commission). 2016. *Petroleum Industry Pricing Review—Final Report*. iccc.gov.pg/wp-content/uploads/2023/08/Petroleum-Industry-Pricing-Review-Final-Report-2016.pdf.

ICCC. 2019a. *2018–19 Sugar Industry Pricing Review—Final Report*. iccc.gov.pg/wp-content/uploads/2023/08/2018-19-Final-report-Sugar-Industry-Pricing-Review.pdf.

ICCC. 2019b. *Petroleum Industry Pricing Review—Final Report*. iccc.gov.pg/wp-content/uploads/2023/08/Petroleum-Industry-Pricing-Review-2019-Final-Report.pdf.

ICCC. 2023. *2023 Stevedoring and Handling Services Pricing Review—Final Report.* iccc.gov.pg/wp-content/uploads/2023/12/Final-Report-2023-Stevedoring-and-Handling-Service-Pricing-Review.pdf.

IFC. 2018. *Papua New Guinea Financial Consumer Protection Diagnostic 2018.* documents1.worldbank.org/curated/en/5419115403909289999/pdf/131286-Wp-PNGFCPReviewReport.pdf

IFC. 2019. 'Going the Distance: Off-Grid Lighting Market Dynamics in Papua New Guinea'. ifc.org/content/dam/ifc/doc/mgrt/png-off-grid-report.pdf.

IFC. 2021. *Markham/Ramu Agricultural Growth Corridor: A Possible Path of Transformational Agricultural Development.* www.ifc.org/content/dam/ifc/doc/mgrt/markham-ramu-report-final.pdf.

Igara, R., W. Kamit and S. Howes. 2021. *Review of the Central Banking Act 2000: Phase One Report.* Independent Advisory Group.

Igara, R. and S. Howes. 2023. *Review of the Central Banking Act 2000: Phase Two Report.* Independent Advisory Group.

Imbun, B. 2015. 'Minimum Wage Debates in a Developing Country Setting: Evidence from Papua New Guinea'. *The Economic and Labour Relations Review* 26 (1): 137–53. doi.org/10.1177/1035304615570807.

IMF (International Monetary Fund). 1992. *Annual Report.* imf.org/external/pubs/ft/ar/archive/pdf/ar1992.pdf.

IMF. 1996. *Annual Report.* imf.org/~/media/Websites/IMF/imported-flagship-issues/external/pubs/ft/ar/96/pdf/_part19pdf.ashx.

IMF. 1999. *Staff Report for the 1999 Article IV Consultation, Supplementary Information.* IMF.

IMF. 2000. 'Press Release: IMF Approves US$115 Million Stand-By Credit for Papua New Guinea'. *IMF*, 29 March. imf.org/en/News/Articles/2015/09/14/01/49/pr0023.

IMF. 2004. 'Papua New Guinea: Staff Report for the 2004 Article IV Consultation'. IMF Country Report no. 04/355.

IMF. 2008. 'Papua New Guinea: 2007 Article IV Consultation—Staff Report; and Public Information Notice on the Executive Board Discussion for Papua New Guinea'. IMF Country Report no. 08/98. www.imf.org/external/pubs/ft/scr/2008/cr0898.pdf.

IMF. 2010. 'Papua New Guinea: 2010 Article IV Consultation—Staff Report and Public Information Notice'. IMF Country Report no. 10/164. imf.org/external/pubs/ft/scr/2010/cr10164.pdf.

IMF. 2020. 'Papua New Guinea: Request for Disbursement under the Rapid Credit Facility-Press Release; Staff Report; and Statement by the Executive Director for Papua New Guinea'. IMF Country Report no. 20/21. imf.org/en/Publications/CR/Issues/2020/06/26/Papua-New-Guinea-Request-for-Disbursement-under-the-Rapid-Credit-Facility-Press-Release-49536.

IMF. 2023. 'Papua New Guinea: Requests for an Arrangement under the Extended Credit Facility and an Extended Arrangement under the Extended Fund Facility—Press Release, Staff Report and Statement by the Executive Director for Papua New Guinea'. IMF Country Report no. 23/126.

IMF. n.d. 'Debt Sustainability Analysis Low-Income Countries'. Accessed 7 September 2023. imf.org/en/publications/dsa

IMF and IDA (International Development Association). 2020. 'Papua New Guinea: Staff Report for the 2019 Article IV Consultation and Request for Staff-Monitored Program—Debt Sustainability Analysis'. 21 February, IMF.

INA (Institute of National Affairs). 2013. 'The Business and Investment Environment in Papua New Guinea in 2012: Private Sector Perspective'. Discussion Paper no. 94, Institute of National Affairs.

Inglis, K. and S. Spark. 2014. 'Interview with Professor Ken Inglis'. In *Australians in Papua New Guinea 1960–1975*, edited by C. Spark, S. Spark and C. Twomey, 213–34. Brisbane: University of Queensland Press.

Islands Business. 2024. 'Public Health Crisis, Indicators Hit All-Time Low, Need Urgent Attention: PNG Doctor'. 15 November. islandsbusiness.com/news-break/png-health-3/.

Ivarature, H. 2022. 'The Hidden Dimension to Political Instability: Insights from Ministerial Durations in Papua New Guinea from 1972 to 2017'. *Asia & the Pacific Policy Studies* 9 (2): 134–46. doi.org/10.1002/app5.352.

Ives, D. 2004. 'Public Sector Reform in Papua New Guinea—the Saga Continues'. *Pacific Economic Bulletin* 19 (1): 80–93.

Jackson, K. 2010. 'People Urged to Oppose Maladina Amendment'. *PNG Attitude*, 27 March, www.pngattitude.com/2010/03/people-urged-to-oppose-maladina-amendment.html.

Jackson, K. 2022. 'Ben Micah: Admission and Contrition'. *Devpolicy Blog*, 22 March. devpolicy.org/on-the-death-of-ben-micah-admission-and-contrition-20220322/.

Jackson, R. 1993. 'Cracked Pot or Copper Bottomed Investment? The Development of the Ok Tedi Project 1982–1991: A Personal View'. Melanesian Studies Centre, James Cook University of North Queensland.

Jackson, R. and D. Hegarty. 1983. 'From Geography to Ideology? The 1982 Elections in Papua New Guinea'. *Australian Geographer* 15 (5): 334–6. doi.org/10.1080/00049188308702836.

Jamaludin, F., V. Klyuev and A. Serechetapongse. 2015. 'What Drives Interest Rate Spreads in Pacific Island Countries? An Empirical Investigation'. Working Paper no. 15/96, International Monetary Fund. doi.org/10.2139/ssrn.2613306.

James, D. 2019a. 'The Lessons We Learned from Papua New Guinea's Last Boom'. *Business Advantage PNG*, 15 April. businessadvantagepng.com/the-lessons-we-learned-from-papua-new-guineas-last-boom/.

James, D. 2019b. 'New Rules, More Independence: Kumul Petroleum's Future'. *Business Advantage PNG*, 27 November. businessadvantagepng.com/new-rules-more-independence-kumul-petroleums-future/.

James, D. 2020. 'Money for Reforms: ADB Offers Papua New Guinea COVID Assistance'. *Business Advantage PNG*, 23 September. businessadvantagepng.com/money-for-reforms-adb-offers-papua-new-guinea-covid-assistance/.

JICA (Japan International Cooperation Agency). 2021. 'Signing of Japanese ODA Loan Agreement with Papua New Guinea: Contributing to the COVID-19 Crisis Response in Papua New Guinea through Provision of Budget Support' [Press release]. www.jica.go.jp/english/information/press/2020/20210304_10_en.html.

Johnson, P. 2010. *Scoping Project: Social Impact of the Mining Project on Women in the Porgera Area*. Porgera Environmental Advisory Komiti.

Johnson, P. 2012. 'Lode Shedding: A Case Study of the Economic Benefits to the Landowners, the Provincial Government and the State, from the Porgera Gold Mine: Background and Financial Flows from the Mine'. NRI Discussion Paper no. 124, National Research Institute.

Joint Standing Committee on Treaties. 2005. *Report 65: Treaties Tabled on 7 December 2004 and 8 February 2005*. Parliament of Australia. aph.gov.au/Parliamentary_Business/Committees/Joint/Completed_Inquiries/jsct/8february2005/report.

Jones, L. and P. McGavin. 2015. 'Grappling Afresh with Labour Resource Challenges in Papua New Guinea: A Framework for Moving Forward'. Discussion Paper no. 96, Institute of National Affairs.

Kabuni, M. 2018. 'Does Political Stability Consolidate Irresponsible Government? PNG 2012–2018'. *Devpolicy Blog*, 16 July. devpolicy.org/does-political-stability-consolidate-irresponsible-government-png-2012-2018-20180716/.

Kabuni, M., M. Laveil, G. Milli and T. Wood. 2022. 'Elections and Politics'. In *Papua New Guinea: Government, Economy, and Society*, edited by S. Howes and L. Pillai, 17–55. Canberra: ANU Press. doi.org/10.22459/PNG.2022.02.

Kama, B. 2014. 'A Victory over Corruption in PNG'. *The Interpreter*, 4 April. lowy institute.org/the-interpreter/victory-over-corruption-png.

Kama, B. 2017. 'PNG in 2017—an Analysis of Papua New Guinea's Political Condition and Trends through to 2025'. *Lowy Institute*, 6 December. interactives. lowyinstitute.org/archive/png-in-2017/png-in-2017-png-political-condition-to-2025.html.

Kalinoe, L. and J. Kiris. 2010. 'Socio-Economic Changes and Their Implications for Customary Land Tenure'. In *The Genesis of the Papua New Guinea Land Reform Program: Selected Papers from the 2005 National Land Summit*, edited by C. Yala, 22–31. Boroko: The National Research Institute.

Kama., B. 2024. *Rethinking Judicial Power in Papua New Guinea: A Mandate for Activism in a Transformative Constitution*. Singapore: Springer. doi.org/10.1007/978-981-97-2946-3.

Kaputin, J. 1982. 'Papua New Guinea's Economic Performance since Independence'. In *Post-Independence Economic Development of Papua New Guinea*, edited by P. Dahanayake, 51–60. Boroko: Institute of Applied Social and Economic Research.

Kaputin, J. 1984. 'The Vulnerability of Small Open Developing Economies to External Factors: Policy Responses in Papua New Guinea'. In *Economic Development and Trade in Papua New Guinea: Proceedings of the Fourteenth Waigani Seminar, 1981*, edited by A Sawyerr, 5–12. Port Moresby: University of Papua New Guinea Press.

Katai, G. 2022. 'Rebate Scheme and Implementation'. Presentation to PNG Tuna Fishing Industry Consultation, 23–24 February, Port Moresby. National Fisheries Authority. fisheries.gov.pg/tuna-fishing-industry-consultation.

Kauzi, G. and T. Sampson. 2009. 'Shock Exposure: Commodity Prices and the Kina'. *Pacific Economic Bulletin* 24 (1): 27–48.

Kavan, P. 2010. 'Informal Sector in Port Moresby and Lae, Papua New Guinea: Activities and Government Response'. *International Journal of Interdisciplinary Social Sciences: Annual Review* 5 (8): 353–70. doi.org/10.18848/1833-1882/CGP/v05i08/51827.

Kavanamur, D., C. Yala and Q. Clements. 2003. 'Introduction: A Mixed Inheritance'. In *Building a Nation in Papua New Guinea: Views of the Post-Independence Generation*, edited by D. Kavanamur, C. Yala and Q. Clements, 1–10. Canberra: Pandanus Books.

KCH (Kumul Consolidated Holdings). 2021. *Annual Review 2020*. kch.com.pg/wp-content/uploads/2021/09/KCH-2020-Annual-Review.pdf.

Kero, G. 2014. 'State Invests K327M'. *The National*, 25 April. thenational.com.pg/state-invests-k327m/.

Ketan, J. 2000. 'The Name Must Not Go Down: Political Competition in Mount Hagen, Papua New Guinea'. PhD thesis, University of Wollongong.

Kiki, A. 1968. *Ten Thousand Years in a Lifetime: A New Guinea Autobiography*. Melbourne: F.W. Chesire Publishing.

Kimas, P. 2010. 'Administration of Land Held under Formal Tenure'. In *The Genesis of the Papua New Guinea Land Reform Program: Selected Papers from the 2005 National Land Summit*, edited by C. Yala, 33–40. Boroko: The National Research Institute.

King, P. 1998. 'January–December 1981'. In *A Papua New Guinea Political Chronicle 1967–1991*, edited by C. Moore and M. Kooyman, 347–54. London: C. Hurst.

King, P., ed. 1989. *Pangu Returns to Power: The 1982 Elections in Papua New Guinea*. Canberra: Department of Political and Social Change, ANU.

King, T. and C. Sugden. 1997. 'Managing Papua New Guinea's Kina'. *Pacific Economic Bulletin* 12 (1): 20–9.

Kisselpar, J. 2016. 'Papua New Guinea Trade Minister says PNG "not interested" in PACER Plus Trade with Australia'. *ABC News*, 5 August. abc.net.au/news/2016-08-05/png-says-no-to-pacer-plus/7695538.

Knutsen, C. and H. Nygård. 2015. 'Institutional Characteristics and Regime Survival: Why Are Semi-Democracies Less Durable than Autocracies and Democracies?' *American Journal of Political Science* 59 (3): 656–70. doi.org/10.1111/ajps.12168.

Kölln, A-K. 2015. 'The Value of Political Parties to Representative Democracy'. *European Political Science Review* 7 (4): 593–613. doi.org/10.1017/S1755773914000344.

Kolma, F. 2019. 'High Court Restores Public Services Commission's Powers'. *Post-Courier*, 29 March. postcourier.com.pg/high-court-restores-public-service-commissions-powers/.

Kolma, F. 2021. 'The Morobe Experience Exposed'. *The National*, 31 December. thenational.com.pg/the-morobe-experience-exposed/.

Kolma, F. 2022. 'Morobe's Seven Bad Years'. *The National*, 14 January. thenational. com.pg/morobes-seven-bad-years/.

Koyama, S. 2004. 'Reducing Agency Problems in Incorporated Land Groups'. *Pacific Economic Bulletin* 19 (1): 20–31.

Kuku, R. 2023a. 'Govt Urged to Ease Log Export Tax'. *The National*, 7 March. thenational.com.pg/govt-urged-to-ease-log-export-tax/.

Kuku, R. 2023b. 'NSO: Population Is 12Mil'. *The National*, 23 August. thenational. com.pg/nso-population-is-12mil/.

Kumoru, L. and L. Koren. 2006. 'Tuna Fisheries Report—Papua New Guinea'. Papua New Guinea Annual Fishery Report, no. WCPFC-SC2-2006. Prepared for the 2nd Science Committee Meeting Manilla, Philippines, August. pacific-data.sprep.org/resource/tuna-fisheries-report-papua-new-guinea-0.

Kumul Petroleum. 2019. 'Kumul Petroleum Puts Records Straight on PNG LNG Revenue'. 14 October. kumulpetroleum.com/news-article/kumul-petroleum-puts-records-straight-on-png-lng-revenue/ (site discontinued).

Kumul Petroleum. 2021. 'Kumul Petroleum Awarded Petroleum Retention Licences to Develop Gas Fields'. 16 April. kumulpetroleum.com/news-article/kumul-petroleum-awarded-petroleum-retention-licences-to-develop-gas-fields/ (site discontinued).

Kurer, O. 2006. 'The Papua New Guinean Malaise: From Redistributive Politics to a Failing State'. *Pacific Economic Bulletin* 21 (1): 84–95.

Kwapena, F. 2021. 'Understanding the Impact of Customary Land Tenure and Reform in Papua New Guinea'. In *Handbook on Space, Place and Law*, edited by R. Bartel and J. Carter, 99–108. Northampton: Edward Elgar Publishing. doi.org/10.4337/9781788977203.00020.

Lakhani, S. and A. Willman. 2014a. *Drivers of Crime and Violence in Papua New Guinea*. Social Cohesion and Violence Prevention Team, Social Development Department, World Bank Group. documents1.worldbank.org/curated/en/919221468284385751/pdf/750580REPLACEM0no020Drivers06004014.pdf.

Lakhani, S. and A. Willman. 2014b. *Trends in Crime and Violence in Papua New Guinea*. Social Cohesion and Violence Prevention Team, Social Development Department, World Bank Group. openknowledge.worldbank.org/server/api/core/bitstreams/472d88d1-f42c-5622-83e7-45d57f92b98c/content.

Langmore, J. 1973. 'Public Policy Pay and Localisation Policy'. In *Alternative Strategies for Papua New Guinea*, edited by A. Clunies-Ross and J. Langmore, 185–209, Melbourne: Oxford University Press.

Langmore, J. 2014. 'A Powerful, Formative Experience: 1963–76'. In *Australians in Papua New Guinea 1960–1975*, edited by C. Spark, S. Spark and C. Twomey, 119–40. Brisbane: University of Queensland Press.

Langmore, J. and R. Berry. 1978. 'Wages Policy in Papua New Guinea'. *Journal of Industrial Relations* 20 (3): 293–302. doi.org/10.1177/002218567802000304.

Lasslett, K. 2017. 'Inside the Somare Bribery Scandal'. *PNGi*, 14 November. pngicentral.org/reports/inside-the-somare-bribery-scandal.

Lasslett, K. 2018. *Uncovering the Crimes of Urbanisation: Researching Corruption, Violence and Urban Conflict*. London: Routledge. doi.org/10.4324/978131 5651798.

Lātūkefu, S., ed. 1989. *Papua New Guinea: A Century of Colonial Impact*. Boroko: The National Research Institute.

Laveil, M. 2019a. 'Predicting the Impact of PNG's 2018 and 2019 Tariff Increases: A Review of PNG's Trade Policy History'. Development Policy Centre Discussion Paper no. 85. doi.org/10.2139/ssrn.3481547.

Laveil, M. 2019b. 'Can PNG Become the Richest Black Nation in the World in Ten Years?'. *Devpolicy Blog*, 14 June. devpolicy.org/can-png-become-the-richest-black-nation-in-the-world-in-ten-years-20190614/.

Laveil, M. 2021. 'Parliamentary Fragmentation in PNG: Is It Getting Worse?' *Devpolicy Blog*, 19 March. devpolicy.org/parliamentary-fragmentation-in-png-202100319-1/.

Laveil, M. 2022. 'Parties in PNG's Elections'. *Devpolicy Blog*, 20 September. devpolicy.org/parties-in-pngs-elections-20220920/.

Laveil, M. 2024. 'Provincial Revenue in PNG: Inequitable, Volatile and Stagnant'. *Devpolicy Blog*, 5 March. devpolicy.org/provincial-revenue-in-png-inequitable-volatile-and-stagnant-20240405/.

Lea, D. 2023. *Papua New Guinea in the Twenty-First Century: The Struggle for Development and Independence*. Lanham: Rowman and Littlefield. doi.org/10.5771/9781666917390.

Leahy, J. 2020. 'Viewpoint'. Oxford Business Group. oxfordbusinessgroup.com/view point/new-rules-john-leahy-principal-leahy-png-law-key-legislative-changes-oil-and-gas-and-extractive.

Leng, A. 2022. 'Connect PNG: The Road to Development?' *Devpolicy Blog*, 11 August. devpolicy.org/connect-png-the-road-to-development-20220811/.

Leng, A. and S. Howes. 2022. 'PNG's Sovereign Wealth Fund: The Clock is Ticking'. *Devpolicy Blog*, 8 November. devpolicy.org/pngs-sovereign-wealth-fund-the-clock-is-ticking-20221108/.

Lepani, W. 2014. 'Reflections: 39 Years of Sovereign Statehood in Papua New Guinea'. SSGM Working Paper no. 2014/8. openresearch-repository.anu.edu.au/bitstream/1885/142145/1/2014_8_Lepani_0_0.pdf.

Levantis, T. 1997. 'The Urban Labour Market in Papua New Guinea, Post-Deregulation'. *Pacific Economic Bulletin* 12 (2): 54–72.

Levantis, T. 2000a. *Papua New Guinea: Employment, Wages, and Economic Development*. Canberra: Asia Pacific Press, ANU.

Levantis, T. 2000b. 'Crime Catastrophe—Reviewing Papua New Guinea's Most Serious Social and Economic Problem'. *Pacific Economic Bulletin* 15 (2): 130–42.

Ley, J. 2014. 'From Colonial Backwater to Vibrant Independent State—in a Decade'. In *Australians in Papua New Guinea 1960–1975*, edited by C. Spark, S. Spark and C. Twomey, 141–62. Brisbane: University of Queensland Press.

Liu, H. 2022. 'The Dynamics of Chinese Businesses in the Pacific'. Unpublished, ANU.

Liu, H. and S. Howes. 2022. 'What Happened to PNG's Air Travel Boom?' *Devpolicy Blog*, 24 February. devpolicy.org/what-happened-to-pngs-air-travel-boom-20220224/.

Locke, S. 2015. 'PNG's Ban on Australian Vegetable Imports Likely to Limit Food Supplies for Australian Refugee Processing Centres'. *ABC News*, 19 August. abc.net.au/news/rural/2015-08-19/png-bans-vegetable-imports-threatening-supplies-to-refugees/6708074.

Lodewijks, J., D. Enahoro and G. Argyrous. 1991. 'Structural Adjustment Issues in Papua New Guinea'. *Economic and Labour Relations Review* 2 (1): 154–71. doi.org/10.1177/103530469100200109.

LoopPNG. 2021a. '106th "Sam Siga" Underway'. 30 November. looppng.com/png-news/106th-%E2%80%98sam-siga%E2%80%99-underway-107245 (site discontinued).

LoopPNG. 2021b. 'Head Bishop Writes to PM'. 3 November. looppng.com/png-news/head-bishop-writes-pm-106252 (site discontinued).

LoopPNG. 2023. 'NPC Process Queried'. 11 June. looppng.com/png-news/npc-process-queried-120754 (site discontinued).

Macintyre, M. and S. Foale. 2004. 'Politicized Ecology: Local Responses to Mining in Papua New Guinea'. *Oceania* 74 (3): 231–51. doi.org/10.1002/j.1834-4461. 2004.tb02851.x.

MacWilliam, S. 2013. *Securing Village Life, Development in Late Colonial Papua New Guinea.* Canberra: ANU E Press. doi.org/10.22459/SVL.05.2013.

MacWilliam, S. 2016. 'Indigenous Commercial Ambitions and Decentralisation in Papua New Guinea: The Missing Driver of Reform'. SSGM Discussion Paper no. 2016/1.

Macdonald-Smith, A. 2023. 'Activist Pressures Weigh on Santos' PNG Growth'. *Australian Financial Review,* 12 December.

Main, M. 2023a. 'Prospects for Peace in Hela'. *Devpolicy Blog,* 1 September. devpolicy.org/prospects-for-peace-in-hela-20230901/.

Main, M. 2023b. 'Hela'. In *Examining Conflict Dynamics in Papua New Guinea,* edited by G. Peake, 21–33. United States Institute of Peace Discussion Paper no. 23-003.

Mako, A. 2012. 'PNG's Experience with Rapid Revenue Growth: Lessons for the Future'. *Devpolicy Blog,* 31 August. devpolicy.org/pngs-experience-with-rapid-revenue-growth-lessons-for-the-future20120831/.

Mako, A. 2013. 'PNG's Rural Decay: A Personal Perspective'. *Devpolicy Blog,* 18 October. devpolicy.org/pngs-rural-decay-a-personal-perspective-20131018/.

Mako, A. 2023. 'The Local "Resource Curse": Missed Opportunities in Porgera, PNG'. *Devpolicy Blog,* 28 June. devpolicy.org/the-local-resource-curse-missed-opportunities-in-porgera-png-20230628/.

Mako, A. and S. Howes. 2024. 'PNG's Development Plan Implies Falling Living Standards'. *DevPolicy Blog,* 25 March. devpolicy.org/pngs-development-plan-implies-falling-living-standards-20240325/.

Manning, A. 1994. 'The Closure of Bougainville Copper Limited's Mine—Lessons for the Mining Industry'. MBA minor thesis, Victoria University of Technology, Melbourne.

Manning, M. 1999. 'Beyond 1999—Some Certainty for Papua New Guinea?' *Pacific Economic Bulletin* 14 (2): 12–23.

Manning, M. 2000. 'Privatisation in Papua New Guinea—Where at and Where to?' *Pacific Economic Bulletin* 15 (2): 91–105.

Manoka, B. and W. Rodrigues. 2013. 'Problems with SoE Regulation—a Poor Prognosis for Papua New Guinea'. Presentation for ANU Pacific Update, 27–28 June. crawford.anu.edu.au/sites/default/files/events/attachments/2013-10/png_update_session_3_-_billy_manoka_-_regulation_of_infrastructure_soes.pdf (site discontinued).

Marape, J. 2021. 'PM Marape Hands over Porgera Framework Agreement to Landowners and Enga Provincial Government'. PM James Marape News Page, 4 June. pmjamesmarape.com/pm-marape-hands-over-porgera-framework-agreement-to-landowners-and-enga-provincial-government/.

Mark, D. 2023. 'RD Tuna Needs US Dollars to Buy Tuna'. *Post-Courier*, 31 March. postcourier.com.pg/rd-tuna-needs-us-dollars-to-buy-tuna/.

Marshall, S. 2007. 'PNG Mobile Company to Continue Operation'. *ABC News*, 25 July. abc.net.au/news/2007-07-25/png-mobile-company-to-continue-operation/2513228.

Marshall, W. 2001. 'Papua New Guinea Government Overturns Minimum Pay Rise'. *World Socialist Web Site*, 26 February. wsws.org/en/articles/2001/02/png-f26.html.

Martin, K. 2015. *The Death of the Big Men and the Rise of the Big Shots: Custom and Conflict in East New Britain*. New York: Berghahn Books.

Masalai i tokaut. 2006. 'Somare Clan Involved in Illegal Logging'. pngforests.files.wordpress.com/2014/02/masalai-43-somare-clan-dives-into-illegal-logging.pdf.

May, R. 1998. 'State, Society and Governance: A Philippines–Papua New Guinea Comparison'. In *Weak and Strong States in Asia-Pacific Societies*, edited by P. Dauvergne, 60–76. Sydney: Allen & Unwin.

May, R. 2001a. 'Introduction: Papua New Guinea at Twenty-Five'. In *State and Society in Papua New Guinea: The First Twenty-Five Years*, edited by R. May, 1–16. Canberra: Australian National University Press.

May, R. (1997) 2001b. 'From Promise to Crisis: A Political Economy of Papua New Guinea'. *Revue Tiers-Monde* 38 (149). Republished in *State and Society in Papua New Guinea: The First Twenty-Five Years*, edited by R. May, 302–23. Canberra: Australian National University Press.

May, R. 2003a. 'Disorderly Democracy: Political Turbulence and Institutional Reform in Papua New Guinea'. SSGM Discussion Paper no. 2003/3.

May, R. 2003b. 'Turbulence and Reform in Papua New Guinea'. *Journal of Democracy* 14 (1): 154–65. doi.org/10.1353/jod.2003.0018.

May, R., ed. 2009. *Policy Making and Implementation: Studies from Papua New Guinea*. Canberra: ANU E Press. doi.org/10.22459/PMI.09.2009.

May, R. 2022. *State and Society in Papua New Guinea, 2001–2021*. Canberra: ANU Press. doi.org/10.22459/SSPNG.2022.

May, R. and R. Anere, eds. 2002. *Maintaining Democracy: The 1997 Elections in Papua New* Guinea. Port Moresby: Department of Political Science, University of Papua New Guinea.

May, R. and R. Anere. 2013. 'Background to 2007 Election: Political Developments'. In *Election 2007: The Shift to Limited Preferential Voting in Papua New Guinea*, edited by R. May, R. Anere, N. Haley and K. Wheen, 11–33. Canberra: ANU E Press. doi.org/10.22459/E2007.09.2013.03.

May, R., R. Anere, N. Haley and K. Wheen (eds). 2013. *Election 2007: The Shift to Limited Preferential Voting in Papua New Guinea*. Canberra: ANU E Press. doi.org/10.22459/E2007.09.2013.

May, R., A. Regan and S. Dinnen. 1997. 'Introduction'. In *Challenging the State: The Sandline Affair in Papua New Guinea*, edited by S. Dinnen, R. May and A. Regan, 1–8. Canberra: National Centre for Development Studies, ANU.

May, R. and M. Spriggs. 1990. *The Bougainville Crisis*. Bathurst: Crawford House Press.

McDonald, H. 2022. 'Papua New Guinea's Election Challenges'. *The Saturday Paper*, 2 July. thesaturdaypaper.com.au/news/ir/2022/07/02/papua-new-guineas-election-challenges#hrd.

McGavin, P. 1991. *Wages, Incomes and Productivity in Papua New Guinea*. Institute of National Affairs.

McGavin, P. 1993. 'The 1992 Minimum Wage Board Determination: Implications for Employment and Growth'. In *The Papua New Guinea Economy: Prospects for Sectoral Development and Broad-Based Growth*, edited by AIDAB, 52–84. International Development Issues no. 30.

McKenna, K., S. Morona and C. Samgay. 2021. 'A Response to "Failed State" Narratives of PNG'. *Devpolicy Blog*, 23 June. devpolicy.org/a-response-to-failed-state-narratives-of-png-20210623/.

McKillop, R. 1981. 'Agricultural Policy Making'. In *Policy Making in a New State: Papua New Guinea 1972–1977*, edited by J. Ballard, 238–56. St Lucia: University of Queensland Press.

McKillop, B., M. Bourke and V. Kambori. 2009. 'Policy Making in Agriculture'. In *Policy Making and Implementation: Studies from Papua New Guinea*, edited by R. May, 57–74. Canberra: ANU E Press. doi.org/10.22459/PMI.09.2009.05.

McLay, A. 2003. 'Reforming Road Maintenance and Rehabilitation: Implementing the National Roads Authority'. *Proceedings of the National Development Forum*. Institute of National Affairs.

McLeod, S. 2003. 'PNG Sends Message to "Developed" Nations'. *ABC News*, 25 October.

McLeod, S. 2005. 'Shoe Incident Sees Australia, PNG Relations Sour'. *ABC News*, 8 April.

McQuillan, K. 2017a. 'Lack of Import Controls Harming Papua New Guinea's Fishing Industry Says Fishing Industry Association's Celso'. *Business Advantage PNG*, 22 March. businessadvantagepng.com/lack-of-import-controls-harming-papua-new-guineas-fishing-industry-says-fishing-industry-associations-celso/.

McQuillan, K. 2017b. 'Why Hosting APEC Will Transform Papua New Guinea'. *Business Advantage PNG*, 8 March. businessadvantagepng.com/why-hosting-apec-will-transform-papua-new-guinea/.

Mejía, J. and and E. Aliakbari. 2022. *Annual Survey of Mining Companies, 2022*. Fraser Institute. fraserinstitute.org/studies/annual-survey-of-mining-companies-2022.

Merriam, R., J. Rowell and S. Kuman. 2020. 'Amendments to PNG Mining Act and Oil and Gas Act'. *Allens*, 18 June. allens.com.au/insights-news/insights/hubs/emerging-with-strength-key-considerations-for-oil-and-gas-industry/PNGs-Oil-and-Gas-Act/.

Micah, B. 2020. 'Ben Micah Says Sorry to the People of PNG for Misusing KPHL Funds'. *PNGBlogs*, 9 March. papua87.rssing.com/chan-7046137/all_p93.html.

Middleton, G. 2000. 'The IMF and World Bank in Papua New Guinea: All Powerful?' Master's thesis, Massey University.

Mietzner, M. and N. Farrelly. 2013. 'Mutinies, Coups and Military Interventionism: Papua New Guinea and South-East Asia in Comparison'. *Australian Journal of International Affairs* 67 (3): 342–56. doi.org/10.1080/10357718.2013.788128.

Migdal, J. 1988. *Strong Societies and Weak States: State-Society Relations and State Capabilities in the Third World*. Princeton: Princeton University Press. doi.org/10.1515/9780691212852.

Ministry of Trade, Commerce and Industry. 2016. *Papua New Guinea Small and Medium Enterprise Policy 2016*. Government of Papua New Guinea. pngsme.org/wp-content/uploads/2019/05/PNG-SME-Policy-2016.pdf.

Mirr, J. 2022. 'Market for SME Sector Planned in Hagen'. *The National*, 18 October. thenational.com.pg/market-for-sme-sector-planned-in-hagen/.

Moore, C. and M. Kooyman, eds. 1998. *A Papua New Guinea Political Chronicle 1967–1991*. Bathurst: Crawford House Publishing.

Morauta, M. 2000. 'Silver Jubilee Address to the Nation'. *Pacific Economic Bulletin* 15 (2): Supplement.

Morauta, M. 2005. 'The Papua New Guinea-Australian Relationship'. *Pacific Economic Bulletin* 20 (1): 159–61.

Morauta, M. 2012a. 'IPBC: Unfinished Business—Speech by Sir Mekere'. Kumul Consolidated Holdings, 12 July. web.archive.org/web/20170811183457/http:/www.kch.com.pg/unfinished-business/.

Morauta, M. 2012b. 'Sir Mekere: PNG Government's "Lamentable Record" in Using Resources Wealth'. *Malum Nalu*, 9 June. malumnalu.blogspot.com/2012/06/sir-mekere-png-governments-lamentable.html.

Morauta, M. 2017. 'Sir Mekere Announces Nomination'. *PNG Observer*, 25 April. mekeremorauta.net/single-post/2017/04/25/sir-mekere-announces-nomination (site discontinued).

Morauta, M. 2021. 'Papua New Guinea's Time of Destiny'. [Speech, 14 July 1999.] *Devpolicy Blog*, 22 August. devpolicy.org/papua-new-guineas-time-of-destiny-20210112-1/.

Morris, M. 2021a. 'Morauta's Masterclass in Economic Reform: Part One'. *Devpolicy Blog*, 15 January. devpolicy.org/morautas-masterclass-in-economic-reform-part-one-20210115-3/.

Morris, M. 2021b. 'Morauta's Masterclass in Economic Reform: Part Two'. *Devpolicy Blog*, 15 January. devpolicy.org/morautas-masterclass-in-economic-reform-part-two-20210115-4/.

Mortimer, R. 1979. 'The Evolution of the Post-Colonial State'. In *Development and Dependency: The Political Economy of Papua New Guinea*, edited by R. Mortimer, G. Kenneth and A. Amarshi, 205–44. Oxford: Oxford University.

Mortimer, R., G. Kenneth and A. Amarshi, eds. 1979. *Development and Dependency: The Political Economy of Papua New Guinea*. Oxford: Oxford University Press.

Mou, F. 2016. 'DSIP Keeps MPs Intact with O'Neill, Says Sungi'. *LoopPNG*, 10 May, looppng.com/content/dsip-funds-keep-mps-intact-pm-o%E2%80%99neill-says-sungi (site discontinued).

Mukherjee, R. 2010. *Provincial Secessionists and Decentralisation: Papua New Guinea, 1985–1995.* Innovations for Successful Societies, Princeton University. successful societies.princeton.edu/publications/provincial-secessionists-and-decentralization-papua-new-guinea-1985-1995.

Murshed, M. 2018. *The Resource Curse.* Newcastle upon Tyne: Agenda Publishing Limited. doi.org/10.1017/9781911116509.

Myles, D. 2023. 'PNG Will Offer Incentives for Final Products'. *FDI Intelligence*, 3 July, fdiintelligence.com/content/interview/png-will-offer-incentives-for-final-products-82537.

Namaliu, R. 1988. 'Policy Statement to Parliament'. [1 July.] *Post-Courier*, 5 July. [Republished 6 April 2023].

Namaliu, R. 1995. 'Politics, Business and the State in Papua New Guinea'. *Pacific Economic Bulletin* 10 (2): 61–5.

Namorong, M. 2014. 'PNG Class Warfare: The Predatory Elite & Its "Willing" Prey'. *PNG Attitude*, 20 February. www.pngattitude.com/2014/02/png-class-warfare-the-predatory-elite-its-willing-prey.html.

Nanau, E. 2020. 'Govt: Increase Export Tax on Logs to Fetch K450M'. *Post-Courier*, 22 January. postcourier.com.pg/govt-increased-export-tax-on-logs-to-fetch-k 450m/.

Narokobi, B. 1986. 'The Old and the New'. In *Ethics and Development in Papua New Guinea,* edited by G. Fugman, 3–16. Goroka: The Melanesian Institute.

National. 2019. 'NAC Director Charged with Official Corruption'. 30 August. thenational.com.pg/nac-director-charged-with-official-corruption/.

National. 2020. 'Bank Plagued by Flaws'. 6 November. thenational.com.pg/bank-plagued-by-flaws/.

National. 2021. 'Judge Stays State's Permit for Wafi-Golpu'. 13 September. thenational.com.pg/judge-stays-states-permit-for-wafi-golpu/.

National. 2022. 'Fisheries Authority Phasing out Rebate Scheme'. 3 March. thenational.com.pg/fisheries-authority-phasing-out-rebate-scheme/.

National Court [of Papua New Guinea]. 2019. *The State vs Paul Paraka, Criminal Law—S 383A, Criminal Code, Misappropriation, Honest Claim of Right Without Intention to Defraud—Guilty, CR (FC) No.118 of 2019.*

National Economic and Fiscal Commission. 2012. *2004–2012 Revenue Report.* nefc.gov.pg/documents/publications/RPR/2004-2012_Revenue_Report.pdf (site discontinued).

National Strategic Plan Taskforce. 2009. *Papua New Guinea Vision 2050.* Government of Papua New Guinea. png-data.sprep.org/dataset/papua-new-guinea-vision-2050.

Nautilus Minerals Inc. 2011. 'PNG Government Confirms Investment in Solwara 1'. *Globe News Wire,* 29 March, globenewswire.com/news-release/2011/03/29/139 9258/0/en/Nautilus-Minerals-Inc-PNG-Government-Confirms-Investment-in-Solwara-1.html.

Nelson, H. 1972. *Papua New Guinea, Black Unity or Black Chaos.* Ringwood: Penguin Books.

Nelson, H. 1982. *Taim bilong masta: The Australian Involvement with Papua New Guinea.* Sydney: Australian Broadcasting Commission. openresearch-repository. anu.edu.au/items/804219f5-0fc2-4d2a-be6f-8ccd80f36a17.

Nelson, H. 2006. 'Governments, States and Labels'. SSGM Discussion Paper no. 2006/1. openresearch-repository.anu.edu.au/server/api/core/bitstreams/8b8b 4797-6b63-4222-b720-6610bf12f946/content

Nelson, H. 2007a. 'The Moti Affair in Papua New Guinea'. SSGM Working Paper no. 2007/1. openresearch-repository.anu.edu.au/bitstream/1885/142155/1/07_ 01wp_Nelson.pdf.

Nelson, H. 2007b. 'The Chinese in Papua New Guinea'. SSGM Discussion Paper no. 2007/3. openresearch-repository.anu.edu.au/bitstream/1885/10107/1/Nelson _ChinesePapua2007.pdf.

Nelson, H. 2009. 'The Incomplete State and the Alternate State in Papua New Guinea'. In *Nation Building, State Building, and Economic Development: Case Studies and Comparisons,* edited by S. Paine, 263–76. New York: M. E. Sharpe.

Nicholas, I. 2019. 'Call for PM to Put Party Leadership up for Challenge'. *Post-Courier,* 30 April. postcourier.com.pg/call-pm-put-party-leadership-challenge/.

Nicholas, W. 2016. 'PNG's SME Policy: The Right Aim but Dubious Means'. *Devpolicy Blog,* 18 July. devpolicy.org/png-sme-policy-right-aim-dubious-means-20160718/.

Nonggorr, J. 1993. 'Resolving Conflicts in Customary Law and Western Law in Natural Resource Developments in Papua New Guinea'. *UNSW Law Journal* 16 (2): 433–57.

North, D., J. Wallis and B. Weingast. 2009. *Violence and Social Orders: A Conceptual Framework for Interpreting Recorded Human History*. Cambridge: Cambridge University Press. doi.org/10.1017/CBO9780511575839.

NSO (National Statistical Office). 2015. *Papua New Guinea 2011 National Report*. Government of Papua New Guinea. png-data.sprep.org/resource/papua-new-guinea-2011-national-report.

NSO. n.d. *2009-2010 Papua New Guinea: Household Income and Expenditure Survey*. Government of Papua New Guinea. documents1.worldbank.org/curated/en/329781468289823696/pdf/PNG-HIES-Statistical-Summary-Tables-Web.pdf.

O'Callaghan, M. 1999. *Enemies within: Papua New Guinea, Australia, and the Sandline Crisis: The Inside Story*. Sydney: Doubleday.

O'Callaghan, M. 2002. 'The Origins of the Conflict'. In *Weaving Consensus: The Papua New Guinea–Bougainville Peace Process*, edited by A. Carl and Sr L. Garasu, 6–11. London: Conciliation Resources.

Ofa, S. 2011. 'Telecommunication Regulatory Reforms and the Credibility Problem: Case Studies from Papua New Guinea and Tonga'. In *The Political Economy of Economic Reform in the Pacific*, edited by R. Duncan, 63–94. Mandaluyong: Asian Development Bank.

O'Faircheallaigh, C. 1986. 'Mineral Taxation in Less Developed Countries: Papua New Guinea's Balanced System'. *American Journal of Economics and Sociology* 45 (3): 291–4. doi.org/10.1111/j.1536-7150.1986.tb02389.x.

Oil Search. 2019. 'Oil Search Clarifies Facts Surrounding UBS Loan'. 29 May. oilsearch.com/__data/assets/pdf_file/0009/35874/190529-Oil-Search-clarifies-facts-surrounding-UBS-loan.pdf (site discontinued).

Okole, H. 2003. 'Enhancing Nation Building through the Provincial Government System in Papua New Guinea: Overtures Toward Federalism'. In *Building a Nation in Papua New Guinea: Views of the Post-Independence Generation*, edited by D. Kavanamur, C. Yala and Q. Clements, 51–68. Canberra: Pandanus Books.

Okole, H. 2012. 'A Critical Review of Papua New Guinea's Organic Law on the Integrity of Political Parties and Candidates: 2001-2010'. SSGM Discussion Paper no. 2012/5.

Okuk, I. 1982. 'Introductory Speech'. In *Post-Independence Economic Development of Papua New Guinea*, edited by P. Dahanayake, 237–40. Boroko: Institute of Applied Social and Economic Research.

Oliver, M. 1998. 'July–December 1988'. In *A Papua New Guinea Political Chronicle 1967–1991*, edited by C. Moore and M. Kooyman, 457–66. London : C. Hurst.

Oliver, M., ed. 1989. *Eleksin: The 1987 National Election in Papua New Guinea.* Port Moresby: University of Papau New Guinea.

Oliver, N. and J. Fingleton. 2008. 'Settling Customary Land Disputes in Papua New Guinea'. In *Making Land Work: Volume Two, Case Studies on Customary Land and Development in the Pacific*, edited by AusAID, 223–40. Commonwealth of Australia. dfat.gov.au/sites/default/files/MLW_VolumeTwo_Bookmarked.pdf.

Olson, M. 1993. 'Dictatorship, Democracy, and Development'. *American Political Science Review* 87 (3): 567–76. doi.org/10.2307/2938736.

Ombudsman Commission of Papua New Guinea. 2018. *An Investigation into the Alleged Improper Borrowing of AU$1.239 Billion Loan from the Union Bank of Switzerland … Final Report.* s3-eu-west-1.amazonaws.com/downloads.pngi portal.org/documents/OC2018_UBS.pdf.

O'Neill, P. 2006. 'The Proposal to Establish District Authorities in the Provinces of Papua New Guinea'. Public Policy in Papua New Guinea Discussion Paper no. 2, ANU.

O'Neill, P. 2012a. 'Speech to the National Press Club Canberra, 28th November 2012'. kundu-jakarta.com/images/doc/PM%27s%20Address%20-%20Australian %20Press%20Club%20Canberra%20(2).pdf.

O'Neill, P. 2012b. 'Papua New Guinea in the Asian Century'. Speech to the Lowy Institute, Sydney, 29 November. *The Lowy Institute.* archive.lowyinstitute.org/ sites/default/files/oneill_papua_new_guinea_in_the_asian_century_0.pdf (site discontinued).

Osborne, D. 2014. 'An Analysis of the Papua New Guinea Sovereign Wealth Fund's Process of Formulation and Progress towards Establishment'. Issues Paper no. 9, The National Research Institute.

Oxford Business Group. 2015. 'PNG Real Estate Prices Rises with Rapid Urbanisation'. oxfordbusinessgroup.com/analysis/png-real-estate-prices-rise-rapid-urbanisation.

Pacific Islands Forum Fisheries Agency. 2021. 'Request for Proposals: To Undertake an Impact Evaluation of the National Fisheries Authority Rebate Scheme in Papua New Guinea'. RFP no. CP01 2122, Pacific Islands Forum Fisheries Agency.

Pacific Mining Watch. 2021. 'K1.1 Billion of PNG LNG Landowner Funds Sitting in Bank Accounts: Marape'. 14 November. mine.onepng.com/2021/11/k11-billion-of-png-lng-landowner-funds.html.

Pandey, M. and S. Howes. 2021. 'PNG: The Hungry Country'. *Devpolicy Blog*, 20 May. devpolicy.org/png-the-hungry-country-20210520/.

Pandey, M. and S. Howes. 2022. 'Have Living Standards Improved in PNG over the Last Two Decades? Evidence from Demographic and Health Surveys'. In *Papua New Guinea: Government, Economy, and Society*, edited by S. Howes and L. Pillai, 163–90. Canberra: ANU Press. doi.org/10.22459/PNG.2022.06.

Parliament of the Commonwealth of Australia. 2005. *Report 6: Treaties Tabled on 7 December 2004 (3) and 8 February 2005*. Commonwealth of Australia.

Patjole, C. 2016. 'Industry Celebrates as O'Neill Caves in on Mining Reform'. *Papua New Guinea Mine Watch*, 6 December, ramumine.wordpress.com/2016/12/07/industry-celebrates-as-oneill-caves-in-on-mining-reform/.

Paul, S. 2021. 'Papua New Guinea Hands Pandora Gas Field to State-Owned Kumul'. *Reuters*, 3 September, reuters.com/article/papua-gas-idUSKBN2FZ0W0.

Payani, H. 2003. 'Bureaucratic Corruption in Papua New Guinea: Causes, Consequences and Remedies'. In *Building a Nation in Papua New Guinea: Views of the Post-Independence Generation*, edited by D. Kavanamur, C. Yala and Q. Clements, 91–106. Canberra: Pandanus Books.

Pearl, H. and H. Joku. 2024. 'PNG Security Forces Shoot 6 People, Kill 1, Near Lawless Porgera Gold Mine'. *RNZ*, 15 October. rnz.co.nz/news/pacific/530788/png-security-forces-shoot-6-people-kill-1-near-lawless-porgera-gold-mine.

Pekic, S. 2021. 'Total Plans Papua LNG FID in 2023'. *Offshore Energy*, 6 May. offshore-energy.biz/total-plans-papua-lng-fid-in-2023/.

Pieper, L. 2004. *Deterioration of Public Administration in Papau New Guinea: Views of Eminent Public Servants*. Paper prepared for AusAID.

PNG Chamber of Mining and Petroleum. 2020. 'Why Is Government Fast-Tracking the Introduction of Production Sharing for Mining and Petroleum'. *PNG Market Screener*, 30 August. marketscreener.com/news/latest/PNG-Chamber-of-Mines-and-Petroleum-lsquo-WHY-IS-GOVERNMENT-FAST-TRACKING-THE-INTRODUCTION-OF-PROD--31203872/.

PNGi. 2019. 'Why Do We Venerate the Architects of Kleptocracy'. *Tokaut Blog*, 19 September. pngicentral.org/reports/why-do-we-venerate-the-architects-of-kleptocracy.

PNGi. 2020. 'Was Peter Graham right to Slam PM Marape over Kumul Minerals Board Shake-Up?' *Tokaut Blog*, 19 October, pngicentral.org/reports/was-peter-graham-right-to-slam-pm-marape-over-kumul-minerals-board-shake-up.

PNGi. 2022. 'UBS Loan Was an "Unnecessary Disaster" for PNG and Its People'. *PNGi Investigates*, 12 April. pngicentral.org/reports/ubs-loan-was-an-unnecessary-disaster-for-png-and-its-people.

PNG Facts. 2020. 'PNG PM Marape Says World Class Hospitals to Be Built in Provinces'. *Papua New Guinea Today*. news.pngfacts.com/2020/05/png-pm-marape-says-world-class.html.

PNG Facts. 2021. 'Maru Calls on Marape Government to Table Reserved Business Bill in Parliament'. *Papua New Guinea Today*. 24 June. news.pngfacts.com/2021/06/marape-calls-on-marape-governmen-to.html.

PNG Facts. 2023. 'PNG PM Marape Tells Youths to Stop Urban Drift and Stay Home'. *Papua New Guinea Today*. pngfacts.com/news/png-pm-marape-tells-youths-to-stop-urban-drift-and-stay-home.

PNG FIU (Papua New Guinea Financial Intelligence Unit). 2011. *Due Diligence in Relation to Government Cheques and Payments*. Issued by the Papua New Guinea Financial Intelligence Unit under Section 14(c) of the Proceeds of Crime Act 2005 on 13 May.

PNG Speaks. n.d. [Home]. Accessed 20 September 2024. pngspeaks.com.

Pokawin, S. 1986. 'Democratisation, Politicisation and Political Leadership in the First Decade'. In *Ethics and Development in Papua New Guinea*, edited by G. Fugmann, 133–8. Goroka: The Melanesian Institute.

Pokawin, S. 1998. 'January–December 1979'. In *A Papua New Guinea Political Chronicle 1967–1991*, edited by C. Moore and M. Kooyman, 330–7. London: C. Hurst.

Pora, P. 1990. *1991 Budget Speech*. Government of Papua New Guinea.

Pora, P. 1991. *1992 Budget Speech*. Government of Papua New Guinea.

Post-Courier. 2007. 'Somare's Son Yanks Permit of Competing PNG Telecom'. 25 July.

Post-Courier. 2019. 'Papua LNG Put on Hold by Landowner's Court Action'. Papua New Guinea Mine Watch, 27 November. ramumine.wordpress.com/2019/11/27/papua-lng-put-on-hold-by-landowners-court-action/.

Post-Courier. 2020. 'Over 25,000 Cases Still Active'. 4 February. postcourier.com.pg/over-25000-cases-still-active/.

Post-Courier. 2022a. 'Supreme Court Dismisses Case'. 1 August. postcourier.com.pg/supreme-court-dismisses-case/.

Post-Courier. 2022b. 'IPA Releases Revised Reserved Industries List'. 18 November. postcourier.com.pg/ipa-releases-revised-reserved-industries-list/.

Post-Courier. 2024. 'ICAC to be Investigated'. 9 October. postcourier.com.pg/icac-to-be-investigated/.

Price, B. 2012. 'O'Neill Backs Emerging Copper-Gold Projects'. *PNG Report*, 12 March.

Pritchett, L. 2022. 'Fewer Adjectives, More Focus on Economic Growth for Development'. *Devpolicy Blog*, 28 July. devpolicy.org/fewer-adjectives-more-focus-on-economic-growth-20220728/.

Proctor, M. 1996. 'Structural Adjustment in Papua New Guinea'. *Pacific Economic Bulletin* 11 (2): 25–30.

PWC. 2016. 'Overview and Commentary on the PNG Government's SME Policy'. pwc.com/pg/en/publications/sme-bulletin/sme-bulletin-png-sme-policy-commentary.pdf.

Quodling, P. 1991. *Bougainville—the Mine and the People*. St Leonards: Centre for Independent Studies.

Regan, A. 1997. 'Preparation for War and Progress towards Peace—Bougainville Dimensions of the Sandline Affair'. In *Challenging the State: The Sandline Affair in Papua New Guinea*, edited by S. Dinnen, R. May and A. Regan, 79–82. Pacific Policy Paper no. 30 and Regime Change/Regime Maintenance Discussion Paper no. 21.

Regan, A. 2019. *The Bougainville Referendum: Law, Administration and Politics*. Canberra: Department of Pacific Affairs, ANU.

Regan, A., K. Baker and T. Oppermann. 2022. 'The 2019 Bougainville Referendum and the Question of Independence: From Conflict to Consensus'. *Journal of Pacific History* 57 (1): 58–88. doi.org/10.1080/00223344.2021.2010683.

Regan, A. and H. Griffin. 2005. *Bougainville before the Conflict*. Canberra: Pandanus Books.

Reilly, B. 2000. 'Democracy, Ethnic Fragmentation and Internal Conflict: Confused Theories, Faulty Data, and the "Crucial Case" of Papua New Guinea'. *International Security* 25 (3): 162–85. doi.org/10.1162/016228800560552.

Reilly, B. 2004. 'Ethnicity, Democracy and Development in Papua New Guinea'. *Pacific Economic Bulletin* 19 (1): 46–54.

Reilly, B. 2006. 'Political Reform in Papua New Guinea: Testing the Evidence'. *Pacific Economic Bulletin* 21 (1): 134–40.

Reuters. 2024. 'TotalEnergies: Papua LNG Project Requires "More Work" to Reach Final Investment Decision'. 8 April. reuters.com/business/energy/totalenergies-papua-lng-project-requires-more-work-reach-final-investment-2024-04-08/.

Reynolds, G. 1983. 'The Spread of Economic Growth to the Third World: 1850–1980'. *Journal of Economic Literature* 21 (3): 941–80.

RNZ (Radio New Zealand). 2006. 'Air Brunei Set to Offer Competition for Papua New Guinea Carrier'. Radio New Zealand International. 3 March. web.archive.org/web/20070927004050/http:/www.rnzi.com/pages/news.php?op=read&id=22604.

RNZ. 2015a. 'PNG Corruption Exposed in Australian Sting'. 24 June, rnz.co.nz/international/pacific-news/277067/png-corruption-exposed-in-australian-sting.

RNZ. 2015b. 'PNG Supreme Court Overturns Grace Period Extension'. 7 September. rnz.co.nz/international/pacific-news/283484/png-supreme-court-overturns-grace-period-extension.

RNZ. 2016. 'PNG Treasurer Sounds Conciliatory Note with Forestry Sector'. 14 November. rnz.co.nz/international/pacific-news/318042/png-treasurer-sounds-conciliatory-note-with-forestry-sector.

Robertson, J. and E. Hui. 2023. 'Papua New Guinea Prime Minister James Marape Orders Corruption Watchdog to Investigate PNG Ports'. *ABC News*, 6 March. abc.net.au/news/2023-03-06/png-pm-james-marape-orders-corruption-probe-into-png-ports/102056752.

Rodrik, D. 2003. 'What Do We Learn from Country Narratives'. In *In Search of Prosperity: Analytical Narratives on Economic Growth*, edited by D. Rodrik, 1–20. Princeton: Princeton University Press. doi.org/10.1515/9781400845897.

Romanyshyn, B. and V. Romanyshyn. 2010. 'Obstacles to Student Success in Papua New Guinea'. Self-published. drive.google.com/file/d/17uQ9VpoOo4QKCqCiNiECyodHFpy8gXOd/view.

Rooney, M. 2015. 'Money and Value in Urban Settlement Households in Port Moresby Part 2: Understanding Spatial Income Inequality through Housing Choices'. SSGM Brief no. 2015/44.

Rooney, M. 2017. '"There's Nothing Better than Land": A Migrant Group's Strategies for Accessing Informal Settlement Land in Port Moresby'. In *Kastom, Property and Ideology: Land Transformations in Melanesia*, edited by S. McDonnell, M. Allen and C. Filer, 111–14. Canberra: ANU Press. doi.org/10.22459/KPI.03.2017.04.

Rowlings, B. 2011. 'Moti: Australia on Trial … and Guilty as Hell'. *Civil Liberties Australia*, 8 December. cla.asn.au/News/moti-australia-on-trial-and-/.

Ruaia, T., S. Gu'urau and C. Reid. 2020. *Fisheries of the Western and Central Pacific Ocean*. Honaira: Forum Fisheries Agency.

Ryan, P. 1991. *Black Bonanza. A Landslide of Gold*. South Yarra: Hyland House.

Saffu, Y. 1988. 'Papua New Guinea in 1987: Wingti's Coalition in a Disabled System'. *Asian Survey* 28 (2): 242–51. doi.org/10.2307/2644825.

Saffu, Y. 1992. 'The Bougainville Crisis and Politics in Papua New Guinea'. *Contemporary Pacific* 4 (2): 325–43.

Saffu, Y. 1998a. 'July–December 1984'. In *A Papua New Guinea Political Chronicle 1967–1991*, edited by C. Moore and M. Kooyman, 385–96. London: C. Hurst.

Saffu, Y. 1998b. 'July–December 1985'. In *A Papua New Guinea Political Chronicle 1967–1991*, edited by C. Moore and M. Kooyman, 405–15. London: C. Hurst.

Saffu, Y. 1998c. 'January–December 1986'. In *A Papua New Guinea Political Chronicle 1967–1991*, edited by C. Moore and M. Kooyman, 416–28. London: C. Hurst.

Saffu, Y. 1998d. 'January–December 1987'. In *A Papua New Guinea Political Chronicle 1967–1991*, edited by C. Moore and M. Kooyman, 429–46. London: C. Hurst.

Saffu, Y. 1998e. 'January–December 1989'. In *A Papua New Guinea Political Chronicle 1967–1991*, edited by C. Moore and M. Kooyman, 467–81. London: C. Hurst.

Saffu, Y. 1998f. 'January–December 1990'. In *A Papua New Guinea Political Chronicle 1967–1991*, edited by C. Moore and M. Kooyman, 482–96. London: C. Hurst.

Saffu, Y., ed. 1996. *The 1992 Papua New Guinea Election: Change and Continuity in Electoral Politics*. Canberra: Department of Political and Social Change, ANU.

Saipan Tribune. 2001. 'PNG-World Bank Director Expelled'. 12 February. saipantribune.com/news/local/png-world-bank-director-expelled/article_428 39636-2cb4-5b24-a54d-fbdecdef8ab0.html.

Salmang, G. 2023. 'Foreign Exchange Affects Procurement of Medicine'. *Post-Courier*, 2 August. postcourier.com.pg/foreign-exchange-affects-procurement-of-medicine/.

Samana, U. 1985. 'The Eight Aims, Development and Decentralization: The Morobe Experience'. In *From Rhetoric to Reality? Papua New Guinea's Eight Point Plan and National Goals after a Decade—Papers from the Fifteenth Waigani Seminar*, edited by P. King, W. Lee and V. Warakai, 209–15. Port Moresby: University of Papua New Guinea Press.

Samana, U. 1988. *Papua New Guinea: Which Way?* North Carlton: Arena Publications.

Samof, K. 2023. 'Are Workers in the Informal Sector Leaving Formal Sector Workers behind in PNG?' *Devpolicy Blog*, 11 April. devpolicy.org/informal-sector-and-formal-sector-workers-in-png-20230411/.

Samof, K. and S. Howes. 2024. 'UPNG Students Think PNG Heading in Wrong Direction. *Devpolicy Blog*, 15 November. devpolicy.org/upng-students-think-png-heading-in-wrong-direction-20241115/.

Sampson, T., J. Yabom, W. Nindim and J. Marambini. 2006. 'Exchange Rate Pass-Through in Papua New Guinea'. *Pacific Economic Bulletin* 21 (1): 20–37.

Sandu, S., M. Yang, X. Shi and Y. Chi. 2020. 'A Governance Perspective on Electricity Industry Development: The Case of Papua New Guinea'. *Energy Policy* 141: 111464. doi.org/10.1016/j.enpol.2020.111464.

Sangetari, P. 2014. 'Leadership Code of Papua New Guinea and Ombudsman Commission's Role in Enforcement to Minimize Corrupt Practices and Ensure Accountably by Leaders in PNG'. The International Ombudsman Institute. theioi.org/downloads/4qj8t/Wellington%20Conference_16.%20Working%20Session%20C_Phoebe%20Sangetari%20Paper.pdf.

Saunders, J. 1993. *Agricultural Land Use of Papua New Guinea*. PNGRIS Publication no.1. AIDAB.

Schmidt, E. 2019. 'Rural Poverty and Undernutrition Widespread in Papua New Guinea'. *Devpolicy Blog*, 23 May. devpolicy.org/rural-poverty-and-undernutrition-widespread-in-papua-new-guinea-20190523/.

Schmidt, E., V. Mueller and G. Rosenbach. 2020. 'Rural Households in Papua New Guinea Afford Better Diets with Income from Small Businesses'. *Food Policy* 97 (101964): 1–15. doi.org/10.1016/j.foodpol.2020.101964.

Schwoerer, T. 2022. 'Plantations, Incorporated Land Groups and Emerging Inequalities among the Wampar of Papua New Guinea'. In *Capital and Inequality in Rural Papua New Guinea*, edited by B. Beer and T. Schwoerer, 33–62. Canberra: ANU Press. doi.org/10.22459/CIRPNG.2022.02.

Scollay, R. 2007. 'Review of the Tariff Reduction Program'. Auckland UniServices Limited. treasury.gov.pg/wp-content/uploads/2023/11/2007-Tariff-Review-Report.pdf.

Searancke, R. 2021. 'CEO of Papua New Guinea Offshore Operator Calls It Quits'. *Upstream*, 5 October. upstreamonline.com/people/ceo-of-papua-new-guinea-offshore-operator-calls-it-quits/2-1-1077364.

Sen, K. 2018. 'PNG is on the Cusp of a Super Cycle in Mining Investment'. *Bluenotes*, 20 April. bluenotes.anz.com/posts/2018/04/png-is-on-the-cusp-of-a-super-cycle-in-mining-investment.

Sepoe, O. 2005. 'Organic Law on the Integrity of Political Parties and Candidates: A Tool for Political Stability'. SSGM Discussion Paper no. 4.

Sepoe, O. 2021a. 'Temporary Special Measures in PNG: Part One—the Story up to 2019'. *Devpolicy Blog*, 10 August. devpolicy.org/temporary-special-measures-in-png-part-one-the-story-up-to-2019-20210810/.

Sepoe, O. 2021b. 'Temporary Special Measures in PNG: Part Two—Latest Developments'. *Devpolicy Blog*, 12 August. devpolicy.org/temporary-special-measures-in-png-part-two-latest-developments-20210812/.

Sharp, T. 2012. 'Following *Buai*: The Highlands Betel Nut Trade, Papua New Guinea'. PhD thesis, ANU.

Sharp, T. 2019. 'Change and Continuity in Papua New Guinea's Marketplaces' *Devpolicy Blog*, 26 September. devpolicy.org/change-and-continuity-in-papua-new-guineas-marketplaces-20190926/.

Sharp, T., M. Busse and R. Bourke. 2022. 'Market Update: Changes in Papua New Guinea's Fresh Food Marketplaces'. *Asia & the Pacific Policy Studies* 9 (3): 483–515. doi.org/10.1002/app5.368.

Shefter, M. 1973. 'Party and Patronage: Germany, England, and Italy'. *Politics & Society* 7 (4): 403–51. doi.org/10.1177/003232927700700402.

Shlezinger, N. 2024. 'Papua New Guinea Businesses Still Face Serious Forex Delays, Despite Interventions'. *Business Advantage PNG*, 23 May. business advantage www.businessadvantagepng.com/papua-new-guinea-businesses-still-face-serious-forex-delays-despite-interventions/.

Singer, H. 1989. 'The 1980s: A Lost Decade—Development in Reverse?' In *Growth and External Debt Management*, 46–56. London: Palgrave Macmillan. doi.org/10.1007/978-1-349-10944-9_5.

Singirok, J. 1997. 'Singirok's Address to the Nation'. *Challenging the State: The Sandline Affair in Papua New Guinea*, edited by S. Dinnen, R. May and A. Regan, 207–16. Pacific Policy Paper 30 and Regime Change/Regime Maintenance Discussion Paper no. 21, ANU.

Smith, A. 1762. *Lectures on Jurisprudence*. Vol. 5. Glasgow edition of the Works and Correspondence.

Smith, A. 2024. 'Gender Norms, Bargaining Power and Intimate Partner Violence: A Case Study in Papua New Guinea'. Development Policy Centre Discussion Paper no. 107, devpolicy.org/publications/gender-norms-bargaining-power-and-intimate-partner-violence-a-case-study-in-papua-new-guinea/.

Somare, M. 1974. 'Achieving with the Eight-Point Improvement Plan'. Address to the Economic Society of Papua New Guinea, 28 January.

Somare, M. 1975. *Sana: An Autobiography of Michael Somare*. Port Moresby: Niugini Press.

Somare, M. 2000. 'Where Did We Go Wrong?' In *Uncertain Paradise: Building and Promoting a Better Papua New Guinea*, edited by Divine Word University, 125–30. Madang: DWU Press.

Somare, M. 2010. 'Where Have We Come from and Where Are We Heading?' In *Living History and Evolving Democracy*, edited by I. Maddocks and E. Wolfers, with contribution from Ron Crocombe, 212–15. Port Moresby: University of Papua New Guinea Press.

Sowei, J. n.d. 'Devolution of Powers through Decentralisation'. Nuku District, nukudistrict.gov.pg/schoolfeeassistanceprogram/ (site discontinued).

Spriggs, M. and D. Denoon, eds. 1992. *The Bougainville Crisis: 1991 Update*. Canberra: Department of Political and Social Change, Research School of Pacific Studies, ANU.

Squires, N. 2004. 'Australian Police Get Warm Reception in Port Moresby'. *South China Morning Post*, 3 December. scmp.com/article/480493/australian-police-get-warm-reception-port-moresby.

Standish, B. 1981. '"Maunten na barat": Policy-Making in Chimbu Province'. In *Policy Making in a New State: Papua New Guinea 1972–1977*, edited by J. Ballard, 280–305. St Lucia: University of Queensland Press.

Standish, B. 1999. 'Papua New Guinea 1999: Crises of Governance'. Parliament of Australia Research Paper no. 4.

Standish, B. 2007. 'The Dynamics of Papua New Guinea's Democracy: An Essay'. *Pacific Economic Bulletin* 22 (1): 135–57.

Stanley, L. 2008. 'The Development of Information and Communication Technology Law and Policy in Papua New Guinea'. *Pacific Economic Bulletin* 23 (1): 16–28.

Stein, L. 1992. 'Structural Adjustment in Papua New Guinea'. *Pacific Economic Bulletin* 7 (2): 25–30.

Stokes, S., T. Dunning, M. Nazareno and V. Brusco. 2013. *Brokers, Voters, and Clientelism: The Puzzle of Distributive Politics*. New York: Cambridge University Press. doi.org/10.1017/CBO9781107324909.

Stella, R. 2003. 'PNG in the New Millennium: Some Troubled Homecomings'. In *Building a Nation in Papua New Guinea: Views of the Post-Independence Generation*, edited by D. Kavanamur, C. Yala and Q. Clements, 11–24. Canberra: Pandanus Books.

Steeves, J. 1996. 'Unbounded Politics in the Solomon Islands: Leadership and Party Alignments'. *Pacific Studies* 19 (1): 115–38.

Stern, N. 2002. *A Strategy for Development*. Washington, DC: World Bank.

Strathern, A. 1993. 'Violence and Political Change in Papua New Guinea'. *Politics, Tradition and Change in the Pacific* 149 (4): 718–36. doi.org/10.1163/22134379-90003110.

Supreme Court of Papua New Guinea. 2013. *In Re Constitutional (Amendment) Law 2008, Reference by the Ombudsman Commission of Papua New Guinea [2013] PGSC 67; SC1302 (19 December 2013)*. Pacific Islands Legal Information Institute. paclii.org/pg/cases/PGSC/2013/67.html.

Supreme Court of Papua New Guinea. 2019. *Kereme v O'Neill [2019] PGSC 7; SC1781 (28 March 2019)*. Pacific Islands Legal Information Institute. paclii.org/pg/cases/PGSC/2019/7.html.

Suwamaru, J. 2020. 'Beneath the Veil of the Kumul Submarine Cable Network'. *Electronic Journal of Informatics* 2: 1–25.

Tarawa, H. 2020. 'Basil Happy to Serve Govt'. *The National*, 21 December. thenational.com.pg/basil-happy-to-serve-govt/.

Tax Justice Network—Australia (TJN) and the Make Exxon Pay Coalition. 2018. 'Is Exxon Paying a Fair Share of Tax in Australia?'. Senate Standing Committees of Economics, Canberra. static1.squarespace.com/static/636a46c59a62847f542195d2/t/637bf133e3f703194fcf075c/1669067062804/Is-Exxon-Paying-a-Fair-Share-of-Tax-A-TJN-Report.pdf.

Tax Review Committee. 2015a. 'Papua New Guinea Taxation Review, Report to the Treasurer Part 1 of 2: Summary of Analysis'. treasury.gov.pg/html/media_releases/files/2016/Tax%20Review%20%20Final%20Report%20vol%201.pdf (site discontinued).

Tax Review Committee. 2015b. 'Papua New Guinea Taxation Review, Report to the Treasurer Part 2 of 2: Detailed Analysis'. treasury.gov.pg/html/media_releases/files/2016/Tax%20Review%20Final%20report%20Vol%202.pdf (site discontinued).

Temu, I., ed. 1997. *Papua New Guinea: A 20/20 Vision*. Canberra: National Centre for Development Studies, ANU.

Temu, I. 2010. 'Long Term Development Strategy and Wealth Creation: A Paradigm Shift Platform'. In *Living History and Evolving Democracy*, edited by I. Maddocks and E. Wolfers, with contribution from R. Crocombe, 108–13. Port Moresby: University of Papua New Guinea Press.

Teskey, G., T. Davda, A. Maaroof and P. Parthiban. 2021. 'Papua New Guinea Governance Update 2021: Steady as She Goes?' National Research Institute Discussion Paper no. 192. pngnri.org/images/Publications/DPNo192_Papua_New_Guinea_Governance_Update_2021-_Steady_as_she_goes_.pdf.

Thomas, A. and J. Trevino. 2013. 'Resource Dependence and Fiscal Effort in Sub-Saharan Africa'. International Monetary Fund Working Paper no. 13/188. doi.org/10.5089/9781484391501.001.

Thomason, J. and P. Kase. 2009. 'Policy Making in Health'. In *Policy Making and Implementation: Studies from Papua New Guinea*, edited by R. May, 117–30. Canberra: ANU E Press. doi.org/10.22459/PMI.09.2009.07.

Thompson, H. and S. MacWilliam. 1992. *The Political Economy of Papua New Guinea: Critical Essays*. Manila: Journal of Contemporary Asia Publishers.

Tinker, H. 1967. 'Broken Backed States: Chaotic, but a High Survival Rate'. *New Guinea and Australia, the Pacific and South-East Asia*, September/October.

Tom, P. 2022. 'Brian Bell Seeks K35M in FX for Major Projects'. *Post-Courier*, 30 March. postcourier.com.pg/brian-bell-seeks-k35m-in-fx-for-major-projects/.

ToRobert, H. 1982. 'Monetary Policy Contributions to Economic Development'. In *Post-Independence Economic Development of Papua New Guinea*, edited by P. Dahanayake, 147–52. Boroko: Institute of Applied Social and Economic Research.

TPA (Tourism Promotion Authority) and Acorn. 2021. *Tourism Satellite Account 2019*. papuanewguinea.travel/wp-content/uploads/2023/10/PNGTSA-2019-Report_PNGTPA.pdf.

Trading Economics. n.d. 'Papua New Guinea—Credit Rating'. Accessed 7 September 2023. tradingeconomics.com/papua-new-guinea/rating.

Transparency International Papua New Guinea. 2010. 'Rehabilitation of Education Sector Infrastructure'. transparencypng.org.pg/rehabilitation-of-education-sector-infrastructure/.

Trebilcock, M. 1982a. 'The Role of the Private Sector in the Economic Development of Papua New Guinea'. Institute of National Affairs Discussion Paper no. 13.

Trebilcock, M. 1982b. 'Public Enterprises in Papua New Guinea'. Institute of National Affairs Discussion Paper no. 13.

Trebilcock, M. 1983. 'Customary Land Law Reform in Papua New Guinea: Law, Economics and Property Rights in Traditional Culture'. *Adelaide Law Review* 9 (1): 191–228.

Tukne, C. 2022. 'Will the Next Government Finally Ban Round Log Exports?' *Act Now!*, 2 June, actnowpng.org/blog/blog-entry-will-next-government-finally-ban-round-log-exports.

Turner, M. 1990. *Papua New Guinea: The Challenge of Independence.* Ringwood: Penguin Books.

Turner, M. and D. Kavanamur. 2009. 'Explaining Public Sector Reform Failure: Papua New Guinea 1975–2001'. In *Policy Making and Implementation: Studies from Papua New Guinea*, edited by R. May, 9–25. Canberra: ANU E Press.

Ukama, P. 2022. 'Prime Minister Marape Inaugurates Papua New Guinea Sovereign Wealth Fund with Kumul Consolidated Holdings Dividend'. *PNG Bulletin*, 10 November. thepngbulletin.com/news/prime-minister-marape-inaugurates-papua-new-guinea-sovereign-wealth-fund-with-kumul-consolidated-holdings-dividend/.

UNDP Human Development Reports. n.d. 'Documentation and Downloads'. Accessed 11 October 2023. hdr.undp.org/data-center/documentation-and-downloads.

UNESCO. 2009. *Investing in Cultural Diversity and Intercultural Dialogue: UNESCO World Report.* UNESCO Digital Library. unesdoc.unesco.org/ark:/48223/pf 0000185202.

UNODC (United Nations Office on Drugs and Crime). 2022. 'Papua New Guinea Targets Good Anti-Corruption Practices to Boost Development'. *United Nations.* 17 June. unodc.org/roseap/en/png/2022/06/anti-corruption-practices-boost-development/story.html.

US State (United States Department of State). 2021. *2021 Investment Climate Statement: Papua New Guinea.*

US State (United States Department of State). 2022. *2022 Investment Climate Statement: Papua New Guinea.*

Vailala. 2020. [Comment on] 'The Porgera Mine in PNG: Some Background'. *Devpolicy Blog*, 20 September. devpolicy.org/the-porgera-mine-in-png-some-background-20200507-2/#comment-765520.

Vatsikopoulous, H. 1995. 'PNG: Under the Spell'. *Pacific Journalism Review* 2 (1): 24–36. doi.org/10.24135/pjr.v2i1.533.

Voigt-Graf, C. 2015a. 'Visitor Arrivals and the Economic Boom in Papua New Guinea'. *Devpolicy Blog*, 6 February. devpolicy.org/visitor-arrivals-and-the-economic-boom-in-papua-new-guinea-20150206/.

Voigt-Graf, C. 2015b. 'The Changing Composition of PNG's Foreign Workforce'. *Devpolicy Blog*, 16 March. devpolicy.org/the-changing-composition-of-pngs-foreign-workforce-20150316/.

Voigt-Graf, C. and O. Sanida. 2015. 'PNG's 2015 Sovereign Wealth Fund Bill: Key Weaknesses and Proposals for Improvement'. *Spotlight with NRI* 8 (4).

Voigt-Graf, C. and F. Odhuno. 2019. 'Assessing the Labour Market Impact of the PNG LNG Project and Implications for Future Projects'. Development Policy Centre Discussion Paper no. 78. doi.org/10.2139/ssrn.3360134.

Voutas, A. 1981. 'Policy Initiative and the Pursuit of Control 1972–74'. In *Policy Making in a New State: Papua New Guinea 1972–1977*, edited by J. Ballard, 33–47. St Lucia: University of Queensland Press.

Waiko, J. 2007. *A Short History of Papua New Guinea.* 2nd ed. South Melbourne: Oxford University Press.

Walton, G. 2016. 'Gramsci's activists: How Local Civil Society Is Shaped by the Anti-Corruption Industry, Political Society and Translocal Encounters'. *Political Geography* 53: 10–19. doi.org/10.1016/j.polgeo.2016.01.009.

Walton, G. and S. Dinnen. 2020. 'Regulating the Growth of Private Security in PNG'. *Devpolicy Blog*, 16 January. devpolicy.org/regulating-the-growth-of-private-security-in-png-20200116/.

Walton, G. and S. Dinnen. 2022. 'Crime and Corruption'. In *Papua New Guinea: Government, Economy, and Society*, edited by S. Howes and L. Pillai, 87–122. Canberra: ANU Press. doi.org/10.22459/PNG.2022.04.

Walton, G. and H. Hushang. 2022. 'The Politics of Free Education in PNG'. *Devpolicy Blog*, 18 January. devpolicy.org/the-politics-of-free-education-in-png-20220118/.

Wari, P. 2016. 'K49M for Schools Gone Missing'. *The National*, 14 April. thenational.com.pg/k49m-for-schools-gone-missing.

Watson, A. 2022. 'Communication, Information, and the Media'. In *Papua New Guinea: Government, Economy, and Society*, edited by S. Howes and L. Pillai, 223–59. Canberra: ANU Press. doi.org/10.22459/PNG.2022.08.

Webster, T. and L. Duncan, eds. 2010. *Papua New Guinea Development Performance 1975–2008*. Boroko: The National Research Institute.

Weise, D. 2002. 'Structural Adjustment Programs in Papua New Guinea: Implementation and Experiences'. Kumul Scholars International 2002 Conference Paper, ANU. openresearch-repository.anu.edu.au/bitstream/1885/40599/3/KSI02-4.pdf.

Wenogo, B. 2022. 'Latest Port Moresby Ban Doomed to Failure'. *Devpolicy Blog*, 25 October. devpolicy.org/latest-port-moresby-ban-doomed-to-failure-20221025/.

Wesley-Smith, T. 1989. 'Pre-Capitalist Modes of Production in Papua New Guinea'. *Dialectical Anthropology* 14: 307–21. doi.org/10.1007/BF01957267.

Wesley-Smith, T. 1992. 'The Non-Review of the Bougainville Copper Agreement'. In *The Bougainville Crisis: 1991 Update*, edited by M. Spriggs and D. Denoon, 92–111. Canberra: Department of Political and Social Change, Research School of Pacific Studies, ANU.

Wesley-Smith, T. 1995. 'Papua New Guinea in Review: Issues and Events, 1994'. *Contemporary Pacific* 7 (2): 364–74.

Wesley-Smith, T. 1997. 'Papua New Guinea in Review: Issues and Events, 1996'. *Contemporary Pacific* 9 (2): 479–87.

WHO (World Health Organisation). 2022. *Noncommunicable Diseases: Progress Monitor 2022*. Geneva: World Health Organization. iris.who.int/bitstream/handle/10665/353048/9789240047761-eng.pdf?sequence=1.

WHO and World Bank. 2023. *Tracking Universal Health Coverage: 2023 Global Monitoring Report*. World Health Organization and World Bank.

Williamson, J. 1990. 'What Washington Means by Policy Reform'. In *Latin American Adjustment: How Much Has Happened*, edited by J. Williamson, 7–20. Washington, DC: Institute for International Economics.

Williamson, J. 2005. 'The Washington Consensus as Policy Prescription for Development'. In *Development Challenges in the 1990s: Leading Policy Makers Speak from Experience*, edited by T. Besley and R. Zagha, 33–53. Washington, DC: World Bank Publications.

Windybank, S. and M. Manning. 2003. 'Papua New Guinea on the Brink'. Centre for Independent Studies, Issue Analysis, no. 30.

Wingti, P. 1985. 'Standing by Our Principles in Tough Times'. In *From Rhetoric to Reality? Papua New Guinea's Eight Point Plan and National Goals after a Decade—Papers from the Fifteenth Waigani Seminar*, edited by P. King, W. Lee and V. Warakai, 15–21. Port Moresby: University of Papua New Guinea Press.

Wiseman, D. 2021. 'Anthony Regan: Bougainville's Prospects for Independence'. *Radio New Zealand*, 2 July. rnz.co.nz/international/pacific-news/446067/anthony-regan-bougainville-s-prospects-for-independence.

Wood, T. 2016. 'Is Culture the Cause? Choices, Expectations, and Electoral Politics in Solomon Islands and Papua New Guinea'. *Pacific Affairs* 89 (1): 31–52. doi.org/10.5509/201689131.

Wood, T. 2017. 'The Papua New Guinea Election Results Database'. *Devpolicy Blog*, 16 March. devpolicy.org/png-election-results-database-20170316/.

Wood, T. 2018. 'The Clientelism Trap in Solomon Islands and Papua New Guinea, and its Impact on Aid Policy'. *Asia & the Pacific Policy Studies* 5 (3): 481–94. doi.org/10.1002/app5.239.

Wood, T. 2022. 'What Went Wrong with the 2022 Elections in PNG?', *DevPolicy Blog*, 19 August. devpolicy.org/what-went-wrong-with-the-2022-elections-in-png-20220819/.

Wood, T. 2023. 'Four Paths to a Better Governed State in PNG'. *Devpolicy Blog*, 27 June. devpolicy.org/four-paths-to-a-better-governed-state-in-png-20230627/.

Wood, T., M. Laveil and M. Kabuni. 2023. 'Troubles and Puzzles: The 2022 General Elections in Papua New Guinea'. *Journal of Pacific History* 58 (4): 444–66. doi.org/10.1080/00223344.2023.2248008.

Woolford, D. 1976. *Papua New Guinea: Initiation and Independence*. St Lucia: University of Queensland Press.

World Bank. 1978. *Papua New Guinea: Its Economic Situation and Prospects for Development*. World Bank.

World Bank. 1982. *A World Bank Country Study, Papua New Guinea: Selected Development Issues*. World Bank.

World Bank. 1990. *Report and Recommendation of the President of the International Bank for Reconstruction and Development to the Executive Directors on a Proposed Structural Adjustment Loan to the Independent State of Papua New Guinea*. World Bank.

World Bank. 1991. *Papua New Guinea: Structural Adjustment, Growth and Human Resource Development*. World Bank.

World Bank. 1993. *Papua New Guinea: Jobs, Economic Growth and International Competitiveness.* World Bank.

World Bank. 1995a. *Report and Recommendation of the President of the International Bank for Reconstruction and Development to the Executive Directors on a Proposed Loan of US$50 Million to the Independent State of Papua New Guinea for an Economic Recovery Program.* World Bank.

World Bank. 1995b. *Project Completion Report: Papua New Guinea Structural Adjustment Loan (Loan 3218-PNG).* World Bank.

World Bank. 1999. *Memorandum of the President of the International Bank for Reconstruction and Development of the Executive Directors on a Country Assistance Strategy of the World Bank Group for the Independent State of Papua New Guinea.* World Bank.

World Bank. 2000. *Report and Recommendation of the President of the International Bank for Reconstruction and Development to the Executive Directors on a Governance Promotion Adjustment Loan in an Amount of US$90 Million to the Independent State of Papua New Guinea.* World Bank.

World Bank. 2002. *Implementation Completion Report: The Independent State of Papua New Guinea Government Promotion Adjustment Loan (Loan No.7021PNG),* no. 23734. World Bank.

World Bank. 2003. *Public Expenditure Review and Rationalization [PERR]: Overview of Discussion Papers.* World Bank.

World Bank. 2004. *Papua New Guinea: Poverty Assessment.* World Bank.

World Bank. 2005. *Economic Growth in the 1990s: Learning from a Decade of Reform.* World Bank Publications.

World Bank. 2017. *World Development Report: Governance and the Law.* World Bank.

World Bank. 2018. *Program Document for a Proposed Development Policy Credit in the Amount of SDR 106.8 Million (US$150 Million Equivalent) to the Independent State of Papua New Guinea for the first Economic and Fiscal Resilience Development Policy Operation (P165717).* World Bank.

World Bank. 2020. *Papua New Guinea Development Policy Operation (P165717): Implementation Status & Results Report.* World Bank.

World Bank. 2021a, *Papua New Guinea Crisis Response and Sustainable Recovery Development Policy Operation.* World Bank.

World Bank. 2021b. *The Changing Wealth of Nations 2021: Managing Assets for the Future.* World Bank.

World Bank Group. n.d.-a. 'Urban Population (% of Total Population)—Papua New Guinea'. Accessed 21 July 2024. data.worldbank.org/indicator/SP.URB. TOTL.IN.ZS?most_recent_value_desc=false&locations=PG.

World Bank Group. n.d.-b. 'Gini Index—Papua New Guinea'. Accessed 20 September 2024. data.worldbank.org/indicator/SI.POV.GINI?locations=PG.

World Bank Group. n.d.-c. 'Worldwide Governance Indicators'. Accessed 20 September 2024. govindicators.org.

World Bank Group. n.d.-d. 'Country Policy and Institutional Assessment'. Accessed 20 September 2024. databank.worldbank.org/source/country-policy-and-institutional-assessment#.

Wrakuale, A. 2012. 'NRI: Monopoly on Rice Bad for PNG Consumers'. *Malum Nalu*, 20 February. malumnalu.blogspot.com/2012/02/nri-monopoly-on-rice-bad-for-png.html.

Xinhua. 2020. 'ADB Approves 250 mln USD Loan to Boost PNG's Covid-19 Response'. 26 November, xinhuanet.com/english/2020-11/26/c_139544892.htm (site discontinued).

Yafoi, M. 2019. 'Disgruntled Landowners Shut Down Billion Dollar Gold and Copper Project'. *Papua New Guinea Mine Watch*, 14 January. ramumine. wordpress.com/2019/01/14/disgruntled-landowners-shut-down-billion-dollar-gold-and-copper-project/.

Yala, C. 2002. 'Melanesian Conflicts'. In SSGM Discussion Paper no. 2002/4, ANU.

Yala, C. 2010a. 'Overview'. In *The Genesis of the Papua New Guinea Land Reform Program: Selected Papers from the 2005 National Land Summit*, edited by C. Yala, 1–10. Boroko: The National Research Institute.

Yala, C., ed. 2010b. *The Genesis of the Papua New Guinea Land Reform Program: Selected Papers from the 2005 National Land Summit*. Boroko: The National Research Institute.

Yala, C. and O. Sanida. 2010. 'Development Planning'. In *Papua New Guinea Development Performance 1975–2008*, edited by T. Webster and L. Duncan, 45–66. Boroko: The National Research Institute.

Yala, C., O. Sanida and A. Mako. 2014. 'The Oil Search Loan: Implications for PNG'. *Devpolicy Blog*, 21 March. devpolicy.org/the-oil-search-loan-implications-for-png-20140321-2/.

Zimmer-Tamakoshi, L. 1997. 'The Last Big Man: Development and Men's Discontents in the Papua New Guinea Highlands'. *Oceania* 68 (2): 107–22. doi.org/10.1002/j.1834-4461.1997.tb02653.x.

Zorn, S. 2018. 'Despite Our Best Intentions: Papua New Guinea's Ok Tedi Mine and the Limits of Expert Advice'. *Mineral Economics* 31: 13–21. doi.org/10.1007/s13563-017-0111-1.